Due Return Date Date	Due Return Date Date

Diplomats and Bureaucrats

DIPLOMATS AND BUREAUCRATS

The First Institutional Responses to
Twentieth-Century Diplomacy in France and Germany

Paul Gordon Lauren

Hoover Institution Press
Stanford University, Stanford, California
1976

*The Hoover Institution on War, Revolution and Peace, founded
at Stanford University in 1919 by the late President Herbert Hoover,
is a center for advanced study and research on
public and international affairs in the twentieth century.
The views expressed in its publications are entirely
those of the authors and do not necessarily reflect
the views of the staff, officers, or Board of
Overseers of the Hoover Institution.*

Hoover Institution Publications 153
Stanford, California
© 1976 by the Board of Trustees of the
Leland Stanford Junior University
All rights reserved
Printed in the United States of America
Library of Congress Catalog Card Number 75-29785
International Standard Book Number 0-8179-6531-9

To my Father and the memory of my Mother,
whose compassion and courage
always will be a source of inspiration to us all

*Nobody can doubt that adaptability to change
is of the first importance in a world as dynamic as
that of the twentieth century. . . .*
— Herbert Butterfield

Contents

PART I

CHAPTER ONE: *The Foundations and Historical Legacy: From King's Court to Ministerial Bureaucracy*

CHAPTER TWO: *The Turning Point: A Changing World, Domestic Criticisms, and Proposals for Reform and Innovation*

PART II

CHAPTER THREE: *The French Response: Reforms and Innovations for the Quai d'Orsay*

CHAPTER FOUR: *The German Response: Reforms and Innovations for the Wilhelmstrasse*

PART III

CHAPTER FIVE: *Diplomatic Pouches and Pocketbooks: New and Expanded Responsibilities for International Commerce*

CHAPTER SIX: Civilisation *and* Kultur: *New and Expanded Responsibilities for International Propaganda*

PART IV

CHAPTER SEVEN: *Epilogue: On the Nature of Institutional Responses and Twentieth-Century Diplomacy*

APPENDIX ONE: *Diplomats and Bureaucrats in the French Ministry for Foreign Affairs, 1900–1925*

APPENDIX TWO: *Diplomats and Bureaucrats in the German Ministry for Foreign Affairs, 1900–1925*

Illustrations

Charts

Abbreviations

AN	Archives nationales, Paris
DDF	*Documents diplomatiques français (1871–1914)*
DP	*Débats parlementaires*
GP	*Die Grosse Politik der europäischen Kabinette 1871–1914*
JO	*Journal officiel de la République française. Lois et décrets*
MAE	Archives diplomatiques du Ministère des Affaires étrangères, Paris
MAE/Chambre, Rapport	Archives diplomatiques du Ministère des Affaires étrangères/Chambre des Députés, Commission du Budget, "Rapport . . . du Budget général . . . (MAE)"
MAE/Sénat, Rapport	Archives diplomatiques du Ministère des Affaires étrangères/Sénat, Commission des Finances, "Rapport . . . du Budget général . . . (MAE)"
NA/DS	National Archives/Records of the Department of State, Washington, D.C.
PA/AA	Politisches Archiv des Auswärtiges Amt, Bonn
PRO/FO	Public Record Office/Foreign Office Correspondence, London
RGB	*Reichsgesetzblatt*
SB	*Stenographische Berichte*

Acknowledgments

It is sincerely a warm pleasure to acknowledge publicly the gener-
ous assistance and encouragement offered by the following individuals and organizations in the preparation of this study:

Professors Gordon A. Craig, Peter Paret, and Gordon Wright of
Stanford University for their sound advice, constructive criticism,
and outstanding personal examples of scholarship;
The Foreign Area Fellowship Program of the Social Science Research Council and American Council of Learned Societies, the
Deutscher Akademischer Austauschdienst, and the Graduate Over-
seas Program of Stanford University for their financial support in
research;
The National Fellows Program of the Hoover Institution for the
appointment as a Peace Fellow and assistance in completing the
manuscript;
M. Jean Laloy, M. Georges Dethan, Mme. Madeleine Glachant,
and Mme. Berger de Nomazy of the *Archives diplomatiques du
Ministère des Affaires étrangères*, and Dr. Klaus Weinandy, Dr.
Theodore Gehling, and Frau Eva Magka of the *Politisches Archiv des
Auswärtiges Amt* all for granting access to heretofore closed mate-
rials, sharing the enthusiasm of new ideas and the rediscovery of
important documents, offering continual help, and extending numer-
ous courtesies;
Dr. Robert Dockhorn of the *Akten zur deutschen auswärtigen
Politik* project, Dr. L. H. Gann and Agnes Peterson of the Hoover
Institution, David Miller of Cambridge University, and Sybil Milton
of the Leo Baeck Institute for their helpful suggestions;
Professor Alexander L. George as a colleague and our students at
Stanford University enrolled in "The Diplomatic Revolution of Our
Time" for urging that I place details within their larger historical
context;
The archivists of the Archives nationales (Paris), Public Record
Office (London), and National Archives (Washington, D.C.) for
services rendered;
The Controller of Her Majesty's Stationery Office for permission
to cite Crown-copyright materials in the Public Record Office;

The librarians of Stanford University, the Hoover Institution, *Bibliothèque du Ministère des Affaires étrangères* (Paris), *Bibliothèque nationale* (Paris), *Universitat Bonn,* Foreign Office Library (London), International Law and Relations Library of University College (London), and of the University of California at Berkeley;

Jane Edwards for her efficient typing;

Mickey Hamilton for her patient guidance through the publication process;

And, particularly, my wife Susan for her constant encouragement and faithful support.

Introduction

Particularly in foreign policy, it is the study and knowledge of the past which best prepares us to understand the present and to prepare for the future.

—French Deputy
Louis Farges

"Autocrat!" "Dictator!" "Tyrant!" These were only a few of the epithets cast at those men who first introduced significant change into the lives of diplomats and bureaucrats in the twentieth century. Their actions aroused the fury of vested interests and the resentment of officials established in the comforts of the *status quo*. The targets of this rage were initiating reforms and innovations in the French and German Ministries for Foreign Affairs. They upset traditional patterns, demanded altered behavior, designed elaborate mechanisms of operation, created carefully defined regulations, applied different techniques, and hired new men. Other contemporaries praised their accomplishments as "far-sighted," "logical," "rational," "highly up-to-date," "most important," "practical," "a genuine and profound reorganization," and "a great reform of modernization."

The programs eliciting these conflicting comments occurred during the first two and a half decades of the twentieth century when European society seemed to be bursting with energy, creativity, and change. Revolutionary discoveries in theoretical physics, psychoanalysis, and applied technology were matched by new forms of art, music, and architecture. Electricity and machines began to transform earlier transportation and communications systems, bringing people closer together. Businessmen and others spoke of "efficiency," "pragmatism," and "rationality" in administrative techniques. International affairs moved to encompass the world beyond the European continent, to proceed at a faster pace, and to grow more complex than ever before in history. The rising popular press, articulate interest groups, and more aggressive parliamentarians promoted major political changes, an end to diplomatic "secrets," and a "democratization" of the old "aristocratic" personnel policies.

The turmoil and ferment arising from the confluence of these pressures was evident several years before the catastrophic outbreak of violence that erupted in 1914, but reached new heights during the First World War. Amid warfare and numerous crises, critics vociferously demanded change and complained that the small, restricted, and remote diplomatic institutions of the past no longer could cope with the complexity and chaos of such drastically transformed conditions. For the French and German Ministries for Foreign Affairs, among others, these upheavals marked a significant historical turning point from which there could be no return.

Astute observers in France and Germany were keenly aware of these developments. They began to understand that so long as a society is fairly stable the problems it presents to men and women tend to be routine and predictable, thus permitting institutions to remain relatively permanent. When change is accelerated, however, more and more novel and unforeseen problems arise, making traditional forms of organization obsolete and inadequate to meet the radically new conditions. Under these circumstances, they saw that in order to maintain control of their destinies they would have to learn how to adapt. They consciously and deliberately responded to their changing environment by designing the imaginative institutional mechanisms and practices now characteristic of all administrations responsible for managing foreign affairs. These responses took the shape of reforms (programs to reorganize, restructure, or reshuffle the already existing order) and innovations (actions to create entirely new arrangements). In the space of a few short years the once simple, traditional, quiet, and isolated ministerial bureaucracies were transformed into the large, complex, rationalized, specialized, and politically active institutions of modern diplomacy that we know today.

This study proposes to explain the nature of these changes and to analyze how the French and German Ministries for Foreign Affairs first reacted to the rigorous, sophisticated, and quantitatively different diplomacy of our own twentieth century. To do this, Chapter One first discusses the foundations and historical legacies of these ministerial bureaucracies. Chapter Two then demonstrates how they were subjected to a changing world, to domestic criticisms, and to numerous proposals for reform and innovation. Chapters Three and Four focus upon the men of action and the purposeful changes made in organizational structures, personnel policies, overseas services, and increased contacts with "outsiders." Chapters Five and Six examine the many new responsibilities assumed by these ministries for complex commercial and propagandistic matters.

Each chapter starts with a short introduction to set the stage, and proceeds to describe the general European milieu, to treat the specific case of France and then that of Germany, and finally to bring the two countries back into a common framework, followed by a few words of conclusion. The only exceptions to this format are the two chapters entitled "The French Response" and "The German Response" in which details of administrative operations are discussed separately. Despite the risk of occasional repetition, these are designed to benefit those specialists primarily concerned with either one country or the other. Finally, Chapter Seven analyzes the larger problems presented by the nature of institutional responses and diplomacy itself.

The French and German Ministries for Foreign Affairs are selected as case studies for several reasons. In the first place, the reforms and innovations in these bureaucracies were the first comprehensive institutional responses to twentieth-century diplomacy. Secondly, European diplomatic institutions traditionally are given an importance far beyond their own geographical borders due to their use as models by other countries around the globe. During the beginning of this century the Quai d'Orsay and the Wilhelmstrasse represented the two most influential, well-established, emulated, and highly respected foreign ministries of continental Europe. Finally—and perhaps most important—when analyzed jointly, these case studies of France and Germany provide the difficult but challenging opportunity of utilizing what the historian Marc Bloch termed "the logic of comparative history" to discover and delineate more universal patterns in human behavior.[1]

The question of responding to twentieth-century diplomacy has become an increasingly important issue to those concerned with managing foreign affairs. One reason for this is that those changes first occurring after the turn of the century have not stopped. They not only continue, but they characterize conditions associated with the diplomacy of our own day: complex commercial and legal questions requiring highly technical competence, sophistication in technology, formal international organizations, expanding numbers of new nations around the entire globe, the increased role of public opinion and propaganda, the growth of outside interest groups with a concern for external relations, the widening involvement of political leaders, and the breakdown of the homogeneity of traditional diplomatic practice, among others.

Another reason is a growing awareness of the fact that as change becomes a permanent and accelerating factor in our lives, adaptability to new conditions becomes the strongest single determinant of survival.[2] In the international sphere this means that former institutions of foreign affairs must either be reshaped or created anew in order to cope effectively with the expanding problems of diplomacy caused by change. Governments throughout the globe consequently are devoting considerable resources—quoting the instructions for a recently established commission—to explore "the changing world

---

1. On the methodology and usefulness of this approach, see the pioneering works of Marc Bloch, "Pour une histoire comparée des sociétés européens," *Revue de synthèse historique*, 46 (décembre 1928), pp. 15–50; Otto Hintze, *Soziologie und Geschichte*, 2nd ed. (Göttingen: Vandenhoeck und Ruprecht, 1964); Max Weber, *Gesammelte Aufsätze zur Wissenschaftslehre*, 2nd ed. (Tübingen: Mohr, 1951); Reinhard Bendix, "The Comparative Analysis of Historical Change," in R. Bendix and Günther Roth (eds.), *Scholarship and Partisanship: Essays on Max Weber* (Berkeley: University of California Press, 1971), pp. 207–24; and the essay by William H. Sewell, Jr., "Marc Bloch and the Logic of Comparative History," *History and Theory*, Vol. 6, No. 2 (1967), pp. 208–18.

2. See Alvin Toffler, *Future Shock* (New York: Bantam Books, 1970); and Warren G. Bennis, *Changing Organizations* (New York: McGraw-Hill, 1966); Frederick Mosher, *Governmental Reorganizations* (Syracuse: Inter-University Case Program, 1967); Louis Gawthrop, *Bureaucratic Behavior in the Executive Branch: An Analysis of Organizational Change* (New York: The Free Press, 1969); and Gerald Caiden, *Administrative Reform* (Chicago: Aldine, 1969).

environment and the manner in which international affairs are conducted" and to investigate "the organization, methods of operation, and powers of all departments, agencies, independent establishments, and instrumentalities . . . participating in the formulation and implementation of . . . foreign policy."[3]

In these recent efforts at reform and innovation, however, those involved find little historical information upon which to draw. They discover a lack of material covering previous attempts to deal with essentially the same problems. The reason is not difficult to determine. The attention of those studying modern history and international relations in the past has focused largely upon three areas: the political substance of major foreign policies, the personalities of leading decision makers, and the events of dramatic crisis situations. As a result, our knowledge of diplomacy frequently has been confined to "high policy" regarding such issues as war or peace, to a restricted number of leaders whose names and actions made headlines, or to sporadic episodes of tension and conflict. Obviously the problems and intricacies of international politics are infinitely more complex than indicated by these few highlights. Integral—but largely neglected—features of diplomacy, particularly in the twentieth century, must include the management of those policies encompassing more subtle commercial or "cultural" questions, the responsibilities of lesser bureaucratic officials in periods of both turmoil and stability, and the actual administrative machinery or organizational context of policy formulation and execution.

These elements can be calculated by focusing upon the nerve center of various types and levels of policy, of numerous civil servants and technical experts, of organized behavior patterns, and of the administration formally charged with managing external relations in an ever-changing environment: the Ministry for Foreign

3. United States, Congress and Office of the President, Commission on the Organization of the Government for the Conduct of Foreign Policy, "Tentative Program," COG/FP COM D 1 (1 August 1973), and "Mandate," COG/FP Staff 1 (15 April 1974). Also see Germany (Federal Republic), Auswärtiges Amt, Kommission für die Reform des Auswärtigen Dienstes, *Bericht der Kommission* (Bonn: Auswärtiges Amt, 1971); I. M. Destler, *Presidents, Bureaucrats and Foreign Policy* (Princeton: Princeton University Press, 1972); and Frederick Mosher, "Some Observations about Foreign Service Reform: 'Famous First Words,' " *Public Administration Review*, Vol. 29, No. 6 (November–December 1969), pp. 600–610.

Affairs. It is this institution of diplomats and bureaucrats which provides the liaison between a government and its agents abroad, sends instructions, receives and analyzes despatches, renders advice, protects nationals overseas, maintains contact with agencies and interest groups, and conducts relations with other countries. This organization is the ultimate focal point of all forces and persons seeking to influence foreign policy. It exists, therefore, as an integral part of society's entire political, social, economic, and intellectual fabric. As such, its behavior and structure reflect with considerable accuracy the impact of the many domestic and international pressures beating upon it.[4] For these reasons, observed one authority years ago, "the functions of the Ministry for Foreign Affairs are the most important and the most difficult of all public administration."[5]

It is hoped that such matters will be illumined by this study of the first institutional responses to twentieth-century diplomacy in France and Germany. It may raise questions and suggest new perspectives on several subjects of wider significance, including the process by which institutions develop and become subject to environmental pressures, the way in which people react to change and attempt to control it, the characteristics of modern diplomacy, the intimate relationship between a bureaucracy and society as a whole, the institutional factors of international relations, the importance of individuals in administrative structures, the interpenetrability of foreign and domestic politics, and the inherent difficulties of actually creating reforms and innovations. Hopefully our understanding of these issues in the recent past will help us to manage change peacefully for the future.

4. Lord Strang, *The Foreign Office* (New York: Oxford University Press, 1955), pp. 21ff.; and Frederick Schuman, "The Conduct of German Foreign Affairs," *The Annals of the American Academy of Political and Social Science* (November 1934), pp. 194, 220.

5. Guillaume de Garden, *Traité complet de diplomatie, ou théorie générale des relations extérieures des puissances de l'Europe* (Paris: Treuttal et Würtz, 1833), 1, p. 10.

— 1 —

The Foundations and Historical Legacy:
From King's Court to Ministerial Bureaucracy

> *Bureaucratization offers above all the optimum possibility for carrying through the principle of specializing administrative functions according to purely objective considerations. Individual performances are allocated to functionaries who have specialized training and who by constant practice learn more and more.*
>
> —Max Weber

The development of bureaucracy as a form of centralized administration provided European governments with a highly effective means of managing state affairs. Indeed, the superiority of such organizations in regulating large-scale operations significantly contributed to the entire historical evolution of the modern nation state. At first this administrative apparatus was rudimentary in nature, with only a small body of select advisors formed in council about the king. As the public nature of affairs increased at the expense of the monarch's own private household matters, it gradually became necessary for bureaucratic institutions to keep pace, expanding in size and growing in competence.

The administrative machinery designed to manage the state's foreign affairs represented a major part of this larger institutional development. As nations grew in power and territory, they completed and expanded at the expense of others, thus forcing issues of external relations to be of growing concern. Leaders in France and in Germany, as in other countries, therefore, designed centralized bureaucratic institutions to manage foreign affairs on a permanent basis. These ministries grew slowly in competence and complexity, however, for their institutional responses to problems were never any greater than the relatively slight domestic and international demands placed upon them.

When viewed from the perspective of the twentieth century, the French and German Ministries for Foreign Affairs—even by the end of the nineteenth century—still existed as rather limited and simple institutions. Business was conducted with small staffs, limited budgets, established traditions, and light work loads. Officials confined their attention to the European continent, to political matters, and to like-minded professionals alone. These conditions of relative simplicity, peacefulness, restricted outlook, and slower pace were appreciated and fostered by the elite diplomatic corps, and even today are recalled fondly as features of the *"gute alte Zeit"*[1] and the "golden age" of diplomacy.[2]

1. The Development of Bureaucracy

The evolution of the modern nation state system from medieval society introduced a new set of centralized administrative institutions to the world. Indeed, the emergence of these organs was concomitant with—and perhaps both cause and effect of—the state's own progression toward concentrated power and authority. In order to achieve territorial unification, political centralization, and economic consolidation, for example, monarchs needed to find a mechanism which could suppress the wide variety of autonomous entities characteristic of feudalism. To establish order and control over public affairs depended upon the ability to eliminate the centrifugal forces of feudal localism, agrarian parochialism, and the independence of provincial estates. The necessary instrument for such a task was found in the development and utilization of a permanent bureaucracy.[3]

1. Heinz Sasse, "Von Equipage und Automobilen des Auswärtigen Amts," *Nachrichtenblatt der Vereinigung Deutscher Auslandsbeamten*, Heft 10, 20. Jahrgang (October 1957), p. 145.

2. Charles Burton Marshall, "The Golden Age in Perspective," *Journal of International Affairs*, 17, 1 (1963), pp. 9–17.

3. Max Weber, *Wirtschaft und Gesellschaft* (Tübingen: Mohr, 1956 ed.), 2, pp. 559ff; Otto Hintze, "Die Entstehung der modernen Staatsministerien," *Historische Zeitschrift*, 100 (1907), pp. 53–111.

Absolute monarchs found that they could assert their authority over most spheres of life through a centralized bureaucratic form of administration. Methodical management could prevail over the less elaborate and more slovenly medieval institutions of the past. Uniform laws and systematic codes, when enforced with the power of the state, could render local customs or individuals obsolete. In short, centrally organized bureaucracy enabled them to transfer decision-making authority away from men known by their neighbors at the community level and establish it at the national level in the hands of professional bureaucrats.[4]

These bureaucrats performed more efficiently, more precisely, more dependably, and far less expensively than the courtiers and royal favorites of the feudalistic system who had no fixed duties, salaries, or expertise. The practice of dispersing offices as personal property to unqualified retainers or royal friends was replaced with one of employing trained experts on a contractual basis. Unabashedly, the new officials themselves stressed their own superiority by advancing the claim that the permanent civil servant represented a distinctive and especially valuable person. Since they sacrificed their entire lives to a collective lofty cause instead of selling their labor to a particular employer, they should be seen as the very embodiment of the state. They argued that such service entitled the bureaucrat to special security, special rights, and a special position of dignity and honor within society.[5]

In contrast with earlier administrative institutions and practices, these officials and the organizational components of *bureaucratie* in France and *Bürokratie* in Germany, as in other nations, began to provide the stability, predictability, and competence necessary for an efficient management of public affairs. Steadiness, increased uniformity, cooperation, and accountability in the discharge of common professional duties was encouraged by stress on collaborative efforts among bureaucrats and on the responsibility of administrative boards. Group action under central supervision further reduced the dangers of excessive graft, favoritism, and personal caprice known in the past.[6]

4. Henry Jacoby, *The Bureaucratization of the World* (Berkeley: University of California Press, 1973), p. 20.

5. Rosenberg, *Bureaucracy, Aristocracy and Autocracy* (Cambridge, Mass.: Harvard University Press, 1958), p. 94.

6. Ibid., p. 96.

By means of enumerated rules, prescribed routines, record keeping, divisions of labor, monetary compensation, and hierarchical authority structures, among other methods, bureaucracy could create well-defined spheres of specialization, develop functional proficiency, establish predictable behavior patterns, and coordinate many diverse activities in order to achieve specific objectives. The advance of bureaucratization, despite its many faults, has been its technical superiority over any other form of large organization. "The fully developed bureaucratic mechanism," wrote Max Weber, "compares with other organizations exactly as does the machine with the non-mechanical modes of production."[7]

As a consequence of these advantages, bureaucracy gradually was adopted as the administrative form by all governments and large-scale organizations. Some critics opposing its development spoke pejoratively of "bureaucracy" as the epitome of tortuous procedures, narrow outlook, rigid rules, duplication of effort, and autocratic officials. Yet their criticisms could not detract from either the utility or the durability of bureaucracy, nor could they retard its remarkable growth. Bureaucracy has been described as "the core of modern government,"[8] "the product of applied reason,"[9] and as part of "the common heritage of contemporary civilization."[10] The historical significance of this phenomenon is difficult to exaggerate, and leads one scholar to write: "Looking back over the past two and a half centuries of continental history the bureaucratic civil service may well pass as the greatest and most enduring achievement of the absolute monarchy, an achievement which, *mutatis mutandis,* survived all the revolutionary changes of the nineteenth century."[11]

The evolution of administrative institutions among the states of Europe proceeded with a remarkably parallel development pattern, although bureaucratization occurred more quickly and with greater success in some countries than in others. Yet governmental organizations evolved in each case as the nation adapted to environmental changes and to new conditions. Early administration, for example,

7. Weber, 2, p. 569.

8. Carl J. Friedrich, as cited in Jacoby, p. 25.

9. Fritz Morstein Marx, *The Administrative State* (Chicago: University of Chicago Press, 1957), p. 25.

10. Rosenberg, p. 13.

11. Walter Dorn, *Competition for Empire* (New York: Harper and Brothers, 1940), p. 21.

first was confined to the private and relatively simple needs of the king's personal household. The expansion of territory to be governed and a gradual increase in the complexity of affairs, however, imposed greater demands upon the monarch. Enlarged responsibilities for revenue collection, commercial protection, internal order, and defense against foreign competitors all tended to force the existing administrative apparatus to expand and move away from the royal family's limited private concerns and from the atmosphere of its court. For this reason the name of the *Conseil du Roi* (King's Council) was changed to the *Conseil d'Etat* (Council of State). In this process one begins to discern the fundamental transformation of the feudal into the public nature of governmental affairs.

With an expansion of responsibilities and the development of bureaucracy, there soon followed a necessary functional differentiation of tasks. Since no group of officials could be expected to have mastery over all aspects of public affairs, each had to specialize in one area or another. Individual departments gradually were established specifically to manage different functions. These early administrative institutions, in turn, served as foundations from which emerged the more sophisticated and complex ministerial bureaucracies of centralized modern government. One such bureaucracy was the ministry responsible for the management of foreign affairs.

2. The Ministry for Foreign Affairs in France

Until the end of the sixteenth and beginning of the seventeenth centuries, no stable organization of bureaucrats existed in France for the management of public affairs. Unity of direction was evident only insofar as authority emanated from the monarch to his few secretaries of state and their clerks. The crown alone determined the legal authorization of administrative measures and operational procedures, and both the king and his servants functioned in an atmosphere largely divorced from public accountability. They made little attempt to create the bureaucratic characteristics of division of labor and specialization. Instead, they discussed matters of state *in plenum* within the king's executive council where foreign affairs could not be distinguished administratively from internal matters, for issues and problems were dispersed arbitrarily among random secretaries.[12] This, in turn, often resulted in competing jurisdictions, ill-defined authority, and much instability.

The first effort to remedy this disadvantageous and inconvenient system was taken by Henri III (1574–1589), a monarch well-acquainted with foreign intrigue and the dangers of hostile alliances. As opponents threatened his authority toward the end of his reign, he suddenly dismissed his four state secretaries and concentrated the management of foreign affairs in the hands of one trusted official named Louis de Révol. According to his ordinance of 1 January 1589, this man henceforth became responsible for all correspondence with foreign countries, which at that time comprised Italy, Piedmont, Savoy, Switzerland, Spain, the Levant, Poland, Sweden, Denmark, Britain, Scotland, and the German states. By entrusting such a duty to a single individual, this ordinance can be said to mark the birth of the position of the French Secretary of State for Foreign Affairs.[13]

Révol and his successors slowly acquired a small staff of permanent bureaucratic officials as the amount of work gradually increased. It soon became apparent that these bureaucrats could contribute significantly to the strength and well-being of the state. By devoting themselves to the service of the crown they provided stability in administration and acquired growing competence in management. In recognition of their worth, the able Henri IV (1589–1610) promoted the faithful personnel who served as *commis* (assistants) and clerks, including those serving immediately under the Secretary of State for Foreign Affairs. He raised their rank, increased their status, enlarged their numbers, and gave them greater responsibility. These officials eventually received regular salaries instead of meager piece-work payment for documents copied by hand. Such changes increasingly indicated the slow but steady rise of a bureaucratic elite.[14]

This evolution of skilled administrators entrusted with greater responsibilities developed further under Cardinal Richelieu. Appointed first minister in 1622, this shrewd, ambitious, and brilliant

---

12. H. Griolet, *Le Ministère des Affaires étrangères* (Paris: Charles-Lavauzelle, 1900), p. 6.

13. Camille Piccioni, *Les premiers commis des affaires étrangères au XVIIe et au XVIIIe siècles* (Paris: Boccard, 1928), p. 14; and Amédée Outrey, "Histoire et principes de l'administration française des affaires étrangères," *Revue française de science politique*, 3, 2 (April–June 1953), pp. 303ff.

14. Piccioni, passim.

leader sought to achieve absolute power for the state. By elevating *raison d'état* as the fundamental principle for all domestic and external policy, Richelieu desired to eliminate governmental inefficiency in its various forms. He launched a thorough investigation into the problems of administration and the specific techniques of management, resulting in major changes for the French navy, economy, bureaucracy, and the organization responsible for foreign affairs. Here his achievements earned the accolades of one diplomat who referred to him as "the model for all statesmen, to whom France owes a very great debt."[15]

Much of his success derived from the fact that Richelieu recognized the importance of establishing and maintaining control, competence, and continuity in the management of external relations. His statute of 11 March 1626 formed a major landmark in creating these features within the French Ministry for Foreign Affairs.[16] The advantages offered by permanence of administration, as he stated in his celebrated passage in *Testament politique,* could never be ignored:

> States receive so much benefit from continuous foreign negotiations, if they are conducted with prudence, that it is unbelievable unless it is known from experience. . . . I am now so convinced of its validity that I dare say emphatically that it is absolutely necessary to the well-being of the state to *negotiate ceaselessly, either openly or secretly, and in all places,* even in those from which no present fruits are reaped and still more in those for which no future prospects as yet seem likely. I can truthfully say that I have seen in my time the nature of affairs change completely for both France and the rest of Christendom as a result of my having, under the authority of the King, put this principle into practice—something up to then completely neglected in this realm.[17]

The practices inaugurated by Richelieu were elaborated during the flowering of French power and culture in the long reign of Louis XIV (1643–1715). Particularly in matters of foreign affairs, Louis

---

15. François de Callières, *On the Manner of Negotiating with Princes,* translated by A. F. Whyte (Notre Dame: University of Notre Dame Press, 1963 ed.), p. 14.

16. Outrey, 3, 2, pp. 304–5.

17. Cardinal de Richelieu, "Que fait voir qu'une négociation continuelle ne contribue pas peu au bon succès des affaires," in *Testament politique,* ed. by Louis André (Paris: Robert Laffont, 1947), p. 347.

and his minister, Jean Baptiste Colbert, stressed the importance of competence, reviewed the detailed aspects of administrative organization and procedure, and insisted upon practical adjustments to grapple effectively with the needs of an expanding policy. Emphasis was placed, for example, upon preserving orderly records, standardized registers, memoirs, and periodic accounts.[18] In order to develop specialized expertise, they created two separate geographical divisions to manage all matters of external relations. The first handled Spain, Portugal, Britain, the German states, and the Papacy, while the other administered affairs with Turkey, the Italian states, Poland, Denmark, Russia, Sweden, and Switzerland.[19]

Administrative specialization also developed with the gradual emergence of distinct internal services. These included the *Cabinet du Ministre* (Minister's Cabinet), the Cypher Bureau, and the *Bureau des Fonds* (Accounting Office) charged with managing the ministerial bureaucracy, issuing passports, conducting surveillance on foreigners, handling matters of protocol, and supervising appointments and transfers.[20] Although such functional differentiation proved necessary, officials themselves often seemed to care much less about the actual form or structure of the institution than about their choice of men to fill these positions. At times this meant that the administrative divisions and the numbers of personnel in each department could be determined more by convenience, opportunity, or personal intrigue than by a rational system of organization.[21] Yet this apparently presented few problems because the staff of bureaucrats remained small, stable, and known personally to the king. Such luxury was permitted in the *ancien régime* by the relative simplicity of the international system and its problems and by the absence of domestic demands upon the conduct of foreign relations. In the eyes of one scholar, these conditions reflected "the glorious era of diplomacy."[22]

18. E. N. Gladden, *A History of Public Administration* (London: Cass, 1972), 2, pp. 147–49; James King, *Science and Rationalism in the Government of Louis XIV, 1661–1683* (Baltimore: Johns Hopkins, 1949), pp. 91, 95, 104, 311; and Richard Sallet, *Der diplomatische Dienst* (Stuttgart: Deutsche Verlags–Anstalt, 1953), pp. 31–53.

19. Piccioni, pp. 27ff.

20. Ibid. A brief account of the development of the archives department can be found in France, Ministère des Affaires étrangères, *Chefs d'État, ministres, grands traités de la France* (Paris: Palais des Affaires étrangères, 1960), p. 3.

21. Outrey, 3, 2, pp. 313, 318.

22. Griolet, p. 6.

This early administrative machinery of foreign affairs met the needs for which it was designed. The organization even received praise from persons highly critical of most other features found in French monarchical government. Before no less ferocious a body than the Committee of Public Safety during the French Revolution, for example, a report describing the advantages of centralized administrative authority forcefully declared: "Under the monarchy, only the Department of Foreign Affairs was well administered. From Henri IV until 1756, the Bourbons did not commit a single mistake."[23]

Despite the dramatic upheavals of the Revolutionary and Napoleonic periods and the turmoil within French political institutions, the ministry responsible for the administration of external affairs remained strong, benefiting from the acquired experience and tradition of the *ancien régime*.[24] Due to its dependence upon experts, the National Convention actually accelerated the process of concentrating administrative competence in matters of foreign policy within a single department. The Decree of 14 February 1793, to illustrate, transferred all authority over French consular services and foreign commercial relations from the Ministry of Marine to the *Ministère des Relations Extérieures* (Ministry for Foreign Relations). Executive orders issued by the Directoire in Year VII and by Napoleon in 1810 required that all official correspondence from and to foreign diplomatic representatives be under the sole jurisdiction of the Ministry. Further decrees elevated the status and security of all diplomats and bureaucrats within the central administration. In addition, the position of the *fonctionnaire public* (civil servant) within the Ministry was advanced by replacing the former subjectiveness of the royal wish with the rudiments of standardization in recruitment, advancement, and discipline among personnel.[25]

The Revolution also portended events of the future by raising serious issues concerning the formulation, control, and execution of a state's foreign policy. What, for example, were the proper roles and respective powers of parliament and the executive branch of government in matters of external affairs? Would the Minister for Foreign Affairs find that his responsibility before the legislature

23. As cited in Frederick Masson, *Le Départment des affaires étrangères pendant la Révolution, 1787–1804* (Paris: Plon, 1877), p. 327.
24. Ibid., p. 496.
25. Outrey, 3, 3 (July–September 1953), pp. 491–500.

increased his political role at the expense of his administrative functions? Could legislative commissions on foreign affairs ever develop sufficient competence to make their influence felt upon the actual administration of policy? Is propaganda able to play any role in international relations? Do periods of domestic upheaval or external crises unleash demands upon institutions for reform? If so, what is the most effective way to institute such changes in response to new conditions?

With the end of the Revolution and the collapse of the Napoleonic Empire, however, these questions of external affairs remained largely unanswered. The restored Bourbon monarchy placed a higher priority upon establishing peace and stability than upon solving these more abstract problems. As a consequence, attention centered upon reconfirming the basic simplicity of the Ministry's structure and operations. Regulations created in 1825 organized the Ministry for Foreign Affairs into three specialized divisions. The important Political Division managed the most crucial matters of international politics. A new Commercial Division indicated that commerce might begin to play a greater role in the relations among states. Finally, the lesser Chancelleries and Archives Division handled questions of protocol, records, diplomatic gifts, passports, and legalizations. General administrative problems, cyphers, accounting, and secretarial services were entrusted to the *Cabinet du Ministre*.[26]

This organization, established during the Restoration, remained essentially the same throughout the entire nineteenth century. The central administration of the Ministry for Foreign Affairs demonstrated remarkably little change, and the vast body of regulations governing French administrative structures continued basically untouched, despite much domestic instability. Minor modifications and brief shufflings of functions occurred occasionally, but these were never more than temporary arrangements.[27] The administration remained small, and the major departments continued as simply

26. Ibid., pp. 505–6; and "Note summaire sur l'organisation de l'administration centrale du ministère des Affaires étrangères depuis 1814 jusqu'en 1877," Appendix 10 in Masson, pp. 539–40.

27. For example, the *arrêté* of 23 March 1832, the *ordonnance* of 13 August 1844, *décret impérial* of 26 December 1869, and the *décrets* of 1 February 1877, 12 January 1880, and 12 May 1891 several of which are found in the original in MAE, Direction du Personnel, Carton 27, "Organisation du Ministère, II. Décrets, Arrêtés, Rapports, Ordonnances, Circulaires, Notes, etc., 1860–1896."

the Political and Commercial Divisions.[28] Throughout this period of traditional diplomacy, the Ministry never increased more in size, complexity, or responsibility than was required by internal domestic pressures and by demands of the international system.

The administration of French foreign policy, in its day-to-day activities, was conducted largely by the Minister for Foreign Affairs. He retained this essential responsibility regardless of the various forms of French government. In fact, the Minister's official description of duties remained exactly the same from Talleyrand to the 1890s: "The negotiation and execution of political and commercial treaties and conventions; correspondence with ambassadors, ministers, diplomatic, and commercial agents."[29] Thus charged with the management of all important matters of French foreign relations, the Minister possessed relatively great freedom of action within the Ministry itself. He was assisted by his own personal cabinet and secretaries who managed the distribution of despatches and much of the internal administrative business. Immediately subordinate to him were the respective Directors of Divisions, followed by their *Sous-Directeurs* (Assistant Directors), *Chefs du Service*, and others, including *rédacteurs, commis principaux, expéditionnaires, secrétaire archivistes, attachés payés*, and *attachés stagiaires*.[30]

The Director of Political Affairs held responsibility for the administration of all political and legal questions connected with foreign countries other than those subjects dealt with directly by the Minister. To facilitate expedition of these matters, a departmental division of labor occurred on the basis of the two basic subdivisions or *sous-directions* first created by Talleyrand: *Nord* and *Midi*. As their titles indicate, these administrative units used geography as the

---

28. MAE/Sénat, Rapport No. 148 (1913), p. 34. Also see PRO/FO 881/129, "Note sur l'organisation intérieure du Ministère des Affaires étrangères, comprenant les modifications apportées à l'ordonnance royale du 13 août, 1844" and idem, "Ordonnance du Roi portant organisation centrale du Ministère des Affaires étrangères du 19 septembre, 1864."

29. France, *Almanach impérial 1805* (Paris: Guyot et Scribe, 1805), p. 120; France, *Almanach impérial 1860* (Paris: Guyot et Scribe, 1860), p. 113; and France, Ministère des Affaires étrangères, *Annuaire diplomatique et consulaire, 1889* (Paris: Berger–Levrault, 1889).

30. The precise number of each category of personnel in all divisions are listed every year prior to 1907 in France, Ministère des Affaires étrangères, *Compte définitif des dépenses de l'exercice 18— –1907* (Paris: Imprimerie nationale, until 1896; then Melun: Imprimerie administrative, 1897–1907).

criterion for the allocation of tasks. The first (in both organizational and political terms) was *Nord*, charged with managing affairs with Britain, Russia, Austria, Prussia and the other German states, the Low Countries, Sweden, Denmark, and the respective colonies of these countries. The second, *Midi*, managed relations with areas of much lesser importance: Spain, Portugal, the Italian states, Switzerland, Greece,the Ottoman Empire, and Morocco.[31]

This administrative division of political affairs thus reflected a most important feature of the nineteenth-century international system: that foreign affairs were confined essentially to those relations among *European* states. Bureaus to manage American, Far Eastern, Southeast Asian, or African affairs remained either nonexistent or subject to a confused and unstable development.[32] Furthermore, these divisions demonstrate the fact that, under this classical system, a very real distinction existed between the Great Powers and those of secondary importance, or the Small Powers. The smaller or weaker states lived as victims, subjects, or pawns in the great chess game of diplomacy. Major decisions were made and enforced by that club of the elite: France, Britain, Russia, Austria, and Prussia. All other states could be used, divided, traded, or sold.

The Commercial Division assumed responsibility for managing all questions relating to French commercial interests abroad and to the commerce of foreigners within France. This involved the preparation of commercial and navigational treaties, advice on the protection of French commerce, monetary conventions, patents, tariffs, consular affairs, and agents of the consular service. The internal division of labor first followed the pattern set by the Political Division with only two geographical sub-units. Yet as dissatisfaction with this system intensified through time, officials found it more practical to differentiate commercial matters by functional criteria. This eventually led to the subdivisions of Commercial Affairs, Con-

31. The geographical distribution for each year can be followed in the respective issues of France, Ministère des Affaires étrangères, *Annuaire diplomatique et consulaire de la République française*.

32. A bureau to manage American and West Indian affairs, for example, was hesitantly created in 1844, suppressed in 1848, and then combined with Indo-China and equally subdivided among both the Political and Commercial Divisions in 1856. Later regulations in 1880, 1883, and 1855 tossed these matters back and forth between *Nord* and *Midi*.

sular Affairs, and Chancellery Affairs, the latter handling tariffs, notarial services, judicial commissions, and passports.[33]

The administrative services of the French Ministry for Foreign Affairs slowly expanded throughout the course of the century. The *Cabinet du Ministre* managed the personal correspondence and appointments of the Minister himself, translations, the cyphering service, opening of despatches, and diplomatic personnel matters. As in Germany, this administrative division between diplomatic and consular personnel led to rivalries and bitterness, with the latter category feeling administratively and politically excluded from important decisions of foreign policy. The *Direction des Fonds et de la Comptabilité* further expedited work relating to the general administration of the Ministry, budget, and account items from salaries to secret funds and diplomatic gifts. An Archives Division completed the organization, being responsible for the preservation, classification, and communication of documents to a few selectively authorized personnel.

By mid-century this institution became firmly established in its impressive residence on the left bank of the Seine at 37, Quai d'Orsay.[34] Located near an ornate bridge later dedicated to Tsar Alexander III and between the great *Esplanade des Invalides* and the *Palais Bourbon*, the building became—and remains to this day—the central administration for the French Ministry for Foreign Affairs. It is from this location that the Ministry derives its now-traditional identification as the "Quai d'Orsay," just as another diplomatic thoroughfare in Berlin was to make the name of "Wilhelmstrasse" synonymous with the German Ministry for Foreign Affairs.

3. The Ministry for Foreign Affairs in Germany

In seventeenth-century Brandenburg the administrative matters of state were managed by a *Geheimer Rat* (Privy Council) over

---

33. The various descriptions of functions can be found in the respective issues of the *Annuaire diplomatique et consulaire de la République française*.

34. France, Ministère des Affaires étrangères, *Le Ministère des Affaires étrangères, residence des Chefs d'Etat, hôtes de la France* (Paris: Ministère des Affaires étrangères, n.d.), pp. 3–5.

which personally presided the Great Elector, Frederick William (1640–1688). The collegial nature of this body emphasized its collective responsibility for all issues of administration. As in France, functional departmentalization did not exist, and the council as a whole considered foreign policy, territorial defense, economic and financial questions, and matters of domestic administration, among others. This cumbersome process of *in plenum* discussions often resulted in delayed decisions, inefficiency, lack of secrecy, and failure to develop specialized competence or permanence among the crown's servants.

The difficulties and problems created by this process slowly became apparent, and the Great Elector decided that political matters, particularly those of foreign policy, should be removed to a smaller, more intimate group of counsellors gathered about himself in his own chamber.[35] Within this smaller cabinet group he assigned the title of *Geheimer Etatssekretarius* (State Secretary) to a specific official responsible for external relations.[36] This action, when combined with the Great Elector's determination to make decisions without restrictions from any other body, sufficiently stripped the privy council of its importance as the center of administration. The decline became dramatically apparent when the council actually was forbidden to discuss matters of external affairs.[37]

As the broad jurisdiction of the early Privy Council narrowed, the tendency for departmental specialization increased. During the end of the seventeenth and beginning of the eighteenth centuries, certain spheres of administration gradually concentrated in the hands of a few officials who demonstrated growing competence and independence in specialized matters. Slowly there emerged those features most characteristic of bureaucratic organizations: the enumeration of permanent responsibilities, specialization, general rules for prescribed routines of organized behavior, and hierarchical levels of authority. In this regard, as in many others, the administration of

35. Rheinhold Dorwart, *The Administrative Reforms of Frederick William I* (Cambridge, Mass.: Harvard University Press, 1953), p. 11.

36. Heinz Sasse, "Zur Geschichte des Auswärtigen Amts," *Mitteilungsblatt der Vereinigung der Angestellten des Auswärtigen Dienstes*, Heft 5, 4 Jahrgang (May 1960), p. 107.

37. See, for example, the order published in G. Schmoller et al., eds., *Acta Borussica. Die Behördenorganisation und die allgemeine Staatsverwaltung Preussens im 18. Jahrhundert* (Berlin: Parey, 1894–1908), 2, 9, pp. 28–30.

foreign affairs proved to be an integral part of the larger development and evolution of Prussian, and later German, institutions.

Frederick William I (1713–1740), with his passion for the minute details of public service, further defined areas of administrative responsibility and began to lay the foundations of a stable organization to manage foreign affairs.[38] He accomplished this in part by charging three men with the management of all external relations. The "Report of the three Privy Counsellors called to the direction of Foreign and Public Affairs" issued during the first month of his reign provides ample testimony to the order of business in the conduct of foreign policy.[39] The counsellors, it states, will have the power to open all letters and reports coming to the crown except those specifically marked "personal." Each item will be accompanied by a receipt from the post office, and the date and contents of each letter will be recorded in a special registry. Decisions will be made by the king himself, although reports of the advisors will be submitted to him in advance. The monarch's decision shall be recorded in writing, with all three counsellors held responsible for the written contents. The countersignature in all matters of administering Prussian foreign affairs, the king noted, shall belong to one of the counsellors, Heinrich Rüdiger von Ilgen.

This last provision for the countersignature of Ilgen is worth particular attention, for it is indicative of the gradual—although somewhat sporadic—tendency in both France and Germany toward concentrating foreign affairs in the hands of a single managing director with a rudimentary supportive staff of subordinate officials.[40] Born in the mid-seventeenth century, Ilgen had been trained for diplomatic service in the typical manner by studying law and political science, and brought to Berlin upon the recommendation of the great mathematician-philosopher, Leibnitz. After 1697 he was the only surviving figure from the reign of the Great Elector who had lengthy experience in the formulation and execution of Prussian foreign policy. This professional expertise, his comprehension of

38. Peter Baumgart, "Zur Gründungsgeschichte des Auswärtigen Amtes in Preussen, 1713–1728," *Jahrbuch für die Geschichte Mittel- und Ostdeutschlands*, 7 (1958), pp. 231–41.

39. "Immediatbericht der drei zur Leitung der auswärtigen und publiquen Affairen berufenen Wirklichen Geheimen Räthe," as published in *Acta Borussica*, 1, 92, pp. 313–16.

40. Dorwart, pp. 47–49.

the operational features of bureaucracy, and Frederick William's personal confidence in him combined to give Ilgen a favored position in the administration of external relations from 1713 to 1728.[41] In fact, his enemies (of whom, as he himself remarked, "unfortunately I have only too many") referred to him as the "omnipotent" managing director for foreign affairs.[42]

Ilgen retained favor until he neared the age of eighty, when Frederick William personally requested a memorandum from him suggesting future reorganization for the small *Department der auswärtigen Affairen* (Department for Foreign Affairs). He informed the king that he did not know of a single person capable of coping with all the demands inherent in the position of director, and loyally stated that he placed his greatest hopes in the king himself for the management of foreign affairs. Beyond that modest suggestion, however, Ilgen proposed reverting to a collegial directorate with two divisions for the department. Secret foreign affairs would be conducted by two ministers and their secretary in one division, and the other would manage more general matters dealing with the Holy Roman Empire, lawsuits in the imperial court, and the rights and privileges of the royal house.[43]

These recommendations of Ilgen were adopted as the basis of reorganization, and in December 1728 the small department for foreign affairs received the king's "Instruction for Lieutenant General von Borck and Privy Counsellor von Cnyphausen in what manner Foreign Affairs and Imperial Matters should be conducted."[44] This new organization received no formal name at that time, but was officially designated in 1733 as the *Cabinetsministerium*.[45] The ministry continued as one of the three supreme organs of Prussian administration, and when the order of importance among state offices was determined later, it ranked above both the General Directory and the Ministry of Justice.[46]

This organization designed to manage external relations expanded slowly, for its administration was not entrusted to a single

41. *Acta Borussica*, 1, p. 808; ibid., pp. 49, 227.

42. Ibid., 4:2, 242, p. 386.

43. The report itself is found in ibid., 4:2, 242, pp. 377ff.

44. Ibid., pp. 397–401.

45. R. Koser, "Die Gründung des Auswärtigen Amtes durch König Friedrich Wilhelm I. im Jahre 1728," *Forschungen zur Brandenburgischen und Preussischen Geschichte*, 2 (1889), pp. 169–70.

46. Dorwart, p. 52.

bureaucrat as it previously had been given to the able Ilgen. Instead, the king increased the number of major officials to three, giving each the significant title of *Kabinetsminister* and the assistance of a secretary corresponding to the French *premier commis*.[47] Further support came from the small staff of the *Geheime Staatskanzlei* (Privy State Chancery) which tediously hand-copied all departmental correspondence. Authority for the control and coordination of this organizational arrangement, as with all other governmental institutions, rested in the person of the king. If he insisted upon exercising his prerogative to conduct policy in person, as in the case of Frederick the Great, the impact upon foreign affairs could be crucial.

As a result of the first Silesian War, Frederick the Great (1740—1786) succeeded in expanding his territory and thrusting Prussia into the position of a major European power. To protect his newly-enlarged state from destruction at the hands of hostile neighbors required skillful administration, the mobilization of resources necessary to support his army, and the ability to conduct a most adroit diplomacy. This goal he accomplished by means of centralized organization and a high degree of discipline and order. The principle, *le roi fait tout*, became an accurate description of the Prussian administrative process. Frederick himself said in referring to his philosophy of administration: "The prince is to the society that he governs as the head is to the body: he must see, think and act for all."[48]

Frederick was a careful observer of France and its institutions, and frequently centered his attention upon the French monarchy's approach to foreign affairs. Following the tradition established by Richelieu, for example, he succeeded in elevating the principle of *raison d'état* as the ultimate test by which the foreign policy of a state should be pursued. He thought the French institutional system extremely inefficient, however, in the actual administration of that policy. Frederick ridiculed the idea that separate ministries could effectively manage different aspects of policy, maintaining that affairs of state should be strictly controlled by the prince. In France, he said, each ministry—including the Ministry for Foreign

47. The title of *Kabinetsminister* remained until the Revolution of 1848. See Sasse, "Zur Geschichte des Auswärtigen Amts," Heft 5, p. 107. For a listing of the ministers from 1728 to 1807, see Koser, p. 175.

48. Frédéric II, "Essai sur les formes de gouvernement et sur les devoirs des souverains," in *Oeuvres historiques de Frédéric II, Roi de Prusse*, 9, pp. 200–201.

Affairs—held so much independence that it could be considered as being ruled by a separate "king."[49] This "defect" would not be fostered under his regime and, although the *Cabinetsministerium* still existed, he deprived it of its independence by conducting his own policy and undertaking direct correspondence with his ambassadors.

This system of personal rule, however, was impermanent by its very nature. Such arrangements are absolutely dependent upon the abilities of a single individual, and quickly collapse under any less able successor. Frederick did not succeed in establishing lasting institutions of administration because, like Bismarck later, his own personality tolerated only subaltern assistants rather than independent and capable collaborators.[50] Personally-tailored administrative organs often provide no established mechanism for change, encourage unquestioned obedience to authority, and prevent the imposition of legal or political checks upon power.

With the death of Frederick the Great, the few ministers and secretaries charged with administering foreign affairs were able to accede to a new status. His passing removed the cloud of excessive restrictions, intrigue, and punishment, permitting these bureaucrats to increase their independence and influence.[51] Less opinionated and less presumptuous monarchs realized that the talents of these officials could be utilized more efficiently by advising and reporting rather than simply writing, copying, or cyphering despatches. Through time this recognition led to a greater differentiation of functions within the Ministry. By 1792, for example, different ranks of personnel had been created in the emerging civil service career: *Vortragende Geheime Räte* (a designation which lasted until 1919), *Geheime Expedierende Sekretäre,* and the lesser persons of the *Büro.*[52]

During the course of German history, the fortunes and development of the Ministry for Foreign Affairs continued to be attuned

49. Frédéric II, "Exposé du gouvernement prussien," in ibid., p. 190. Also see Hintze, p. 81.

50. On this point see Gerhard Ritter, *Frederick the Great: A Historical Profile*, translated by Peter Paret (Berkeley: University of California Press, 1968), pp. 154–55; and Rosenberg, p. viii.

51. Gladden, II, p. 165; and Rosenberg, passim.

52. Koser, p. 180; and Sasse, "Zur Geschichte des Auswärtigen Amts," Heft 5, pp. 109, 112.

closely to the international and domestic currents of the time. In this tradition, the upheavals of the French Revolution and the Napoleonic periods proved to be no exception. The collapse of the old Prussian administrative system at the hands of Napoleon's army not only exposed the weaknesses of the earlier regime but offered new opportunities for change. The collegial nature of ministerial leadership, for instance, was soon dissolved because of its unmanageable nature.[53] Following the French example, individual ministers received the right to have direct access to the king and to be made directly responsible to him. More specifically, some of the first Stein-Hardenberg reforms succeeded in introducing an organizational reconstruction of the institution designed to manage foreign affairs.

The resulting *Preussisches Ministerium der auswärtigen Angelegenheiten* (Prussian Ministry for Foreign Affairs) was given much greater autonomy than its predecessor under Frederick the Great. As a consequence, diplomats and bureaucrats within the organization had more opportunities to express their own opinions. Yet the Ministry's structure and organization still remained small and simple. Division of labor occurred only insofar as matters of international relations could be separated into either political or nonpolitical categories. The king's Decree of 27 October 1810, for example, simply created two major administrative units: the Political and the Commercial Divisions. The first section was charged with the general administration of all political matters between Prussia and other states. The second managed internal administrative matters, commercial and financial issues, consulates, boundaries, passports, and all other questions "not pertaining to high political affairs."[54]

Further establishment of this arrangement resulted from the 1819 purchase of the residence at Wilhelmstrasse 76 in Berlin. Located not far from the *Wilhelmsplatz* and flanked by a palace belonging to Prince Radziwill, the impressive building and its spacious garden were purchased from the Russian Minister Alopeus. "On either side right and left of the staircase," recorded one contemporary in describing its exterior, "crouches a sphinx—mute, deep-gazing, and

53. Gustav Roloff, "Die Neuorganisation des Ministeriums des Auswärtigen von 1798–1802," *Forschungen zur Brandenburgischen und Preussischen Geschichte*, 7 (1894), pp. 97–111.

54. As cited in Sasse, "Zur Geschichte des Auswärtigen Amts," Heft 5, p. 112.

doubtless profoundly wise, which the stranger may regard as an intimation that he stands on the threshold of a mysterious region, inaccessible to most mortals."[55] This building housed the central administrative core of the Prussian—later German—Ministry for Foreign Affairs, and its two stone sphinxes guarded the portals of German diplomacy until the end of the Second World War.[56]

The 1810 division of the Ministry into two sections remained—except for brief periods of turmoil and crisis—the essential structural foundation of the organization throughout the entire nineteenth century.[57] This was the institution that Otto von Bismarck inherited upon ascending to power in 1862 and with which he forged policies that would transform the diverse Prussian states system into the unified nation-state of Germany. In this process, the Ministry for Foreign Affairs became successively that of Prussia (*Preussische Ministerium des Auswärtigen Angelegenheiten*), of the North German Confederation (*Auswärtiges Amt des Norddeutschen Bundes*) in 1867, and of united Germany (*Auswärtiges Amt des Deutschen Reiches*) following the new constitution of 1871.[58] The Wilhelmstrasse of the new German Empire thus represented an extension of the former Prussian Ministry for Foreign Affairs as it had developed from the Hardenburg era, and until 1919 there still existed no organic division between the two. As a consequence of this combined role, the Ministry was responsible not only for the relations between Germany and foreign countries, but also for those between the central government and the federal German states.[59]

55. Moritz Busch, *Bismarck: Some Secret Pages of His History* (New York: Macmillan, 1898), 1, p. 427.

56. For a brief history, see Herbert von Hindenburg, *Das Auswärtige Amt im Wandel der Zeiten* (Frankfurt am Main: Societäts–Verlag, 1932), p. 6.

57. See PA/AA, Büro des Reichsministers, Aktenzeichen 2, Band 1, copy of Report No. 862 from Finance Minister Wirth to the President of the Reichstag, "Organisationspläne der Reichsministerien," dated 8 November 1920, p. 2; and Sasse, "Zur Geschichte des Auswärtigen Amts," Heft 5, pp. 114–16.

58. The designation of *Amt* (Office) was personally selected by Bismarck under the rationale that foreign affairs constituted a branch of the personal business of the Chancellor, and that its administration should thus be in a Foreign Office responsible to him. In view of its development and history before and after the Bismarckian period, however, the institution is referred to throughout this study as the German Ministry for Foreign Affairs. See Heinz Sasse, "Die Entstehung der Bezeichnung 'Auswärtiges Amt,' " *Nachrichtenblatt der Vereinigung Deutscher Auslandsbeamten*, Heft 10, 19. Jahrgang (October 1956), pp. 85–89.

59. American Historical Association, *A Catalogue of Files and Microfilms of the German Foreign Ministry Archives, 1867–1920* (Oxford: Oxford University Press, 1959), pp. xiii–xvi.

Foreign policy in the new Reich received direction from the able but domineering hands of Bismarck who, as Imperial Chancellor and Prussian Foreign Minister, was appointed by the Kaiser and responsible to him alone. The *Staatssekretär* (State Secretary) followed as his immediate subordinate and was directly responsible for the management of the Ministry for Foreign Affairs. The new constitution, however, made no changes in the internal structure of the organization. Bismarck recommitted the Ministry to the concept of two major divisions of political and non-political matters.[60]

Throughout the nineteenth century responsibility for all major activity of international politics rested in the hands of the exclusive inner circle of the Political Division, first called *Abteilung I* and then *IA*, but referred to by the intimates simply as "A."[61] The annual official description of its functions told the story tersely and simply: *"höhere Politik."*[62] This division held charge of all important problems of foreign policy, including colonial affairs, until 1890.[63] It also exercised a considerable degree of control over the work of the other departments which were obliged to submit to it for countersignature all matters with political implications. Questions involving railway construction or foreign loans, for example, which would normally be handled by those specializing in commercial affairs, often had to be submitted to the Political Division.[64]

Abteilung I itself and the daily work of the Ministry was administered by the State Secretary with the assistance, after 1881, of an Under State Secretary. Within the division internal distribution of duties remained very unstructured, as specific responsibilities frequently followed individuals rather than being assigned to permanent administrative positions. Functional subject matter rather than

60. PA/AA, Politisches Archiv und Historisches Referat, Aktenzeichen 12, "Geschichte der alten 2. (staatsrechtlich-handelspolitischen) Abteilung," pp. 1–3 and passim. Another *Abteilung* had been briefly established in 1854, but then discontinued.

61. Joseph Maria von Radowitz, *Aufzeichnungen und Erinnerungen*, ed. by Hajo Holborn (Berlin: Deutsche Verlags, 1925), 1, p. 255.

62. See, for example, Germany, Reichsamt des Innern, *Handbuch für das Deutsche Reich, 1874* (Berlin: Carl Heymanns, 1874), p. 51, and idem., *Handbuch für das Deutsche Reich, 1894* (Berlin: Carl Heymanns, 1894), p. 43.

63. A separate but short-lived *Kolonial Abteilung (IV)* was created in 1890, but in 1907 was removed entirely from the Ministry and established as the *Reichskolonialamt*.

64. PA/AA, Politisches Archiv und Historisches Referat, Aktenzeichen 11, "Geschichte der Politischen Abteilung 1870–1920," p. 2.

geography provided the basis for a rudimentary division of labor, and only gradually did certain *Vortragende Räte* (counsellors)— such as the powerful Friedrick von Holstein—become responsible for individual countries or specific territorial areas.[65] In turn, these officials received support from the *Ständiger Hilfsarbeiter* (assistants) and from the *Expedienten* (clerks). Again, as in France, their perspective of international politics in the nineteenth century was confined largely to the continent of Europe. When a subordinate once suggested seeking more cordial relations with the United States, Bismarck furiously rejected the whole notion because, as he explained, Americans "don't matter at all."[66]

The Commercial-Legal Division (*Abteilung II*) held responsibility for matters of trade and commerce. Some of its duties included the management of commercial and financial policy, the consular service, currency, grievances and claims, postal issues, and navigational questions. This division similarly managed all legislation and issues involving international law until 1885 when officials created a separate Legal Division (*Abteilung III*). Traditional attitudes, however, still held commercial matters in much lower esteem than the work of the seemingly omnipotent Political Divison. Diplomats and bureaucrats sometimes were assigned here for disciplinary reasons, and in frustrated moods they said among themselves that "Division II equals *capitis diminutio.*"[67] To make this separation of political from non-political questions even more explicit, the respective bureaus were housed in different buildings—the Commercial Division being in the "other house."[68]

In keeping with early attempts at business management techniques and thus prophetic of future administration within the Ministry, distribution of work within the Commercial Division proceeded in accordance with defined areas of specialization and competence.

---

65. Ibid., pp. 5–6. Also see PRO/FO 881/1296, Enclosure No. 2 to the despatch from Buchanan (Berlin) to Hammond, 1 June 1864. No differentiation is listed in the *Handbuch für das Deutsche Reich* until after the reforms.

66. Bismarck, as cited in Friedrich von Holstein, *The Holstein Papers*, ed. by Norman Rich and M. H. Fisher (Cambridge: Cambridge University Press, 1955), 2, p. 125.

67. Ibid., p. 29.

68. PA/AA, Politisches Archiv und Historisches Referat, Aktenzeichen 13, "Geschichte der Handelspolitischen Abteilung des A.A., 1885–1920," pp. 3ff.; Radowitz, 1, p. 261; and PRO/FO 881/1296, Enclosure No. 2 to the despatch from Buchanan (Berlin) to Hammond, 1 June 1864.

Specified *Referate* (subdivisions) gradually were established in the Division to regularize the administration of international commercial affairs. Included in these units, for example, one finds groups such as railroads, posts and telegraphs, and insurance; commercial relations with European states, patents, and customs exemptions; another includes navigation, maritime commerce, and fishing questions.[69]

During the nineteenth century the administrative functions of managing the Ministry for Foreign Affairs itself and its personnel expanded slowly. Essential internal matters of accounting, personnel, and budget affairs received greater recognition when separated from the Legal-Commercial Division in 1879. At the same time officials also established a separate Personnel Division as *Abteilung IB*, although in 1895 the responsibility for personnel of the diplomatic service was attached—as were other important matters—to the powerful *IA*.[70] With this control and its continual supervision over examinations and recruitment,[71] the Political Division could assure that the formulation, content, and execution of policy were determined by diplomats and bureaucrats drawn heavily from the aristocracy. This prerogative enabled the German Ministry for Foreign Affairs, like its French counterpart, to contribute significantly to the prevailing conditions of European diplomacy in the nineteenth century.

4. The Milieu of Nineteenth-Century European Diplomacy

Envisaging the construction of a new building to house the French Ministry for Foreign Affairs, François Guizot voiced certain requirements with which he thought to assure tranquillity and peace. "The *Hôtel* of the Minister," he said, "must be isolated; that is to say, detached from other buildings, surrounded by a court and a

---

69. PA/AA, Politisches Archiv und Historisches Referat, Aktenzeichen 13, pp. 20–21.

70. Ibid., Aktenzeichen 10, "Geschichte der Personalienabteilung, 1879–1920," pp. 1 and passim. There also existed a small Central Department to receive and distribute correspondence, a Cyphering Department, and a Registry Department.

71. Ibid., Aktenzeichen 11, pp. 1, 12–19.

The Quai d'Orsay During the Nineteenth Century
"Rien ne venait troubler la sérénité de ses bureaux."

garden, [and] distant from the public thoroughfare."[72] His statement proved to be both literally and figuratively prophetic, for the Ministry, its administrative functions, its personnel, and much of its policy, were to be isolated from the general public view. The same phenomenon occurred in Germany, where contemporaries described parts of the Wilhelmstrasse as "holy ground, unapproachable for the profane world, and only accessible to the Levites and priests."[73]

Throughout the nineteenth century both the French and the German Ministries for Foreign Affairs experienced few public restrictions upon policy formulation, content, or execution. Such a milieu enabled them to maintain a relatively closed "family" system of personnel, and to enjoy a relaxed atmosphere of bureaucratic simplicity and limited hours of work. This judgment is confirmed by the memoirs of men who actually lived and worked in this period of diplomacy. In the words of one old ambassador: "Nothing ever came to disturb the serenity of our offices."[74]

The daily atmosphere within the Ministry at Paris, for example, was relaxed enough to foster a tradition at the Quai d'Orsay: "*le thé de cinq heures.*"[75] Visiting members of French missions abroad and permanent officials of the central administration gathered here to leisurely socialize on a regular basis. The Political Division and the Commercial Division had time to compete with each other over who could provide the best cup of tea. In a similar vein, one employee of the Wilhelmstrasse fondly recalled its "beautiful old shady trees . . . where the nightingales beneath their spreading branches celebrate the budding springtime and the sunrise" and described the locale as "specially charming and indeed fairy-like."[76]

---

72. François Guizot in 1844, as cited in France, Ministère des Affaires étrangères, *Le Ministère des Affaires étrangères, résidence des Chefs d'Etat, hôtes du la France,* p. 4.

73. Busch, 1, p. 424.

74. René Millet, "Les Ministères: Ministère des Affaires étrangères," *La Revue hebdomadaire,* 10 (March 1911), p. 177.

75. A description of this tea-time is provided by Comte de Saint-Aulaire in his *Confession d'un vieux diplomate* (Paris: Flammarion, 1953), pp. 31ff.; La Roche, *Au Quai d'Orsay* (Paris: Hachette, 1957), pp. 11ff.; and F. Charles-Roux, *Souvenirs diplomatiques d'un âge révolu* (Paris: Fayard, 1956), p. 92, among many others.

76. Busch, 1, p. 446.

Working hours were limited in both ministries. A note issued by French Foreign Minister Freycinet as late as 1885, for example, required only five to six hours of work each day.[77] Over twenty years later, one observer described the situation in Paris as still "very slack."[78] Although Bismarck frequently placed strict demands upon his subordinates when personally in Berlin,[79] he was not always present and the prestigious Political Divison still had no fixed or scheduled hours for daily work.[80] Even insiders spoke of the general laxness among these diplomats and bureaucrats,[81] claimed that they "haven't enough to do,"[82] and complained that many "spend their time strolling about, and . . . are more often to be found out shooting than in their office."[83] Officials in other European capitals shared in this relaxed and less complicated mood of nineteenth-century diplomacy and admitted that they too generally "did not begin work until midday, so that there was plenty of time for exercise."[84] Porters still met horse-drawn carriages, there was time to read all correspondence, rooms were small, typewriters unknown, budgets limited, and the use of firewood for heat seemed to confirm the family atmosphere and make the Ministries even more cozy.[85]

One of the primary reasons for the tradition of afternoon teas, in the words of one ambassador, could be found in the motive of fostering a "common spirit, doctrine, and manners" among the diplomats and bureaucrats.[86] This promotion of a distinct *famille diplomatique* enabled departmental directors to know "not only the

77. Note of 6 November 1885 in MAE, Direction du Personnel, Carton 27, "Organisation du Ministère, II, Décrets, Arrêtés, Rapports, Etc., 1860–1896."

78. Comment by Edward Grey, on Despatch No. 455 from Bertie (Paris) to Grey, 18 November 1906, in PRO/FO 371/74.

79. This is the other mood portrayed in Busch, 1, pp. 424ff. and 444. Sasse, "Zur Geschichte des Auswärtigen Amts," Heft 5, p. 114, also stresses the working hours for lesser employees.

80. Radowitz, 1, p. 259.

81. Holstein, 2, pp. 192–93.

82. Herbert Bismarck, as cited in ibid., 2, p. 57.

83. Lothar Bucher, as cited in Busch, 2, p. 243.

84. Lord Vansittart, *The Mist Procession* (London: Hutchinson, 1958), p. 43.

85. See Heinz Sasse, "Von Equipage und Automobilen des Auswärtigen Amts," pp. 145–48; MAE/Chambre, Rapport No. 3318 (1914), 1, pp. 200–1; Radowitz, 1, p. 260; Saint-Aulaire, *Confession d'un vieux diplomate*, pp. 26–27; and Millet, p. 180.

86. Saint-Aulaire, *Confession d'un vieux diplomate*, p. 32.

names, but also the attitudes, of all . . . from chief of mission to the last attaché."[87] Members of this special family knew each other, possessed common origins, belonged to the same student associations, enjoyed mutual social connections, and worshipped together. The composition of officials in the Wilhelmstrasse's Personnel Division from 1879 to 1919, for example, included 82 percent Prussians and 91 percent Protestants.[88] As late as 1914 the German foreign service included eight princes, twenty-nine counts, twenty barons, and fifty-four untitled noblemen, with only eleven commoners.[89] Experienced officials therefore advised their young prodigies to "go to parties as much as possible," and even in republican France to recognize the crucial importance of a good aristocratic position.[90] One contemporary later described how it would have been "sacrilege" to change this European system:

> it was generally acknowledged that these great affairs were the special business of kings, nobles and aristocratic persons. Ambassadors, Foreign Secretaries, diplomatists of all grades, even clerks . . . all belonged to the aristocratic caste. They alone were supposed to have the manners and to speak the language of the 'Courts' in which great affairs were transacted. They alone could be trusted with the secrets which had to be imparted to the inner ring.[91]

The concept of a diplomatic family in the nineteenth century is more than mere metaphor, for very real family connections abounded among those responsible for foreign affairs. The family of Johann Bernstorff, for example, had such a long tradition of service to the Prussian and then German state that Kaiser Wilhelm II could introduce the ambassador with the words, "His father was my father's friend."[92] Bernhard von Bülow's relatives actually had

87. Millet, p. 180. Also see Radowitz, 1, p. 254.

88. PA/AA, Politisches Archiv und Historisches Referat, Aktenzeichen 10, pp. 87–88. In the Legal–Commercial Department from 1871 to 1885, 90 percent of the personnel were Prussians and 93 percent were Protestants. See idem, Aktenzeichen 12, pp. 75–76.

89. Rudolf Morsey, *Die Oberste Reichsverwaltung unter Bismarck, 1867–1890* (Münster: Aschendorffsche Verlagsbuchhandlung, 1957), p. 246n.

90. Bernhard Fürst von Bülow, *Denkwürdigkeiten* (Berlin: Ullstein, 1931), pp. 289, 313–14. Also see Outrey, 3, 3, p. 504.

91. J. A. Spender, *The Public Life* (London: Cassell, 1925), 2, p. 40.

92. Graf Johann Bernstorff, *Erinnerungen und Briefe* (Zürich: Polygraphischer Verlag, 1936), p. 12.

lived at 76 Wilhelmstrasse at the beginning of the century, and Bismarck asked the elder Bülow, whom he appointed as Secretary of State for Foreign Affairs, "Wouldn't you like to make a diplomat of your eldest son?"[93] Similarly, one of the men most responsible for the future reforms and innovations at the Quai d'Orsay was the son of a former Minister for Foreign Affairs, Marcelin Berthelot.

At times, members of the *corps diplomatique* even considered themselves to be members of a cosmopolitan, culturally homogeneous, European family. They spoke a common language, read the same Marten's *Guide diplomatique*,[94] defended similar social and political institutions, and fostered a certain consensus on the nature of the international system. They were each "players of the great game" that "had rules of its own which were known to all initiates."[95] Although somewhat idealistic, the words of French Foreign Minister Guizot contained much substance: "Professional diplomats constitute in Europe a distinct society, which has its particular maxims, understandings, manners and desires, and maintains in the midst of the disagreements or conflicts of the states it represents, a tranquil and permanent unity."[96]

One particular advantage afforded by this "family" tradition lay in the area of personnel recruitment. Although examinations for the services existed and sometimes were difficult,[97] final determination upon entrance remained liable to subjective judgments. This assured the maintenance of like-minded individuals with sufficient social standing who could, in the words of one of its members, "guarantee the fraternity."[98] Bernstorff remarked, "The attaché's sole salvation was the fact that in the Foreign Ministry the spirit of Bismarck still prevailed, and that it had already been decided before

93. Bülow, 4, p. 288.

94. See, for example, ibid., p. 273; and Busch, 1, p. 450.

95. Spender, 2, p. 48.

96. François Guizot, *Mémoires pour servir à l'histoire de mon temps* (Paris: Michel Lévy Frères, 1859), 2, p. 266. On this point also see Gabriel Hanotaux, "L'Europe qui naît," *La Revue hebdomadaire*, 48 (30 November 1907), p. 563, a copy of which is also in file in PA/AA, Abteilung IA, Frankreich 105 Nr. 1, Band 26, Despatch No. 753 from Radolin (Paris) to Bülow, 5 December 1907.

97. For one who emphasizes the difficulty of the exams, see Lysbeth Muncy, *The Junker in the Prussian Administration under William II, 1888–1914* (Providence, R.I.: Brown University Press, 1944), p. 47, who claims that Bismarck also said that "birth could not be an excuse for inefficiency."

98. Saint-Aulaire, *Confession d'un vieux diplomate*, p. 33.

the oral examination whether the candidate should pass or not."[99] Bismarck himself, for example, had written with his own hand in the general instructions for the test: "I reserve the right to accept the candidate for the diplomatic service if I think him suitable, though he may not have passed the examination."[100] In the French examination it was even possible to fail completely in questions regarding economic geography and yet become an esteemed ambassador.[101]

The luxury of such subjective recruitment practices could still be afforded, in part, because the daily affairs of international politics were either unknown or of little concern to most of the public. Due to official policy and limited communication systems, a very real shortage of information could explain much of the public apathy and the lack of knowledgeable critics. Further legal restrictions, however, assured that executive control over external policy would remain largely unimpaired by legislative pressure, and left little room for popular scrutiny of either policy or procedures of the respective Ministries for Foreign Affairs.

The French organic laws of 1875, for example, placed control of foreign affairs clearly in the hands of the President and his Cabinet rather than under the authority of the legislature.[102] The President could negotiate and even ratify treaties, informing the chambers only "when the interest and safety of the state permit."[103] Thus, although ministerial responsibility existed under the parliamentary system of France, the legislators could render judgment upon most policy only *ex post facto* and, in the words of one frustrated participant, "on accomplished facts."[104] No permanent commissions for foreign affairs existed in either chamber, and the *ad hoc* creation of

99. Bernstorff, pp. 25–26.
100. Ibid.
101. Saint-Aulaire, *Confession d'un vieux diplomate*, p. 13.
102. L. Duguit, *Les Constitutions et les principales lois politiques de la France depuis 1789* (Paris: Librairie générale de droit et de jurisprudence, 1925), p. 324.
103. Certain treaties, however, such as those involving peace, commerce, or territorial exchanges, required approval. Consent was needed for declarations of war, although no declarations were ever given for the conquest of Indo-China in 1884, the Dahomey Expedition of 1892, or the suppression of the Boxer Rebellion of 1900. Similarly, the chambers were never consulted in the 1878 Treaty of Berlin, the French alliance with Russia, the 1889 agreement on Africa, or the Franco-German 1911 convention on Morocco.
104. Joseph Barthémly, *Démocratie et politique étrangère* (Paris: Félix Alcan, 1917), pp. 130–38.

temporary *bureaux* for policy considerations with members chosen by lot prevented not only effective legislative supervision but also the development of well-informed criticism.

The German Constitution similarly established that external relations would be conducted by the Chancellor acting under the sole authority of the Emperor and responsible to him alone.[105] Only the *Bundesratsausschuss für die auswärtigen Angelegenheiten* (Bundesrat Committee for Foreign Affairs) could be considered as a permanent body in any way concerned with international politics. Bismarck's domination of diplomacy, however, assured that this committee's advice would be ignored. After its first meetings in 1871, the committee met only once more during the entire course of the nineteenth century, and that was in 1879. Its lack of power and ludicrously infrequent sessions left it without influence and virtually impotent.[106]

Neighboring diplomats and bureaucrats of the French and German Ministries for Foreign Affairs thus lived and functioned within the same milieu of traditional European diplomacy. The similarity of goals and the similarity of needs meant that there would be little variance between the internal management, decision-making procedures, or organizational structures of either the Quai d'Orsay or Wilhelmstrasse. The contrast existed rather in the fact that their respective historical legacies had implanted potentially different opportunities for instituting reforms and innovations, although this did not become apparent until the turn of the twentieth century.

Despite the slow and uncertain development of parliamentary government in France, for example, the organic laws of 1875 provided at least the seeds of investigation and criticism. The latent power of the purse within the Assembly's budget commissions furnished a potential means with which to influence the organization that made and executed external policy. Moreover, the ministerial instability inherent in popular elections afforded greater opportunity for individual initiative and for proposals of change to emerge from within the bureaucracy itself.

---

105. Ernst Rudolf Huber, *Deutsche Verfassungsgeschichte seit 1789* (Stuttgart: Kohlhammer, 1963), 3, pp. 809ff.; and Friedrich Thudichum, "Die Leitung der auswärtigen Politik des Reichs," *Jahrbuch für Gesetzgebung, Verwaltung und Rechtspflege des Deutschen Reiches* (1876), pp. 323–47.

106. Ernst Deuerlein, *Der Bundesratsausschuss für die auswärtigen Angelegenheiten, 1870–1918* (Regensburg: Josef Habel, 1955).

In Germany, on the other hand, the legacy left by such domineering personalities as Frederick the Great and Bismarck and the continued existence of monarchical government provided appreciably fewer opportunities for effective criticism and little mechanism for peaceful or gradual institutional change. The tradition of authority and discipline imposed specifically upon the Ministry for Foreign Affairs, as expressed by one of Bismarck's subordinates, assured that few knowledgeable officials would dare to question operations or to propose reorganization: "The strictest order prevails from top to bottom, unconditioned obedience is the rule, and, as is right and proper, every one obeys without protest or contradiction, whatever his own opinion may be. Everything downstairs moves at the bidding of *one* absolute subordination. . . . There must be no stoppage caused by this or that individuality. Acquiescence is the first and highest law."[107]

Such conditions guaranteed that there would be few proposals for reform or innovation. Both the French and German Ministries for Foreign Affairs remained secure, for the system under which the diplomats and bureaucrats operated provided the stability acquired from long tradition. As described by one contemporary, "they inherited it, saw no alternative to it, [and] did their best with it."[108] Any criticisms that did exist were either personal vendettas or isolated voices often suggesting only vague solutions for specific problems. Political, financial, and personal factors, when combined with strong personalities or the security of routine and fear of alterations, proved to be sufficient obstacles in preventing major change.[109] The words written on the cover of one dossier containing reform proposals starkly summarize the fate of most: "Rejected."[110]

As a consequence, the organizational structure of the German Ministry for Foreign Affairs remained essentially the same through-

107. Busch, 1, pp. 444–45.
108. Spender, 2, p. 41.
109. MAE, Direction du Personnel, Carton 28, "Projet de Réorganisation de l'administration centrale, 1899–1900"; Paul Boell, *Les Scandales du Quai d'Orsay* (Paris: Nouvelle librairie Parisienne, 1893); Morsey, pp. 121–22; Holstein, 2, pp. 130, 192, 241, 284; and Sasse, "Zur Geschichte des Auswärtigen Amts," *Mitteilungsblatt der Vereinigung der Angestellten des Auswärtigen Dienstes,* Heft 6, 4. Jahrgang (June 1960), pp. 136–37.
110. MAE, Direction du Personnel, Carton 28, "Projet de Réorganisation de l'administration centrale, 1899–1900."

out the century—"simple and clear."[111] Similarly, an official of the
Quai d'Orsay could still say in 1877 that "the organizational system
remains nearly identical with the system adopted by Talleyrand."[112]
In the qualified judgment of the former archival director, "The
principal quality of the early organization of the central services of
Foreign Affairs appears to have been its simplicity, its unencum-
bered character, the fact that it was conceived for the most immediate practical necessities and without theoretical preconcep-
tions, and always remained easy to manage and easy to adapt."[113]

* * * *

The world in which the French and German ministerial bureaucracies developed thus existed as one of relatively simple demands,
limited complexity, and fixed principles. "The air was strictly reserved for real birds," wrote intellectual Paul Valéry from France.
"Electricity had not yet lost its wires. Solid bodies were still fairly
solid. Opaque bodies were still quite opaque. Newton and Galileo
reigned in peace. Physics was happy and its references absolute.
Time flowed by in quiet days: all hours were equal in the sight of the
Universe. Space enjoyed being infinite, homogeneous, and per-
fectly indifferent to what went on in its august bosom."[114]
    The domestic and international milieu of the nineteenth century
could tolerate subjective standards of personnel recruitment, promotion, salaries, and discipline among the diplomats and bureaucrats. The Ministries for Foreign Affairs could manage with a strict
organizational separation of political from commercial affairs, "international" questions basically confined to the continent of
Europe, restricted administrative responsibilities for commercial or
propaganda matters, and bureaucracies of limited numbers. Recal-
ling a period as late as the 1890s, one European diplomat captured a
mood of this earlier century which now seems so distant:

    111. Schuman, "The Conduct of German Foreign Affairs," p. 194. Also see the
judgments of Irmtraut Schmid, "Der Bestand des Auswärtigen Amts in Deutschen
Zentralarchiv Potsdam," Archivmitteilungen, Heft 2/3 (1962), p. 74.
    112. Masson, p. 545. Also see Piccioni, p. 27.
    113. Outrey, 3, 4 (October–December 1953), p. 720.
    114. Paul Valéry, The Outlook for Intelligence (New York: Harper and Row,
1963 ed.), p. 126.

Our barometer was set fair, and no other reading permissible. It was a round of green dawns and golden eves, leaf drifts and snow-balls, of discipline divine or parental, withheld but present. There were murmurs when the tot of income-tax grew by a few coppers, but there was no inkling of its capacity for transforming society, or of the need for change. The skies of metaphor were unclouded. It really did look like peace in our time, in everyone's time. . . . The 'have-nots' of the early nineties had cause for complaint in all conscience, but knew not our present fears of extinction. The most modest 'haves' enjoyed comfort enough for their good. There were few bathrooms and ice was rare; but calm abounded, and straw was spread before the houses of the sick; there were no telephones, no cars, no deaths on the road or in the air. There were less nerves, less noise; perhaps after all the world would give that peace which the prayer-book said it couldn't.[115]

115. Vansittart, pp. 18–19.

— 2 —

The Turning Point:
A Changing World, Domestic Criticisms, and
Proposals for Reform and Innovation

The incessant development of questions treated by the Ministry for Foreign Affairs, the necessity for rapid solutions, and the new acuteness of political and economic struggles on all points of the globe no longer permit us to keep indefinitely an organization that goes back to an earlier period in which political activity scarcely exceeded the limits of Europe and in which telegraphic communications did not exist.

–from a proposal submitted to the
French Ministry for Foreign Affairs

Beginnings are not easily ascribed to a particular moment in time, for newer features often emerge before the older ones are entirely erased. It would be artificial, therefore, to suggest that at the turn of the century the world and its diplomacy suddenly became "modern." Yet the years following 1900 were not a mere twilight to the nineteenth century. The period prior to the First World War burst with energy, discovery, and development, marking a beginning of many of our present-day concerns and achievements.[1]

Revolutionary innovations in theoretical physics, psychoanalysis, and applied technology were matched by new forms of art, music, and architecture. Electricity and machines began to transform antiquated transportation and communication systems. Businessmen and others spoke of "efficiency," "pragmatism," and

1. The most recent exponent of this interpretation is Oron Hale, in his excellent synthesis, *The Great Illusion, 1900–1914* (New York: Harper and Row, 1971). Also see the earlier Paul Morand, *1900* (Paris: Les Éditions de France, 1931).

"rationality" in administrative techniques. International affairs encompassed the world rather than confining themselves to the European continent, proceeded at a faster pace, and became more complex. The popular press, articulate interest groups, and more aggressive parliamentarians all demanded drastic domestic reform, an end to hidden diplomatic "secrets," and a "democratization" of the "aristocratic" personnel policies of the past.

The ferment arising from this turmoil was evident several years before the outbreak of violence in 1914 and reached its climax during the First World War. Critics complained that the small, isolated, restricted, and traditional diplomatic institutions could not cope with the complexities of dramatically transformed conditions. For the French and German Ministries for Foreign Affairs, among others, these pressures led to an historical turning point and signalled that major changes lay in store for twentieth-century diplomacy.

1. A Changing World

"Thought had more than once been upset, but never caught and whirled about in the vortex of infinite forces. Power [in 1900] leaped from every atom, and enough of it to supply the stellar universe. . . . Man could no longer hold it off. Forces grasped his wrists and flung him about as though he had hold of a live wire or a runaway automobile."[2] This was the way Henry Adams saw the dawn of the new and dynamic twentieth century. His essay on "A Law of Acceleration" is filled with terms of energy and motion: "dynamic theory," "immense volume of force," "unlimited power," "new forces," and "the inadequacy of old implements of thought."[3] To quote one student of the period, "the time vibrated with a search for new forms and new realms."[4]

That traditional modes of thought and institutions soon would be broken by revolutionary innovations was given dramatic proof in the

2. Henry Adams, *The Education of Henry Adams: An Autobiography* (Boston: Houghton Mifflin, 1918), p. 494.

3. Ibid., pp. 489–98.

4. Barbara Tuchman, *The Proud Tower: A Portrait of the World Before the War, 1890–1914* (New York: Macmillan, 1966), p. 337.

physical sciences. Here, growing restlessness and energetic creativity questioned established canons and banished old landmarks. In theoretical physics, for example, Max Planck's 1900 quantum theory of energy, followed in 1905 by Albert Einstein's dissertation on relativity, soundly shook the Newtonian concept of the universe. Concepts of discontinuity, and relativity of mass, time, and space opened new perspectives to twentieth-century minds. Further research on X-rays, radioactivity, and molecular structural theory led toward the study of atomic rather than chemical phenomena.

New dimensions were appearing in the study of human behavior and philosophy. Sigmund Freud, Adler, and Jung expounded innovative doctrines of psychoanalysis. Ernst Troeltsch, Sorel, Durkheim, and Max Weber opened new approaches to the study of society and bureaucracy. The immediate popularity of William James' *Pragmatism* and Henri Bergson's *L'Evolution creatrice* in 1907 indicated further attacks upon nineteenth-century thought. "In all countries, and among a great many thinkers," wrote Bergson, "the need is strongly felt for a philosophy more genuinely empirical, more closely related to immediate needs, than is found in traditional philosophy."[5]

Change was in the air, and artists sensitive to the times sought to break out of old strictures and to experiment with new forms. Exuberant productions by Stravinsky and the Imperial Russian Ballet dazzled European cities in 1910 and thereafter, revolutionizing choreography and stage production. The works of Strauss, Debussy, and Schönberg repudiated romanticism in music and opened creative possibilities for modern composers. The founding of the *Deutscher Werkbund* in 1907 and the pioneering work of Frank Lloyd Wright, Perret, Behrens, and Walter Gropius led architecture and design to emphasize functional over ornamental considerations.[6] In art riotous color and distorted lines emerged from Matisse and the *Fauves,* while Kirchner, Heckel, and Schmidt-Rottluff organized *Die Brücke* to develop their ideas of Expressionism. Picasso and Braque followed with the geometric forms of Cubism,

5. Henri Bergson, letter of 10 July 1905 to the editor, *Revue philosophique,* 60 (July–December 1905), p. 230.

6. It is interesting to note that Edmund Schüler, the man most responsible for the major innovations in the Wilhelmstrasse, was particularly fascinated by the work of these new architects. See PA/AA, Politisches Archiv, "Ministerialdirektor a.D. Schüler."

(courtesy Bibliothèque national)

(courtesy Auswärtiges Amt)

Old Horses and New Automobiles:
A Time of Change at the Quai d'Orsay and Wilhelmstrasse
(Circa 1910)

and the Italian Futurists were fascinated with another dynamic feature of the new century—machines, speed, and power.[7]

At the turn of the century Europeans were experiencing one of those discontinuous leaps forward in invention and the practical application of technological advancement that marked industrial progress.[8] Writers began to refer to the nineteenth century as the "Century of Steam" and to the twentieth as the "Age of Electricity," for lighting, power, and municipal transportation steadily increased in Paris and Berlin as elsewhere. Applied science in the internal combustion engine, airplanes, automobiles, and motion pictures directly affected the lives of millions, affecting also the internal and overseas operations of the Ministries for Foreign Affairs. The Wilhelmstrasse replaced its horse-drawn carriage with an automobile.[9] The Quai d'Orsay began to value typing ability above other clerical skills,[10] and installed electric lights and an elevator.[11] Telegraphy was used increasingly in international transactions, destroying many former barriers to communication.

The wireless telegraph and Louis Blériot's sensational crossing of the English Channel by airplane in 1909 influenced future foreign relations by nullifying limitations upon distance, upon national boundaries, and—most crucially—upon time. Increased speed of communication and transportation soon led to changes characteristic of twentieth-century diplomacy such as shortened elapsed time between transmission and receipt of diplomatic despatches, increased impersonalization of business affairs, exercise of greater control by the Foreign Ministries over missions abroad, and reductions in the length of time available for making decisions. The

7. See René Huyghe and Jean Rudel, *L'Art et le monde moderne* (Paris: Libraire Larousse, 1969), 1; and Karl Wörner, *Die Musik in der Geistesgeschichte* (Bonn: Bouvier, 1970). One of the men most responsible for reforms in the French Foreign Ministry, Philippe Berthelot, was extremely fond of these new forms of art and, to the chagrin of his colleagues, used them in decorating his Quai d'Orsay office. See La Roche, p. 32.

8. On this point see Hale, pp. 56ff.

9. Sasse, "Von Equipage und Automobilen des Auswärtigen Amts," pp. 145–148. An item for "frais de voitures" first appears in the budget for the Quai d'Orsay in 1907, as indicated in France, Ministère des Affaires étrangères, *Compte définitif des dépenses de l'exercice 1907*.

10. MAE, Comptabilité, "Décrets et décisions ministérielles," Carton 44, No. 74, Arrêté of 8 March 1900 signed by Délcassé.

11. Ibid., Carton 53, No. 1113, "Note pour le Ministre" of 25 March 1907.

minister and his administrative bureaucracy, for example, increasingly were forced by technology to choose between alternatives, to give instructions, and to assume responsibilities without the relaxed luxury of contemplation and careful judgment enjoyed by their predecessors.[12]

Some of this speed, energy, and dynamic creativity of the new century first was displayed at the monumental 1900 International Exposition held in Paris within view of the Quai d'Orsay. Here fifty million people inspected the latest demonstrations of man's growing ability to harness the world's resources. The categories of the various exhibition halls testified to the scope of this bursting inventiveness: machinery, textiles, civil engineering and transportation, mining and metallurgy, chemical industries, and electricity. An ominous portent of the future, however, lay in the number of visitors standing spellbound before the exhibits of Schneider-Creusot's long-range cannon and Vickers-Maxim's rapid-firing machine guns.[13]

Although weapons always seem to hold a strange fascination for the world's inhabitants, it was no accident that these armament displays received so much attention. The European diplomatic system and its acceptable norms of behavior, like the new technology and art forms, were rapidly changing. After the dismissal of Bismarck in 1890, German foreign policy fell to epigoni, often incapable of following their former master's sense of responsibility and proportion, and unable to maintain the delicate Bismarckian alliance system.[14]

Added to the growing intensity and frequency of conflicts among the European Powers over commercial rivalries and colonial differences, this led to increasing uncertainty about the state of international politics and to a concomitant expansion of naval and army estimates. Citizens of this century would spend more money on armaments than ever before, would make corresponding proposals for disarmament, and would begin to realize the implications of arms

12. Walter Zechlin, *Diplomatie und Diplomaten* (Stuttgart: Deutsche Verlags-Anstalt, 1935), p. 17; and the introduction by M. de Fleuriau in Emanuel Levis-Mirapoix, *Le Ministère des Affaires étrangères* (Angers: Société anonyme des Editions de l'ouest, 1934), p. x.

13. Tuchman, pp. 269–270; and Morand, *1900*, pp. 71–130.

14. Graf von Monts, *Erinnerungen und Gedanken*, ed. by K. Novak and F. Thimme (Berlin: Verlag für Kulturpolitik, 1932), pp. 287ff.; and Gordon A. Craig, *From Bismarck to Adenauer: Aspects of German Statecraft* (New York: Harper and Row, 1965 ed.), pp. 21–42.

races and technological obsolescence.[15] In 1905, for example, new management techniques and scientific technology were applied to laying the keel of *H.M.S. Dreadnought*, thereafter rendering obsolete all existing fleets. This merely fed the fears that produced it.

Uneasiness intensified as one ominous development or crisis followed another, and observers fearfully watched the international system and diplomatic norms they knew in the previous century begin to strain and crack under the stress. The Boxer Rebellion in 1900, the outbreak of war between Russia and Japan, the basic outlines of the Schlieffen Plan in 1904, massive public uprisings in Russia, Kaiser Wilhelm's proclamations about *Weltpolitik* and his provocative visit to Tangiers in 1905 all placed considerable pressure upon the old diplomatic edifice and institutions. The mood began to change from shared values of cooperation to competition, and suspicions grew on all sides. As one diplomat records: "There was a noticeable difference of atmosphere between 1900 and 1907, [and] the old good humor was dissolving in vinegar."[16]

Under such strains, numerous pre-war crises, and growing commercial rivalries for overseas markets, statesmen sought to discard some of their former practices and acquire new allies.[17] During the search for new forms in art, music, architecture, and technology, European diplomats began replacing the old with new alliance structures. Breaking away from its long tradition of "splendid isolation" and freedom from "entanglements" in peacetime, Britain signed a formal alliance with Japan in 1902. The time had come, said Lord Lansdowne, to stop being "swayed by any musty formulas or old-fashioned superstitions."[18] This accord was followed by the Anglo-French *Entente cordiale* in 1904 and the British-Russian agreement three years later. Together, these treaties constituted a striking reversal of previous policy and the creation of a new alliance

15. Quincy Wright, *A Study of War* (Chicago: University of Chicago Press, 1965 ed.), pp. 670–71.

16. Vansittart, p. 67.

17. See Pierre Renouvin, *Histoire des relations internationales*, tome 6, *Le XIXe siècle, II: de 1871 à 1914, l'apogée de l'Europe* (Paris: Hachette, 1955), especially "Les forces profondes," pp. 136–56, and "Le nouveau groupement des états européens," pp. 204–5.

18. Lansdowne, 13 February 1902, in Britain, House of Lords, *The Parliamentary Debates*, 102 (London: H.M.S.O., 1902), col. 1176.

system. The results divided Europe into two armed camps and arranged the opposing powers that would soon face each other during the First World War. According to one observant French diplomat, these events marked a "great turning point of world politics."[19]

Ambassador Paléologue's choice of the term "world" politics was no mistake, for it signified yet another major change during these early years: the rise of Africa, Asia, and America to positions of increasing importance in international relations. Smoldering resentment against European imperialism ignited in 1899 when President Kruger of distant South Africa dared to assert his independence and issued an ultimatum to Great Britain. The resulting Boer War and the British difficulty in smashing resistance indicated some of the problems to be faced in the new century. The Boxer Rebellion in China similarly struck out against past European encroachments by inaugurating a program of terrorism against the hated foreigner, assassinating ambassadors, destroying legations, and burning customs houses. One journalist saw this as "writing on the wall" and felt that he was "watching the end of one immensely long age in the world's history and the beginning of another."[20]

Perhaps the most unnerving signal of the emergence of non-European countries in international politics occurred when the news reached Europe in 1905 that "little Japan" had sent the pride of the Russian Baltic Fleet to the bottom of the Tsushima Straits. Japan's victory stunned the Old World. It gave notice that Western imperialism henceforth would be much more difficult than in the past. "There are all these peoples of all races," said Jean Jaurès later, "who have seemed inert . . . and sunk deep in an eternal sleep, who are now awakening, demanding their rights, and flexing their muscles."[21]

As if the victory of an Asiatic over a European power in the Russo-Japanese War was not sufficiently shocking, an offer to mediate between the belligerents came not from the chancelleries of

19. Maurice Paléologue, *Un grand tournant de la politique mondiale 1904–1906* (Paris: Plon, 1934).
20. Sir Valentine Chirol, *Fifty Years in a Changing World* (London: Cape, 1927), p. 207.
21. Jean Jaurès, 2ᵉ séance of 28 June 1912, in France, Chambre, *DP*, p. 923.

Europe, but from the President of the United States. Riding on a new wave of involvement in international affairs, Theodore Roosevelt offered his good offices—and threatened to use his newly-found power. This moved one French ambassador to enter in his diary: "Something new and unexpected has happened—something which seems to presage important developments in world politics. For the first time in its history, the United States of America is intervening in the affairs of Europe."[22]

These changes in the expanding international system are well represented by the maps used and produced by the cartography sections of the Ministries for Foreign Affairs. The atlases in the *Annuaire diplomatique et consulaire*, for example, even as late as the 1890s, contained only a small number of maps. Most of these concerned nations on the European continent, thus accurately reflecting the perspective of nineteenth-century diplomacy. There existed only a single map of North America, another of the entire Asian land mass, and one very superficial representation of Africa. Such Euro-centric priority had sufficed for the diplomacy of an earlier era but grew increasingly obsolete after the turn of the new century when—in the words of one diplomat—geography became "a grand new subject."[23]

Maps now were required to reflect the *international* aspects of foreign policy, and cartographers were pressed to use greater sophistication in their work. Africa emerged from a single page showing only a continental mass to two maps in 1901—*Afrique du Nord* and *Afrique du Sud*—and eventually to three plates delineating individual national boundaries prior to the First World War. By 1903 the map of the United States was considerably more detailed than it had been two years earlier.[24] The crude, one-page representation of the entire area of Asia soon developed into two plates, East and West. Japan, once shown with only five cities, acquired twenty-three by 1910–11, and China was covered with place names and

22. Paléologue, *Un grand tournant*, p. 364.

23. Vansittart, p. 40.

24. Maps of the United States indicated no cities west of Galveston until one reached Los Angeles or San Francisco. The new 1903 map, however, provided considerable detail, adding such places as Atlanta, Buffalo, Albany, Milwaukee, Memphis, Tucson, Santa Fe, Sacramento, Carson City, Salt Lake City, Cheyenne, Omaha, Salem, Olympia, and Tacoma.

detailed insets. Neither the countries nor the names were new, but in the past they had been ignored. This cartographical attention indicated that America, Africa, and Asia would play major roles in twentieth-century diplomacy.[25]

Examination and comparison of the amount of correspondence conducted during these years also gives evidence that non-European areas of the globe were growing in importance for international politics.[26] To illustrate, during the period from 1907 to 1910, the total written correspondence between the Wilhelmstrasse and the German embassies in such European capitals as Madrid, Luxemburg, and Copenhagen actually decreased. At the same time, however, notable increases occurred in that between the Ministry in Berlin and the missions in such non-European cities as Washington, Addis Ababa, and Buenos Aires.[27] Officials clearly saw their perspectives turning from a limited continental arena toward a more extensive global theatre.[28] It was no idle boast when Count von Balestrem proudly proclaimed that Germans, in these days, "did not go in for anything less than world politics."[29]

"The affairs of the world now interest all the world," wrote Gabriel Hanotaux, who—in 1907 rather than at the end of the First World War—proclaimed the passing of the old and the birth of a new diplomatic system. He spoke of the "logic of history," "world-wide

25. Based upon an examination of maps in France, Ministère des Affaires étrangères, *Annuaire diplomatique et consulaire de la République française,* from the 1880s through 1925, noting the dramatic changes from 1900 to 1914. Also see the new efforts required on behalf of the French *Bureau géographique* in MAE, Comptabilité, "Décrets et décisions ministérielles," Carton 50, No. 237, "Note pour le Ministre," 10 May 1906. The period also saw the addition of expenses "für kartographische Arbeiten" in Africa in the budget for the German Ministry for Foreign Affairs. See PA/AA, Politisches Archiv und Historisches Referat, "Etat 1903," "Etat 1904," and "Etat 1905."

26. Annual registry charts found in PA/AA, Abteilung 1A, Deutschland 149, Band 15, Nr. I 30471/84435, "Übersicht über den Geschäftsverkehr (Ein- und Ausgänge) bei den kaiserlichen und königlichen Missionen in Jahre 1908"; idem, Nr. I 30471/84435 for 1909; and idem, Nr. I 30602/84675 for 1910. Although less precise, for the increases of correspondence to and from the Quai d'Orsay, see France, MAE/Chambre, Rapport No. 3318 (1914), pp. 80–81.

27. Correspondence with Washington, for example, was 13,083 in 1907, 14,959 in 1908, 15,600 in 1909, and 16,212 by 1910.

28. Hammann, *Deutsche Weltpolitik, 1890–1912* (Berlin: Hobbing, 1925), pp. 36ff.; among others.

29. Count von Balestrem, as recounted in Paléologue, *Un grand tournant,* p. 428.

repercussions'' of political events, and the impact of scientific discoveries upon politics. The combination of these various features,
concluded Hanotaux, would result in many "new problems" and
"new tasks" for twentieth-century diplomacy.[30]

The new problems and tasks were immense. The expansion of the
diplomatic arena to include new geographical areas, advancing
sophistication in communications and transportation, armament
races, crises within the European system itself, and growing complexity in international relations began to severely strain the French
and German Ministries for Foreign Affairs. These institutions and
their bureaucracies had been required heretofore to respond only to
the limited demands of traditional nineteenth-century diplomacy.
Such limitations were reflected in their structural organization and
personnel. How long the Quai d'Orsay and Wilhelmstrasse could
survive in this new century was increasingly open to question, not
only from the external international sphere for which they were
responsible, but also from the domestic context of which they were a
part. A French report that international affairs now were becoming
"world-wide" simultaneously spoke of internal agitation and declared: "Domestic political factors [also] condition the way in which
governments consider foreign policy."[31]

2. French Criticisms and Proposals

"La révolution Dreyfusienne" is the term applied to that crisis of
the Third Republic which had serious consequences for French
domestic politics.[32] The Army's false accusation of treason against
Captain Alfred Dreyfus sparked violent political and parliamentary
fights, street demonstrations, fanatical plots, strikes, and venom
which spilled from pulpits and the press. The resulting struggles
often were seen as battles between justice and raison d'état,
civilianism versus militarism, anti-clericalism against the Church,
socialism in combat with aristocracy, and respect for individualism
instead of anti-Semitism. As such, the crisis became the point of

30. Hanotaux, pp. 561–70.
31. MAE/Sénat, Rapport No. 114 (1910), pp. 4, 13.
32. The term was first used by Georges Sorel, La révolution Dreyfusienne
(Paris: Rivière, 1909).

departure for "*société moderne*" and French politics of the twentieth century.[33]

The most immediate consequences of the Dreyfus affair were the rallying of those committed to "*la défense républicaine*" and the election in 1899 of Waldeck-Rousseau as premier. When this occurred, in the words of one scholar of modern France, "the Third Republic reached a major political turning point."[34] Henceforth, members of the Radical Party would replace the Moderates as the fulcrum of French republican politics, and until the Second World War seldom would be out of power. What distinquished this first cabinet was not only that the key posts were held by Radicals, but that one of its members—Millerand—was the first Socialist to cross the ideological boundary and cooperate with a bourgeois government. These events signalled that many institutions of the past—particularly the military, the religious, the political, the economic, and the diplomatic establishments—would be subjected to increasing scrutiny and criticism.

Indeed, one of the characteristics of diplomacy in this century would be expanded public concern and involvement in international relations to a degree heretofore considered unimaginable. This was soon made most explicit by Deputy Fernand Dubief who, in introducing the annual budget for the French Ministry for Foreign Affairs before the Chamber, declared that it was first necessary

> to discover if the orientation given to our foreign policy is in conformity with the interests and aspirations of our republican democracy.
>
> The strength of memories and traditions that reign at the Quai d'Orsay tend to maintain activity which, if it has the precious advantage of assuring continuity of plans, also has the troublesome disadvantage of retarding the necessary evolution required by new political and economic conditions. Moreover, it obscures a clear vision of our interests in the new times.[35]

33. This is the opinion of J.-J. Chevallier, *Histoire des institutions politiques de la France moderne, 1789–1945* (Paris: Dalloz, 1958), p. 446. That the Ministry for Foreign Affairs was well aware of the smallest details is documented by the personal account of their own agent in the case, Maurice Paléologue, in *Journal de l'affaire Dreyfus, 1894–1899: L'affaire Dreyfus et le Quai d'Orsay* (Paris: Plon, 1955).

34. Gordon Wright, *France in Modern Times* (Chicago: Rand McNally and Company, 1966), p. 325.

35. MAE/Chambre, Rapport No. 2640 (1902), p. 1.

Along with new inventions and energy, a search for innovative artistic forms, an expanding diplomatic system, and dynamic economic development, these *temps nouveaux* now included bursting domestic pressure. For the French Ministry for Foreign Affairs this meant an increasing barrage of criticism of its nineteenth-century administration, operations, policies, personnel selection, and isolation from the public. Complaints, criticism, and proposals for reform emerged from parliament in debates and committees, from the press, from members of the diplomatic and consular services, and from the newly confident and knowledgeable chambers of commerce. One legislative specialist spoke of "new methods" and "the progressive ascension of the people," and predicted that the public "in gradually raising itself to an understanding of the great problems of domestic and foreign policy, [would] participate more and more in the control and direction of public affairs."[36]

The first requisite for effective and intelligible guidance of foreign relations is adequate information. Yet the demands for this objective and the protests against "secret diplomacy" were not made during the First World War, as is so often assumed, but several years earlier.[37] "The problems of foreign policy have not been brought before this Assembly," observed the eloquent Jean Jaurès in 1911, who warned that the danger for international relations rested in "deceitful combinations . . . hatched in hidden diplomacy."[38] Senator Raymond Poincaré spoke of the importance in hearing "the wish of the Chamber,"[39] and Deputy Albert Bedouce, in discussing the details of foreign negotiations, declared: "The Chamber wants to hear those [from the Ministry for Foreign Affairs] who do not wish to speak."[40] Deputy Ernest Roche similarly deplored the "secrets" of diplomacy, denounced the fact that parliament and the country were never consulted in foreign affairs, and called for "*une politique*

36. Ibid., Rapport No. 2661 (1906), pp. 2, 4.

37. Nor were such cries even a creation of the twentieth century as Felix Gilbert has observed in *Towards the Farewell Address* (Princeton: Princeton University Press, 1961), particularly Chapter 3: "Novus Ordo Seculorum," pp. 44ff. These early criticisms, however, had a restricted audience and a limited impact upon European diplomacy.

38. Jean Jaurès, 13 January 1911, in France, Chambre, *DP*, pp. 37–38.

39. MAE/Sénat, Rapport No. 165 (1911), p. 36.

40. Albert Bedouce, 2ᵉ séance of 15 March 1912, in France, Chambre, *DP*, p. 957.

de pleine lumière."[41] Count Albert de Mun protested the "obscurities" and "chancellery mysteries" of diplomatic intercourse. When he claimed that Frenchmen could learn the truth better from the debates in foreign assemblies, particularly the German Reichstag, he received rousing applause ranging from the political Right to the Left.[42]

These protests also must be seen in their entire European and global context. Those in France and Germany who wanted to make diplomacy more responsive, representative, and effective were in the forefront of a much larger movement. It was not uncommon in America, for example, to find respectable critics calling the State Department "notoriously disorganized,"[43] or describing it as an organization directed by an "uncertain chief paltering platitudes," composed of "coddling cheap politicians," and supported by an "incompetent horde of retainers infesting foreign capitals."[44] The Foreign Office in London came under similar attack as an editorial in *The Times* asked, "Who, then, makes war?"

> The answer is to be found in the Chancelleries of Europe, among the men who have too long played with human lives as pawns in a game of chess, who have become so enmeshed in formulas and the jargon of diplomacy that they have ceased to be conscious of the poignant realities with which they trifle. And thus will war continue to be made, until the great masses who are the sport of professional schemers and dreamers say the word. . . . If that word is ever to be spoken, there never was a more appropriate occasion than the present.[45]

Such attacks on the Ministry for Foreign Affairs and the conduct of external relations, however, could not be sustained in public debates. As several scholars have noted, issues of international

---

41. Ernst Roche, 8 March 1912, in ibid., pp. 825–26.

42. Albert de Mun, 14 December 1911, in ibid., pp. 1350–52. For similar comments, see Flaissières, 29 March 1913, in France, Sénat, *DP*, pp. 476ff.; *Le Petit Parisien*, 28 October 1906; and *Le Gaulois*, 15 August 1908.

43. James D. Whelpley, "Our Disorganized Diplomatic Service," *Century*, 87 (November 1913), p. 126.

44. "The Loss of Mr. Moore," *Literary Digest*, 48, 11 (14 March 1914), p. 540, citing the *New York Tribune*.

45. *The Times* (London), 26 November 1912. For more material on British criticisms, see Zara Steiner, *The Foreign Office and Foreign Policy, 1898–1914* (Cambridge: Cambridge University Press, 1969), pp. 164–71.

politics generally were obscured because the interests and orienta-
tions of most parliamentarians and their constituents lay in French
domestic struggles.[46] Yet in blaming the members of parliament for
abdicating their responsibilities to watch over the conduct of French
foreign relations, one must not ignore the work of their committees
or overlook the constitutional and political restrictions inhibiting
public discussion of policy. The Ministry for Foreign Affairs, for
example, which was required to answer only those questions
approved by a majority vote of the Chambers, could simply ignore
interpellations and written questions by claiming immunity in the
name of "the interests and security of the nation." These limitations
were formidable deterrents against opposition in open debate. To
circumvent such restrictions, parliamentarians wishing to exert
control over the Quai d'Orsay discovered a useful mechanism in
their power of the purse.

Each year the Chamber's *Commission du Budget* and the Senate's *Commission des Finances* prepared reports on the accounts of
the various French ministries, including the Ministry for Foreign
Affairs. Early in the new century the annual report began to provide
a means of direction, criticism, and supervision over the administration of the Quai d'Orsay itself. The Chamber's reports grew to
several hundred pages in length, giving details of the Ministry's
organization and operations and providing analyses of virtually all
proposed yearly expenditures, including the amounts spent for
salaries, correspondence, diplomatic representation, maintenance,
official contributions, and numerous other items.

Since cooperation of the Quai d'Orsay staff was required by law,
much accurate information about the bureaucracy and internal operations of the Ministry thus became exposed to serious investigation. Several of these annual reports were used as a basis for discussion, elaboration, and even criticism of the substance of French
foreign policy. That these commissions were taken seriously is
evidenced by the quality of men who served as committee members[47] and by the explicit statements regarding their watch-dog

---

46. Barthélemy, pp. 130ff.; and John C. Cairns, "Politics and Foreign Policy:
The French Parliament, 1911–14," *The Canadian Historical Review,* 34 (September 1953), pp. 245–76.

47. Among those who served on the Chamber's commission between 1900 and
1925 were Paul Deschanel, Louis Marin, Paul Doumer, L.-L. Klotz, Sarraut,
Albert Thomas, Paul-Boncour, Jules Roche, Lucien Hubert, Painlevé, Viviani,
Chautemps, comte Albert de Mun, Caillaux, Noblemaire, Leon Blum, Herriot,
Bonnet, and George Bonnefous.

functions and responsibilities.[48] Their strength so impressed the reform-minded British ambassador that he claimed "the President of the Commission of the Budget is, or can make himself, the most powerful man in the House outside the Ministry."[49]

The terms of reference for the respective commissions were not properly foreign policy, but rather the investigation and scrutiny of the Ministry's administration, bureaucratic staff, and operations. In this capacity the committees rendered their most effective service by providing intelligent criticism and proposing major changes for the Quai d'Orsay. The 1901 report, for example, called for administrative reform and warned that the formulation and execution of foreign policy in the twentieth century would be conducted under much greater supervision than in the past: "It seems that the Ministry for Foreign Affairs often lives only from day to day, with funds disbursed at random, without order or standards, with exaggerated numbers of personnel who yet are irregularly and insufficiently paid. At the Quai d'Orsay, one has, in short, a remarkable spectacle of an administration in which there is a neglect of duties on a massive scale."[50]

Others spoke of administrative abuse in the Ministry,[51] of "archaic" and "ambiguous" regulations,[52] "incredible administrative disorder"[53] and even of the Quai d'Orsay's "administrative 'monster.' "[54] This deplorable mess was due, some argued, to the fact that French Foreign Ministers in the past had concerned themselves primarily with "high politics" and not with the important administrative features of their duties.[55] The time had come, said Deputy Paul Deschanel, to recognize that "the organization is, in certain respects, defective, and *no longer seems to respond to our present necessities.*"[56]

48. See MAE/Chambre, Rapport No. 333 (1907), p. 7; and idem, Rapport No. 2661 (1906), p. 4.

49. PRO/FO 371/1116, Despatch No. 36 from Bertie (Paris) to Grey, 17 January 1911.

50. MAE/Chambre, Rapport No. 2640 (1902), pp. 21–22.

51. MAE/Sénat, Rapport No. 337 (1908), p. 4.

52. H. Pognon, *Lettre à Monsieur Doumergue, Président du Conseil, Ministre des Affaires étrangères, au sujet d'une réforme du Ministère des Affaires étrangères* (Paris: Figuière, 1914), p. 117.

53. MAE/Sénat, Rapport No. 165 (1911), p. 3.

54. *Le Temps*, "Bulletin de l'étranger, Réformes diplomatiques," 18 November 1906.

55. See, for example, ibid.

56. MAE/Chambre, Rapport No. 333 (1907), p. 2 [my emphasis].

As an active and relentless *rapporteur* of the Quai d'Orsay's annual budget report for several years, Deschanel acquired a detailed understanding of the Ministry's internal administration and operations. Using these reports as a forum, he led a sustained and intelligent attack against specific features of the French Ministry for Foreign Affairs, and received well-deserved recognition when reforms were finally instituted.[57] He first realized that the old division of labor appeared irrational in the twentieth century, and that a more realistic and efficient system should be devised. "The division of affairs between the Political and the Commercial Departments," for example, now seemed "forced and arbitrary."[58]

Critics sounded this theme of an old, outdated division of affairs again and again. "One no longer knows how to make a rational distinction," argued A. Gervais, "between a 'political' and a 'commercial' act."[59] "How can the 'political' affairs of, say, China, be separated from the 'commercial' affairs of that same country? The same holds true for America. . . . These former abstractions no longer make sense."[60]

A more rational administrative division, the critics proposed, would be one based upon a geographical structure in which political and commercial affairs were considered together, with work divided on the basis of global location. "The division founded purely upon geography," said Deputy Gervais, "appears to be the most rational."[61] This reorganization, many suggested, if accompanied by coordination and permanence, would prevent duplication of effort and internal competition, and would result in better policy. More specifically, such a remedy might offer an institutional, administrative means for diplomats and bureaucrats to deal effectively with the new non-European areas such as the Americas or Far East. This reorganized administration, many asserted, would be more in keeping with the spirit of the times, more "rational," "sensible," "logi-

57. Among many comments, see *Le Temps*, 15 May 1912; and PRO/FO 371/250, Despatch No. 609 from Bertie (Paris) to Grey, 26 December 1907. It is interesting to note that the Wilhelmstrasse also watched Deschanel's activities as *rapporteur*, as evidenced in PA/AA, Abteilung IA, Frankreich 108, Band 18, Despatch No. 188 from Lancken (Paris) to Bülow, 16 May 1909.

58. MAE/Chambre, Rapport No. 333 (1907), p. 2.

59. Ibid., Rapport No. 2661 (1906), p. 249. Also see p. 120.

60. *Le Temps*, 18 November 1906. Also see MAE, Direction du Personnel, Carton 28, "Projet de Réorganisation de l'Administration centrale, 1899–1900."

61. MAE/Chambre, Rapport No. 2661 (1906), p. 252.

cal," and "efficient." French chambers of commerce claimed that such a new organizational structure also would be "more profitable."[62]

Other critics deplored the financial mismanagement at the Quai d'Orsay. Those who criticized the Ministry for managing funds "at random" on an irregular day-to-day basis[63] were followed by those who urged a more careful and precise surveillance of the way in which the public's money was spent.[64] Deschanel's calm and reasoned approach soon gave way to the harsher words of Raymond Poincaré, proclaiming that "an incredible administrative disorder has reigned for several years at the Ministry for Foreign Affairs and the most elementary public accounting rules have been disregarded with unparalleled perseverance."[65] The contradictory and diverse systems of accounting and the lack of adequate public surveillance he—and the national *Cour des Comptes*—found inexcusable. Poincaré therefore demanded "a rational reorganization" and declared: "The need for a rapid and profound reform compels recognition."[66]

Scandals always seem to serve as effective catalysts for exposing weakness and abuse, and from this particular phenomenon the Quai d'Orsay (like its counterpart in Germany) was not to be immune. Franz Hamon, the Ministry's accounting director, during the spring of 1911 was accused of deviously mismanaging funds. *"L'Affair Hamon"* exposed to all France that the financial administration of the Ministry for Foreign Affairs was under no careful audit or public scrutiny and that its director, if so inclined, could siphon off gain for himself and his friends. Now, with added force and fresh ammunition, Deschanel could declare: "We insist anew that the Department put an end to these perpetrated irregularities."[67]

As the scandal demonstrated, no administrative organization, however cleverly devised, can operate itself; ultimately it depends upon its own trained and dedicated staff. Nor did this feature of administrative science escape the eyes of the Ministry's critics who

62. See, for example, the many comments from various members of commerce as reproduced in ibid., pp. 134ff. Also see Chapter Five.

63. MAE/Chambre, Rapport No. 2640 (1902), pp. 21–22.

64. Ibid., Rapport No., 361 (1911), p. 180.

65. MAE/Sénat, Rapport No. 165 (1911), p. 3.

66. Ibid., p. 21. The details of the complaints are found on pp. 3–27.

67. MAE/Chambre, Rapport No. 1237 (1911), p. xxii. The details of the Hamon scandal can be traced in idem, Rapport No. 3318 (1914), 1, pp. 208–51; and *Le Temps*, "Ce qu'on dit au quai d'Orsay," 2 May 1911.

argued for better selection and permanence among personnel, crying: "fewer agents and more money."[68] Inadequate salaries and the lack of objective criteria for establishing pay scales led only to "insufficient work," the employment of "amateurs," instability with no permanent direction, and great financial disparities among the staff of the central administration.[69] The confusion resulting from such irregularities, claimed Deschanel, affected not only salaries, but vacations, advancement, retirement, general *esprit de corps*, and internal accounting techniques as well.[70] Other critics were less euphemistic about the treatment of diplomats and bureaucrats. They spoke of "ministerial absolutism," administrative "lackeys," "byzantine" and "absolutely immoral" regulations, "anarchy," and even "camarillas" and "mafias" that controlled the uncertain fate of staff and agents.[71] More important politically was the charge that such low salaries and arbitrary practices were "anti-democratic."

Many critics argued that insufficient payment—particularly for young attachés—permitted only those persons *avec fortune* to enter the staff of the central administration or to become members of the diplomatic and consular corps. It was well known that such personnel of the nineteenth century were recruited from the aristocratic class. Arising from the turmoil of the Dreyfus affair and the ascendance of the Radical Socialists, protest and criticism became more vocal and insistent. In his first ministerial declaration, for example, Georges Clemenceau asserted that French diplomats adequately must reflect the new republican régime, and word of a possible "purge" was used openly.[72] "I understand very well," said one Senator, "that the present situation assuredly is suitable for the *fils de famille*; but it is shameful for a democracy which must open all careers, even the highest, to new men with merit even though they

68. MAE/Chambre, Rapport No. 2661 (1906), p. 120.

69. Ibid., Rapport No. 2640 (1902), p. 22; idem, Rapport No. 333 (1907), pp. 3–4; and idem, Rapport No. 1237 (1912), p. xx.

70. Ibid., Rapport No. 2015 (1909), pp. 164–65; and idem, Rapport No. 1237 (1912), pp. 123–25. This opinion is confirmed by much internal memoranda, as evidenced in MAE, Comptabilité, "Décrets et décisions ministérielles," Carton 51, "Note pour le Ministre," from Hamon to Pichon, 12 November 1906; and Carton 59, "Note pour le Ministre," Hamon to Pichon, 26 December 1910.

71. Pognon, pp. 47, 61, 79, 106, 130.

72. See, for example, *L'Echo de Paris*, 18 November 1906.

may not be accompanied with money."[73] The Assembly, declared Deschanel, should end the elitism of this system and now force reforms upon the French Ministry for Foreign Affairs.[74]

The abuses, stagnation, and irrational organization within the institution of the Quai d'Orsay, many claimed, were duplicated in the overseas services as well. Reforms suggested for one were paralleled closely by proposals for the other. "The diplomatic and consular organization of France," declared Deputy Gervais, "should also be reformed and strengthened, established upon a solid basis, and in a sweeping way."[75] As new geographical areas required systematic management in the bureaucracy at Paris, so too the suppression, transformation, and creation of foreign posts should be conducted in a "methodical" and "rational" manner. It must be recognized, he said, that the world was "on the path of development and transformation."[76] Proposals recommended that several old posts in Europe be terminated in favor of newer missions in the more dynamic areas of China, Japan, and the Americas.

Critics contended that just as the Ministry itself no longer should be divided on the basis of "political" and "commercial" matters, so must the antiquated, corresponding distinction between the diplomatic and consular services be abolished. As specific divisions of geography should be established in the central administration, so must the services be divided in accordance with specialized geographical "zones" based upon area, language, and culture. The objective to be reached in both the Ministry and the services was thus the same: specialization and expertise in order to respond efficiently and rationally to the demands of the new international system and its diplomacy.[77]

The external environment, however, is never an independent variable in foreign policy formulation and execution, as the French overseas services (like the Quai d'Orsay itself) discovered when faced with pressure of a more domestic nature. Like the Ministry,

---

73. Charles Dupuy, 15 January 1907, in France, Sénat, *DP*, p. 89.

74. MAE/Chambre, Rapport No. 333 (1907), pp. 2–4, 137–39, among others.

75. Ibid., Rapport No. 2661 (1906), p. 247.

76. Ibid., p. 252.

77. Ibid., Rapport No. 2661 (1906), pp. 244ff.; idem, Rapport No. 333 (1907), pp. 203ff.; idem, Rapport No. 2015 (1909), pp. 66–73; and idem, Rapport No. 2749 (1910), p. 55.

the diplomatic and consular services were questioned about past recruitment of aristocrats, promotion and transfer practices, low salaries, and insufficient traveling expenses. Such criticism was levelled with particular force by the informed, aggressive, and articulate chambers of commerce.[78] They argued that new demands fierce competition, and the sheer expanding importance of economics in international relations neither could nor would tolerate the blatant past discrimination of the "political" diplomats against the *corps consulaire*; nor could they accept the old game in which advancement was more rapid for the staff in Paris than for those on overseas missions.

Many critics maintained that the practices of the nineteenth century were inefficient, unrepresentative, expensive for the taxpayer, unfair and insecure for the personnel themselves, and unresponsive to new international and domestic conditions. The days of the amateur, they said, had disappeared. The irregularities and arbitrariness of the past must be replaced by standardization and objective regulations (a *statut des fonctionnaires*). Organizational confusion must be superseded by rational authority structures and efficient management techniques.[79] In short, asserted one deputy, "the services of the Ministry must be organized like those of a *grande maison de banque*."[80]

Some claimed that like a great banking house the Quai d'Orasy should not only defend, but actively promote French interests abroad. A more active, aggressive role by the Ministry for Foreign Affairs, asserted the critics, would be particularly important both in international commerce and in propaganda.[81] One senator urged that such innovations be created "with discernment, method, and perseverance."[82] Another advised, "Do not imitate your predecessor, *Monsieur le Ministre*," for now is the time to "speak little and

78. See Chapter Five.
79. MAE/Chambre, Rapport No. 333 (1907), pp. 3–5, 205ff.; France, Sénat, *DP*, 15 January 1907, p. 89; MAE/Chambre, Rapport No. 2015 (1909), pp. 76–82; idem, Rapport No. 361 (1911), pp. 140ff.; idem, Rapport No. 1237 (1912), pp. xx–xxii; and Pognon, pp. 108–40.
80. MAE/Chambre, Rapport No. 2661 (1906), p. 252. Also see Chapters Five and Six.
81. See, for example, Paul Bluysen, 14 June 1912, in France, Chambre, *DP*, p. 460; and ibid., p. 2.
82. MAE/Sénat, Rapport No. 439 (1907), p. 17.

act much . . . watch over our interests . . . in a word, be tenacious . . . and imitate the German diplomats."[83]

3. German Criticisms and Proposals

"The year 1906 has been a remarkable one as regards Germany," remarked the British ambassador in Berlin, "as during the course of it the change which has come over public opinion in political questions, more especially in connection with the relations between the people and the Government, and even the Emperor himself, has become evident. No doubt this change has been gradual in its development, but it has only been in the course of this year that it has become apparent. When I first came to Berlin, eleven years ago, I was told that the attitude of an ordinary German in reading a newspaper was to ask whether the statements contained in it were official." If the answer was in the affirmative, he reported, the German reader would treat the contents with attention and respect, but if not, the same person would attach little importance to what he read.

> Now anything published by authority is received with suspicion and closely criticized, and constant attacks have been made. . . . The first manifestations of this change came under my notice during the sittings of the conference at Algeciras, when I was astonished to hear people in society, to whose individual opinion no great weight was attached, openly criticizing the action of the Government. "What," they asked, "had Germany to seek in Morocco?" . . . This, and similar questions, were symptomatic of a general feeling that foreign affairs of Germany were not skillfully dealt with.[84]

The fear that French encroachments endangered German interests and the resulting Moroccan episode had brought foreign affairs before the eyes of the public, and many Germans thought—and said—that the Wilhemstrasse's policy had been woefully bungled. Berlin's insistence on an international conference at Algeciras and the forced resignation of French Foreign Minister Delcassé not

83. Pognon, p. 152. Also see MAE/Chambre, Rapport No. 3318 (1914), p. 182.
84. PRO/FO 371/260, Despatch No. 238, "Confidential," from Lascelles (Berlin) to Grey, 24 May 1907.

Paul Deschanel

Ernst Bassermann

French and German Parliamentarians: Criticism and Proposals
for Reform in the Ministries for Foreign Affairs

only increased tension with France, but dramatically demonstrated Germany's diplomatic isolation. Striving for prestige, she was stung with humiliation, and critics openly began to ask why.

A great deal of the criticism concentrated not so much on the mistaken *policy* as upon the decision-making *process*. Parliamentarians levelled attacks against the Kaiser himself and his system of "dilettantism" and "personal rule" in managing external relations. National-Liberal Deputy and leading critic Ernst Bassermann said, "So long as a great statesman like Bismarck guided our foreign policy we could submit to his guidance. But now we will take the liberty of criticizing . . . and it will be well in the future if the people of Germany will show more interest in foreign affairs. . . . The times are past when we remained silent before such a state of things, and, moreover, we will take the liberty of discussing it in the Reichstag."[85]

The impact of Algeciras also precipitated a series of misfortunes and resignations at the Wilhelmstrasse. Soon after the first meeting of the conference Baron von Richthofen, Secretary of State for Foreign Affairs, succumbed to an apoplectic stroke. Chancellor von Bülow shortly thereafter suffered a seizure that disabled him for months. The same day witnessed the departure of another pivotal figure in the shaping of German foreign policy—Friedrich von Holstein.

Holstein's forced retirement, according to contemporary observers, "creates a great gap in the continuity of German foreign policy, and makes it, too, at a critical time. . . . It is not possible to fill the place of such a man."[86] The impact of his strong will, his abilities, knowledge, and experience in European politics had provided evidence of the power of a permanent bureaucrat upon policy formulation. Having "grown up and trained in the diplomatic school of Prince Bismarck,"[87] he had been one of the major bulwarks of the traditional Ministry for Foreign Affairs. "His resignation," some

---

85. Ernst Bassermann, in *Kölnische Zeitung*, 6 November 1906. See the subsequent interpellation, debate, and criticisms on 14 and 15 November 1906 in Germany, Reichstag, *SB*, 1905–06, 5, pp. 3619ff.

86. *The Times*, 19 April 1906, as enclosed in PA/AA, Abteilung IA, Deutschland 122 Nr. 2, Band 2, Despatch No. 391 from Metternich (London) to Bülow, 19 April 1906.

87. *Norddeutsche Allgemeine Zeitung*, 9 May 1909. With Holstein's death, said *La Liberté* of 10 May 1909, "Bismarck died for the second time."

predicted, "following upon the death of von Richthofen, will without doubt bring about great changes in the Wilhemstrasse."[88]

Furious over his dismissal and rabid for revenge, Holstein sought
to destroy the man whom he considered responsible—Kaiser
Wilhelm's close friend and court favorite, Prince Philipp Eulenburg.
In the process he assisted in exposing a major scandal. "Your aim of
many years—my removal—has now at last been achieved, . . ."
wrote Holstein to Eulenburg. "But there are two sides to everything. I am now free, I need exercise no restraint, and can treat you
as one treats a contemptible person with your characteristics."[89]
Such vindictiveness was used by the "feared and fearless editor" of
Die Zukunft, Maximilian Harden, to spread lurid evidence of per-
version, intrigue, and blackmail before a bewildered German public.
"All this would be their own private affair," wrote Harden, "if they
did not belong to the inner circle of the Kaiser's Round Table."[90]
The Establishment itself was on trial and the scandal became
another catalyst for mounting public criticism against the Emperor's
personal political régime in general and the Wilhelmstrasse in particular. The center of the affair, Eulenburg, was a former ambassador with connections in the Foreign Ministry.

Attention focused upon the way in which foreign policy decisions
were made and executed, and parliamentarians openly used the
word Kamarilla.[91] The press expressed fear of the dangers involved
in the "cabinet policy of the Kaiser" and doubted the abilities of
those charged with the management of German external relations.[92]
Brutal colonial scandals magnified the Wilhelmstrasse's inept administration even more.[93] The public's interest in foreign affairs

88. *Journal des Débats*, 22 April 1906.

89. Holstein, 4, p. 419.

90. Maximilian Harden in *Die Zukunft* of 17 November 1906, as cited in
Norman Rich, *Fredrich von Holstein: Politics and Diplomacy in the Era of Bismarck and Wilhelm II* (Cambridge: Cambridge University Press, 1965), 2, p. 769.

91. In the debate of 15 November 1906, in Germany, Reichstag, *SB*, 1905–06,
5, pp. 3619–50.

92. *Kölnische Zeitung*, 6 November 1906; *National Zeitung*, 15 May 1906;
Frankfurter Zeitung, 18 April 1907; and *Die Zukunft*, 8 April 1907, to name but a
few. This critical atmosphere was exacerbated further by the publication of Hohen-
lohe's controversial memoirs and German policy toward the Hague disarmament
conference.

93. See the wealth of material on this subject in PA/AA, Abteilung IA,
Deutschland 122 Nr. 2, Bände 1, 2, and 3.

grew, and it became more difficult to silence the critics. One particularly astute analyst made the following observation:

A generation ago the German public took but little interest in general foreign affairs, except in those which affected her relations with her neighbors, France and Russia, and these were left in full confidence in the hands of Prince Bismarck. Things have changed since then: colonies have been acquired; a big navy has been constructed; the Kaiser by his incessant journeys has attracted the attention of his people to foreign countries and their affairs, and finally the great increase of Germany's economic development and consequent power of expansion, have all contributed to create a spirit of discontent in wide circles with the personal régime of the Kaiser and have inspired a more vigorous criticism of the Imperial *Weltpolitik*.[94]

He stated further, "That public opinion is knocking louder every day at the door of the Berlin Foreign Office for information is not to be wondered at, and it is in great part the result of the Kaiser's personal methods of conducting the affairs of the Empire."[95]

Even these complaints, however, faded in comparison with the blast of criticism ignited by one of the Kaiser's most explosive personal blunders: the *Daily Telegraph* affair. An interview with Wilhelm II slipped through the Wilhelmstrasse where, according to Holstein, officials treated it like a "hot potato" and "pure dynamite."[96] The contents appeared in the English *Daily Telegraph* of 28 October 1908. With typical indiscretion, the Kaiser attempted on his own to improve Anglo-German relations by telling the public that he had abstained from a policy designed "to humble England to the dust," and had worked out a campaign plan for the British against the Boers (a plan which, by a curious coincidence, bore striking similarity to that which they actually adopted). He then asserted that "Germany must have a powerful fleet" to protect her commerce and interests "in any quarter of the globe."[97] "The Interview" was

94. PRO/FO 371/260, Despatch No. 48 from Cartwright (Munich) to Grey, 6 May 1907.

95. Ibid. This interpretation is confirmed by other skillful foreign observers, as evidenced in MAE, Allemagne, politique intérieure, dossier général, NS 3, Despatch No. 223, "Très-confidentiel," from Bihourd (Berlin) to Pichon, 18 November 1906.

96. Holstein, 1, p. 172.

97. *Daily Telegraph*, "The German Emperor and England, Personal Interview, Frank Statement of World Policy," 28 October 1908.

disturbing to Britain,[98] but German public opinion and the leaders of all political parties were infuriated at this irresponsible performance by the crown and Foreign Ministry. The *Daily Telegraph* affair exploded into a domestic crisis of major proportions.[99]

Appearing so soon after the Eulenburg scandal, this new mistake seemed incredible. "I am convinced that something must be DONE," wrote Harden. ". . . I will demand, *crûment*, immediate abdication."[100] In the Reichstag, critics lashed out with unprecedented fury against the process of policy formulation that permitted such rash interference in German external relations. Some even declared that the moment had come to introduce a constitutional form of government with ministerial responsibility.[101] "We want constitutional guarantees," said Deputy Heine, that such irresponsibility would never occur again.[102] The *Deutsche Tageszeitung* vigorously attacked the Kaiser for his constant meddling, and the *Berliner Tageblatt* cried that "this state of affairs is intolerable to any self-respecting nation" and "the German people no longer intend to allow its most vital interests to depend upon the haphazard decisions of one solitary individual."[103] The *Börsen Courier* declared:

> From whatever point they are viewed, His Majesty's remarks are calculated to produce a most unfortunate effect, such as will serve to show afresh the dangerous position in which our foreign policy has been placed for the last quarter of a century, by the impossibility of reckoning or controlling the personal interference of the Sovereign in diplomatic activity.[104]

---

98. In a short marginal note Eyre Crowe recorded: "The ways of the Berlin Foreign Office are often odd, but this story seems almost incredible." PRO/FO 371/463, note on Despatch No. 61, "Confidential," from de Salis (Berlin) to Grey, 31 October 1908.

99. Rich, 2, pp. 819ff.; and Germany, Auswärtiges Amt, *GP*, 24, "Deutschland und die Westmäche, 1907–1908," pp. 167ff. October was also the month of the Bosnian Crisis which added to general anxiety and focused public attention on foreign affairs.

100. Harden to Holstein, 29 October 1908, as in Holstein, 4, pp. 591–92.

101. Germany, Reichstag, *SB*, 233, pp. 5375–439.

102. Heine, 11 November 1908, in ibid., p. 5428.

103. *Deutsche Tageszeitung* and *Berliner Tageblatt*, as found in PRO/FO 371/463, W18, File 37537.

104. *Börsen Courier*, as found in ibid.

"*Meine Herren,*" declared Bassermann in full debate, "the Reichstag cannot abdicate in this question of foreign policy decision making. The center of criticism must be here in the parliament."[105] The dependence of effective supervision upon sufficient information led German deputies, like their French colleagues, to deplore the operations of *Geheimdiplomatie* (secret diplomacy). They decried the fact that the Reichstag was neither consulted nor informed on matters of international politics, and abhorred the Ministry's "mystery mongering"[106] Even members of the diplomatic corps themselves admitted the existence of an unhealthy "atmosphere of mystery that surrounded diplomatic procedure."[107]

The oppressive Bismarckian legacy of executive control, constitutional and political limitations upon legislative participation in foreign affairs, and an overwhelming preoccupation with domestic politics still inhibited Reichstag discussion.[108] The right of interpellation on international politics thus was deterred and seldom granted by the Chancellor or Foreign Minister. Some deputies asked unsuccessfully for a standing Reichstag committee on foreign affairs;[109] others, like their counterparts in Paris, attempted to circumvent the restrictions by discussing external policy and operations when Wilhelmstrasse officials came before the parliament to acquire annual appropriations.[110]

Critics wishing greater control over the formulation and execution of German foreign policy sought to implement what they considered to be the potentially more effective Bundesrat's Committee for

105. Bassermann, 10 November 1908, Germany, Reichstag, *SB*, 233, p. 5379.

106. See the debates of 19, 20, 23 November 1900, in Germany, Reichstag, *SB*, pp. 9ff.; 10, 11 November 1908, idem, 233, pp. 5373ff.; Philipp Scheidemann, on 31 March 1909, idem, 236, p. 7905; and Germany, Nationalliberalen Zentralvorstandes, *Von Bassermann zu Stresemann: Die Sitzungen des nationalliberalen Zentralvorstandes, 1912–1917,* edited by Klaus-Peter Reiss (Düsseldorf: Droste, 1967), p. 136 [hereafter cited as Reiss].

107. Wilhelm von Schoen, *Erlebtes: Beiträge zur politischen Geschichte der neusten Zeit* (Berlin: Deutsche Verlags-Anstalt, 1921), p. 111.

108. Johann Sass, *Die Deutschen Weissbücher zur auswärtigen Politik, 1870–1914* (Berlin: Walter de Gruyter and Co., 1928), passim; and Eckart Kehr, *Der Primat der Innenpolitik,* ed. by Hans-Ulrich Wehler (Berlin: Walter de Gruyter and Co., 1970), particularly pp. 149–75.

109. Sass, pp. 102–6; and the ridicule of the proposal in *Kladderadatsch,* 22 November 1908.

110. Such debates, for example, are found on 5 April 1906, in Germany, Reichstag, *SB*, 216, pp. 2648ff.; 2 December 1912, idem, 286, pp. 2497ff.; and *Vorwärts,* "Die auswärtige Politik in der Budgetkommission," 4 April 1913.

Foreign Affairs, as provided within the Constitution. This was the body on which Bavaria had insisted at the time of national unification to assure that the federal states would be informed and consulted regularly on external affairs. For years members of this *Bundesratsausschuss für die auswärtigen Angelegenheiten* had tried to play a greater role in German foreign relations.[111] It took the public reaction to the *Daily Telegraph* affair to encourage them. "Who governs the German Empire?" demanded the *Bayerischer Kurier*, challenging the federal states to assert their authority in external affairs.[112] "If the Committee of the Bundesrat had met regularly and frequently," said Dr. Günther in the Saxon Landtag, "the misdirection and impulsiveness" of the Kaiser's foreign policy "would have been impossible."[113]

Wilhelm II's personal role in the *Daily Telegraph* interview, however, was only one aspect of the criticism levelled against the methods of German diplomacy. Much of the blame for this blunder fell upon the stately, sphinx-guarded doorstep at Wilhelmstrasse 76. Reichstag critics fumed that professional bureaucrats in the Ministry had failed in their responsibility by permitting the interview material to pass through their hands. Under Bülow, said the *Kölnische Volkszeitung*, the Wilhelmstrasse conducted foreign affairs with no established policy and lived only "from hand to mouth."[114]

The Wilhelmstrasse found its organization and operations exposed to public censure and scrutiny as never before. Like its French equivalent on the Quai d'Orsay, it was forced to learn that foreign and domestic politics were more interrelated than in the past. The *Daily Telegraph* affair—called the "November assault" by the State Secretary[115]—drew public attention to the mismanagement of German foreign affairs, exposed a deep-seated discontent, and demonstrated an unforeseen potential for criticism of the Ministry. The press, political parties and pressure groups, chambers of commerce, diplomatic and consular personnel, and members of the Reichstag demanded comprehensive reforms. Only a few years

111. See Deuerlein, pp. 133ff.

112. *Bayerischer Kurier*, 6 November 1908.

113. Dr. Günther, as cited in PRO/FO 371/463, Despatch No. 46, "Confidential," from Findlay (Dresden) to Grey, 18 November 1908.

114. *Kölnische Volkszeitung*, 10 November 1908.

115. Schoen, p. 100.

earlier this institution had been described as "inaccessible to most mortals."[116] Now, said Bassermann in public, the affair clearly demonstrated the need to consider "the reorganization of the Wilhelmstrasse."[117] He was echoed by the conservative deputy, Liebermann von Sonnenberg, in the Reichstag: "That the Ministry for Foreign Affairs must be reformed is now thoroughly beyond all dispute."[118]

Even Freiherr von Schoen, the new Secretary of State for Foreign Affairs, referred to the Wilhelmstrasse as a "defective organization . . . so out of date it had to be replaced with something newer and better."[119] He described the quantity and detail of work in twentieth-century international relations as overwhelming and unmanageable with a nineteenth-century institution. "The burden of the office" was so great on his immediate predecessors that it had killed Hartmann von Richthofen—a "man who enjoyed work"— and forced Heinrich von Tschirschky to resign to save his health.[120] Others confirmed the expanding volume and complexity of the work and declared that the administration and numbers of personnel were inadequate to meet the new demands.[121]

Some critics blamed the Wilhelmstrasse's inefficiency and confusion upon an administrative apparatus that perpetuated an outdated system of division of labor. The same theme had been directed against the Quai d'Orsay in Paris: that in the twentieth century it was increasingly irrational to divide affairs into strictly political and commercial categories. They proposed a more realistic organization into a *Regionalsystem,* involving geographical divisions.[122] Under Reichstag pressure, even Kiderlen-Wächter as personal representa-

---

116. Busch, 1, p. 427.

117. Bassermann, 10 November 1908, in Germany, Reichstag, *SB*, 233, p. 5378.

118. Liebermann von Sonnenberg, in ibid., p. 5404.

119. Schoen, pp. 52, 118; and in the debate of 10 December 1908, in Germany, Reichstag, *SB*, 233, p. 6107.

120. Schoen, p. 51.

121. See even the relatively mild statements by Kiderlen-Wächter and Dirksen, 11 November 1908, in Germany, Reichstag, *SB*, 233, pp. 5433, 5435–36. Also see the material in PA/AA, Abteilung IA, Deutschland 122 Nr. 2, *secr.*, Band 1.

122. Schoen, p. 118. The only geographical distribution which occurred existed as sub-units within the respective Political and Commercial Divisions. See PA/AA, Abteilung IA, Deutschland 149, Band 10, A. 7579, "Geschäftsverteilung der politischen Abteilung," of 24 April 1906 after Holstein's departure; idem, Band 11, A. 8886 of 5 June 1907; and idem, Band 12 of the same series for the unnumbered 1908 listing.

tive of the State Secretary admitted that administrative burdens had increased greatly as German policy and business interests expanded around the globe and as commercial and political matters became enmeshed.[123]

The industrialists, manufacturers, and exporting firms were particularly concerned, knowledgeable, and vocal about the relation between foreign politics and commerce. Much more should be done, they argued, to capture and safeguard world markets for German firms, noting that the Wilhelmstrasse had failed in this phase of its responsibilities. Such was the thrust of the petition submitted in 1907 by Gustav Stresemann on behalf of major commercial interests.[124] A hard-hitting memorandum to the Ministry for Foreign Affairs followed from Bernhard Dernburg, a man hailed in the press as representing "up-to-date business methods." He lambasted the "defective" system of managing Germany's foreign commerce, declaring that the Commercial Division had little systematic contact with the *Reichsamt des Innern* (Interior Ministry) on economical matters. Even worse, the diplomatic and consular services lacked the basic knowledge or techniques of business matters in a new world of modern telegraphs, railroads, and steamships.[125]

Critics also found fault with the lack of standardization and administrative abuses within the Wilhelmstrasse. In accounting matters, for example, a "rather delicate question" arose when ambiguous, subjective criteria were used to determine annual Christmas gratuities being paid out of funds granted for other purposes.[126] Others attacked the Press Bureau, claiming that its irresponsibility created great administrative and political havoc. Its small size was accused of being inadequate to influence public opinion sufficiently.[127] Colonial scandals exposed additional mismanagement within

123. Kiderlen-Wächter, 11 November 1908, in Germany, Reichstag, *SB*, 233, p. 5433; and marked with red pencil on the copy filed in PA/AA, Abteilung IA, Deutschland 122, Nr. 2, Band 3.

124. See PA/AA, Abteilung IA, Deutschland 122 Nr. 2, *secr.*, Band 1, A.2254, circular of 4 February 1909; and PA/AA, Politisches Archiv und Historisches Referat, Aktenzeichen 13, p. 49.

125. PA/AA, Abteilung IA, Deutschland 122 Nr. 2, *secr.*, Band 1, "Neuorganisation des Ausw. Amtes," Denkschrift from Dernburg to Under State Secretary Stemrich, 26 November 1908.

126. Schoen, p. 103.

127. See, for example, *Allgemeine Zeitung*, "Die Presse und die deutsche Weltpolitik," 16 April 1906, among many others, and Chapter Six.

the Ministry for Foreign Affairs, forcing even Bülow to admit that "our present organization . . . is inadequate."[128] The confusion resulting from this whole absolutist system of foreign policy, said Scheidemann, "remains one of an Offenbach comic opera."[129]

Much administrative abuse, confusion, and lack of standardization, of course, resulted from the unusual position, personality, and interfering practices of the Kaiser. Chief executives seldom have good working relations with the bureaucratic machinery formally charged with the management of foreign relations, and in this respect Wilhelm II certainly provided no exception. Even foreign diplomats recognized the existence of "the traditional struggle between the Wilhelmstrasse and the Palace."[130] In addition to his personal interference and impulsiveness in diplomacy, burdened officials found the Kaiser's marginal notes on important despatches to be terribly disconcerting or useless in the rational management of affairs. Holstein despaired that His Majesty wanted "to make foreign policy himself, without contradiction from the professional bureaucracy,"[131] and sadly observed: "The Kaiser's dislike of the Foreign Ministry is almost pathological and is recognized as such by the people concerned."[132]

Many critics also knew of Wilhelm's interference in personnel policy, and they vigorously attacked his seemingly uncontrolled, subjective power over Wilhelmstrasse appointments and dismissals. Several men had been "put on ice" by his direct intervention.[133] Yet the higher officials in the Ministry acted in much the same manner. Holstein's own control over personnel matters was notorious, and even someone as well-placed as Bernstorff observed that "to visit the Foreign Ministry and not see Holstein was like Rome without

---

128. Bülow, 29 March 1906, in Germany, Reichstag, *SB*, 216, p. 2417; and the comments by Dr. Spahn and others during the same debate.

129. Scheidemann, 15 March 1910, in Germany, Reichstag, *SB*, 260, p. 2143.

130. MAE, Allemagne, politique intérieur, dossier général, NS 4, Despatch No. 105, "Absolument confidentiel," from Cambon (Berlin) to Pichon, 4 June 1907.

131. Holstein, 4, p. 406.

132. Ibid., 1, p. 173. One can imagine that teeth were particularly set on edge when the Kaiser once noted that he had carried through a successful policy "while," in his own words, "the Foreign Ministry had shat in its pants." See Rich, 2, p. 732.

133. Holstein, 1, p. 175.

the Pope."[134] "Posts simply must not be filled according to the purely private feelings of the highest persons in the State," warned the *Kölnische Zeitung*.[135] Others claimed that such abuses were not only unfair but dangerous since they crushed vital initiative and demoralized both the diplomats and bureaucrats.[136]

Politically more serious were those critical accusations that echoed an issue sounded in Paris: this lack of standardization within the Ministry for Foreign Affairs was not only unfair and inefficient, but also smacked of "absolutism" and reinforced aristocratic bias. Common knowledge held, for example, that "next to brains, the other two 'b's' (birth and bank account)" were of crucial importance in the Wilhelmstrasse.[137] The lengthy unpaid probationary period followed by low salaries, in addition to the explicit requirement for a private income, assured heavy discrimination in favor of the German political and social elite.[138] The time had come, said the critics, to open careers to talent, to destroy the family "clique," and to instill "new blood."[139] Even Schoen admitted that "there was great justification" for complaints against the traditional aristocratic and plutocratic practices of the Wilhelmstrasse which "*were no longer consistent with the spirit of the times.*"[140]

This criticism also included the diplomatic and consular services, for many contended that the missions abroad represented mere extensions of the confused organization and administrative abuses at the Ministry. They saw a shameful duplication of the obsolete emphasis upon the geographical area of Europe, the rigid functional

134. Bernstorff, p. 27. Also see the numerous press clippings about Holstein's control of personnel questions on file in PA/AA, Abteilung IA, Deutschland 122 Nr. 2, Band 4.

135. *Kölnische Zeitung*, 6 November 1906.

136. *Hannoverscher Courier*, "Unsere auswärtige Politik," 3 September 1907; and Reiss, citing Professor Eugene Leidig in 1913, pp. 143–44.

137. Zechlin, p. 74.

138. Erich Kordt, *Nicht au den Akten* (Stuttgart, Union Deutsche Verlagsgesellschaft, 1950), p. 30; and Paul Seabury, *The Wilhelmstrasse: A Study of German Diplomats Under the Nazi Regime* (Berkeley: University of California Press, 1954), pp. 6–8.

139. Bassermann, 30 April 1907, in Germany, Reichstag, *SB*, 228, p. 1247; debates of 10, 11 November 1908, idem, 233, pp. 5373ff.; Wiemer, 10 December 1910, idem, 262, p. 3570; and Reiss, p. 144.

140. Schoen, p. 112 [my emphasis].

separation of "political" from "commercial" affairs, subjective policies, and the same antiquated methods. In personnel recruitment as well, the services only reinforced an "exclusive circle" of aristocrats, a practice that no longer could be tolerated by the growing democratic spirit of twentieth-century diplomacy.[141]

Business and shipping interests, like their French competitors, stressed the new century's need for "systematic" and "rational" management, especially in the economic aspects of foreign policy. Overseas services, like the Wilhelmstrasse itself, needed to take a more "active" and "energetic" role in protecting and expanding German interests abroad. The expansion and complexity of responsibilities in the diplomatic and consular services required increased specialization in legal, technical, and linquistic abilities. Many foreign posts had changed little since the days of Bismarck, lacked systematic salary standards, and—exactly like their central administration in Berlin—now were in need of a "thorough reform."[142]

Such reforms, however, appeared nearly impossible under the existing system of German government, or what the Reichstag referred to as "this monarchical problem." While other countries developed democratic institutions, the constitutional framework of the Reich remained as it had been created by Bismarck in the nineteenth century. Chancellor Bethmann Hollweg bluntly said to those deputies demanding ministerial responsibility and reforms in the management of foreign relations: "That attitude, gentlemen, assumes the existence of a different constitutional system to that which prevails in Germany."[143]

141. *Frankfurter Zeitung*, "Etwas von diplomatischen Dienst," 20 December 1908; *Norddeutsche Allgemeine Zeitung*, 28 January 1909; *Neue Preussische Zeitung*, "Nationale auswärtige Politik und die deutsche Diplomatie," 9 May 1914; 5 December 1908, Germany, Reichstag, *SB*, 233, pp. 5995ff.; and PA/AA, Abteilung IA, Deutschland 122 Nr. 2, Bände 3, 4, and 5.

142. Among many examples, see the "Denkschrift, betreffend die Neuregelung der Besoldungen der Auslandsbeamten," in PA/AA, Politisches Archiv und Historisches Referat, "Etat für das Auswärtige Amt auf das Rechnungsjahr 1914," pp. 62–65; the Dernburg Denkschrift of 26 November 1908 in PA/AA, Abteilung IA, Deutschland 122 Nr. 2, *secr.*, Band 1, A.S.1752; and Heinz Sasse, "Zur Geschichte des Auswärtigen Amts," *Mitteilungsblatt der Vereinigung der Angestellten des Auswärtigen Dienstes,* Heft 7, 4 Jahrgang (July 1960), pp. 161–62.

143. Bethmann Hollweg, 9 December 1913, in Germany, Reichstag, *SB*, 291, p. 6281.

The *Daily Telegraph* affair led to demands by many members of the Reichstag for the immediate retirement of Bülow, constitutional limits on the Kaiser's imperial power in external relations, and drastic changes in the Ministry for Foreign Affairs. Although little change resulted at the time, *Die Post* wrote: "The Chancellor was saved, but the Prusso-German Monarchy suffered on the 10th of November 1908 the greatest defeat since the year 1848." The editorial concluded:

> The Reichstag, by lacking the moral courage to dismiss a Chancellor of ordinary abilities, has chosen a way which must inevitably lead to the undermining of the foundations of the Monarchy. In times to come, however—and no one can say how far or how near they may be—when all Europe will be convulsed, the Germans too will have to ask themselves 'Republic or British Constitution?' and then the recent debate in the Reichstag will furnish to all opponents of autocratic rule an endless quarry of irrefutable arguments.[144]

4. Convulsions of the First World War

The European diplomatic system of the nineteenth century had dramatically changed by 1914, but it collapsed during the First World War. The domestic criticism of diplomacy and demands upon the French and German Ministries for Foreign Affairs that had emerged earlier seemed to explode during the years of war and devastation. These were the convulsions envisaged by *Die Post* and others. As Jean Jaurès predicted immediately before his assassination: "When typhus finishes the work begun by bullets, and as death and misery strike all, men will turn on their rulers, whether German, French, Russian or Italian—and demand an explanation for all those corpses."[145]

Europe and the world staggered in disbelief as over four years of slaughter indiscriminately killed and disabled men, women, and

---

144. *Die Post,* as found in PRO/FO 371/463, W18, File 37537. The protest against the Zabern affair of 1913 also inflamed these arguments against the monarchy.

145. Jean Jaurès, 29 July 1914 speech in Brussels, as reproduced in *L'Humanité*, 30 July 1914.

children—"leaving the dead like a million bloody rugs."[146] The century's new science and technology unleashed unimaginable forces of destruction that revolutionized modern warfare, obliterated the old distinction between civilian and combatant, and laid waste entire provinces. Empires crumbled and crowns fell from the heads of the German Hohenzollerns, Austrian Hapsburgs, and Russian Romanovs. The war precipitated democratic and communist revolutions, brought about direct American intervention into European affairs and a redistribution of world power, loosened the ties of empires abroad, and created new states from the ashes of old monarchies. In leaving little distinction between "victor" and "vanquished," the conflict further signalled the final collapse of the limited features of nineteenth-century warfare and diplomacy. Moreover, the internal and external dimensions of such extended conflict profoundly damaged the earlier cultural, moral, and psychological homogeneity of European civilization. Years of death and exhaustion left, in the mournful words of Erich Maria Remarque: "Fields of craters within and without."[147] "The old Europe that we had known in 1914," said one French diplomat, "ceased to exist."[148]

In accordance with the prediction of Jean Jaurès, people indeed demanded an explanation for the dead and maimed bodies scattered throughout Europe. Many argued that a small number of scheming diplomats within the confines of "secret diplomacy" had failed to keep the peace, aggravated prewar tensions, and bore primary responsibility for the holocaust. "The art of secret diplomacy is the worst survival of past absolutism," proclaimed one critic, [149] while another stated flatly: "The old ambassadorial system has failed and is discredited."[150] Woodrow Wilson concluded that this "compli-

---

146. F. Scott Fitzgerald, *Tender Is the Night* (New York: Scribner, 1951 ed), p. 125. For an important essay on the impact of this struggle on warfare and diplomacy, see Gordon A. Craig, "The Revolution in War and Diplomacy," in *War, Politics and Diplomacy: Selected Essays* (New York: Praeger, 1966), pp. 194–206.

147. Erich Maria Remarque, *All Quiet on the Western Front* (New York: Fawcett World Library, 1968 ed.), p. 162.

148. Georges Bonnet, *Le Quai d'Orsay sous trois républiques* (Paris: Fayard, 1961), p. 40.

149. *Vorwärts,* "Krieg und Diplomatie," 26 May 1915.

150. Trevelyan, 19 March 1918, in Britain, House of Commons, *The Parliamentary Debates,* 104 (London: H.M.S.O., 1918), p. 846.

cated network of intrigue and espionage . . . unerringly caught the entire family in its meshes."[151]

The mood of desperation and anger is captured in Remarque's bitter novel, *All Quiet on the Western Front*:

> "But what I would like to know," says Albert, "is whether there would not have been a war if the Kaiser had said No. . . . Well, if not him alone, then perhaps if twenty or thirty people in the world had said No."
>
> "That's probable," I agree, "but they damned well said Yes."
>
> "It's queer, when one thinks about it," goes on Kropp, "we are here to protect our [German] fatherland. And the French are over there to protect their fatherland. Now, who's in the right? . . . just you consider, almost all of us are simple folk. And in France, too, the majority of men are laborers, workmen, or poor clerks. Now just why would a French blacksmith or a French shoemaker want to attack us? No, it is merely the rulers. I had never seen a Frenchman before I came here, and it will be just the same with the majority of Frenchmen as regards us. They weren't asked about it any more than we were."
>
> "Then," asks Tjaden, "what exactly is the war for?"[152]

As the war continued with its rising fatalities, heavier hardships, and suppressed civil liberties, an uneasy domestic political truce in the French *union sacrée* and German *Burgfrieden* began to crumble. Greater numbers of citizens refused to accept their government's official explanations, and asked—with Remarque's young, battle-weary soldier, Tjaden—why the war was being fought.[153] The disclosure of various "war aims" and "peace points" indicated that the diplomats apparently had learned nothing from the war. Secret treaties formulated *in camera* during hostilities actually delineated zones of influence and protectorates, plans for territorial acquisition, and promises of future economic penetration—all this in stark contrast with the official slogans of a war for freedom and self-defence. In the opinion of one scholar, "these treaties represent the

151. Woodrow Wilson, as cited in Bernadotte Schmitt, *Triple Alliance and Triple Entente* (New York: Holt, 1934), p. 1.

152. Remarque, pp. 122–124.

153. P. Golay, "Pour les Peuples," in *L'Aube: Revue politique et littéraire*, 1 October 1917, considered important enough to file in PA/AA, Abteilung 1A, Frankreich 105 Nr. 1, Band 32.

most vivid incarnation of the spirit, the techniques, and the objectives of the Old Diplomacy."[154]

To many critics these secret wartime agreements vividly illustrated the connection between methods of diplomatic negotiation and the actual content of international agreements. They claimed, for example, that ministerial bureaucracy and its diplomats used secrecy not only to conduct negotiations, but to hide the damaging features of "power politics," "armament races," "rival alliances," "imperialist annexations," and "trade wars" from an increasingly alert, vocal, and critical public.[155] Lenin's April Theses and Woodrow Wilson's Fourteen Points of 1917 were notable expressions, among many others,[156] of the idea that diplomacy in this century must differ in its origins, objectives, and methods from that of the past. These spokesmen demanded that there must be "adequate machinery for democratic control" over foreign policy, "open covenants of peace openly arrived at" instead of clandestine bargains, and even new institutions capable of facilitating peaceful political and economic change. "Foreign policy must be placed under effective parliamentary control," reiterated the German socialist Eduard Bernstein, and "secret treaties must be abolished."[157]

For twentieth-century diplomacy, however, the writings and activities of socialists like Bernstein had significance far beyond their content. They indicated that citizens would attempt to bypass the

154. From the extremely interesting study by Arno J. Mayer, *Wilson vs. Lenin: Political Origins of the New Diplomacy, 1917–1918* (New York: World Publishing Co., 1964), pp. 17, 208–14, 279–80.

155. Ibid., pp. 7 and 57; and Comité pour la Reprise des Relations Internationales, *Seconde conférence socialiste internationale de Zimmerwald: Les résolutions* (Paris: Féderation des Métaux, 1916). Max Weber, 2, pp. 580–81, for example, notes that bureaucratic administration always tends to increase its professional superiority and hide its actions from criticism by keeping its knowledge and intentions secret.

156. In emphasizing the significance of Lenin and Wilson, it is important to acknowledge the foundation of criticism upon which they constructed their ideas. In addition to those sources already cited in this chapter, see Milorad M. Drachkovitch, *Les Socialismes français et allemand et le problème de la guerre, 1870–1914* (Geneva: Droz, 1953); and M. Swartz, *The Union of Democratic Control in British Politics During the First World War* (Oxford: Clarendon Press, 1971).

157. Eduard Bernstein, *Die parlamentarische Kontrolle der auswärtigen Politik,* Zentralorganisation für einen dauernden Frieden (The Hague: Martinus Nijhoff, 1916); and Ludwig Quessel, "Die Kontrolle der auswärtigen Politik," *Sozialistische Monatshefte,* 22. Jahrgang, 3 (October 1916), pp. 1087–91.

traditional diplomacy of the Ministries for Foreign Affairs and the professional diplomats to take matters into their own hands. Numerous international conferences held by socialist and labor organizations during the war consistently disregarded official bureaucracy and discussed international relations, the causes and aims of the war, and the faults of nineteenth-century diplomacy.[158] At these public meetings it was common to hear French socialists like Albert Thomas support recognition of "the common will of the people" in the conduct of foreign relations,[159] or his German counterparts demand the immediate "suppression of secret diplomacy."[160] As deaths rose on the battlefield, aggressiveness increased among the critics. Deputy Pierre Renaudel cried, "We not only have the right, but the duty to be informed. We will no longer be satisfied with vague words given to us. I demand the texts. . . . As responsible parliamentarians we demand to know what negotiations have been carried out in Russia! On whose initiative? What about? What has been signed? What letters exchanged?"[161]

Such boldness was abhorrent to those trained in traditional diplomatic methods,[162] but indicated yet another sign of the future. As the trench war continued and domestic pressure mounted, the professional *corps diplomatique* found itself bypassed by military personnel or untrained political "amateurs." The First Proclamation of the Petrograd Soviet urged all people to "take into their own hands the decision of the question of war and peace."[163] "Diplomats were invented simply to waste time," said Lloyd George in expressing his contempt for the professionals, and declared bluntly: "I want no

158. Parti Socialiste et Confédération Générale du Travail, *Le Memorandum des socialistes des pays alliés* (Paris: Simart, 1918); and Angelica Balabanoff, *Die Zimmerwalder Bewegung, 1914–1919* (Leipzig: Hirschfeld, 1928).

159. AN, Fonds Albert Thomas, 94 AP 357, dossier "Attitude des socialistes françaises."

160. Ibid., 94 AP 406, "Résponse de la délégation allemande"; idem, 94 AP 358, dossier "Congrès International Socialiste de Stockholm"; and *Manchester Guardian*, "Six Peace Programmes: A Comparison of the Main Proposals," 20 August 1917.

161. Pierre Renaudel, in France, Assemblée nationale, Chambre des Députés, Comité secret du 1er juin 1917, *Comptes-rendus in-extenso des comités secrets de la Chambre des Députés, 1916–1917* (Paris: Imprimerie des Journaux officiels, 1925), p. 518.

162. Among many examples, see MAE, Direction politique et commerciale, Papiers des Agents: Philippe Berthelot, Carton 4, undated note by Loyson, "Mission en Angleterre."

163. The Petrograd Soviet, as cited in Mayer, p. 192.

diplomats."[164] Even the untrained socialists Albert Thomas and Philipp Scheidemann were sent by their respective governments on international missions.[165] This assault upon the career corps continued at the Paris Peace Conference. Here the politicians Lloyd George, Clemenceau, Orlando, and Wilson—referred to by one official as "The Dread Amateur"[166]—often rejected the advice offered by their staff experts and relied upon personal intuition to solve intricate international problems.

In addition to destroying the nineteenth-century framework, to accelerating criticism of traditional diplomacy, to increasing the contempt for professional diplomats and bureaucrats, and to facilitating the employment of amateurs, the First World War contributed another element that would greatly influence the French and German Ministries for Foreign Affairs and future international relations. This was experimentation with new forms of centralized administrative techniques of control and organization.

The confusion following initial hostilities soon led to the stark realization that a total mobilization of national resources was essential to survival. Shortages, bottlenecks, and profiteering convinced many leaders that only centralization could save them. They insisted that massive interministerial administrative efforts be made to coordinate policy, supply, production, distribution, prices, and the use of manpower. "New forms and methods must be found," said the innovative Walter Rathenau, who claimed that "organization is able to take up any issue, however difficult it may be, and can find new means to solve problems."[167]

This resulted in an enormous proliferation of new offices, committees, commissions, departments, and various centralized services

---

164. Lloyd George, as cited in A. L. Kennedy, *Old Diplomacy and New* (London: John Murray, 1922), pp. 364–65.

165. AN, Fonds Albert Thomas, 94 AP, Cartons 181, 182, 185, and 190; PA/ AA, Abteilung IA, Weltkrieg Nr. 11, adh 1., "Akten betr. den Krieg 1914, Unternehmungen u. Aufwiegelungen gegen unsere Feinde durch die Sozialdemocratie bezw. die Arbeiterschaft."

166. Vansittart, p. 176.

167. Walther Rathenau, *Deutschlands Rohstoffversorgung*, Vortrag gehalten in der "Deutschen Gesellschaft 1914" am 20. Dezember 1915. Stenogramm H. Geitner Veröffentlicht mit Genehmigung des preussischen Kriegsministeriums (Berlin: Fischer, 1918), pp. 18, 26. French reaction to German organizational and management abilities can be seen in the interesting wartime collection of essays in Jean Labadié (ed.), *L'Allemagne, a-t-elle le secret de l'organisation?* (Paris; Bibliothèque de l'opinion, 1916).

under governmental control in all belligerent countries. *"C'est la guerre d'organisation,"* said French observers, *"c'est la guerre d'administration."*[168] These experiments in administrative techniques and centralized organization, asserted Rathenau, demonstrated "a new departure" which "has no precedent in history, which will have a decided influence on the war, and which in all probability is destined to affect future times."[169] Such military and economic mobilization was essential, according to a French analyst, but the rational preparation for total war also called for yet another element: "diplomatic mobilization."[170]

The increased vigor with which critics proposed reforms and innovations for the French and German Ministries for Foreign Affairs was set in this general wartime context of a search for new solutions and administrative forms. Wartime confusion, loss of experienced personnel in battle, influx of "newcomers," and growing contempt for traditional diplomacy made the Quai d'Orsay and the Wilhelmstrasse particularly susceptible to criticism and less able or willing to resist change. Many critics argued that the war proved it to be more than ever necessary to "abandon obsolete methods."[171]

The Ministry's central administration in Paris, which had undertaken major institutional reforms prior to the outbreak of hostilities, came under sharp attack for still being "a prisoner of its traditions" and for failing to respond adequately to the requirements of war.[172] The professionals were attacked for their immobility in a time of crisis, for systematically ignoring public opinion, and for being inadequately skilled in technical and commercial matters.[173] Critics

168. Comité de propagande socialiste pour la Défense nationale, *Les Socialistes dans la Nation et pour la Nation* (Paris: Librairie de l'Humanité, 1916), p. 3. Also see MAE, Direction politique et commerciale, Papiers des Agents: Philippe Berthelot, Carton 3; and MAE/Sénat, Rapport No. 226 (1918), pp. 47–50.

169. Rathenau, p. 5.

170. MAE/Chambre, Rapport No. 4108 (1918), p. 4.

171. France, Assemblée nationale, Chambre des Députés, Annexe au procès-verbal de la séance du 22 juin 1916, Rapport No. 2234, "Proposition de loi ayant pour object la réform de l'organisation des consulats," par Henry Lémery, et al., p. 2 [hereafter cited as France, Chambre, Rapport No. 2234, "Proposition"].

172. MAE/Chambre, Rapport No. 4108 (1918), p. 3. For a treatment of these pre-war reforms, see Chapter Three.

173. This criticism is briefly summarized in MAE/Chambre, Rapport No. 4108 (1918), pp. 3–10. Also see the demands for greater parliamentary participation as expressed in *Le Temps*, 21 June 1917.

proposed a more "rational," "systematic," and "modern" organization of affairs, the employment of specialists for complex problems in international relations, better methods of promotion, adequate salaries to attract talent and destroy the monopoly of wealth, and more rigorous means for recruiting and training of personnel.[174] One spokesman anticipated a "complete recasting" of those French institutions concerned with external affairs, and the Chambre declared:

> The experience of the war demonstrates the necessity to create immediately reforms in the organization and the methods of work within the Ministry for Foreign Affairs, as in the recruitment and promotion of diplomatic and consular personnel.[175]

Despite much early criticism, but unlike the Quai d'Orsay, the German Ministry for Foreign Affairs had instituted no significant reorganization before the First World War. This fact, aggravated by serious diplomatic blunders during the war,[176] brought demands for immediate reform in the Wilhelmstrasse. All the criticisms aimed at the Ministry before 1914 resounded with increased and unprecedented fury. If the armies of most of the world were now turned against Germany, said one group of critics, "the fault must lie singularly with the Ministry for Foreign Affairs."[177]

This blunt statement was reinforced in a remarkably detailed, "strictly confidential" memorandum prepared by a group of more than one hundred Hamburg businessmen and submitted to the German Chancellor and Ministry for Foreign Affairs. The report summarized in frank terms the major faults of the administration and

174. Among many wartime proposals, see *Le Figaro,* "La Réforme des Consulats," 1 July 1916; MAE/Chambre, Rapport No. 4108 (1918), pp. 5–16; and MAE/Sénat, Rapport No. 226 (1918), pp. 47ff.

175. A Chambre *ordre du jour,* as cited in MAE/Chambre, Rapport No. 4108 (1918), p. 10.

176. Most notable were the outcries raised by the Zimmermann Telegram, the proclamation of a Polish Kingdom in 1916, unrestricted submarine warfare and the resulting entrance of the United States in the war on the side of the Entente, and the Graf Luxburg affair.

177. Cited in an undated memorandum by Paul von Schwabach and given to Töpffer as found in PA/AA, Handakten des Unterstaatssekretär Töpffer, Aktenzeichen 13, Band 1; and in Heinz Sasse, "Zur Geschichte des Auswärtigen Amts," Heft 7, p. 162. For a treatment of the new reforms that did occur before 1914, see Chapter Four.

operations of the Wilhelmstrasse. The entire structural organization of the Ministry, said these critics, was "inadequate" to meet the demands of the twentieth century. Principles and methods of management were irrational and simply "wrong." The bureaucratic officials of the past had represented only dynastic interests and had received "insufficient knowledge" of technical, commercial, or propaganda matters. Training emphasized theoretical abstractions at the expense of practical skills. Furthermore, the lack of sufficient funds greatly inhibited the efficient operation of the Wilhelmstrasse, fostered the wealth monopoly and discouraged needed talent from entering the service of the state. "Time urgently presses," asserted the critics, "and the work of reform must be taken in hand immediately!"[178]

Some Reichstag deputies renewed demands for permanent, institutional means to influence policy and to supervise the operations and procedures of the Wilhelmstrasse. "This fearful war," said Bassermann, "has demonstrated to us the necessity of a more active participation by the Reichstag in questions of foreign policy."[179] Other critics insisted that the administrative structure of the Ministry be completely reorganized along geographical lines rather than the antiquated political-commercial distinction. New divisions should be created within the organizational structure to promote aggressive German commerce and propaganda. "Modern," "efficient," and "rational" business techniques must be systematically applied to the magagement of foreign affairs. Latin script should replace the obsolete and difficult German *fraktur* to facilitate speed in reading and decision making. Personnel must be well-trained specialists, familiar with practical in contrast to theoretical aspects of international relations, and be rigorously selected on the basis of talent rather than birth or wealth. Promotion, salaries, and transfer should be based upon standardized practices, and the old cleavage between diplomatic and consular services abolished.[180]

178. Ausschuss für Neugestaltung des Auslandsdienstes, *Hamburger Vorschläge zur Neugestaltung des deutschen Auslandsdienstes* (Hamburg: April 1918), pp. 6–15, and filed under PA/AA, Handakten des Unterstaatssekretär Töpffer, Aktenzeichen—[see 13], Beiband [hereafter cited as PA/AA, *Hamburger Denkschrift*].

179. Bassermann, 11 October 1916, in Germany, Reichstag, *SB*, 308, p. 1741.

180. In addition to all the German wartime sources already cited see the secret memorandum by Max M. Warburg, "Betr. Amtliche Vertretung Deutschlands im

"In the completely changed circumstances brought about by the war," declared one memorandum of proposals, "the earlier procedures can simply no longer be maintained."[181]
As we shall see, this experience of devastating war enabled further reorganization and innovation to take place in France and broke down previous barriers to make significant reform possible in Germany. Critics of both the Quai d'Orsay and Wilhelmstrasse understood the challenge sounded loudly in the Chamber of Deputies:

> It is not only necessary to complete the best possible [ministerial] organization for the present, but to also prepare it for the future. The war, which has transformed so many things, will bring profound changes in our diplomatic and consular institutions. They now ought to adapt themselves not only to new requirements, but also to the new political, economic and social configuration which will emerge as a result of the conclusion of peace.[182]

* * * *

These many criticisms and proposals for new diplomatic institutions, while generated by immediate pragmatic considerations, were part of a much larger movement in the search for new forms and solutions to problems of the twentieth century. Evidence of this quest appeared as art, music, philosophy, science, applied technology, alliance systems, and ideas for managing international relations all reflected creative invention. Technological, international, and domestic pressures loosened many established traditions and practices of the past, making change and reform both possible and necessary.

Auslande," "Geheim," dated Hamburg, March 1918, and found in PA/AA, Handakten des Unterstaatssekretär Töpffer, Aktenzeichen—[see 13]; Wilhelm Schrameier, *Auswärtiges Amt und Auslandsvertretung: Vorschläge zur Reform* (Berlin: Curtius, 1918); and Wahrhold Drascher, "Zur Organisation unseres Auslandsdienstes," *Das Neue Deutschland*, 23, 5. Jahrgang (September 1917), pp. 639–42.

181. From a memorandum submitted to the Chancellor by the Chambers of Commerce of Bremen, Hamburg, and Lübeck, as reproduced in *Export* of 20 July 1918, and as found in PRO/FO 371/3481, Despatch No. D/3391 from War Intelligence Department to Foreign Office, 31 August 1918.

182. MAE/Chambre, Rapport No. 4108 (1918), p. 7.

The material and mental exhaustion of the First World War accelerated this process to a point where the former moorings of society were ruptured often beyond recognition. "An extraordinary shudder ran through the marrow of Europe," wrote Paul Valéry after the experience. "She felt in every nucleus of her mind that she was no longer the same, that she was no longer herself."[183] Romain Rolland sensed the feeling and cried: "Adieu, Europe, queen of thought and guide of humanity! You have lost your way."[184]

Yet the turmoil of the new century and the extent of the war not only destroyed the old, but forced peoples and governments — for sheer survival—to seek out and create new remedies and new institutions. To be fully appreciated, the reorganizations in the French and German Ministries for Foreign Affairs must be seen within this extensive process of destruction and creation. For if so viewed, one sees not only the intimate connection between foreign and domestic politics, but also that diplomacy and its institutions are integral parts of the political, military, social, economic, and intellectual elements within society as a whole. Dynamic changes in one area either permit, encourage, or actually force reforms and innovations in another.

183. Valéry, p. 24.
184. Romain Rolland, "Aux peuples assassinés," in *Demain: Pages et Documents*, 11/12 (November–December 1916), p. 266.

PART II

— 3 —

The French Response:
Reforms and Innovations for the Quai d'Orsay

The obligations of our diplomacy have expanded with the development of affairs. The organization of the central administration of the Ministry for Foreign Affairs no longer seems to correspond exactly with the needs of our politics or of external policy. A careful examination of the organization and operation of the Ministry's various services has led me to recognize that this administration could use beneficial modifications. Under these conditions, therefore, I have the honor to submit for your consent a project of reform.

—Foreign Minister
Stephen Pichon

The increasing pressure of domestic critics, when combined with the growing complexity and rapid pace of world politics, forced the Ministry for Foreign Affairs to shed its cocoon of tradition and isolation. Effective management of diplomacy required more elaborate and specialized administrative structures, improved managerial techniques, better qualified technicians systematically recruited on the basis of merit, and a greater use of modern technological inventions. The pragmatic realities of politics at home and abroad required a "more rational organization," "logical methods of work," "systematic techniques," and permanent mechanisms to manage "the necessities of modern diplomacy."

The French response to these new conditions took the form of major institutional changes within the Quai d'Orsay. Dynamic transformations occurred in the organizational structure, personnel policies, overseas services, and the Ministry's relations with outside interest groups. There was specialization and expansion in geographical, functional, and administrative responsibilities, greater sophistication in management procedures, standardization in personnel policy, and a more realistic distribution of representation abroad. These and other changes formed essential components of a larger modernization process within French society, leading a contemporary scholar to observe: "Nowadays—at any rate since the upheaval of 1914–1919—bureaucracy in France, governmental as well as unofficial, is obviously in transition: a transition from the nineteenth-century *milieu* of individualized production by artisans, craftsmen, clerks, and small-scale managerial officials guided by rule-of-thumb methods, to a more 'rationalized,' specialized twentieth-century technique of management."[1]

1. Men and Methods of Action

The dynamic changes affecting European society during the first two decades of the twentieth century forced an analysis of the failures of traditional institutions.[2] Many administrative structures and practices of the past were now considered grossly inadequate to cope with the complexities of the new century. Some officials sought refuge in custom. Others, however, eagerly responded to the modern challenge with creative reforms and innovations. Indeed, said one deputy in the French Chamber, "the very future of a country depends upon the spirit of enterprise with which it adapts itself to these new conditions."[3]

The accomplishments of industrial growth, commercial expansion, technological development, intellectual achievement, artistic expression, and scientific discovery convinced many reformers that rational effort could achieve positive results. It seemed possible to

1. Walter Rice Sharp, *The French Civil Service: Bureaucracy in Transition* (New York: Macmillan, 1931), p. vi.

2. On this point, see Pierre Legendre, *Histoire de l'administration de 1750 à nos jours* (Paris: Presses universitaires de France, 1968), pp. 90ff.

3. France, Assemblée nationale, Chambre des Députés, Commission de l'administration générale, Rapport No. 4285, Annexe au procès-verbal de la séance du 6 février 1918, "Rapport fait au nom de la commission de l'administration générale, départementale et communale chargée d'examiner les propositions de loi et de résolution concernant la réorganisation administrative de la France," par Jean Hennessy, p. 2.

either seize or create an opportunity for change. The future was subject to men and methods of action. To those concerned with the reform of governmental or managerial institutions, for example, a new approach to administrative science appeared very promising.

To many reformers, the assumptions and practices of traditional bureaucracies demonstrated only stark obsolescence. It seemed ludicrous that institutions should continue to be confined by rigid formalism or antiquated legalism. Others were disturbed that university faculties still considered administration as an "art" restricted to privileged groups and taught the virtues of limited governmental activity. To many who desired reform, the solution appeared in developing new approaches to business techniques, to managerial operations and control, and to the larger problems of public administration. Foremost in this movement were those in the more pragmatic schools of engineering and technology, and their leading French spokesman, Henri Fayol.

Fayol first drew attention with a speech in 1900 and a pioneering article entitled "Administration industrielle et générale" several years later.[4] He approached administration as a science. Management, he declared, must be considered a deliberate enterprise designed to accomplish a specific task. This should make it possible to develop techniques of providing efficient service within bureaucratic organizations. His elaboration of theoretical concepts like division of labor, assignment of responsibility and authority, specialized technical functions, organizational hierarchy, discipline, and personnel control opened new perspectives toward administrative science and managerial skills. The striking influence of "Fayolism"— even in Britain and the United States—the creation of the First International Congress of the Science of Administration, and the appearance of crusading writing on bureaucracy and *les fonctionnaires,*[5] all gave ample evidence that institutions—like other elements within the society of which they were an integral part—soon would be subjected to major transformations.

4. Both reprinted in Henri Fayol, *Administration industrielle et générale: Prévoyance, organisation, commandement, coordination, contrôle* (Paris: Dunod, 1920).

5. Charles Benoist, *La crise de l'état moderne; L'organisation du travail: le travail, le nombre et l'état* (Paris: Plon, 1905); Henri Chardon, *Le pouvoir administrative* (Paris: Perrin, 1912 ed.); and George Demartial, *La réforme administrative: ce qu'elle devrait être* (Paris: Cornély, 1911), among others.

The political emergence of *la République radicale* in France during 1906 gave reform-minded leaders their first chance. Unlike most of their counterparts in Germany who had to wait until after the First World War, they now appeared to have a base from which to launch effective efforts for significant change in society. Following a sweeping electoral success, Premier Georges Clemenceau vigorously asserted: "The country has made known its desire to emphasize and to accelerate the work of reform." He spoke of "modern societies," the need for civil liberties, social justice, protection of the working masses and the creation of a new Ministry of Labor, and even alluded to a progressive income tax. The military, he said, must be "imbued with the spirit of democracy," professional syndicalists must be permitted to organize, and the various branches of government must be encouraged to institute "administrative reorganization." In addition, asserted the new premier, French foreign policy must be made "republican."[6] It is in this context of movement that Foreign Minister Stephen Pichon heeded Clemenceau's call for "energetic action," and the following day created a commission to study reforms for the Quai d'Orsay.

Pichon charged this important *Commission des réformes administratives* with "studying the reforms that could be introduced in the internal and overseas services of the Ministry for Foreign Affairs."[7] The creation, composition, and operating procedures of this group indicated the manner in which most of the French reforms and innovations would be instituted, except for a few cases where the Foreign Minister decided to act more or less on his own. That is, this commission and a number of others were created by ministerial order.[8] Each was composed almost exclusively of professional diplomats and bureaucrats who met to consider strategies of reform for specific objectives;[9] thus each body could proceed with a temporary

6. Georges Clemenceau, 5 November 1906, in France, Chambre des Députés, *Débats parlementaires*, pp. 5–6. Also see Pichon's involvement in the reform movement in *Rappel*, 26 February 1907; and *Le Temps*, 22 September 1908. Reorganizations also occurred at this time in the Ministries of Interior, War, Public Works, and Post and Telegraph.

7. *Arrêté* of 6 November 1906, as in France, *JO*, 3 May 1907, p. 3269.

8. See MAE, Direction politique et commerciale, Papiers des Agents: Philippe Berthelot, Carton 12, letter from Berthelot to Paul Claudel, 4 August 1907; ibid., Direction du Personnel, Carton 86, "Commission de Réorganisation de la comptabilité et de l'architecture, 1911"; MAE/Chambre, Rapport No. 2015 (1909), p. 166; and idem, Rapport No. 6339 (1919), pp. 197–98.

9. MAE/Chambre, Rapport No. 1237 (1912), p. 99, indicates that a notable

arrangement of "multiple advocacy," permitting several well-informed, individual viewpoints to be heard.[10] Moreover, during sessions of "search" (obtaining and sharing relevant information) and "analysis" (evaluation of proposals and the appropriateness of alternative options), these commissions carefully considered both the comments of numerous critics and opinions solicited from others concerned with international affairs.[11]

Following this deliberation, the Foreign Minister received all recommendations emerging from each commission for his personal consideration and "choice" (selection of a particular course of action from a number of alternatives). Final decisions regarding enactment or implementation would be made by the Minister himself, resulting in either a simple *arrêté* for minor changes or a *décret* approved and co-signed by the French President for more important matters. Any decrees relating to salaries required the signature of the Minister of Finances as well. Under such arrangements, therefore, the actual details of all reforms and innovations affecting internal and overseas operations never were imposed upon the Quai d'Orsay, despite many external criticisms and pressures. Instead, they emerged for specific objectives over a period lasting between 1907 and 1920[12] from diplomats and bureaucrats personally involved in the Ministry for Foreign Affairs.[13] The commission first created by Pichon carried the names of MM. Crozier, ambassador, Gavarry and Thiébant, ministres plénipotentiaires, and in the important role

---

exception was the inclusion of leading critic Paul Deschanel on one of these commissions.

10. See Alexander L. George, "The Case for Multiple Advocacy in Making Foreign Policy," *American Political Science Review*, 64, 3 (September 1972), pp. 751–85.

11. See, for example, MAE, Direction du Personnel, Carton 85, "Textes et projets de réforme antérieur à 1912"; and MAE/Chambre, Rapport No. 2015 (1909), pp. 53–73.

12. The precise dates of each reform and innovation, plus subsequent modifications, are provided in detail in the footnotes.

13. Michael Crozier, in *Le phénomène bureaucratique* (Paris: Editions du Seuil, 1963), pp. 258–59, 291–92, 360–61, presents the thesis that reforms and innovations in the French bureaucracy can be enacted only if they encompass the entire organization *en bloc*, are instituted all at once, and are a result of a sudden crisis. The evidence in this study, which shows a pattern of specificity for objectives, the enactment of changes over a period of time, and the relatively calm manner of internal approach, does not support his argument. Instead, this thesis of the otherwise perceptive Crozier appears to be more applicable to the German case.

Philippe Berthelot

of *rapporteur*, an embassy secretary first class named Philippe Berthelot.

Son of Marcellin Berthelot (one of the founders of modern chemistry, Senator, and once Minister for Foreign Affairs), Philippe had easy access to the foreign service without examination and soon distinguished himself in a meteoric career.[14] Like the man who would reform the German Ministry for Foreign Affairs, he began in the consular service and then rapidly moved into the central administration. Here his industry, amazing memory, and grasp of the minute details within international relations eventually made him *le fonctionnaire*—"the indispensable cog,"[15] and "the most important of the permanent officials at the Quai d'Orsay."[16] Admirers and adversaries alike recognized his tremendous talents, "incomparable intelligence," and "unequalled mastery" of diplomacy.[17] His desire for power, self-confident bearing, impressive appearance, and piercing eyes all confirmed his description as "a well-liking cat with no use for mice."[18] No one else could match his service within all the important offices of the Quai d'Orsay, including the politically advantageous *Cabinet du Ministre* and eventually the position of Secretary General itself. This wide experience acquired as a bureaucrat in the central administration in Paris made him a veritable specialist on ministerial operations. Furthermore, he brought to his work rational techniques—described by insiders as his "methode"[19]—and a well-known "disdain for conventional forms."[20] Such expertise, combined with his personal characteris-

14. France, Ministère des Affaires étrangères, *Annuaire diplomatique et consulaire 1931*, pp. 220–21; and the account in August Bréal, *Philippe Berthelot* (Paris: Gallimard, 1937).

15. Sharp, p. 7.

16. Richard Challener, "The French Foreign Office: The Era of Philippe Berthelot," in Gordon A. Craig and Felix Gilbert (eds.), *The Diplomats* (New York: Atheneum, 1968), 1, pp. 69–70.

17. PA/AA, Abteilung IA, Frankreich 105 Nr. 1, Band 31, A.S. 1944, note from Haussen (Berne?) to Auswärtiges Amt, 7 May 1916; PRO/FO 371/6981, notes by Villiers and others on Despatch No. 975 from Hardinge (Paris) to Foreign Secretary, 26 December 1921; NA/DS, Index 851.021/9, Despatch No. 65 from Dawson (Paris) to Secretary of State, 2 August 1921; and Joseph Paul-Boncour, *Entre deux guerres* (Paris: Plon, 1945), 2, p. 339; among others.

18. Vansittart, pp. 246–47, who also records that Berthelot had "a professional mind equal to Crowe's."

19. Paul Morand, *Journal d'un attaché d'ambassade* (Paris: Gallimard, 1963), p. 163.

20. LaRoche, p. 96.

CHART I

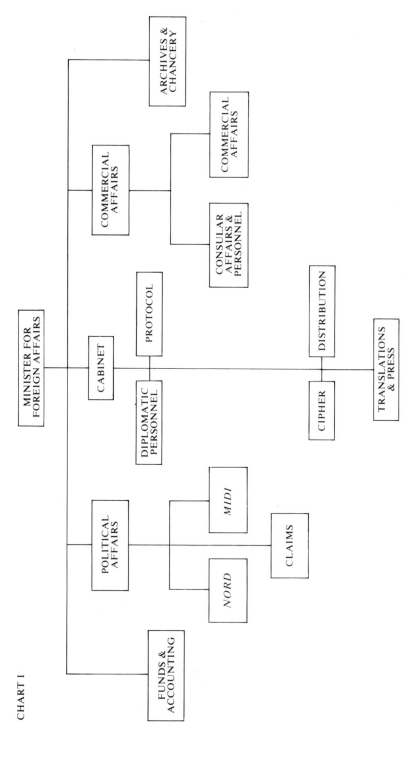

MINISTER FOR FOREIGN AFFAIRS

CABINET
— PROTOCOL
— DIPLOMATIC PERSONNEL

ARCHIVES & CHANCERY

COMMERCIAL AFFAIRS
— COMMERCIAL AFFAIRS
— CONSULAR AFFAIRS & PERSONNEL

POLITICAL AFFAIRS
— MIDI
— NORD
— CLAIMS

FUNDS & ACCOUNTING

DISTRIBUTION
— CIPHER
— TRANSLATIONS & PRESS

THE FRENCH MINISTRY FOR FOREIGN AFFAIRS:
BASIC NINETEENTH-CENTURY ORGANIZATION

tics, made it possible for Philippe Berthelot to become largely responsible for most of the major reforms and innovations of the Ministry.

Berthelot made his attitude clear in a detailed analysis of the theoretical and practical aspects of instituting necessary change. With Pichon's blessing, he asserted that the Ministry for Foreign Affairs should respond to the new demands of diplomacy, referring to the enormously increased burdens imposed by domestic criticism and by international events. "It is considered that the methods of the Quai d'Orsay have become obsolete and no longer correspond to the requirements either of our politics or of our world situation." Of the former, he declared:

> No one is entirely satisfied with the organization of the Ministry: The public considers that our diplomacy is not sufficiently adapted to our system of parliamentary democracy. Commercial interests believe that the consular service does not provide useful and necessary reports. . . . Parliament and the press occasionally regret the vague information emanating from the Quai d'Orsay. . . . Even the diplomatic agents themselves complain of the old routine which often paralyzes initiative, the lack of precise regulations for recruitment and promotion, insufficient salaries and the questionable allocation of personnel.
>
> A project of genuine and complete reform must take account of all these factors and endeavor to give the greatest satisfaction to each one.[21]

His solution involved the creation of permanent institutional mechanisms and practices such as a "logical" organizational structure, a "rational" division of labor, an "effective" operation of specialized responsibility, and the utilization of certain "modern" and "efficient" techniques of management.

---

21. Berthelot, in the "Rapport de la commission des réformes administratives du Ministère des Affaires étrangères," as reproduced in France, *JO*, 3 May 1907, pp. 3269–75 [hereafter cited as Berthelot, "Commission des réformes administratives"]. Pichon's own ideas can be found in France, *JO*, 3 May 1907, pp. 3265–66; *Le Temps*, "Propos diplomatiques. Les Réformes au Quai d'Orsay," 17 November 1906; and MAE/Sénat, Rapport No. 28 (1912), p. 16.

2. Organizational Structure

To begin a major institutional reform of the Ministry for Foreign Affairs, said Berthelot, it was necessary to recognize one of the basic structural defects of the old organization: the distinction between "political" and "commercial" affairs. This division "had ceased to correspond with the real nature of affairs" in the twentieth century, and thus "could no longer be maintained." He asserted that "in the great majority of cases, political and commercial considerations are intertwined, and nothing is more arbitrary and dangerous than to require their dissociation in an abstract manner and to treat them separately."[22] Describing the rationale of such arguments as "unquestionable," President Fallières and Foreign Minister Pichon signed a decree establishing the new, unified *Direction des Affaires politiques et commerciales* (Political and Commercial Division).[23] As the name implied, it now would treat these questions together, striving to assure greater unity in French foreign policy and to set the stage for thorough reorganization.

"The logical consequence" in reforming the Ministry structurally, declared Berthelot, would be to follow this initial unification with a specialized subdivision based upon a geographical division of labor.[24] To manage affairs according to specific territorial areas not only provides the advantage of distinguishing one country from "the rest of the world," but also imposes a certain degree of unity in terms of language, political and religious tradition, and historical experience. Critics, of course, frequently attacked the inadequacy of the Euro-centric administration and the simplistic units of *Nord* and *Midi* for managing the affairs of the entire globe. To respond to this basic reality of twentieth-century politics, a series of decrees instituted the specialized geographical divisions maintained by the Ministry to this day: the most important were *Europe, Amerique, Asie et Oceanie,* and *Afrique.*[25] Charging each section with permanently coordinating all aspects of foreign policy directed

22. Berthelot, "Commission des réformes administratives," pp. 3269–70.
23. Decree of 29 April 1907, in France, *JO,* 3 May 1907, pp. 3266–69.
24. Berthelot, "Commission des réformes administratives," p. 3270.
25. Decree of 29 April 1907, in France, *JO*, 3 May 1907, pp. 3266–69; Decree of 29 January 1912, in idem, 8 February 1912, p. 1226; and Decree of 23 July 1918, in idem, 31 July 1918, pp. 6642–44.

toward these respective groups of countries, such reforms gave institutional recognition to the emergence of non-European areas and confirmed the new global nature of international politics.

Geographical divisions represented a major step in the proper direction toward reorganization, Berthelot asserted, but it remained equally important to recognize that all affairs could not be administratively based upon geography alone. "It is necessary to combine geographical distribution with a division based upon subject matter." Diplomacy of this century demanded functional "specialists," trained in technical affairs and capable of "more scientific" administration than in the past. The directors of various geographical sections, therefore, should be assisted at all times by experts capable of providing advice on the increasingly complex and detailed matters of commerce, finances, and the nuances of international law.[26]

The force of this rationale led immediately to the decree by Pichon creating specialized "technical counselors" for commerce, finance, and legal affairs.[27] The new *Conseiller commercial et financier* was charged with maintaining constant contact with the geographical sections, preparing treaties of commerce, assuring competent management of *"la doctrine économique française,"* and providing advice on all economic consequences of external policy and the general financial conditions of foreign countries. In addition, this bureau and its postwar successor, *Relations commerciales,* received responsibility for establishing close contact with, and for actively encouraging, French financial and industrial concerns conducting operations abroad.[28] Furthermore, said the same reforming decrees, the Ministry's office of *Jurisconsulte* (Legal Expert) now would be strengthened, raised in administrative status, and charged with all major technical matters of public and private international law. A specialized section of *Affaires de Chancellerie et du Contentieux* (Chancery and Administrative Claims) henceforth would be responsible for questions of conflicts in laws, extradition,

---

26. Berthelot, "Commission des réformes administratives," p. 3271.

27. Decree of 29 April 1907, in France, *JO*, 3 May 1907, p. 3268. Also see MAE/Chambre, Rapport No. 2015 (1909), pp. 24–26.

28. See France, Ministère des Affaires étrangères, *Annuaire diplomatique et consulaire 1920.* Also see more detail in Chapter Five.

naturalization, privileges and immunities, general claims, and judicial affairs, among others.[29]

This functional specialization, continued Berthelot, also should be applied to yet another area: international conventions and unions.[30] His reasoning for this recommendation lay in the fact that with the increase in contact and interdependence among nations, many individuals actively considered the advantages of collective efforts to solve common problems. As a result, private and governmental organizations began signing conventions to standardize certain practices or joining unions to share resources and information on a wide variety of subjects.[31] The creation of the International Labor Office in 1900, the International Association of Chambers of Commerce five years later, and the International Office of Public Health founded in Paris during 1907 all seemed to indicate the future direction of international organizations. For this reason, Berthelot and others urged that the Quai d'Orsay possess a special section to deal with this proliferation of cooperative efforts.

In response, decrees instituted a new department for *Affaires administratives et des Unions internationales* (Administrative Affairs and International Unions).[32] They now charged the Ministry for Foreign Affairs with permanent responsibility for technical questions of international conventions and unions, including those of railroads, canals, consular agreements, international rivers and navigation, weights and measures, and relief matters. The list also encompassed hygiene, labor, police regulations and maritime security, postal and monetary accords, agricultural diseases, copyright and patent protection, and even meteorological and seismological

29. See Decree of 29 April 1907, in France, *JO,* 3 May 1907, p. 3268; Decree of 13 December 1910, in idem, 8 January 1911, p. 162; Decree of 29 January 1912, in idem, 8 February 1912, p. 1226; Decree of 23 July 1918, in idem, 31 July 1918, pp. 6642–44; MAE/Chambre, Rapport No. 2015 (1909), pp. 144ff.; and idem, Rapport No. 2749 (1910), pp. 145–46. Other specialists created at this time include the *conseiller pour les affaires douanières* and *conseiller pour les affaires religieuses.*

30. Berthelot, "Commission des réformes administratives," p. 3271.

31. See MAE/Chambre, Rapport No. 4108 (1918), pp. 41ff.

32. Decree of 29 April 1907, in France, *JO,* 3 May 1907, p. 3268; Decree of 13 December 1910, in idem, 8 January 1911, p. 162; Decree of 8 September 1912, in idem, 22 September 1912, p. 8269; and Decree of 23 July 1918, in idem, 31 July 1918, p. 6643.

affairs. French membership in numerous functional committees of the League of Nations after the First World War further accelerated this trend of institutional involvement in an extremely wide range of human activities.[33] It seemed to confirm that in this century, diplomacy—like warfare—was becoming "total."

Such activity by the Ministry in so many aspects of human life, particularly at a time of intense international competition and armed conflict, brought forth other major institutional innovations such as administrative bureaus specifically designed to influence public opinion. The early creation of a small section to influence the press,[34] for example, grew to major proportions during the years of warfare. Many considered its activity to be so crucial to foreign policy that a decree of 1920 established the more elaborate *Service d'Information et de Presse* (Press and Information Service) which remains at the Quai d'Orsay today.[35] Utilizing this department with technology like the wireless telegraph and new techniques such as the modern press conference, the Ministry sought to achieve a desired effect among the public at home and abroad.[36] The additional creation of a new *Service des Écoles et des Oeuvres françaises à l'étranger* (Service of French Schools and Works Overseas) designed to extend culture and propaganda abroad soon led to an explosive expansion of administrative subdivisions for every major geographical location around the globe, supported by numerous functional sections. Its offices included those for universities and schools, hospitals and welfare, the glories of French language and literature, artistic and cinematic productions, tourism, and international sports. Its activities indicated that "culture" would become an important tool for diplomacy in the twentieth century.[37]

Several other specialized bureaus also evidenced the impact of this pragmatic desire for effectiveness in coping with new diplomatic problems, as reformers either created or strengthened further organizational components in order to provide more technical service

---

33. MAE/Chambre, Rapport No. 3131 (1922), pp. 46–125.
34. Decree of 29 April 1907, in France, *JO*, 3 May 1907, p. 3268.
35. Decree of 2 September 1920, according to Outrey, 3, 4, pp. 715–16.
36. MAE/Chambre, Rapport No. 802 (1920), p. 68.
37. See, for example, ibid., pp. 159ff.

and expert advice. Berthelot criticized the *Sous-Direction des Archives* (Archives Department), to illustrate, for

> editing catalogues of old files and publishing historical documents of the sixteenth or seventeenth centuries, but neglecting contemporary items. It is more important for the Ministry that its archive services are able to find rapidly needed information and examples of precedent in modern documents. The archives of the Ministry for Foreign Affairs must serve it by making policy—and not history![38]

Responding to this criticism, the archivists began to concentrate on more recent research, on modern filing systems, and on becoming a more integral part of "the centralized and active life" of the Quai d'Orsay.[39]

Officials of the Ministry sadly recognized that in this new age of nationalism, other countries increasingly insisted upon breaking past tradition by using their own language rather than French in diplomatic intercourse.[40] For this reason, reformers reluctantly enlarged the *Service des Traducteurs* (Translation Service).[41] "The complexity of geographical questions . . . boundary changes, exploration and discovery, new routes of international communication, etc." as described in one report,[42] resulted in reorganization and increased work loads for the *Service géographique* (Geographical Service).[43] Finally, the Ministry's response to growing armed conflict in international relations found form in the creation of a *Service des affaires militaires* (Military Affairs).[44]

38. Berthelot, "Commission des réformes administratives," pp. 3274–75; and the confirmation of these attitudes as expressed by other reform advocates in MAE/Chambre, Rapport No. 2015 (1909), pp. 26ff.; among others.

39. The words are those of Berthelot, in "Commission des réformes administratives," p. 3375. The resulting decrees are the Decree of 29 April 1907, in France, *JO*, 3 May 1907, p. 3268; and Decree of 23 July 1918, in idem, 31 July 1918, p. 6642.

40. Saint-Aulaire, *Confession d'un vieux diplomate*, p. 37; among others.

41. Berthelot, "Commission des réformes administratives," p. 3273; MAE/Chambre, Rapport No. 3318 (1914), 2, p. 14; and idem, Rapport No. 6339 (1919), p. 179.

42. MAE/Chambre, Rapport No. 1230 (1908), pp. 418–19.

43. See Decree of 29 April 1907, in France, *JO*, 3 May 1907, p. 3268; Decree of 19 July 1912, in idem, 24 July 1912, p. 6668; and Decree of 23 July 1918, in idem, 31 July 1918, p. 6642.

44. Decree of 13 August 1910, in France, *JO*, 14 August 1910, p. 7036. This was subdivided in 1912 and 1918 among the European, American, and Asian departments as the *Service des attachés militaires et navals*. The *Services de Guerre* was created only for the duration of the war.

The "logical division of affairs" desired by Berthelot, Pichon, and numerous others thus became instituted within the Quai d'Orsay by the creation of new *geographical* and *functional* departments. This arrangement placed a premium upon specialized competence in particular areas or in narrowly defined types of problems. Yet complex questions of foreign affairs seldom fall exclusively within the domain of a single bureau. Indeed, the infinite ramifications of most external policy involve overlapping jurisdictions of numerous offices and individuals. This creates the classical problem of coordination and the integration of various—and often competing—parts to the whole.[45] Berthelot recognized the practical problems of this theoretical concept of administrative science, observing that innovative, expanded, and reorganized bureaucracies simply do not operate by themselves.[46] Effective coordination, management, and control of organizations depend upon efficient *administrative* departments, working techniques, and operating procedures.

In the past, the Ministry had been strongly criticized for operating within "water-tight compartments." "The disadvantages of this system," claimed Berthelot, "were carried to the extreme by the artificial separation of affairs and the high, defensive walls maintained between the bureaus. Nothing was organized to inform one department what took place in its neighboring office, with which it seldom communicated"—all of which seriously impaired any coordinated effort at policy making or implementation. This necessitated action "to create a centralized mechanism capable of receiving and distributing general as well as specialized information, and assuring a constant exchange not only between the internal services of the Ministry, but with the foreign missions as well. In a word, to have an active system of circulation."[47]

The institutional means of creating this flow of information and channelling of advice took shape in the innovative *Bureau des Communications* (Communications Bureau). New decrees charged this department with receiving material from various diplomats and

45. See Graham Allison and Morton Halperin, "Bureaucratic Politics: A Paradigm and Some Policy Implications," *World Politics*, 24 Supplement (Spring 1972), pp. 40–79; and Crozier, pp. 218–19.

46. Berthelot, "Commission des réformes administratives," pp. 3271–72.

47. Ibid. Also see MAE, Personnel, "Décrets et Arrêtés," Carton 40, *Arrêté* of 12 May 1918 by Pichon.

bureaucrats and then distributing all important information—at least in summary—throughout the Ministry and to overseas posts. These provisions now required relevant reports to be printed and circulated in order that each office might be informed of the work of its colleagues down the hall. They further provided that significant articles appearing in either the domestic or the foreign press be distributed among interested departments, and that such information be filed systematically in dossiers using new techniques of alphabetical classification to assure rapid retrievability.[48]

This interest in speed and efficiency also encouraged the Ministry to employ the latest inventions of applied technology to expedite its operations. The swift carriages of typewriters increasingly replaced the scribe's slowly moving pen.[49] Rapid duplicating machines and hectographs reproduced reports once copied by hand.[50] Modern electric lights superseded wax candles and greasy oil lamps.[51] Time-saving telephones[52] and "streamlined" automobiles made ministerial operations proceed faster than ever before in history.[53] Even the annual budget began to include an exciting and suggestive item of the times: *"machines et moteurs."*[54]

The monetary cost of all these enlarged services and staffs, new bureaus and divisions, and modern technological devices grew to unprecedented proportions. The Ministry's expenditures seemed to

48. Decree of 29 April 1907, in France, *JO*, 3 May 1907, p. 3268; Decree of 14 September 1917, in idem, 15 September 1917, p. 7300; MAE/Chambre, Rapport No. 1230 (1908), pp. 429–30; and idem, Rapport No. 3318 (1914), 1, pp. 83–84.

49. MAE, Comptabilité, "Décrets et décions ministérielles," Carton 44, No. 74, *Arrêté* of 8 March 1900 by Delcassé; idem, Carton 69, No. 156, *Arrêté* of 2 March 1916 by Jules Cambon; and MAE, Personnel, "Décrets et Arrêtés," Carton 38, dossier "Mai, 1916."

50. MAE/Chambre, Rapport No. 3318 (1914), 1, pp. 82–84.

51. MAE, Comptabilité, "Décrets et décisions ministérielles," Carton 61, No. 856, *Arrêté* of 30 December 1911; idem, Carton 69, No. 377, *Arrêté* of 17 May 1916; among others.

52. Ibid., Carton 58, No. 244, *Arrêté* of 30 May 1910; MAE, Direction politique et commerciale, Papiers des Agents: Philippe Berthelot, Carton 4, "Note sur le Bureau de Londres," 26 February 1916; and MAE, Personnel, "Décrets et Arrêtés," Carton 42., *Arrêté,* of 10 December 1919.

53. MAE, Comptabilité, "Décrets et décisions ministérielles," Carton 69, No. 378, *Arrêté* of 17 May 1916; La Roche, p. 23; PA/AA, Abteilung IA, Frankreich 108, Band 21, Despatch No. 492 from Wedel (Vienna) to Auswärtiges Amt, 7 June 1919.

54. See France, Ministère des Affaires étrangères, *Compte définitif des dépenses de l'exercice 1910.*

leap—to use a twentieth-century term—by quantum levels. One observer described the phenomenon as "staggering."[55] In 1800, for example, expenditures totalled no more than 5,923,732 francs. One hundred years later the figure indicated an amount of only 16,898,042 francs. Yet, thereafter, the budget's expansion appeared as follows:[56]

1905	18,356,852	current value francs
1910	21,613,947	
1915	30,379,380	
1920	52,237,679	
1925	105,041,503	
1930	299,599,724	

The total number of chapters in each budget appropriation demonstrates still another side of this same financial expansion and growing complexity. The sum of individual divisions within the annual budget, to illustrate, averaged less than twenty-five before 1900. In contrast, by 1907 this figure had risen to forty-one chapters, by 1919 to seventy-six, and by 1922 to eighty-six separate divisons.

The details involved in such major increases indicated the necessity to eliminate old methods and to adopt more sophisticated techniques of business accounting. Accordingly, reformers enacted more exacting standards of professional specialization, competence, and responsibility. Further regulations for the expanded staff in the *Division des Fonds et de la Comptabilité* (Funds and Accounting) required that the Minister of Finance now countersign the appointment of the bureaucrat assigned to the new position of *Controleur des dépenses engagées* (Controller). The Quai d'Orsay's own financial operations also became subjected to much greater scrutiny by experts in the national *Cour des Comptes* and legislative commissions in order to assure "absolute regularity."[57]

55. Note by Villiers on Despatch No. 3469 from Cheetham (Paris) to Foreign Secretary, 13 December 1921, in PRO/FO 371/6977.

56. Based upon France, Ministère des Affaires étrangères, *Compte définitif des dépenses de l'exercice*—for the years 1880 through 1930. Also see the discussion in MAE/Chambre, Rapport No. 3318 (1914), 1, pp. 198–207.

57. See MAE, Direction du Personnel, Carton 86, "Commission de Réorganisation de la Comptabilité et de l'architecture"; MAE/Chambre, Rapport No. 1230 (1908), 1, pp. 108–10; idem, Rapport No. 3318 (1914), 1, pp. 93–251; and, 2, pp. 15–16; and idem, Rapport No. 4108 (1918), pp. 50–54.

In this search for standardization lies an essential key to under-standing basic reform within any bureaucratic organization in gen-eral and the Ministry for Foreign Affairs in particular. The essence of effective management in a bureaucracy depends upon regularity and predictable behavior resulting from clearly established rules of organized performance patterns. Well-defined duties must be dele-gated to permanent, differentiated departments operating together to achieve institutional goals and objectives. Berthelot, Pichon, and others within the Quai d'Orsay realized this feature of administra-tive science to a remarkable degree. They explicitly stated that their entire ministerial reorganization was based upon the principle of precisely defined, specialized responsibilities at all levels of the organizational hierarchy. Such precise delegation of authority and duties, they claimed, would enable effective management and con-trol of all operations and efforts. In additon, they anticipated that standardized procedures would enhance performance by sig-nificantly reducing the number of intermediaries inserting them-selves between the actual work of information gathering and analysis on the one hand, and eventual foreign policy decision on the other.[58]

The central source of such decision-making responsibility, both before and after the reforms, rested in the *Ministre des Affaires étrangères* (Minister for Foreign Affairs). His authority extended to all aspects of policy determination, its execution, and the general conduct of relations with foreign countries. Both the substance of external policy and the internal management of the Quai d'Orsay therefore could be conditioned by his individual personality, at-titudes, beliefs about the international system, and operational codes.[59] In order to check the arbitrary use of such power, reform-ers made it clear that members in the Minister's personal *Cabinet* and *Bureau du Personnel* were expected to support his decisions only if they could maintain the principles of "precision," "regulari-ty," and "professional merit."[60]

58. See Berthelot, "Commission des réformes adminsistratives," pp. 3272–73; Pichon's comments in France, *JO*, 3 May 1907, p. 3266; and Deschanel, in MAE/Chambre, Rapport No. 1230 (1908), 2, p. 7.

59. MAE/Chambre, Rapport No. 2020 (1921), p. 47; and La Roche; among others.

60. See Berthelot, "Commission des réformes administratives," pp. 3272–73.

CHART II

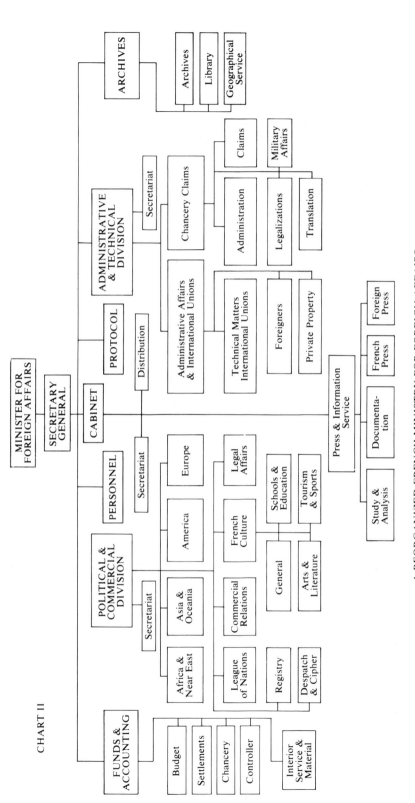

MINISTER FOR FOREIGN AFFAIRS

SECRETARY GENERAL

CABINET

PERSONNEL
— Secretariat

PROTOCOL
— Distribution

ADMINISTRATIVE & TECHNICAL DIVISION
— Secretariat

ARCHIVES
— Archives
— Library
— Geographical Service

POLITICAL & COMMERCIAL DIVISION
— Secretariat

FUNDS & ACCOUNTING
— Budget
— Settlements
— Chancery
— Controller
— Interior Service & Material

Africa & Near East
Asia & Oceania
America
Europe

League of Nations
Commercial Relations
French Culture
Legal Affairs

Registry
General
Schools & Education

Despatch & Cipher
Arts & Literature
Tourism & Sports

Administrative Affairs & International Unions
Chancery Claims

Technical Matters International Unions
Administration
Claims

Foreigners
Legalizations
Military Affairs

Private Property
Translation

Press & Information Service
Study & Analysis
Documentation
French Press
Foreign Press

A REORGANIZED FRENCH MINISTRY FOR FOREIGN AFFAIRS: RESULTS OF REFORMS AND INNOVATIONS, 1907–1920

Although the most stable of all French ministerial posts,[61] the position of Minister for Foreign Affairs still saw the arrival and departure of numerous men, causing particular difficulties in continuity and steady administration at the Quai d'Orsay.[62] This handicap of most parliamentary democracies became especially evident during the First World War as politicians of all sorts came and went. To control the resulting problems, new decrees created the innovative and powerful office of *Secrétariat général* (Secretary General), an administrative post that would be "independent of the vicissitudes of politics" and would serve as "the principal direction of all ministerial services" since it was held by a permanent, professional bureaucrat.[63] Those who created this position—made famous by Berthelot himself—sought to complete the far-reaching structural reorganization of the Ministry by providing the means to insure managerial stability, the opportunity for sustained planning, and skilled guidance in foreign affairs.

3. Personnel

Bureaucratic organizations, however brilliantly designed, simply cannot function by their own accord. Formal vertical and horizontal structural arrangements, carefully differentiated task assignments, innovative management techniques, and useful technological tools all ultimately depend upon living human beings for efficient operation. People are the source of judgment and performance abilities, responsibility and role assumption, managerial and decision-making skills. It is necessary, therefore, that every administrative institution seriously consider the training, hiring, compensation, and general welfare of its personnel.

61. Frederick L. Schuman, *War and Diplomacy in the French Republic* (New York: McGraw-Hill, 1931), pp. 29–30.

62. See MAE/Chambre, Rapport No. 1237 (1912), p. xx, pointing to the example of the British Permanent Under Secretary of State; idem, Rapport No. 802 (1920), pp. 3–7; La Roche, pp. 30, 111–12; and Pognon, p. 38.

63. Briand's Decree of 30 October 1915, in France, *JO*, 31 October 1915, p. 7852; Pichon's Decree of 19 December 1917, in idem, 21 December 1917, p. 10447; and Millerand's Decree of 20 January 1920, in idem, 23 January 1920, p. 1214, among others. The Ministry also began to experiment with a *Sous-secrétaire d'Etat* at this time, as evidenced by the Decree of 13 February 1912, in idem, 14 February 1912, p. 1447; and Decree of 21 June 1914, in idem, 23 June 1914, p. 5459; among others.

French governmental institutions, including the Ministry for Foreign Affairs, began to recognize the importance of personnel policy, particularly during the rise of a campaign known as administrative syndicalism. This movement among state functionaries sought to create statutory guarantees against the arbitrary action emerging as a result of the expansion of official services and their corresponding political abuses. Their grievances against subjective interference in appointments and promotions, nepotism, favoritism, and *l'arbitraire* became especially intense during the Dreyfus Affair and subsequent separation of Church and State. Official espionage, secret notes and dossiers, dismissals, and transfers or disciplinary action due to political or religious beliefs aggravated the problems even further. For thousands of civil servants caught in this caldron, a solution appeared in organizing *associations* and *syndicats de fonctionnaires* to demand fixed rules for their recruitment, examination, promotion, salaries, discipline, and retirement.[64]

It was no coincidence, therefore, that comprehensive reforms and innovations on the Quai d'Orsay would include a response to this larger movement within society for standardization in personnel policies. "It seems to me," said one critic, "that in a Republic calling itself egalitarian and democratic, the laws that apply to the workers also should apply to the agents of the Ministry for Foreign Affairs!"[65] For this very reason, several organizers created the *Association professionelle des agents du Ministère des Affaires étrangères*. With this body, they sought to exert continual pressure upon the Ministry in order to assure that any institutional changes would contain an objective *statut des fonctionnaires*, a law specifying and guaranteeing the rights of all ministerial officials.[66]

Many of the rank and file within the Quai d'Orsay concurred with those outside critics who argued that any structural reorganization of the Ministry would be useless if unaccompanied by guarantees for

64. See the accounts presented in Alexander Lefas, *L'Etat et les fonctionnaires* (Paris: Giard et Brière, 1913); and Henri Chardon, *L'Administration de la France: les fonctionnaires* (Paris: Perrin, 1908); among others.

65. Pognon, p. 105.

66. France, Assemblée nationale, Chambre des Députés, Commission de l'Administration générale, Rapport No. 1213, Annexe au procès-verbal de la 2e séance du 11 juillet 1907, "Rapport fait au nom de la Commission de l'administration générale, départmentale et communale, des cultes et de la décentralisation chargée d'examiner le projet de loi sur les Associations de fonctionnaires," par Jules Jeanneney, Annexe XI, p. 179.

its personnel. Effective performance, they claimed, could result only after creating an encouraging milieu and incentive system. Statutory regulations would enhance stability, general *esprit de corps*, quality of recruitment, reward of talents, and specialization of skills.[67] We must, said one report, "defend in practice the principle of professional merit among agents against internal arbitrariness and the abuse of political interference."[68] Another exhorted that "our diplomats be better recruited, better selected by means of a more prolonged and conclusive preparation, better administered, better housed, better paid, better supervised and stimulated, better known and loved. May our diplomats of tomorrow be worthy of our soldiers!"[69]

To assure this improvement in selection and recruitment of talent, some of the first innovative decrees regulating personnel matters created new, rigorous, professional examination procedures.[70] No longer would it be sufficient for candidates to be merely loyal, industrious, or nominated by influential contacts as in the past. These regulations demanded that officials in the Ministry and members of the overseas missions possess advanced knowledge or specialized technical skills to cope with twentieth-century diplomacy. All candidates, for example, became responsible for possessing degrees "in law, letters, or sciences," or for holding a diploma from one of the special professional schools, such as the influential *Ecole libre des Sciences politiques*.[71]

67. See, for example, MAE/Chambre, Rapport No. 1230 (1908), 1, pp. 324–81; idem, Rapport No. 1237 (1912), pp. 113–14; and idem, Rapport No. 6339 (1919), pp. 198–200 (the paragraphs of which are specially marked with pencil in the Quai d'Orsay's copy of this report).

68. MAE, Direction du Personnel, Carton 85, "Affaires étrangères. Textes et projets de réforme antérieur à 1912," dossier "Réforme. Rapports 1912."

69. MAE/Chambre, Rapport No. 2020 (1921), p. 160.

70. Decree of 24 April 1900, in France, *JO*, 6 May 1900, pp. 2837–38; Decree of 17 January 1907 in idem, 20 January 1907, pp. 448–50; Decree of 20 December 1920, in idem, 23 December 1920, pp. 21306–7; and MAE, Personnel, "Décrets et Arrêtes," Carton 44, the Decree of 15 June 1920. The position of *attaché de chancellerie* was recruited by means of special examinations as provided by the Decrees of 24 May 1908, 10 December 1910, 29 March 1919, and 7 March 1921, among others.

71. Sharp, p. 112, indicates that this school soon became recognized as the normal recruiting ground for the upper levels of the French administration and foreign services. From 1905 to 1927, for example, 153 out of 192 appointees to diplomatic and consular vacancies had diplomas from the *Ecole*.

In addition to the traditional requirements of age and military obligation, stated these new regulations, each candidate now must enter the central administration as a bureaucrat of the Ministry for a probationary period of three months. This experience, said Deschanel, would provide "an excellent school in which to learn how to handle and classify affairs."[72] Candidates had to follow instructions carefully and perform practical tasks under the direction of a special probationary commission composed entirely of professionals from the Quai d'Orsay itself. The latter would then quantitatively score each candidate according to his "professional aptitude" (based upon a precise scale ranging from 0 to 20), the results being multiplied by a factor of two and added to the final marks obtained in written and oral examinations.

The reformed examination procedures themselves soon were regarded as "an exceedingly rigorous and mentally fatiguing operation enduring a minimum of seventeen hours" and as "the 'stiffest' of any given for entry into government service."[73] A carefully selected board of examiners administered a grueling series of written and oral tests according to explicit scoring procedures. Even the subject matter of these examinations reflected the new trends of diplomacy in the twentieth century. Language requirements confirmed the declining use of French by including possible examinations in English, German, Spanish, Italian, Russian, or Arabic. Essays and presentations on diplomatic history no longer could be confined to the European continent, but included subjects from the world at large, including topics on America, Asia, and Africa. Numerous questions concerned the merchant marine, chambers of commerce, industrial property, imports and exports, customs regulations, tariffs, economic geography, civil law, and both private and public international law, further reflecting the Ministry's reaction to the growing importance of commercial and legal transactions in international relations. Detailed examination regarding telegraph lines, submarine cables, railway transit dues, currency exchanges, standardization of weights and measures, international unions, and regulations for stockbrokers clearly indicated the new complexities and

72. MAE/Chambre, Rapport No. 1230 (1908), p. 381.
73. Sharp, p. 145. Only the *agrégation* for *lycée* and university professors rivaled this examination for difficulty.

extent of diplomatic problems. Moreover, they gave notice that the age of the amateur was over.[74]

These new decrees also emphasized the priority placed upon specialists by guaranteeing that the higher administrative positions within the Quai d'Orsay specifically be reserved for those agents with overseas experience. That is, that the most important bureaucrats be recruited exclusively from the ranks of the most important diplomats. According to these regulations, the positions of director and assistant director, *chef de service, chef* and *sous-chef de bureau,* editing and sorting clerks, *secrétaire interprète* and *archiviste,* and *attaché au chiffre* now were to be filled only by persons who had served abroad.[75] Such requirements endeavored to provide protection against unqualified and unprofessional political appointments, and to assure that decision makers in Paris could complement any *theoretical* considerations with their own personal experiences in *practical* international politics.[76]

To attract and maintain this high standard of professional talent, additional reforms sought to guarantee better levels of monetary compensation and to provide personal security. They raised salary levels and fixed objective payment scales in accordance with clearly established hierarchical rank.[77] Each raise was based upon a standardized amount, and even probationary candidates received payment during their provisional period. Further reforms required promotion in either grade or salary to be based upon professional

74. France, L'Ecole nationale d'administration, *Concours d'entrée et scolarité* (Paris: Imprimerie nationale, 1951), pp. 204–5, provides evidence that these same themes contrasting traditional diplomacy with that of the twentieth century can be seen in the more recent examinations.

75. MAE/Chambre, Rapport No. 3318 (1914), 2, pp. 8–9; and Decree of 11 July 1918, in France, *JO,* 16 July 1918, pp. 6198–99, indicates that technical specialists such as accountants, cyphering agents, translators, geographers, and librarians were recruited separately.

76. See the Decree of 11 April 1916, in France, *JO,* 18 April 1916, pp. 3281–82; Decree of 15 June 1918, in idem, 26 June 1918, pp. 5511–12; and the comments in MAE/Chambre, Rapport No. 2020 (1921), pp. 11–12; La Roche, p. 228–29; and Henry K. Norton, "Foreign Office Organization," *The Annals of the American Academy of Political and Social Science,* Supplement to CXLIII (1929), pp. 24–26.

77. Decree of 29 April 1907, on France, *JO,* 3 May 1907, p. 3266; Decree of 8 September 1911, in idem, 22 September 1911, pp. 8266–67; Decree of 8 September 1911, in idem, 22 September 1911, pp. 8266–67; Decree of 31 March 1915, in idem, 2 April 1915, p. 1820; and Decree of 22 February 1920, in idem, 7 March 1920, p. 3750, among many others.

merit rather than on seniority alone. They also instituted precise disciplinary procedures and an administrative council to determine regulated sanctions. Agents received the legal right to consult their own confidential dossiers.[78] These new regulations even extended to minor service employees of the Quai d'Orsay who received guaranteed monetary compensation for overtime work, regular hours, weekly rests, and increased annual leave.[79]

The very mention of overtime is indicative of the increasing pace of work at the Ministry for Foreign Affairs. Daily working hours were lengthened and memos spoke of "more modern methods capable of yielding better results in the speed of handling affairs."[80] Officials made efforts to adopt "more rapid" techniques, to purchase new maps, to open subscriptions for contemporary periodicals, to hire larger numbers of women typists and telephone operators, and to employ more secretaries for handling the seemingly uncontrollable "*avalanche du papier.*"[81] Even the offices of the Ministry overflowed the facilities of the Quai d'Orsay and physically expanded to additional buildings and apartments scattered throughout Paris.[82] To complete this picture, the administrative staff that had numbered only 142 in 1907 reached the remarkable figure of 600 by the year 1921.[83]

The institutional mechanism designed to manage this small army of officials became the reformed *Service du Personnel* (Personnel

78. Decree of 11 April 1916, in France, *JO,* 18 April 1916, pp. 3281–82; Decree of 15 June 1918, in idem, 26 June 1918, pp. 5511–12; Decree of 21 July 1918, in idem, 31 July 1918, p. 6642; and Decree of 14 April 1920, in idem, 5 May 1920, p. 6687.

79. See MAE/Chambre, Rapport No. 2749 (1910), p. 172; and idem, Rapport No. 3318 (1914), 2, pp. 23–24.

80. MAE, Comptabilité, "Décrets et décisions ministérielles," Carton 52, "Note pour le Ministre," from Hamon to Pichon, 26 July 1907.

81. Berthelot, "Commission des réformes administratives," pp. 3271–72; MAE, Personnel, "Décrets et Arrêtés," Carton 29, *Arrêté* of 28 December 1907 by Pichon; MAE/Chambre, Rapport No. 802 (1920), pp. 73–76; idem, Rapport No. 3131 (1921), pp. 139–40.

82. MAE/Chambre, Rapport No. 4792 (1923), pp. 23–24; and idem, Rapport No. 3131 (1922), pp. 189–90.

83. See *Le Temps,* "Le nombre des fonctionnaires des affaires étrangères," 22 July 1921; and MAE/Chambre, Rapport No. 3131 (1922), pp. 128–33. This number was reduced, however, with budgetary cuts imposed during the interwar years. See France, *JO,* 6 May 1922; and MAE, Comité chargé de rechercher et de proposer toutes mesures tendant à la suppression ou à la réduction des dépenses publiques, "Rapport général au President du conseil," August 1935.

Service).[84] New decrees gave this office responsibility for *all* personnel questions, thus seeking to eliminate the earlier distinctions made between those persons employed at the Ministry, in the diplomatic corps, or in the consular service. To prevent despotic control by any single individual over the fate of every agent, all nominations and promotions henceforth were made in collaboration with the Ministry's other higher officials. The office's duties also included examining budgetary questions on salaries, making recommendations for membership in the prestigious Legion of Honor, and "carrying into effect the reforms recommended by the lessons of experience."[85] Most important, these reforms detached this Personnel Service from the notoriously intriguing influence (some called it "vengeance")[86] of the hand-picked *Cabinet du Ministre*, and established it as an autonomous department.[87]

4. Overseas Services

Major reorganizations and innovations in the Quai d'Orsay's central administrative structure and far-reaching reforms in personnel policy marked the beginning of the entire French response to twentieth-century diplomacy. Effective direction of external relations depends both upon the efficiency of bureaucratic management at home and upon the operations of overseas services in other lands. With good reason, therefore, Senator Charles-Dupuy asserted: "The reorganization of the Ministry's foreign services is no less necessary than those of the internal administration."[88]

As described by Deschanel, however, reforming the diplomatic and consular services often brings forth "very special difficulties. The reform of the central administration is able to take effect immediately," he said, primarily because it raises only a minimum of budgetary, personnel, or status questions. "It is not the same with

---

84. Decree of 29 April 1907, in France, *JO*, 3 May 1907, p. 3269; Decree of 23 July 1918, in idem, 31 July 1918, pp. 6642–43; among others; and MAE/Chambre, Rapport No. 3318 (1914), 1, pp. 84–85.

85. MAE, Commission de Réorganisation, "'Rapports présentes à la Commission de réorganisation de l'Administration centrale," Année 1933, pp. 123ff. and 153.

86. Pognon, p. 105 and passim.

87. Specifically by the Decree of 23 July 1918, in France, *JO*, 31 July 1918, p. 6642.

88. MAE/Sénat, Rapport No. 337 (1908), p. 8.

the reorganization of our posts throughout the world, which raises so many of these delicate problems."[89] Yet despite very real and numerous complications, reformers sought to establish new missions and to suppress obsolete ones, to permit exchanges between the overseas services, to raise salaries, to create technical attachés, and to enact a general *statut* for both diplomatic and consular personnel.

Any reform of statutory guarantees for such personnel policies as recruitment, promotion and discipline, many argued, should be applied equally to the bureaucrats in the Quai d'Orsay and to their overseas counterparts. The abuses of arbitrariness were none the less real when distant from Paris. At times the inability to argue one's case or to secure objective treatment in person brought much grief to those stationed abroad.[90] They often said "that the more one resides in the sunshine of the Quai d'Orsay, the better one advances."[91] Such abusive practices, argued many critics and agents alike, could be eradicated only by standardized guarantees—a legal *statut de la carrière diplomatique et consulaire*.

One of the most "essential" and "indispensable" requisites for these statutory regulations, said Deschanel, must be "the guarantee against arbitrary admission."[92] Among the first reforms, therefore, ministerial decrees required that candidates for either the diplomatic or consular service pass the same competitive *concours d'entrée* required of all bureaucrats.[93] The resulting standardized examinations were lengthy and rigorous procedures that required professional qualifications rather than personal friends. In addition, a probationary period of three months under the eyes of a collective commission in the central administration further sought to check subjective influences or intrigue. The result of these new entrance

89. MAE/Chambre, Rapport No. 1230 (1908), 2, p. 10. Also see MAE, Direction du Personnel, Carton 85, "Affaires étrangères. Textes et projets de réforme antérieur à 1912," report entitled "Notes preliminaries—Conditions pratiques d'application de la Réforme."

90. For one vivid example among several, see Pognon, passim.

91. MAE/Chambre, Rapport No. 2020 (1921), p. 126, repeating the statement describing conditions before the reforms.

92. Ibid., Rapport No. 2015 (1909), p. 81.

93. The examinations are described in greater detail in the previous section of this chapter. See, in particular, footnote 70; the additional Decree of 15 November 1920, in France, *JO*, 28 November 1920, p. 19366; and the comments in MAE/Sénat, Rapport No. 148 (1913), pp. 54–58; and MAE/Chambre, Rapport No. 2020 (1921), pp. 82–91.

and testing requirements, observed Deputy Louis Marin, was "to close almost completely the door of careers based upon favoritism."[94]

More rigorous selection procedures and demands for specialized skills also called for corresponding forms of reward and incentive. "In addition to better guarantees for satisfaction and *moral* security," declared one report in the Chamber, "appreciably greater *material* advantages are absolutely imperative in a revision of the regulations for agents and an increase in their salaries."[95] Diplomatic and consular representatives, along with numerous critics, often complained of payment in the overseas services, describing it as "notoriously insufficient," "absurdly low," "the real wages of famine," and "very inferior" for "the dignity of a great and rich nation like France."[96] Low monetary rewards, they claimed, only contributed to "*la crise de personnel*" by failing to pay adequately meritorious service, by discouraging recruitment of talented young men, and by exposing ludicrously inequitable practices. "Why, for example," asked Deschanel, "does the French embassy counselor in Rome receive only 14,000 francs when his colleagues of exactly the same rank in London and St. Petersburg are paid nearly 24,000 francs?"[97] A more rational, equitable, and efficient system of salaries, several critics suggested, would be based upon systematic and standardized scales proportional to degrees of individual responsibility, size of family, distance required for travel, and living costs at various foreign locations.[98]

To correct these weaknesses and abuses, the reforms of the French overseas services made provision for remuneration increases and adjustments. Several ministerial decrees not only raised salaries, but specifically created differentiated criteria for computing payments.[99] They established salaries in accordance with (1)

94. MAE/Chambre, Rapport No. 3318 (1914), 1, p. 121.

95. Ibid., Rapport No. 2020 (1921), p. 93.

96. See MAE, Direction du Personnel, Carton 85, "Affaires étrangères. Textes et projets de réforme antérieur à 1912"; MAE/Sénat, Rapport No. 148 (1913), p. 45.

97. MAE/Chambre, Rapport No. 361 (1911), p. 141, repeating a statement first made in 1907.

98. Ibid., pp. 141–44; and MAE/Sénat, Rapport No. 28 (1912), p. 27.

99. Decree of 22 September 1913, "Traitement des agents des services exterieurs," as summarized in MAE/Chambre, Rapport No. 3318 (1914), 1, pp. 128–29; Decree of 15 November 1920, in France, *JO*, 28 November 1920, pp. 19368ff.; and MAE/Chambre, Rapport No. 3131 (1922), p. 7.

professional grade, (2) specific overseas post, and (3) cost of living at each foreign mission. Allowance for rank accompanied each agent regardless of his location, with post and living expenses determined by geographical region, importance, size, and currency exchange conditions. An additional indemnity for *charges de famille* was provided to those representatives with children. "This new method of calculating salaries of foreign service officers is excellent," said the frequently critical Louis Marin, "and will give much satisfaction to the large majority of agents."[100] Even before these reforming decrees were formally enacted, *Le Temps* declared: "Public opinion will welcome this equitable overhaul of salaries with unanimous approval. It is a good piece of work: practical, far-sighted and humane. Moreover, it is so rare that a reform actually succeeds like this!"[101]

Further reforms sought to provide agents with even greater security during the course of their professional careers.[102] New regulations established provisions for leaves of absence, recall or transfer to the Paris administration, rights of substitute representatives, and legal definitions of activity and retirement. They instituted explicit procedures for disciplinary matters, describing the composition of an innovative Disciplinary Council, establishing its terms of reference, and defining limits of penalty imposition. In addition, these ministerial decrees fulfilled another long-advocated requirement: "a precise regulation of advancement."[103] Henceforth, promotion would be based upon professional competence rather than upon seniority alone, although a prescribed minimum period of service was required in each preceding rank before advancing to the next level. The purpose of these various reforming provisions, said one internal memorandum, could be seen as the desire to avoid abuses, to provide equitable treatment, and to regulate the matters of diplomatic and consular personnel "with precision."[104]

Further measures dealt with the traditional conflict between the

100. MAE/Chambre, Rapport No. 3318 (1914), 1, pp. 122, 128.

101. *Le Temps,* 15 May 1912.

102. See, for example, the Decree of 22 September 1913, signed by Pichon, in France, *JO,* 27 September 1913; and Decree of 15 November 1920, signed by Georges Leygues, in idem, 28 November 1920, pp. 19365–70.

103. MAE/Chambre, Rapport No. 2015 (1909), p. 83; among others.

104. MAE, Direction du Personnel, Carton 85, "Affaires étrangères. Textes et projets de réforme antérieur à 1912," dossier "Réforme. Rapports 1912."

diplomatic and consular services which long had impeded efficient operation of French missions abroad and harmed healthy staff relations at home. Jealousies and rivalries had been aggravated institutionally by separate recruiting and examination procedures, divided personnel bureaus, distinct "political" and "commercial" divisions, and completely separated careers. The resulting lack of personal contact inhibited understanding or appreciation of one service for the other, and often fostered prejudice. "Diplomats are persuaded," wrote one consular agent, "that the consular corps is worthless," recounting that when he once identified himself as a member of the "other" service, a diplomat replied: "Consuls are very . . . very . . . very . . . respectable men, yes . . . very respectable; and I assure you that I regard them highly. But still, *Monsieur,* you know as well as I that consuls are not diplomats!"[105]

Checking this internecine friction, therefore, became "one of the principal ideas" in reforming the overseas services.[106] New provisions sought to reduce existing distinctions, to create opportunities for collaboration, and to promote exchanges among the diplomatic and consular careers. The *statuts de la carrière* thus were established on an equal basis for each of the services. The same entrance examination applied to both, with successful candidates permitted to choose between one branch or the other depending upon their respective scores. A single *Service du Personnel* started to administer affairs for *all* officials, whether located at home or abroad, and additional actions initiated the process of "unifying" the services by following the example of the structural reorganization within the Ministry itself.

The unification of political and commercial matters under the same division at the Quai d'Orsay, said one report, should be the prelude to a similar reform for the interpenetrability of the diplomatic and consular careers. "All the reasons and all the arguments that induced the fusion of political and commercial affairs in the central administration also militate in favor of a reform accomplished on the same basis and responding to the same needs for a better functioning of our foreign services."[107] New ministerial de-

105. Pognon, pp. 111–12.

106. MAE/Sénat, Rapport No. 337 (1908), p. 10.

107. MAE/Chambre, Rapport No. 2020 (1921), p. 57. The same idea is also expressed by Deschanel in idem, Rapport No. 2015 (1909), p. 82.

crees therefore created an equivalence of rank between the overseas services.[108] This gave agents the novel opportunity to interchange their positions on a corresponding level between the diplomatic and the consular careers. Such innovation, said Deputy Noblemaire, represented the "logical" response to new political conditions.[109]

In the same report on the Ministry for Foreign Affairs, Noblemaire declared that any changes made for the services also must recognize another major feature of twentieth-century diplomacy: "the utility of technical attachés in overseas posts." The complexity and technical nature of international affairs could no longer tolerate amateurs. Control of events demanded well-trained experts capable of contributing specific skills: "The best means to renovate the methods of work in foreign posts will be by the establishment of *specialized* aptitudes, knowledge, and competence around each chief of mission."[110] In response, the Ministry began creating new technical attachés, thus expanding the overseas staffs to unprecedented proportions.[111] In addition to the traditional military and naval attachés assigned to important posts, there now appeared other specialists for those matters destined to play increasingly important roles in world politics, including commerce, agriculture, finance, culture, and press relations. At the Berlin embassy alone, by 1922 France had added specialized services for economics, politics, industry, and finances, and needed still more advisors for legal and farming affairs.[112]

Sending agents abroad, officials of the Quai d'Orsay discovered, raised more than one question about the overseas services. After resolving the issue of *who* would represent French interests in other lands, they also had to determine *where* such persons would be sent.

108. See the Decree of 22 September 1913, Decree of 15 November 1920, and the Decree of 19 August 1921; as summarized in MAE/Chambre, Rapport No. 1230 (1908), pp. 376–79; idem, Rapport No. 3318 (1914), 1, p. 123; idem, Rapport No. 2020 (1921), pp. 74–75, 82–83; PRO/FO 369/971, Memorandum of 9 January 1918; Schuman, p. 42; and Sharp, pp. 324–25. The complete amalgamation desired by some, however, was not realized.

109. MAE/Chambre, Rapport No. 2020 (1921), pp. 74–75.

110. Ibid., pp. 75, 80; and idem, Rapport No. 3131 (1922), p. 5.

111. See, for example, the discussion in Jean Baillou and Pierre Pelletier, *Les Affaires étrangères* (Paris: Presses universitaires de France, 1962), pp. 151–52, 158; and Ludwig Dischler, "Der auswärtige Dienst Frankreichs" (Hamburg: unpublished dissertation, 1952), 1, pp. 91–95.

112. See MAE/Chambre, Rapport No. 3131 (1922), pp. 188–89; among others.

Solicited opinions from the representatives themselves,[113] as well as a "meticulous investigation,"[114] revealed dissatisfaction with the inability of existing posts to meet the demands imposed by the changing international system. One agent said that "the Russo-Japanese War has profoundly changed the political and economic conditions of countries in East Asia," and urged the creation of a new vice-consulate in Vladivostok.[115] Another suggested that recent transformations in Africa necessitated establishing missions there.[116] Critics also asked the Ministry to justify the anomaly of having eighteen consular missions in Spain while maintaining only seven or eight in the entire United States.[117] "The evolution of international phenomena," declared one report, "has compelled us to recognize that while in one part of the world events have rendered formerly necessary posts now useless, on other points of the globe they have driven us to the creation of entirely new posts."[118]

Agreeing to this argument, innovators within the Ministry instituted a program for the "reorganization of posts" and designed to reform, to "methodically revise," and to "remake" the French diplomatic and consular map of the world. They did not simply or indiscriminately enlarge the number of foreign missions. Indeed, some of the old, traditional posts—including several in Europe— were eliminated because of expense or obsolescence. Others, however, were expanded in size or newly created in order to cope with the changed political and economic realities of global affairs. Just as the Quai d'Orsay created new bureaus in the central administration for the Far East, America, and Africa, so it now responded with new overseas missions in these same geographical areas. Increased French representation occurred in such distant and diverse locations as Paraguay, Argentina, South Africa, the Congo, Liberia, Egypt, Afghanistan, Japan, Canada, and the United States. Addi-

---

113. Encouraged by Deschanel and others, Ministers Léon Bourgeois and Pichon sent circular inquiries to agents stationed abroad for their opinions. See MAE/Chambre, Rapport No. 2015 (1909), pp. 53ff.; and Le Temps, 17 November 1906.

114. The words are Pichon's, in MAE/Sénat, Rapport No. 28 (1912), p. 25.

115. See MAE/Chambre, Rapport No. 2015 (1909), p. 71.

116. Ibid., p. 73.

117. Debate of 15 January 1907, in France, Sénat, DP, p. 90.

118. MAE/Chambre, Rapport No. 3318 (1914), 1, p. 133. Also see idem, Rapport No. 1230 (1908), pp. 92–323.

tional missions followed after the First World War in such nations as Poland, the Soviet Union, and Czechoslovakia.[119]

This extensive expansion of posts, of course, meant that the political, economic, and cultural policies of France, in the words of Louis Marin, increasingly would clash with foreign rivals on "so many different points of the globe." Yet this development in the overseas services—like reforms in the organizational structure and personnel policies—was essential, because "the acuteness of international problems" had become "more intense than ever before."[120]

5. Relations with "the Outside"

Public demand for greater participation in matters of foreign affairs, noted Berthelot in his lengthy report on reforms and innovations, constituted one of the primary reasons for instituting major changes in the Quai d'Orsay.[121] Criticism poured from many sources even before the war against the abuses of "secret diplomacy" and ministerial operations hidden from outside scrutiny. Parliamentarians, political parties, chambers of commerce, private businessmen, the press, and members of the general public insisted upon being consulted and informed about questions involving external relations. Response to this pressure indicated that diplomacy in this century no longer would—or could—be transacted solely within the peaceful confines of a secluded ministry.

The direction of foreign affairs long had been considered an exclusive function of executive power. Political philosophy, traditional practice, constitutional provisions, legislative ignorance, and public apathy all permitted a system in which policy could be formulated and executed far from the *Palais Bourbon*. In the new century, however, parliamentarians of all parties felt that they had remained silent and subservient long enough, and demanded far-reaching changes. Their earlier acquiescence turned to vocal protest, and the

119. See MAE/Chambre, Rapport No. 2015 (1908), pp. 66ff.; idem, Rapport No. 3318 (1914), 1, pp. 134ff.; idem, Rapport No. 6339 (1919), pp. 210ff.; idem, Rapport No. 2020 (1921), pp. 144–45; and NA/DS, Index 851.021/14, Despatch No. 445 from Simons (Paris) to Secretary of State, 24 April 1925.

120. MAE/Chambre, Rapport No. 3318 (1914), 1, p. 181; among others.

121. Berthelot, "Commission des réformes administratives," p. 3269.

resulting cries reached major proportions. Said one contemporary, "for democracies, the parliamentary control of foreign policy now has become more than ever before a problem of the first magnitude."[122]

Numerous efforts within the legislature, therefore, attempted to exert greater influence upon the Ministry for Foreign Affairs. The budget commissions of both the Chamber of Deputies and Senate, for instance, began to use their power of the purse as an effective lever for prying open once-closed ministerial doors. Their annual reports exposed the details of internal operations and personnel policies. These yearly accounts soon developed into highly effective platforms of relentless criticism, and provided a means of proposing reforms for every bureau of the Quai d'Orsay. The surveillance potential of these respective budget commissions, however, was inherently restricted by terms of reference that allowed them only to examine strictly administrative and financial matters rather than substantive policy.[123] Parliamentarians seeking greater control over more significant questions of international politics thus looked toward the idea of creating permanent commissions for foreign affairs.

Prior to the twentieth century, no standing institutional mechanism existed for legislative supervision of external policy. Early committees operated merely on an *ad hoc* basis to consider specific treaties or questions of foreign relations as they arose, and their influence was minimal. Critics sought to change this impotent system and give legislators greater control over policy by advocating the establishment of permanent commissions. Their pressure, when combined with persistent efforts on the part of deputies like Louis Marin, succeeded in creating the Chamber's standing committee first known as the *Commission des Affaires extérieures, des protectorats et des colonies* (1902), then as the *Commission des Affaires extérieures* (1915), and finally as the *Commission des Affaires étrangères* (1920).[124] Senators established a similar committee, and

---

122. S. R. Chow, *Le contrôle parlementaire de la politique étrangère en Angleterre, en France et aux Etats-Unis* (Paris: Sagot, 1920) p. 7.

123. Recognition of this limitation can be seen, for example, in MAE/Sénat, Rapport No. 140 (1906), p. 3; and MAE/Chambre, Rapport No. 3318 (1914), 1, p. 3.

124. France, Chambre, *DP*, 17 November 1902, pp. 2624ff.; idem, 29 January 1915, pp. 68–78; idem, 23 January 1920, pp. 36–40; and Maurice Schumann, "La Commission des Affaires étrangères," in J. Basdevant et al., *Les Affaires, étrangères* (Paris: Presses Universitaires de France, 1959), pp. 21–55.

thus assured that both houses now would have institutional means of obtaining information and exerting influence upon French foreign policy.[125]

These permanent legislative commissions prepared reports on treaties and other matters of external relations, kept in constant communication with the Quai d'Orsay through their *rapporteurs d'information,* submitted inquiries and received replies, and called officials before them for testimony and discussion. Moreover, the prestigious chairmanship of each body was awarded only to highly qualified parliamentarians, and to men noted for their expertise in foreign affairs.[126] As a result, observers said within just a short period of time that these commissions constituted "the most active and effective" instruments of legislative supervision, "the nearest approach yet devised to an effective organ of parliamentary control and direction of foreign policy and the exercise of an appreciable, if somewhat imponderable, influence on the activities of the Ministry."[127]

In response to this increased supervision of their activities by parliamentarians, diplomats and bureaucrats of the Quai d'Orsay instituted several new practices. More time and talent were allocated to answer questions and draft replies to legislators. The Foreign Minister and other high officials scheduled appointments for personal appearances before the parliamentary commissions.[128] Later, they even created a *Secrétariat législatif* (Legislative Secretary) and "parliamentary attachés" to facilitate transactions with senators and deputies.[129] Parliamentarians had never received such attention, and some seemed a bit unsure of how to adjust. For this

125. France, Sénat, *DP,* 4 February 1915, p. 32.

126. The list includes Deschanel, Barthou, Leygues, and Paul-Boncour in the Chamber, with Freycinet, Clemenceu, de Selves, Poincaré, and Doumergue in the Senate. Each of these men except Deschanel served as Foreign Minister.

127. Schuman, pp. 25–26. Also see Barthélemy, *Démocratie et politique étrangère,* pp. 130–31; idem, *Essai sur le travail parlementaire et le système des commissions* (Paris: Delagrave, 1934), pp. 257–77; and the private letter from Paul Deschanel to Francis Bertie, "Note concernant la Commission des Affaires extérieures et la Commission du budget," 24 January 1911, in PRO/FO 371/900.

128. See, for example, MAE, Comptabilité, Carton 59, "Décrets et décisions ministérielles," Decree of 1 December 1910; and Barthélemy, *Essai sur le travail parlementaire,* pp. 262–67.

129. MAE, Commission de Réorganisation, "Rapports presentés à la Commission de réorganisation de l'Administration centrale," Année 1933, pp. 239–46.

reason, Deputy Louis Barthou suggested to his colleagues that they appreciate these innovations, but that they remember that "a just mean must be found before the two extremes of the diplomacy of the public street and the *secret du roi*; between the constitutional prerogatives of the Government and the legitimate demands of public opinion and Parliament."[130]

Legislators represented only one segment of those "outsiders" demanding more information on matters of international politics. Other critics considered ludicrously inadequate the occasional communiqués, the inspired "leaks" to the press,[131] the infrequent words spoken in the Chambers, and the short comments made on *faits accomplis*. Journalists and other articulate citizens wanted more than mere scraps from the table. "In a democratic society," asserted one spokesman, "public opinion must be accurately informed."[132] In a democracy like France, admitted Pichon, the people should have the right to be informed on those matters of international politics that can profoundly affect their destiny.[133]

Under this pressure to check the bureaucratic propensity toward privacy and secrecy,[134] Pichon signed a decree instituting a *Bureau des Communications*. Charged, in part, with establishing direct communication with the press, this department began to receive journalists daily. Conferences and discussions slowly opened those doors once closed to all but the intimate diplomats and bureaucrats. In addition, this bureau initiated the practice of circulating analyses and summaries of relevant information to interested parties, including the President of the Republic, various Cabinet members, legislative commissions, and business groups.[135]

This new practice of actively and regularly communicating information to "the outside" accelerated during and after the First World

130. Louis Barthou, as cited in PRO/FO 371/3753, Despatch No. 315, "Confidential," from Derby (Paris) to Foreign Secretary, 4 February 1920.

131. See LaRoche, pp. 14–15; and PRO/FO 800/165, private letter from A. Nicolson (London) to Bertie (Paris) of 11 October 1912 complaining of indiscretions.

132. MAE/Chambre, Rapport No. 2661 (1906), p. 125.

133. Pichon, in a report dated 9 March 1907, as found in MAE, Personnel, "Lois, Ordonnances, Décrets et Arrêtés," Carton 29.

134. On this characteristic of bureaucracies, see Weber, 2, 559ff.

135. Decree of 29 April 1907, in France, *JO*, 3 May 1907, p. 3268; and MAE/Chambre, Rapport No. 2015 (1909), pp. 22–24.

War. Increased public pressure against "secret diplomacy," when combined with enemy propaganda deliberately designed to influence opinion, convinced many of the necessity for further institutional innovations. The vast wartime *Maison de la Presse* under Berthelot's own dynamic leadership pumped hundreds of thousands of books, brochures, films, and newspaper articles into the public view. Yet even this proved to be only a beginning, as many officials including Pichon urged that a closer liaison between the Ministry and others should be considered as "indispensable."[136] For this reason, an additional ministerial decree created the new *Service d'Information et de Presse*.[137] Its staff held press conferences, published documentary collections, issued pamphlets, and developed a wireless communications system for overseas broadcasts. The Ministry now possessed the means to disseminate information at home and around the world. Such activity and public relations services actually existing within the once-isolated Quai d'Orsay broke with the past, and ministerial press bureaus became permanent fixtures in twentieth-century diplomacy.

These institutional means to maintain constant communication between the Quai d'Orsay, parliament, the press corps, and the general public indicated the Ministry's growing involvement with those various "outsiders" interested in aspects of foreign affairs. Additional innovations broadened this circle even further to include other ministries, foreign governments, international organizations, commercial concerns, and other interest groups. New provisions made the Foreign Minister or his representative integral parts of any intra-ministerial committee responsible for various questions of defense or foreign policy, such as the *Conseil supérieur de la défense nationale* or the *Commission interministerielle permanente de l'immigration*.[138] Particularly after the war, officials of the Quai

136. MAE, Direction politique et commerciale, Papiers des Agents: Stephen Pichon, Volume 6, undated note "Relations avec la Presse étrangère."

137. Outrey, 3, 4, pp. 715–16. For more details, see Chapter Six.

138. See France, *JO,* 18 November 1921, pp. 12734–35; and idem, 31 July 1920, p. 10894. By the Decree of 23 July 1918, the Sous-Direction of Administrative Affairs and International Unions became charged with acting as a permanent intermediary between the Ministries for Foreign Affairs, Interior, and War. The results of this intraministerial cooperation are clearly evident in AN, Ministère de l'Intérieur, Direction des Renseignements, Carton No. F⁷ 13.424, "Rapports d'agents secrets," and Carton No. F⁷ 13.425, "Notes générales."

d'Orsay greatly expanded their roles on multinational commissions by instituting permanent staffs for the *Services de la Conference des Ambassadeurs* and the various *Commissions fluviales internationales*.[139] An elaborate *Service français de la Société des Nations* for the League of Nations in Geneva and involvement in the Permanent Court of International Justice committed the Ministry to active participation in worldwide organizations.[140] The creation of *attachés commerciaux* and a "Commercial and Financial Counsellor" within the central administration signalled conscious attempts to establish and maintain permanent contact between the Ministry for Foreign Affairs and French businessmen.[141] Finally, additional outsiders were given an opportunity to express their opinions by new provisions which required that positions on the Quai d'Orsay's board of examiners be selected only after consultation with the Minister of Commerce, chambers of commerce, civil administrators, and university educators.[142]

*   *   *   *

In first explaining the basic rationale for reforming the Quai d'Orsay, Philippe Berthelot noted the importance of "adapting to new conditions and to the necessities of modern diplomacy."[143] He recognized, with so many of the critics, that the realities of both international and domestic politics required major institutional changes within the Ministry for Foreign Affairs. Responding to these pressures of twentieth-century diplomacy, therefore, ministerial decrees created new, permanent mechanisms to manage French foreign relations more effectively and efficiently.

Within the central administration, this response first found form in the structural unification of political and commercial affairs, in the creation of geographical divisions and numerous functional

139. See MAE/Chambre, Rapport No. 4792 (1923), pp. 185–95; and Ministère des Affaires étrangères, *Compte définitif des dépenses de l'exercice 1921–1925.*

140. MAE/Chambre, Rapport No. 3131 (1922), pp. 46–125; and idem, Rapport No. 4792 (1923), pp. 158–85.

141. Among other sources, see MAE/Chambre, Rapport No. 361 (1911), pp. 158–67. Also see Chapter Five.

142. See references in footnote 70.

143. Berthelot, "Commission des réformes administratives," p. 3269.

specialists, in the employment of more sophisticated administrative bureaus and management techniques, and in the utilization of new technological inventions. In personnel policy the reforms initiated important legal standardization for recruitment, examination, compensation, promotion, and discipline procedures. For the diplomatic and consular corps, reforming decrees instituted an equivalent *statut* in personnel matters, permitted transfer between services, suppressed obsolete missions, and created new posts and technical attachés where needed. Further innovations established permanent liaisons between the Quai d'Orsay and other ministries, international organizations, foreign governments, parliament, the public at large, and even private interest groups.

These achievements are impressive, considering the reluctance or inability of most bureaucratic organizations to institute change of any kind.[144] Even before the reforms and innovations reached completion, therefore, several of the Ministry's most relentless critics began to praise the accomplishments. Louis Marin spoke of the response as "considerable progress," "a work of importance," and "a genuine and profound reorganization."[145] Deschanel referred to the French Ministry for Foreign Affairs as an institution now becoming established on "a new base and more adapted to modern necessities."[146]

144. See, for example, Crozier, pp. 257–61; Weber, 2, 577ff.; and the more detailed discussion in Chapter Seven.

145. MAE/Chambre, Rapport No. 3318 (1914), 1, pp. 121, 132.

146. Ibid., Rapport No. 361 (1911), p. 139.

— 4 —

The German Response:
Reforms and Innovations for the Wilhelmstrasse

> *Everywhere the question is one of reconstruc-*
> *tion, mostly reconstruction on the basis of the*
> *ruins of the old. . . . I know that people say that in*
> *the Foreign Ministry everything goes on in the*
> *same old sluggish way. Those who say so, how-*
> *ever, have no insight into either the changes that*
> *have already taken place or those in preparation.*
> *I have no inclination to live with the criticisms*
> *directed against my predecessors. . . . I am*
> *firmly determined to bring about reforms in the*
> *Ministry for Foreign Affairs.*
>
> –Foreign Minister
> Brockdorff-Rantzau

The demands and complexities of international politics experienced by French diplomats and bureaucrats burst with even greater
force upon their German counterparts. The pressures of war and
defeat, aggravated by vociferous domestic criticism during the empire's collapse and revolution, indicated an end to the traditional
operations of the Wilhelmstrasse. "Public opinion of all shades is
unanimous in condemning the Foreign Ministry," noted one observer. "Even the extreme Right," he continued, "otherwise favor-
ably disposed to the Bismarckian system, admit that this is its
weakest point. Germany today universally recognizes that the reform is urgent."[1] The critics maintained that efficient administration
of foreign affairs under such drastically changed conditions necessitated a more "logical" and "expanded" organizational structure,

1. Report of 31 October 1919 from the Director of Military Intelligence (War
Office) to the Under Secretary of State for Foreign Affairs, in PRO/FO 371/3778.

"rational" techniques of management, "systematic" personnel policies, "specialists," and the application of "modern" technology.

The German response to these international and domestic pressures upon diplomacy resulted in major institutional changes within the Ministry for Foreign Affairs. Reforms and innovations transformed the central administration, personnel policies, representation abroad, and liaison with outside interest groups. As such, they became integral features of the entire Weimar experience which, in the words of one scholar, symbolized "a new start" and expressed "the impulse for reform."[2]

1. Men and Methods of Action

The domestic and international upheavals besetting Europe from the turn of the century to the early twenties seriously convulsed the foundations of many hallowed institutions. Massive criticism and demands for reform gave dramatic evidence of a deep discontent with antiquated structures and established practices. Many Germans, therefore, sought adequate responses to the challenges in instituting necessary change. Some individuals looked for practical applications of new developments within industrial management and administrative science, and increasingly spiced their suggestions with expressions of "modern techniques," "systematic organization," "business efficiency," "up-to-date procedures," and "scientific training."[3] Others hoped to benefit from the experience gained elsewhere, and looked toward their neighbors and competitors in France for solutions.

With reference to reorganizing the institutions designed to manage external relations, the French example received the most attention by far. Newspaper articles, Reichstag speeches, diplomatic despatches, and internal ministerial memoranda indicate that—long

2. Peter Gay, *Weimar Culture: The Outsider and Insider* (New York: Harper and Row, 1968), pp. 1, 38.

3. Among many examples, see PA/AA, Abteilung IA, Deutschland 122, Nr. 2, Band 2; Theodor Vogelstein, "Der Stil des amerikanischen Geschäftslebens," in *Süddeutsche Monatshefte*, 2 (July–December 1906), pp. 80–100; and Arnold Brecht and C. Glaser, *The Art and Technique of Administration in German Ministries* (Cambridge: Harvard University Press, 1940), passim.

before the outbreak of war—reforms and innovations at the Quai
d'Orsay often were observed with an interest toward emulation.[4]
Some critics, like Ernst Bassermann, declared that as a consequence of its changes the French Ministry for Foreign Affairs was
"much better organized" than its German counterpart. He further
suggested bluntly that the Wilhelmstrasse should institute the same
modifications.[5]

Confronted with proposals that the French reforms be used as a
model, officials in the German Ministry for Foreign Affairs frequently argued that such reorganization would be either unnecessary or dangerous. Bülow boasted, for example that under his able
direction the Wilhelmstrasse had worked "faultlessly."[6] In a typical
ploy, Kiderlen-Wächter conjured up the time-tested formula of tradition and the great master. "The organization of the Ministry," he
warned, "originates from a great age—from the era of Prince
Bismarck—and that ought to make us particularly cautious before
we undertake any new alterations."[7]

The crisis produced by the *Daily Telegraph* affair shattered this
mystique of past perfection. By exposing gross mismanagement, it
seriously shook public apathy and governmental complacency. "A
deep and lasting indignation has taken hold of the people," recorded
one contemporary in the flood of unprecedented criticism. The
Reichstag parties, he said, demanded "the immediate retirement of
Prince Bülow, constitutional limitations of the Imperial Power, and
drastic changes in the Ministry for Foreign Affairs."[8] Attacks of
this nature eroded the self-satisfaction among higher officials, forcing them to recognize the existence of an out-dated institution.

4. *Vossische Zeitung*, "Die Umgestaltung des Auswärtigen Amts," 8 July
1910; Kiderlen-Wächter's speech on 11 November 1908, in Germany, Reichstag,
SB, 233, p. 5433; Despatch No. 387 from Lancken (Paris) to Bethmann-Hollweg,
22 September 1910, in PA/AA, Abteilung IA, Frankreich 105, Nr. 1, Band 28; and
the undated, unsigned note concerning the French press article on "Ein Projekt der
Reform," in Handakten des Unterstaatssekretär Töpffer, Aktenzeichen 13,
Beilage.

5. Ernest Bassermann, 10 November 1908, in Germany, Reichstag, *SB*, 233,
p. 5378.

6. Bülow, 10 November 1908, in ibid., p. 5396.

7. Kiderlen-Wächter, 11 November 1908, in ibid., p. 5433; and again on 12
December 1910, in idem, 262, p. 3592.

8. PRO/FO 371/463, Despatch No. 43, "Confidential," from Findlay (Dresden) to Grey, 10 November 1908.

Under pressure, Bülow reluctantly admitted that the Wilhelm-strasse possibly contained certain defects,[9] and Kiderlen-Wächter announced that reforms perhaps would be forthcoming.[10] The resulting personnel and internal procedural changes intro-duced some modifications within the Ministry prior to the war and demonstrated that at least slight alterations could be made. This fostered additional dissatisfaction among many who realized that these early reforms represented only minor and half-hearted efforts to respond to twentieth-century diplomacy.[11] "Attempts were re-peatedly made to reorganize the Ministry thoroughly," claimed Schoen later, "but they came to nothing. We had to manage as best we could with trifling remedies and alleviations of technical difficul-ties. More important changes had to be postponed until a more favorable moment."[12]

That moment struck at the Wilhelmstrasse with the First World War and its aftermath. This traumatic experience exacerbated pres-sures to the breaking point, and critics vowed that Germany never would return to the tradition-ridden nineteenth-century world. Even Chancellor Bethmann-Hollweg, during the war and in the face of strong conservative opposition, spoke of the necessity for a *Neuorientierung* within institutions. He declared that "the new era and the new nation are here!"[13] and warned that the country's survival depended upon its ability to respond effectively to "the spirit of the times."[14]

These words came too late, however, for in the wake of military defeat and exhaustion, the German Empire itself collapsed. The

9. Bülow, 10 November 1908, in Germany, Reichstag, *SB*, 233, p. 5396.

10. Kiderlen-Wächter, 11 November 1908, in ibid., p. 5433.

11. Among many examples, see *Vossische Zeitung*, 8 July 1910; and *Deutsche Marke*, "Arbeit für den Staatssekretär von Jagow!" 5 January 1913; both of which are also filed in PA/AA, Abteilung IA, Deutschland 122 Nr. 2, Band 5.

12. Schoen, p. 118. Also see PA/AA, Abteilung IA, Deutschland 122 Nr. 2, *secr.*, Band 1, A.S. 68, memorandum from Schoen in the folder marked "Neuor-ganisation des Ausw. Amtes"; and the unnumbered circular from Mathieu dated 24 February 1909.

13. Bethmann-Hollweg, 27 February 1917, in Germany, Reichstag, *SB*, 309, p. 2375.

14. Bethmann-Hollweg, 14 March 1917, in Germany, Prussia, Landtag, *SB*, pp. 5254–59.

army's nerve cracked, mutiny spread, and revolt spread throughout the country. Kaiser Wilhelm abdicated his throne, socialists created new institutions to direct revolution and control change,[15] and people heard the proclamation of a new Republic. "Germany is now on the road from an autocratic to a democratic state," cried *Vorwärts*.[16] The *Frankfurter Zeitung* spoke of "The New Germany,"[17] and circulars boldly proclaimed: "The hour has struck!"[18] When the reins of political power passed to the Majority Socialists in November 1918, the administrative bureaucracies and civil service were transferred from a government committed to traditional vested interests and placed in the hands of one pledged to reform and innovation.[19] In the words of a legation secretary, this provided the opportunity and "the psychological moment for radical reorganization of the internal structure of the Ministry for Foreign Affairs."[20]

As new constitutional provisions, electoral and taxation laws, ministerial reorganizations, and civil liberties swirled throughout Germany, pressure increased to force radical change in the Wilhelmstrasse.[21] Letters, articles, and various memoranda poured into the Ministry at such a hectic rate that special procedural instructions were necessary simply to manage their registration and distribution.[22] Private citizens, business interests, politicians, diplomats, and even bureaucrats themselves criticized the organization

15. Germany, Volksbeauftragen, *Die Regierund der Volksbeauftragen, 1918–1919*, edited by Erich Matthias and Susanne Miller (Düsseldorf: Droste, 1969).

16. *Vorwärts*, "An Deutschlands Männer und Frauen!" 18 October 1918.

17. *Frankfurter-Zeitung*, "Das neue Deutschland" columns, 1–6 November 1918.

18. An unnumbered note entitled "An Deutschlands Jugend!" in PA/AA, Abteilung I A, Deutschland 122 Nr. 2, Band 6, and signed by Bernstorff, Bernhard W. Bülow, Harry Kessler, Prittwitz, Stumm, and Trautmann, among other diplomats.

19. On this point, see Seabury, p. 9.

20. Kuno Tiemann, *Das Auswärtige Amt, die Notwendigkeit seiner Reorganisation* (Berlin: Verlag Neues Vaterland, 1920), p. 6.

21. The reorganizations that occurred in the other governmental ministries are summarized in Report No. 862 from Finance Minister Wirth to the President of the Reichstag, "Organisationspläne der Reichsministerien," dated 8 November 1920 and found in PA/AA, Büro des Reichsministers, Aktenzeichen 2, Band 1.

22. See, for example, I. 31658/31758, note of 11 September 1918 circulated to the registering clerks, in PA/AA, Abteilung I A, Deutschland 149, Band 27; and the new job description provided by I. 37541, "Geschäftsverteilung der Abteilung I," dated 6 December 1919, in Band 31 of the same series.

and practices of the past and proposed reforms for the future.[23] The new Foreign Minister, Brockdorff-Rantzau, recognized the validity of their comments and the strength of their numbers and declared before the National Assembly meeting at Weimar that he was "firmly determined" to institute change.[24] Yet as he, his assistant Helmut Töpffer, and his immediate successor Hermann Müller grew increasingly enmeshed in the Paris peace negotiations, the moving force behind reforms and innovations became the Personnel Director, Friedrich Edmund Schüler.

Born in the Berlin suburb of Spandau to the family of a Prussian Major General, Schüler had ready access to the educational and cultural opportunities of Wilhelminian society.[25] His "mental abilities and acute intelligence" showed at an early age, and he distinguished himself in music, architecture, and interior design. Professional advancement and service to the state appeared to be greater in law, however, and Schüler immersed himself in legal studies at Lausanne, Leipzig, Munich, and Berlin. After a lengthy apprenticeship and the difficult advanced state legal examination, he took an extended vacation and travelled throughout Europe for nearly a year visiting numerous countries and seeking to perfect the French and English languages. This experience so aroused his interest that on his return to Germany he applied for extrance into the foreign service.

On the 11th of December, 1900, Schüler received a summons to appear at the Wilhelmstrasse for probationary exercises, and six

---

23. Among numerous examples, see *Neue Berliner Zeitung*, "Frische Luft im Auswärtigen Amt!" 24 January 1919; letter of 27 January 1919 from the Vereinigung der mittleren Auslandsbeamten to Töpffer and enclosure "Anregungen der Vereinigung der mittleren Auslandsbeamten zur Personalreform des Auswärtigen Dienstes"; the printed "Bemerkungen zu der umstehenden schematischen Darstellung der Laufbahnen des auswärtigen Dienstes," dated April 1919 and signed by "Der Beirat der Bürobeamten des Auswärtigen Amtes"; all in PA/AA, Handakten des Unterstaatssekretär Töpffer, Aktenzeichen 13, Band 1. Also see the material in Nachlässe Ulrich von Brockdorff-Rantzau, idem, Aktenzeichen 14, Band 1; and Abteilung IA, Deutschland 122 Nr. 2, Band 6; among others.

24. See *Deutsche Allgemeine Zeitung*, "Reichsminister Graf Brockdorff-Rantzau über den Frieden. Deutsche Nationalversammlung," 11 April 1919.

25. This biographical information is based upon Schüler's career outline located in the personnel files of the Auswärtiges Amt; and a special memorandum entitled "Ministerialdirektor a. D. Schüler," dated 6 December 1954, in PA/AA, Politsches Archiv.

(courtesy *Auswärtiges Amt*)

Friedrich Edmund Schüler

days later he formally began his career in the German Ministry for Foreign Affairs. His knowledge of legal and commercial affairs was first sought by the consular corps. Stationed for brief periods in Constantinople, Sarajevo, Smyrna, Addis Ababa, and Kharkov, he gained practical experience in foreign lands, met influential German diplomats, and demonstrated outstanding professional abilities. Annual evaluations by superiors, for example, referred to Schüler's "brilliant qualities."[26] Others described him as a "highly gifted, creative personality."[27]

These talents soon were recognized by the Ministry, and in November 1906 when the first French Reform Commission was named for the Quai d'Orsay, Schüler entered the consular section of the Wilhelmstrasse's Personnel Division as a known, zealous advocate of change. From this new position in the central administration he could observe the internal operations and personnel practices of the ministerial bureaucracy. This experience confirmed Schüler's belief that the pressing demands of twentieth-century diplomacy required drastic changes. When the 1918 collapse and revolution finally swept old obstacles and opposition away, he became the man charged with transforming his ideas into reality.

Schüler was assigned to direct a special commission created specifically for the study of proposals demanding major reorganization.[28] Although subjected to great outside pressure and criticism, this commission's search and evaluation of an incredibly large number of suggestions nevertheless proceeded with extensive comments from the Wilhelmstrasse's diplomats and bureaucrats themselves.[29] The actual decisions about internal reforms and innovations were made within the Ministry itself, as indicated in the numerous *Verfügungen* (decrees) signed by Schüler, an Under State Secretary, or

26. This comment comes from a report by Stemrich, who later became Under State Secretary, as recounted in ibid.

27. Johannes Sievers, "Aus meinum Leben" (Berlin, 1966), p. 351.

28. Otto Schifferdecker, *Die Organisation des Auswärtigen Dienstes im alten und neuen Reich* (Heidelberg; privately printed, 1931), p. 45.

29. See the "Reorganisationspläne," dated 15 April 1919 from Naumann; and the "Denkschrift der Expedienten des Auswärtigen Amtes über den Geschäftsbetrieb in dieser Behörde," of March 1919 signed by "Die planmässigen Expedienten des Auswärtigen Amtes"; all in PA/AA, Handakten des Understaatssekretär Töpffer, Aktenzeichen 13, Band 1.

the Minister for Foreign Affairs. Personnel dislocations and complicated peace negotiations restricted the two latter, however, and the permanent bureaucrat—Friedrich Edmund Schüler—grew in power and influence. He soon gained the reputation as "a man of extraordinary energy, a passionate craving for work, and an iron will verging on a dictator's obstinacy."[30] His influence upon the German institutional response to twentieth-century diplomacy became so overwhelming that the resulting internal changes are still known as "the Schüler Reforms."[31]

2. Organizational Structure

In introducing his public pledge to institute major changes in the Wilhelmstrasse, Brockdorff-Rantzau asserted, "the question is one of structural reform in the organization."[32] He recognized—like so many of the critics—the inadequacy of maintaining the traditional "monopoly" of power in *Abteilung IA*, the obsolete Euro-centric orientation, and the administrative separation of international affairs into arbitrary "political" or "commercial" categories. Twentieth-century diplomacy required more precision and greater sophistication, leading Rantzau to promise: "Instead of this division of departments as heretofore prevailing, I shall introduce the system of distinction by geographical regions. . . . In the future, the departments will be distinguished by the great cultural regions of the world to which they belong."[33]

30. *Berliner Tageblatt*, 27 December 1920.

31. Heinz Sasse, *Auswärtiges Amt, 1870–1970* (Bonn: Auswärtiges Amt, 1970), pp. 33, 35. Contemporaries also used the label "Schüler Reforms," as evidenced in *Frankfurter Zeitung*, "Das Auswärtige Amt," 25 December 1920; and letter of 30 December 1920 from Simons (Bärenfels) to Haniel, in PA/AA, Büro des Reichsministers, Aktenzeichen 2, Band 1; among others. In using this designation it should be noted that Schüler's direct influence was felt primarily from 1918 to 1920 and that some changes had occurred earlier and others took place after his forced retirement. Information on the dates of the reforms and innovations can be found in the footnotes.

32. Brockdorff-Rantzau, 10 April 1919, in Germany, Nationalversammlung, *SB*, 327, p. 933.

33. Ibid. Finance Minister Wirth stated that this recognition of the obsolete nature of traditional divisions was "the central idea" behind reorganization. See PA/AA, Büro des Reichsministers, Aktenzeichen 2, Band 1, copy of Report No. 862 from Wirth to the President of the Reichstag, "Organisationspläne der Reichsministerien," dated 8 November 1920, p. 3.

CHART III

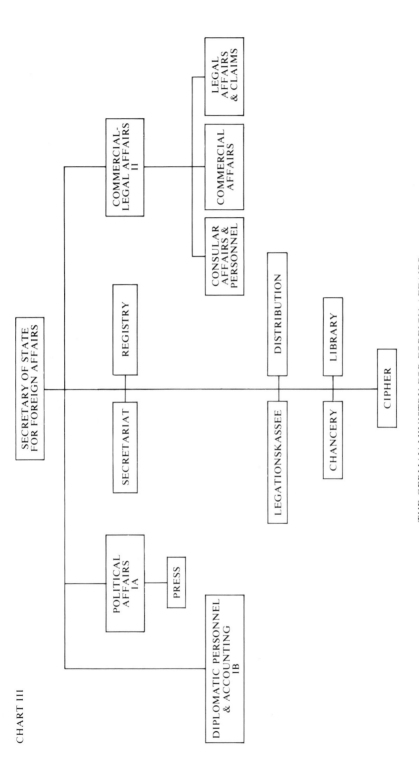

THE GERMAN MINISTRY FOR FOREIGN AFFAIRS:
BASIC NINETEENTH-CENTURY ORGANIZATION

Charged with achieving this objective, the energetic Schüler abolished the old Political Division with its "mystic veil of clouds"[34] and introduced a long-awaited *Regionalsystem*. He organized the administrative combination of political and commercial matters under groups specializing in specific locations, following the example of the French. New *Länderabteilung* (geographical divisions) were designed to manage relations with the expanding community in world politics. Each became responsible for a particular region: Western Europe; Central Europe and the Balkans; England, the Americas, the Near East, and Africa; Russia, Poland, and Scandinavia; and Asia.[35] Under this arrangement, observed one press report, "administrative operations no longer would be divided into hierarchical stories where one noble level existed for the elite of statesmanship with the attics and basements of the Ministry for the inferior groups."[36] Each department managed all the multiple political, economic, legal, and propagandistic aspects of policy relating to its specific region. "In this way," said Rantzau, "the treatment of individual countries can be subjected to greater concentration, and a number of real specialists will be trained who possess a comprehensive knowledge of their particular country in all its relations."[37]

This emphasis upon specialization became an essential feature of the German institutional response to twentieth-century diplomacy. Schüler recognized that expertise was required both for individual countries and for those problems of international relations which extended beyond the confines of regional boundaries. To complement and assist the new geographical divisions, therefore, he

34. These words are from Theodore Wolff in the *Berliner Tageblatt*, 27 December 1920.

35. PA/AA, Abteilung III, Geschäftsgang Ia, Band 1, No. 527, circular of 21 December 1921; and ibid., Politisches Archiv, "Geschäftsverteilungspläne," Bände 1–2. See Schüler's first arrangements as indicated in "Geschäftsverteilung innerhalb des Auswärtigen Amts," signed by Schüler on 19 March 1920, in idem, "Geschäftsverteilungspläne," Band 1. Also see the experiments evidenced by PA/AA, Abteilung IA, Deutschland 149, Band 22a, "Geschäftsverteilung der politischen Abteilung 1916"; and H. Wolgast, "Die auswärtige Gewalt des Deutschen Reichs unter besonderer Berücksichtigung des Auswärtigen Amtes: ein Ueberblick," *Archiv des öffentlichen Rechts*, N.F. 5, Heft 1 (1923), p. 49.

36. *Berliner Tageblatt*, 27 December 1920.

37. Brockdorff-Rantzau, 10 April 1919, in Germany, Nationalversammlung, *SB*, 327, p. 933.

created technical departments staffed with experts in commercial, financial, and legal affairs.

Building upon the sophistication that had been developing in the former Commercial Division since the early 1900s,[38] Schüler set up the *Aussenhandelsstelle* (Office of Foreign Trade). This introduced into the Wilhelmstrasse many new specialists in international commerce and finance. Subsequent innovations brought in even more experts to staff such new bureaus as *Sonderreferat für Wirtschaftspolitik* (Special Department for Economic Policy), *Referat für wirtschaftliches Nachrichtenwesen,* which gathered and distributed trade intelligence, and *Referat Rohstoffwirtschaft* (Raw Materials Department). They now collectively had the means to provide comprehensive advice to the Ministry on complex technical aspects of commercial treaties, reparations payments and indebtedness, foreign loans, international business information, overseas markets and competition, availability and movement of natural resources, shipping routes, customs duties, and export regulations.[39]

A new premium also was placed upon technical competence in the Ministry's management of difficult legal transactions. As the *Rechtsabteilung* (Legal Division) expanded with the growing demands of international and domestic politics, functional tasks became increasingly varied and specialized.[40] Particularly under Schüler, this office grew rapidly. Organizational tables displayed new subdivisions for international law, civil matters and consular jurisdiction, constitutional and labor issues, taxation affairs, inheritance and private papers, and legalizations concerning foreigners in Germany.[41] The juristic complexities of the lengthy Versailles settlement and the need for favorable interpretations of its provisions

38. PA/AA, Politisches Archiv und Historisches Referat, Aktenzeichen 13, "Geschichte der Handelspolitischen Abteilung des A.A., 1885–1920," pp. 27–36 indicates that differentiation in job assignments increased from 1907 to the outbreak of the First World War.

39. Ibid., Politisches Archiv, "Geschäftsverteilungspläne," Band 1, passim. More will be said about the Ministry's involvement in commerce in Chapter Five.

40. Ibid., Politisches Archiv und Historisches Referat, Aktenzeichen 10, "Geschichte der Personalienabteilung," p. 2, indicates that in 1902 the Legal Department first created three separate subdivisions: *Volkerrecht, Staatsrecht,* and *bürgerliches Recht.*

41. Ibid., Politisches Archiv, "Geschäftsverteilungspläne," Band 1, 1920 and thereafter.

led to creation of a special *Friedensabteilung* (Peace Department),[42] and a separate offiice for *Abrüstung* (Disarmament) provided the administrative means to supervise all military articles.[43] These bureaus became so significant in diplomacy that one newspaper claimed "the activities of the Ministry have been influenced almost exclusively by lawyers," and even complained of diplomats being "supplanted by legal advisors."[44]

The scope of administrative activity increasingly encompassed greater varieties of human activity.[45] Agreements designed to facilitate cooperation in some of the more practical aspects of interstate relations assigned new responsibilities to bureaus charged with commercial and legal matters such as the department for *Schiffahrtwesen* (Maritime Affairs and International Conventions). In transportation and communication matters alone, diplomats and bureaucrats were responsible for knowing all international accords relating to postal services, telegraphs, marine cables, standardization of railway systems, airplane and automobile traffic, navigational aids, and signals. Other items included monetary and copyright agreements, opium smuggling, fishing privileges, mental health, hospitals, medical questions, and veterinary affairs.[46]

Innovations created to influence human attitudes further demonstrated this expansion into diverse areas by the Ministry for Foreign Affairs. In response to pressures imposed by new dimensions of international rivalry and the popular demand for news, changes at the Wilhelmstrasse—like those on the Quai d'Orsay—established permanent administrative mechanisms designed to shape and inform public opinion. A small one-man office expanded

42. Ibid., Abteilung IA, Deutschland 149, Band 30, note from Sell to Zentralbüro, 14 July 1919; and idem, Politisches Archiv, "Geschäftsverteilungspläne," Band 1, "Organisationplan" dated April 1919 and "Verzeichnis der Referate der Friedensabteilung" of 1919.

43. Robert Dockhorn, "The Wilhelmstrasse and the Search for a New Diplomatic Order, 1926–1930" (Madison: unpublished dissertation, 1972).

44. *Kölnische Volkszeitung*, 30 May 1921; also Herbert von Dirksen, *Moskau, Tokio, London: Erinnerungen und Betrachtungen* (Stuttgart: Kohlhammer, 1949), pp. 55–56.

45. PA/AA, Politisches Archiv, "Geschäftsverteilungspläne," Band 2, "Sacheinteilung der Registraturen der Landerabteilung," dated 1 April 1928.

46. Ibid., Politisches Archiv und Historisches Referat, Aktenzeichen 13, "Geschichte der Handelspolitischen Abteilung des A.A., 1885–1920," pp. 31–35; and idem, Politisches Archiv, "Geschäftsverteilungspläne," Band 1, 1920 and thereafter.

after the *Daily Telegraph* affair and was formally designated as a separate *Presse Abteilung* (Press Bureau) in 1915.[47] In the First World War its functions multiplied to massive proportions under the new *Nachrichtenabteilung* (Press and Information Division). After the war Schüler's reforms installed an even more elaborate *Vereinigte Presseabteilung der Reichsregierung* (Press and Information Service of the German Government) responsible for all public information activities around the world.[48]

Indeed, reaching the public in all parts of the globe through a variety of means now seemed to be a proper domain for propaganda activities directed by the Ministry. Recognizing the importance of popular support for policies at home and abroad and the propagandizing efforts of competitors—particularly the French—Schüler created the *Kultur Abteilung* (Cultural Division).[49] This new department, along with a separate *Schuld Referat* designed to handle questions of war guilt, was planned to influence public opinion. He mobilized many different resources to achieve this objective, and indicated that instruments of twentieth-century diplomacy would include art, music, literature, educational and medical facilities, tourism, films, and theatrical productions.[50]

To facilitate the operation of all these new departments in their expanded functions, further reforms and innovations instituted an increased number of technical services. The creation of a *Politisches Archiv* (Archives Department) with a reorganized and systematically catalogued *Bibliothek* (Library) provided written and published background material necessary for decision making.[51] In response to the introduction of extensive conference diplomacy and

47. Ibid., Politisches Archiv und Historisches Referat, Aktenzeichen 10, "Geschichte der Personalienabteilung," p. 3; and I. 8622/50106, *Verfügung* of 15 April 1915 from Jagow, in idem, Presse Abteilung, Beiakten I, Band 1.

48. A.N. 17411, *Verfügung* of 24 November 1919, in PA/AA, Presse Abteilung, Beiakten 1; and idem, Politisches Archiv, "Geschäftsverteilungspläne," Band 1, the "Geschäftsverteilung der Presse Abteilung der Reichsregierung" of 1919 and the various structural arrangements of the following years. See Chapter Six for a more detailed discussion.

49. I.A. 2482, *Verfügung* of 10 September 1920 from Schüler in PA/AA, Politisches Archiv, "Geschäftsverteilungspläne," Band 1.

50. See ibid., Abteilung IA, Deutschland 149, Band 30, A.N. 13649, note from Freytag, dated 29 August 1919.

51. Irmtraut Schmid, "Der Bestand des Auswärtigen Amts im Deutschen Zentralarchiv Potsdam, II. Teil: 1920–1945," *Archivmitteilungen*, Heft 4 (1962), p. 126n.

the decline of French as the language of negotiations, the new *Sprachendienst* (Translation Service) introduced more interpreters for multi-lingual transactions.[52] A *Kartographisches Büro* (Geographical Service) for worldwide cartographical information, a more sophisticated *Chiffierbüro* for secret ciphered messages ("brought to a state of efficiency which should exclude the possibility of any failures such as took place during the war"),[53] and a new *Etikette* section for protocol advice were established to give the Wilhelmstrasse as much practical assistance as possible.[54]

The creation of such specialized divisions provided the Ministry for Foreign Affairs with permanent institutional means to manage a large variety of specific problems. In the twentieth century, however, the complexities of many matters in international relations often defy rigid structural categorization. Innovative *geographical* and *functional* departments, although necessary for a division of labor, offer no guarantee of efficient performance. In fact, the proliferation of differentiated units and offices in any organization actually can increase the difficulties of coordinating these diverse efforts. To facilitate integration and minimize unnecessary delays, duplication, and competition requires that administrators use rational management techniques. With this feature of bureaucratic behavior in mind, therefore, those concerned about reforming the Ministry also instituted new procedures and *administrative* departments.

Traditionally the Wilhelmstrasse operated within the practice of each office working in isolation. One bureau knew little of the activities of another. Some described this arrangement as nothing short of "organized confusion,"[55] and attacked the Bismarckian system in which "cooperation with the secrecy-shrouded Department A did not exist."[56] As one insider recalled, "Rarely was this

52. Sasse, "Zur Geschichte des Auswärtigen Amts," Heft 7, p. 165. The employment of "outsiders" untrained in traditional diplomacy and French also necessitated the more frequent use of translators.

53. The words are those of Foreign Minister Simons, 24 January 1921, as cited in PRO/FO 371/6008, Despatch No. 156 from Kilmarnock (Berlin) to Foreign Secretary, 25 January 1921.

54. See PA/AA, Politisches Archiv, "Geschäftsverteilungspläne," Band 1, "Stand vom August 1923," Referat N.

55. *Berliner Tageblatt*, 6 October 1919.

56. Ibid., 27 December 1920.

Chinese Wall ever surmounted."[57] To remedy this condition and encourage interoffice communication, Schüler created daily ministerial conferences in which the Minister, his assistants, and the divisional directors would meet each morning to discuss problems and to share mutually relevant information concerning international issues. "This new arrangement of cooperation by officials in close personal contact," noted one contemporary observer, "is of indispensable importance to achieve common opinions and a unifying *esprit de corps.*"[58]

To achieve even greater cooperation and efficiency, further innovations changed some of the more mundane—yet basic—features of bureaucratic operations. Job descriptions of each individual's official responsibilities became explicit and detailed.[59] New instructions systematized coding arrangements, established classification schemes, and tightened internal security.[60] Greater standardization was introduced in working procedures, in the distribution of materials, and in the rapid circulation of carbon copies to interested colleagues.[61] A new administrative *Ministerial-Bürodirektor* (Office Director) managed logistical problems arising from these changes and kept all internal operations running smoothly.[62]

The application of technological inventions indicates another aspect of this search for bureaucratic efficiency. Handwritten notes in careful script, manually-lit oil lamps reeking "poisonous air" and

---

57. Ottmar von Mohl, as cited in ibid.

58. Wolgast, p. 55.

59. See, for example, PA/AA, Abteilung IA, Deutschland 149, Band 31, I. 37541, "Geschäftsverteilung der Abteilung I," dated 6 December 1919 and signed by Hermann Müller.

60. Some of the earliest appeared after the *Daily Telegraph* affair, as evidenced by I. 29687, *Verfügung* of 9 November 1908 by Kiderlen-Wächter in ibid., Abteilung IA, Deutschland 149, Band 12. Also see Nr. 301, *Verfügung* of 12 November 1919 by Schüler, in idem, Abteilung III, Geschäftsgang 1, Band 1.

61. I. 14056, *Verfügung* of 26 April 1918 from Bussche; Nr. 56, *Verfügung* of 11 February 1920 from Hermann Müller; and the "Geschäftsordnung für das Auswärtige Amt," dated 18 March 1920 from Schüler; all in ibid., Abteilung III, Geschäftsgang 1, Band 1; and I. G. 2331, an unsigned circular "An die Leiter sämtlicher Arbeitseinheiten und die Eingangsstelle," of 8 July 1921, in Presse Abteilung, Beiakten II, Band 1, among others.

62. See the listings in Germany, Reichsministerium des Innern, *Handbuch für das Deutsche Reich, 1922* (Berlin: Carl Heymanns Verlag, 1922), p. 58.

"evil gases,"[63] horse-drawn carriages, and slow-travelling despatches no longer were sufficient for the rapid pace of twentieth-
century diplomacy. The Ministry began to use electric lights and
automobiles,[64] typewriters and telephones,[65] telegraphs, the latest
teletype machines, and other "modern" office equipment.[66] Ambassadors who only a short time before had calculated correspondence time in terms of days and weeks now thought of hours and
minutes.[67] Telephonic communications occurred instantaneously.

The extensive use of such inventions, combined with the expansion of ministerial departments, soon necessitated considerable appropriations. An abrupt rise in expenditures indicates that those
internal circulars urging economizing among officials did so with
good reason.[68] Budgets that once reached only 7,227,490 marks in
1875, or 9,481,315 marks in 1890 disappeared with the nineteenth
century.[69] Expenses now seemed to expand with no restraint:[70]

1905	16,728,382	current value marks
1910	19,018,488	
1914	21,065,337	
1920	312,338,005	

These annual expenditures soon reached such heights that when

---

63. The words are those of Busch, 1, p. 429, describing the interior of the late
nineteenth-century Wilhelmstrasse.

64. Sasse, "Von Equipage und Automobilen des Auswärtigen Amts," pp.
147–48.

65. See PA/AA, Abteilung IA, Deutschland 122 Nr. 2, Band 2, A. 7418,
Despatch from Metternich (London) to Bülow, 19 April 1906 for an early example
of typewriters; and discussions about the use of the telephone in 1914 in idem,
Abteilung IA, Deutschland 149, Band 17.

66. Many examples of telegraphic communications are evident in ibid., Abteilung IA, Deutschland 149, Band 18 and thereafter; while discussions of the
Hughes-Apparat are available in ibid., Band 26 of the same series.

67. See the difference in time, for example, between Radolin's carried Despatch No. 373 from Paris on 9 April 1906 and his telegraphic message No. 161 dated
one month later in ibid., Abteilung IA, Frankreich 87, Band 85.

68. Among several examples, see I. A. 2074, note of 19 June 1921 from Rosen;
and I. G. 101, Hauszirkular of 27 March 1922, both in ibid., Abteilung III,
Geschäftsgang 1, Band 2.

69. Germany, RGB 1874 (Berlin: Decker, 1874), pp. 158, 170; and RGB 1890
(Berlin: Reichsdruckerei, 1890), pp. 28, 36.

70. These figures are based upon the sum of chapters 4, 5, 6, and 2 in the
Ministry's annual budget until 1919, although the year 1915 was unavailable in this

compared to the other large Foreign Ministries in the world, the appropriations for the Wilhelmstrasse represented both the greatest total amount and the highest percentage of any national budget.[71]

To administer these extensive financial operations and concomitant staff affairs more systematically, reforms abolished the former scattering of internal management functions and created the new, consolidated *Personal- und Verwaltungs Abteilung* (Personnel and Administrative Division).[72] This department's gradual growth changed to rapid acceleration. Specialized subdivisions administered accounts of budgets and payments, travel expenses, currency values, and the settlements of salaries and pensions. Other sections managed the physical buildings, technical machinery, ministerial procedures, and general organization.

The direction of this entire bureaucratic apparatus was placed in the hands of the new *Reichsminister des Auswärtigen* (Minister for Foreign Affairs). His position occupied the top rung of the organizational hierarchy and gave him ultimate responsibility for all policy decisions. In order that this burden did not become oppressive, particularly when combined with increasing international and domestic demands upon the Minister's time, reformers designed other administrative changes which included making the *Staatssekretär* (State Secretary) the highest-ranking civil servant in the Wilhelmstrasse and thus providing an equivalent to the Secretary General in the Quai d'Orsay. The innovative posts of *Ministerialdirektor* (Director) and *Ministerialdirigent* (Deputy Director) for the major divisions assured that they also would be guided by experienced diplomats and bureaucrats.[73] The rationale behind these developments was the desire to guarantee both competence in administration and stability in the midst of political vicissitudes.

---

particular archival series. In 1920 this scheme of chapters is replaced by another. The detailed budget data found in the archives for the years following 1922, however, increasingly becomes unintelligible due to the fact that uncontrolled inflation pushes expenses into the billions and makes officials change the printed figures from month to month. See PA/AA, Politisches Archiv, special series "Haushalt des Auswärtigen Amtes."

71. Norton, pp. 60–63, comparing the German Ministry for Foreign Affairs with those of France, Britain, Italy, and the United States.

72. See I. 37524/151488, *Verfügung* of 6 October 1918 from Matthieu, in PA/AA, Abteilung IA, Deutschland 149, Band 28; and idem, Politisches Archiv, "Geschäftsverteilungspläne," Band 1, passim, sections on *Abteilung I*.

73. Germany, Reichsministerium des Innern, *Handbuch für das Deutsche Reich 1922*, pp. 58–59.

CHART IV

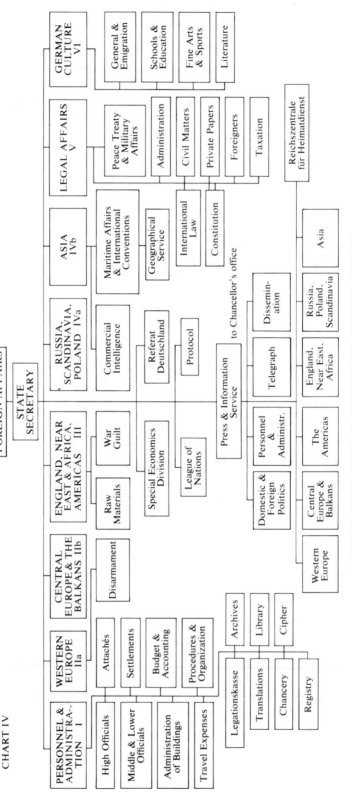

A REORGANIZED GERMAN MINISTRY FOR FOREIGN AFFAIRS:
RESULTS OF REFORMS AND INNOVATIONS, 1908–1923

"This whole reform plan has been carefully and ably thought out,"
announced one newspaper, "but of course everything new depends
upon the new men who are chosen."[74]

3. Personnel

The effectiveness of any administrative system cannot be judged
solely upon the symmetry, neatness, or logical arrangements of its
structural pattern. Vertical directions of command, lateral relationships of advice, prescribed working procedures, and office machinery are useless unless properly handled by qualified people of flesh
and blood. According to one authority on public administration, the
source of bureaucratic rationality, responsibility, competence, and
continuity lies not in its organizational design, but in its career civil
servants.[75]

Specific legal statutes and a long imperial tradition had governed
the personnel matters of *Reichsbeamten* (German public officials)
including those at the Ministry for Foreign Affairs.[76] These codes
and the profession of civil service were often considered as "outstanding characteristics" of the state itself.[77] Special positions
entailed specific duties, responsibilities, rights, and privileges.
Statutory regulations, for example, guaranteed selection, routine
promotion, salary levels, discipline procedures, and pensions. In an
appointment of career status, an official could anticipate lifetime
security except in cases of gross incompetence, incapacity, or mal-
feasance of duty.

Despite these advantages, however, many features of such traditional laws and practices came under increasingly severe criticism in
the twentieth century, with the rise of civil servant associations and
the growth of public interest in administrative personnel policies.[78]
Particularly after Germany's collapse and revolution, these groups

74. *Berliner Tageblatt*, 6 October 1919.
75. Morstein Marx, pp. 5, 34–53, 74.
76. The most important statute is the law of 31 March 1873, in Germany, *RGB
1873*, pp. 61–90.
77. Fritz Fleiner, *Institutionen des deutschen Verwaltungsrechts* (Tübingen:
Mohr, 1928 ed.), pp. 93–94.
78. See Adolf Grabowsky, *Die Reform des deutschen Beamtentums* (Gotha:
Perthes, 1917), among others.

applied vocal and organized pressure to bring about significant change.[79] The results included revisions in the general civil service law,[80] new constitutional provisions,[81] and other innovative statutes.[82] The republican Constitution, for example, now guaranteed the freedom of association and political opinion for public officials, the inviolability of "duly acquired rights" including salary and insurance benefits, access to personal record, opportunity to participate in legislative assemblies, and the abolition of discrimination against women in the civil service.

Even these provisions only provided guarantees of a general nature. The relegation of much appointive authority to individual ministries meant that they could autonomously determine the details of such policies as affected recruitment, entrance qualifications, examination procedures, and probationary training. According to one observer, "this legislation was so general in character that the Foreign Ministry was for all practical purposes left free to lay down such rules as it desired with regard to its personnel."[83] The abuses permitted by this subjective system, argued the critics, resulted in the higher Wilhelmstrasse posts being monopolized by a wealthy, monarchical, Protestant, aristocratic, class-conscious, inbred clique. Some called for an "iron broom" to sweep out these elements,[84] while Deputy Wels demanded the end of elitism and "the beginning of a new epoch" in staffing practices.[85] In this democratic spirit of Weimar, Brockdorff-Rantzau asserted:

> Besides the structural reforms of the organization, I have also begun a reform of the personnel policies of the Ministry for Foreign Affairs. . . . The choice of candidates for the highest positions will be

79. Albert Falkenberg, *Die deutsche Beamtenbewegung nach der Revolution* (Berlin: Verlag für Sozialwissenschaft, 1920).

80. "Reichsbeamtengesetz" of 18 May 1907, in Germany, *RGB 1907*, pp. 245–78.

81. The text of the Constitution is found in Germany, *RGB 1919*, pp. 1383–418. Particularly relevant are Articles 39 and 128–31.

82. See, for example, the "Personalabbauverordnung" of 27 October 1923, in Germany, *RGB 1923*, pp. 999–1010; and Heinz Sasse, "Die Entwicklung des gehobenen Auswärtigen Dienstes," *Nachrichtenblatt der Vereingung deutscher Auslandsbeamten*, 22. Jahrgang, 10 (1959), p. 202.

83. Frederich Schuman, "The Conduct of German Foreign Affairs," p. 197.

84. *Leipziger Volkszeitung*, "Solf geht. Wann folgen die andern?" 13 December 1918.

85. Wels, 26 July 1919, in Germany, Nationalversammlung, *SB*, 328, p. 1985.

based upon a broader foundation, and the custom of reserving these posts for a small, select circle now will be abolished.[86]

Essential to any organization in its recruitment of qualified persons is an effective selection process which places a premium upon professional merit rather than social or political status. In recognition of this fact, and in the long-standing German tradition of entrance requirements for civil servants, some of the first personnel reforms abolished the former prerequisite for a statement of financial worth and instituted an elaborate battery of more objective, specialized examinations and regulations.[87] Entrance into the Ministry's higher service now required that prospective candidates possess a university education, thorough competence in at least English and French, a certain amount of legal knowledge, and if possible, typing skills and the "practical business experience" necessary for twentieth-century diplomacy.[88]

New regulations also required that all applicants submit to a preliminary two-hour written examination and two twenty-minute tests of foreign languages. Success in this first hurdle then would lead to the official admission as *Anwärter* (candidates) and the beginning of a very lengthy probationary period. Like their French counterparts, potential diplomats and bureaucrats were required to work and learn within the Minstry for Foreign Affairs under the watchful eyes of experienced professionals. Upon completion of this training period and an extensive course which included experience with diplomatic archives, candidates would be eligible to take the comprehensive *Abschlussprüfung* (foreign service examination).

The final and severe series of tests, according to the new standardized regulations, was administered by a standing select committee composed of distinguished professors, prominent businessmen,

86. Brockdorff-Rantzau, 10 April 1919, in ibid., 327, p. 933.

87. *Norddeutsche Allgemeine Zeitung*, "Bestimmungen über den Eintritt in den diplomatischen Dienst," 1 May 1908, indicates the nature of the first reformed regulations of the twentieth century that established a solid foundation for the examination procedures described here.

88. This discussion is based upon the "Entwurf eines Gesetzes über den auswärtigen Dienst," "Prüfungsordnung für die diplomatisch-konsularische Abschluss-Prüfung," and the "Ordnung für den Ausbildungsgang der Anwärter für den auswärtigen Dienst," filed under December 1920–January 1921 in PA/AA, Büro des Reichsministers, Aktenzeichen 2, Band 1.

members of the Personnel Division, the Legal Advisor, State Secretary, and Foreign Minister himself.[89] Their supervision first extended to the difficult linquistic examination now consisting of three hours of written work plus an oral test for each language, with both English and French being obligatory. Candidates then prepared written answers, lengthy themes, and finally oral responses to detailed questions of diplomatic relations. The committee included among the requisite topics "modern" history and "contemporary" politics, social conditions, money and credit, accounting, financial systems, world trade and commerce, private and public legal transactions, and international law. The extremely high standards of this new testing procedure soon were described as "exacting" and "grilling,"[90] eventually reaching the point where one of the examiners doubted his own ability to pass and characterized the examination as "entirely too difficult."[91]

Such rigorous requirements sought to guarantee that the higher Wilhelmstrasse positions would be occupied by "only the very best"[92] or "first-rate, expertly-trained individuals."[93] "The old practice of placing officials carelessly," said Foreign Minister Simons, "led to a rather dilettante treatment of affairs. Now this is less admissible than ever before, because the demands made for a thorough knowledge . . . have become considerably greater than they used to be. Consequently, our officials must specialize."[94] He further suggested that this more competent management could be achieved by combining some of the *theoretical* aspects of administration and decision making at Berlin with the *practical* experience of overseas service in "an interchange of officials between the central Ministry and posts abroad."[95] As a result, the foremost

89. For an example of the men serving on this committee, see Anlage 1 of I.F. 124/25, note from Rathenau to "Die Herren Mitglieder des Prüfungsausschusses," dated 22 February 1922 in ibid., Büro des Reichministers, Aktenzeichen 2, Band 3.

90. Norton, pp. 33, 35.

91. Julius Curtius, *Sechs Jahre Minister der deutschen Republik* (Heidelberg: Winter, 1948), p. 148.

92. Graf Monts, in *Berliner Tageblatt*, "Unsere Diplomatie," 3 June 1917.

93. The words are those of Brockdorff-Rantzau, 10 April 1919, in Germany, Nationalversammlung, *SB*, 327, p. 933.

94. Simons, 24 January 1921, before the Hauptausschuss des Reichstags, as cited in *Deutsche Allgemeine Zeitung*, "Das Auswärtige Amt," 25 January 1921.

95. Ibid.

bureaucratic positions became filled with "men of long diplomatic experience and high diplomatic rank."[96]

Other innovations instituted by Schüler in attempting to raise professional standards included the recruitment of qualified personnel as "new blood" from other fields such as the Ministries of Finance and Justice, chambers of commerce, private industry, and business.[97] Higher salary scales for all personnel and even monetary compensation for attachés in probationary training reduced the need for independent wealth and attracted greater talent,[98] proving the accuracy of Brockdorff-Rantzau's statement that "today—and today more than ever before—one can secure good work only by good pay."[99] Advancements were carefully supervised by a collective board of Wilhelmstrasse officials emphasizing a policy in which "individual capacity and demonstrated fitness entirely supersede seniority as the basis of promotion"[100] Finally, the new Constitution assured administrative due process in any disciplinary actions and protected all tenure privileges.[101]

The importance of such standardized procedures increased with the expansion of personnel and the amount of work handled by the Ministry. Despatches, letters, packages, newspapers, and other printed matter flooded the Wilhelmstrasse. Items of correspondence for *Abteilung IA* alone had numbered 20,922 in 1900 and by 1918 reached 61,510.[102] Complaints of oppressive work loads were voiced publicly, and in response officials found it necessary to add more and more administrators, cipherers, librarians, stenographers,

96. Schuman, "The Conduct of German Foreign Affairs," p. 196. Also see Seabury, p. 16. By 1922, for example, all the officials occupying the central administration's important posts of *Ministerialdirektor*—Gneist, Mutius, Rümelin, Schubert, Maltzan, Knipping, Köpke, and Heilbron—had long experience in the foreign service.

97. See, for example, the document listing the former occupations of new officials as filed without number or signature under July–August 1921, in PA/AA, Büro des Reichsministers, Aktenzeichen 2, Band 2.

98. "Besoldungsgesetz" of 15 July 1909 in Germany, *RGB 1909*, pp. 573ff.; idem, 30 April 1920 in *RGB 1920*, pp. 805ff.; and the revisions of 26 October 1922 in idem, *RGB 1922*, pp. 811ff.

99. Brockdorff-Rantzau, 10 April 1919, in Germany, Nationalversammlung, *SB*, 327, p. 933.

100. Norton, p. 43, particularly referring to the higher grades.

101. See the previous discussion of the constitutional provisions regarding civil servants; and Kraus, pp. 219ff.

102. PA/AA, Politisches Archiv und Historisches Referat, Aktenzeichen 11, "Geschichte der Politischen Abteilung," Anlage 3, pp. 4–7.

typists, telephone operators, printers, and porters. A bureaucracy requiring only 179 staff members in 1907 grew by 1923 to a staff of nearly 600.[103] The size of ministerial departments swelled beyond the physical capacity of the original Wilhelmstrasse facilities and spread to supplementary offices located on other streets throughout Berlin.[104] A doorkeeper is quoted as commenting to one diplomat: "The German Reich keeps getting smaller and smaller, but the Foreign Ministry gets bigger and bigger!"[105]

Managing this enlarged staff and the expanded facilities became the responsibility of the new Personnel and Administrative Division. By uniting *all* personnel matters within this single administrative unit, Schüler—like his French counterparts—sought to abolish traditional organizational confusion and discriminatory distinctions among the various services.[106] Centralization eliminated the former arrangement under which "the three careers—diplomatic, consular, and ministerial—strictly were separated from each other."[107] Furthermore, the creation of an independent division and the establishment of collective boards to manage examinations and promotions reduced political intrigues to a minimum. Through such reforms and innovations in the central administration Schüler hoped to provide a more rational organization, to expedite operations, and to raise professional standards of competence.

4. Overseas Services

Structural and personnel changes in the Wilhelmstrasse were signs of a more comprehensive German response to twentieth-

103. Schifferdecker, p. 38; and "Haushalt des Auswärtigen Amts für das Rechnungsjahr 1923," in ibid., Politisches Archiv. This figure, however, was reduced temporarily in the wake of subsequent budgetary pressures. Also note the striking similarity of these figures with the number of personnel at the Quai d'Orsay as indicated in Section 3 of Chapter Three.

104. See PA/AA, Abteilung III, Geschäftsgang 1, Band 2, "Übersicht über die Unterbringung der einzelnen Abteilungen des Auswärtigen Amts," dated 1921, among other sources that indicate the addition of other addresses including Wilhelmstrasse 74, Mauerstrasse 66/67, Charlottenstrasse 50/51, Bunsenstrasse 2, Wilhelmplatz 8/9, and Nollendorfstrasse 21/21a.

105. As cited in Dirksen, p. 29.

106. See PA/AA, Politisches Archiv und Historisches Referat, Aktenzeichen 10, "Geschichte der Personalienabteilung."

107. *Berliner Tageblatt*, 27 December 1920.

century diplomacy. Schüler and others realized that centralized bureaucracy, however rationally organized and competently operated, cannot perform by itself all the multiple functions required to manage external relations. The crucial tasks of reporting, representation, negotiation, and protection of interests abroad must be handled by the overseas service. One legation secretary consequently declared that the reforms applied to the central administration in Berlin "must find expression in the organization of the foreign missions and services as well."[108]

Just as Schüler applied the principles of competency and specialization to the Ministry, so he now directed them toward the overseas services. In the past, many claimed, a preoccupation with social status had led to dilettantism and the exclusion of qualified persons from overseas service. "Our foreign representatives were much too exclusive," asserted critics, and too concerned with the nobility-wealth monopoly to develop the technical skills necessary for intricate diplomacy.[109] "This money and birth aristocracy naturally must be abolished," said Foreign Minister Hermann Müller, declaring: "The German Republic now must bring a group of new men into its foremost diplomatic posts. But that is not enough. Above all we also must assure—and this is almost more essential—that in the future the basis of selection is broadened."[110]

Reforms therefore were directed toward reducing the influence of family connections and assuring the use of talented personnel. The new Constitution stated that "all citizens without distinction are to be admitted to public offices in accordance with the provisions of the laws and in correspondence with their qualifications and accomplishments."[111] To guarantee such abilities for the higher foreign service positions, standardized entrance requirements demanded a university education, competitive preliminary tests, a lengthy probationary period under the supervision of professionals, and a difficult and comprehensive final examination.[112] Schüler

108. Tiemann, p. 36.

109. Dr. Löwe, "Die Reform des Auswärtigen Dienst," *Der Volksstaat*, Nr. 4 (25 January 1919), p. 34.

110. Hermann Müller, 23 October 1919, in Germany, Nationalversammlung, *SB*, 330, p. 3355.

111. Article 128, in Germany, *RGB 1919*, p. 1407.

112. These requirements and examinations are treated at greater length above in Section 3 of this chapter.

placed a premium upon ability above all other factors by emphasizing "practical" training in choosing candidates,[113] and by searching
personally for new foreign service officers with experience in business, banking, journalism, administration, and domestic politics.[114]

This more objective procedure of initial recruitment was followed
by financial reforms and innovations, for as Deputy Felix Waldstein
stated in debate: "The matter of personnel selection, essential to the
reorganization, is closely connected with the question of salaries."[115] In the past, low monetary compensation permitted only
those persons with considerable private means to embark on a
career in the foreign service, and this reinforced the traditional
social, political, and economic monopoly of the wealthy and well-
placed. Waldstein therefore advised: "Whoever would abolish the
former aristocratic and plutocratic character of our diplomatic representatives and foreign service must so establish the diplomats that
they can live not poverty-stricken, but on their official income."[116]

"The reform of the foreign service, as I said at the outset, will cost
money," declared Müller, but he asserted that "these financial
questions must be overcome."[117] Accordingly, the material incen-
tives and career security provided for bureaucrats in the Wilhelmstrasse were extended to their overseas service counterparts.[118]
Increases in standardized professional rank and salary scales also
included supplementary allowances for the cost of living at foreign
posts, size of family, and other expenses.[119] As civil servants, these
agents enjoyed new benefits provided by the Constitution, including
the inviolability of duly earned rights, pensions and provisions for

113. "Ordnung für den Ausbildungsgang der Anwärter für den auswärtigen
Dienst," in PA/AA, Büro des Reichsministers, Aktenzeichen 2, Band 1.

114. As evident by section "Auslandsbehörden" in the unnumbered, unsigned
document filed under July–August 1921 in ibid., Band 2; the "Besetzung der
diplomatischen Posten in Europa," dated 5 March 1923 in idem, Band 3 of the same
series; and Berliner Tageblatt, 27 December 1920.

115. Waldstein, 23 October 1919, in Germany, Nationalversammlung, SB, 330,
p. 3352.

116. Ibid.

117. Hermann Müller, 23 October 1919, in ibid., p. 3356.

118. See "Anregungen der Vereinigung der mittleren Auslandsbeamten zur
Personalreform des Auswärtigen Dienstes" of January 1919, as found in PA/AA,
Handakten des Unterstaatssekretär Töpffer, Aktenzeichen 13, Band 1.

119. See footnote 98 above; and Berliner Tageblatt, 6 October 1919. In the event
of transfer, officials would still retain their salary of rank.

dependents, and the guaranteed right to inspect their personal dossiers.[120] Hereafter, disciplinary penalties of suspension, pay reduction, or temporary retirement could result "only under the conditions and through forms prescribed by law."[121] A collective promotion and assignment board within the Ministry further sought to protect these rights and to encourage advancement by demonstrated professional ability and achievements rather than by seniority alone.[122] Such provisions provided security for individual careers and promoted a favorable *esprit de corps*.

Other changes attempted to resolve the fundamental problem of the distinction between the diplomatic and the consular corps. Different entrance requirements, segregated personnel management, and unequal "political" and "commercial" divisions had served to institutionalize discrimination and to keep these services "totally separated."[123] Such a separation bred hostility, retarded efficient administration at home and abroad, and often condemned highly qualified persons to second-rate careers. Coming from the consular corps himself, Schüler personally had experienced this discrimination and his determination to abolish the distinction between the services became so strong that people openly spoke of his *"furor consularis."*[124]

In order to eradicate these practices of the past and to meet demands of the future, Schüler abolished the individual administrative offices for each service and replaced them with a single Personnel Division responsible for all staffing affairs.[125] This was followed by a decree which included the following statement: "In connection with the reorganization of the foreign service, it is now resolved that diplomatic and consular affairs are merged into a unified career with the same conditions and the same training."[126]

120. Germany, *RGB 1919*, particularly pp. 1407–08. Such total coverage for all national *Beamter* under the Constitution precluded the need for a separate *statut de la carrière diplomatique et consulaire* as in France.

121. Article 129, in ibid., p. 1407.

122. Norton, p. 49; and Schuman, "The Conduct of German Foreign Affairs," p. 202.

123. Löwe, p. 34.

124. *Berliner Tageblatt*, 27 December 1920.

125. *Deutsche Allgemeine Zeitung*, "Veränderungen im Auswärtigen Amt," 11 December 1918.

126. I. 45672, *Verfügung* of 2 December 1918, signed by Solf, in PA/AA, Abteilung IA, Deutschland 149, Band 28.

Thus began a comprehensive unification of the services to correspond with the structural reorganization of the Ministry. The application of the same entrance requirements accompanied an equivalence of rank, salary, and qualifications for promotion.[127] This encouraged greater cooperation in common tasks, exchanges between career branches, and the movement of ability into useful positions. Many trained in consular work, for example, now entered high-level posts because they showed greater competence in managing complex commercial and financial aspects of foreign policy than did their diplomatic colleagues.[128] Such unification of the two services, in the judgment of one official, represented "the fundamental enactment of Schüler's entire reform."[129]

Further innovations instituted new technical advisors or attachés to assist these agents while abroad. Like their Berlin colleagues, overseas representatives found that they required expert help with the expanding volume and complexity of international affairs. Greater numbers of specialists therefore became attached to missions in foreign lands. Joining the military and naval advisors [130] were attachés for trade, finance, agriculture and forestry, and press affairs.[131] The Weimar Republic added still others by creating cultural, social, and labor attachés because—in the words of Müller—these issues "will play a great role in the future."[132]

In addition to the size of overseas staffs, the number of foreign missions was expanded as never before, leading French observers to describe the appearance of one German post after another as a

127. Norton, pp. 48–49; and Schuman, "The Conduct of German Foreign Affairs," p. 196.

128. See Ernst von Weizsäcker, *Erinnerungen* (München: List, 1950), p. 60; and Seabury, p. 174n.

129. PA/AA, Politisches Archiv, "Ministerialdirektor a. D. Schüler."

130. Article 179 of the Treaty of Versailles, as found in Germany, *RGB 1919*, pp. 934–35, temporarily prohibited the activity of military, naval, and air attachés abroad. Yet for an excellent treatment of their activity after the war, see Manfred Kehrig, *Die Wiedereinrichtung des deutschen militärischen Attachédienstes nach dem Ersten Weltkrieg (1919–1933)* (Boppard am Rhein: Boldt, 1966).

131. See PA/AA, Abteilung IA, Deutschland 122 Nr. 2, Band 3, Despatch No. 1266 from Metternich (London) to Bülow, 28 December 1908; Abschrift zu J. Nr. 2307/11, "Technische-diplomatische Vertretungen" of 1911, in idem, Band 5 of the same series; *Hannoverscher Courier*, "Presseattachés," 11 April 1909; and Wolgast, pp. 64–65.

132. Hermann Müller, 23 October 1919, in Germany, Nationalversammlung, *SB*, 330, p. 3356.

"remarkable development" proceeding at an incredibly "rapid progression."[133] In response to the demands imposed by international transactions, nearly fifty new foreign missions were created between 1900 and the outbreak of war in 1914.[134] That these posts should be established around the globe became evident after defeat, for, as one diplomat asserted: "Following this collapse, the continent of Europe is no longer to be regarded as the decisive factor in world politics and world economics."[135]

Wartime hardships and the temporary difficulty of reestablishing missions with former belligerents[136] also introduced changes in representation abroad. The new Constitution, in providing that "the direction of relations with foreign states is exclusively a function of the Reich," centralized authority within the Wilhelmstrasse and abolished the former anomaly of sending representatives from the separate German federal states.[137] The elimination of obsolete posts and the creation of new ones in widely diverse geographical areas ranging from the Soviet Union and Eastern Europe to Asia, Africa, and the Americas[138] further indicated that the overseas services—like the ministerial administration in Berlin—now might be able to cope more efficiently with twentieth-century diplomacy.

5. Relations with "the Outside"

Other reforms and innovations signalled that in this century, the German Ministry for Foreign Affairs no longer would be permitted

133. MAE/Chambre, Rapport No. 3318 (1914), 1, pp. 196–98; and idem, Rapport No. 4108 (1918), p. 5.

134. The *Etat* series in PA/AA, Politsches Archiv, indicates that the budget provided for 130 foreign missions in 1900 and for 176 in 1914.

135. Tiemann, p. 36.

136. For example, see the note dated January 1919 and labeled "Der Reichsregierung (Herrn Volksbeauftragten Ebert) vorzulegen," in PA/AA, Nächlasse Brockdorff-Rantzau, Aktenzeichen 14, Band 1; the "Projet de lettre au président de la délégation allemand," dated 25 July 1919, in PRO/FO 372/1248; and *Berliner Tageblatt*, 6 October 1919.

137. See Articles 6 and 78, in Germany, *RGB 1919*, pp. 1384, 1398. This also formally abolished the Prussian Ministry for Foreign Affairs. The federal states, however, could still maintain diplomatic relations with the Vatican, the Reich itself, and with each other. See Kurt Wahl, "Die deutschen Länder in der Aussenpolitik," *Tübinger Abhandlungen zum öffentlichen Recht*, 22 (1930), pp. 102ff.

138. See the *Etat* series in PA/AA, Politisches Archiv, particularly those annual budgets following 1920; and *Frankfurter Zeitung*, 8 October 1921; among others.

to operate within its traditional luxury of isolation from public scrutiny and negligible contact with "outsiders." Rising pressure from politicians, from business interests, from journalists, and from vocal members of the public at large demanded an end to the imperial arrangement of "an aristocratic collegium unapproachable to the ordinary mortal, like the table of the Holy Grail."[139] The bloodshed of the First World War swelled the ranks of these critics, while defeat and the collapse of the monarchy crushed much of the former resistance to change. According to Dr. Preuss, as architect of the new republican Constitution, it was time to eliminate the antiquated vestiges of secret diplomacy.[140]

Accordingly, the determined delegates at the Weimar National Assembly made particular efforts to assure that the Constitution would strengthen legislative power to influence external policy. They abolished the system under which the leading official of the Wilhelmstrasse existed merely as an administrative agent of the Chancellor and Kaiser. Specific constitutional provisions created a new Minister for Foreign Affairs who became not only responsible to the Reichstag, but even subject to dismissal by a vote of no confidence independent of the rest of the Cabinet.[141] As the first occupant of this position, Brockdorff-Rantzau clearly indicated that he understood the significance of such a change toward parliamentary democracy when he announced:

> Ladies and Gentlemen! The German Government has confirmed me in my office as Minister for Foreign Affairs. Accordingly, it is both my right and my duty to give you an account of the main principles with which I intend to direct the external policy of the state. The former government was not recognized unreservedly as being responsible in negotiations, for it lacked the confirmation of the will of the people. This deficiency is now removed. The will of the people has found expression in the democratic principle of majority rule. . . .

139. The words are those of Theodore Wolff, in *Berliner Tageblatt*, 6 October 1919. See Chapter Two above.

140. Dr. Preuss, 8 February 1919, in Germany, Nationalversammlung, *SB*, 326, p. 14, among other occasions.

141. Articles 50, 54, 56, in Germany, *RGB 1919*, pp. 1393–94.

I know that I shall be called to account. . . . I know that I shall hold my office only as long as you are satisfied.[142]

The same parliamentarians further broke with the past by restricting executive authority and by providing guarantees for their own participation in foreign affairs. Although the new President inherited many of the former powers of the Kaiser, including accreditation of ambassadors and command of the armed forces, his acts now required countersignature by the Chancellor and the Foreign Minister who were responsible to the legislature. Moreover, the Constitution explicitly stated that declarations of war, conclusions of peace, alliances, and treaties relating to subjects within the jurisdiction of the Reich hereafter would acquire validity only upon parliamentary consent.[143]

In addition, the delegates created the long-awaited special committee to deal with external policy. Building upon persistent efforts for reform during the war,[144] the Constitution instituted a new *Reichstagausschuss für auswärtige Angelegenheiten* (Reichstag Committee for Foreign Affairs) on a permanent basis. Explicit provisions guaranteed that it could deliberate when the rest of the legislature was not in session and even during the interval between a dissolution and the convocation of another Assembly. This committee also was given investigative rights permitting requests for information, the collection of evidence, and demands for the physical presence of the Chancellor or Foreign Minister in order to answer questions.[145] Further constitutional clauses required that the Reichsrat, or upper legislative house, and its corresponding committee also be kept informed of the conduct of external relations.[146]

The activity of these permanent mechanisms for legislative scrutiny of ministerial operations and policy soon demonstrated that these parliamentarians intended to exercise their newly-acquired

142. Brockdorff-Rantzau, 14 February 1919, in Germany, Nationalversammlung, *SB*, 326, p. 6.

143. Article 45, in Germany, *RGB 1919*, p. 1392. Also see the earlier law of 28 October 1918, in idem, *RGB 1918,* p. 1274.

144. Debates of 11 and 26 October and the Resolution of 27 October 1916, in Germany, Reichstag, *SB*, 308, pp. 1703–42, 1808–34, 1857.

145. Articles 33 and 35, in Germany, *RGB 1919*, pp. 1389–90.

146. Articles 65 and 67, in ibid., p. 1395.

rights. They asked questions, submitted interpellations, called upon the Minister for information, and debated matters of foreign affairs with unprecedented aggressiveness.[147] Committee members appeared at the Wilhelmstrasse itself to receive briefings from officials.[148] Enlarged appropriation powers and close examination of annual expenditures provided additional opportunities for legislative control. One observer wrote that with this change, the consideration of the Foreign Ministry's budget now proceeded "with the same meticulous attention to detail as in France."[149]

Like their French counterparts on the Quai d'Orsay, diplomats and bureaucrats of the Wilhelmstrasse realized that they had to respond to these "new times" of increased parliamentary inspection and participation. Accordingly, the Ministry arranged for drafting answers to questions, making official appearances, and instructing staff members to assist the legislative bodies "as much as possible."[150] A special bureau called *Parlamentarischer Untersuchungsausschuss* was created to deal with investigative commissions,[151] followed by a more permanent section of *Referat Deutschland (D)* (Office of German Affairs).[152] Its new duties included advising on the increasingly intimate interrelationship between foreign and domestic politics and serving as a liaison between the Wilhelmstrasse and the Reichstag, Reichsrat, legislative committees, and various political parties.[153]

147. See NA/DS, Index 811.03/113, Despatch No. 1457 from Schurman (Berlin) to Secretary of State, 31 August 1926, enclosure entitled "Report on the Legislative Control of Germany's Relations with Foreign Countries," based upon discussions with the Legal Division of the Wilhelmstrasse; and the various Reichstag foreign policy debates of the early 1920s.

148. As indicated in Despatch No. 85, "Secret," from D'Abernon (Berlin) to Foreign Secretary, 24 January 1922; and Report No. 940, "Secret," from the Secret Intelligence Service to Foreign Office, 30 October 1922, both in PRO/FO 371/7536.

149. Norton, p. 5.

150. A. 26524, instruction from Boyé to Abteilung A.N., 7 October 1919, in PA/AA, Presse Abteilung, Beiakten II, Band 1.

151. See ibid., Politisches Archiv, "Geschäftsverteilungspläne," Band 1, the unnumbered chart covering the period until June 1920.

152. I. A. 3201, *Verfügung* of 10 November 1920, from Simons, in ibid., Büro des Reichsministers, Aktenzeichen 2, Band 1; and the brief descriptions of "Sonderreferat D" in idem, Politisches Archiv, "Geschäftsverteilungspläne," Band 1.

153. The sordid activities of this section under the later Nazi period should not detract from its original purpose and its valuable service under the Weimar Republic.

From the perspective of parliamentarians, the immediate purpose of such contact with the Ministry was to provide knowledgeable information concerning foreign affairs. Many critics, starved for accurate facts after a wartime diet of propaganda, demanded that official materials be made available for authorized inspection.[154] Under pressure, therefore, personnel of the Wilhelmstrasse began to provide legislative investigating committees with heretofore secret diplomatic documents.[155] Gradually, they made more and more material available to an ever-larger group of people. As a result, boasted Müller, a "new spirit" could reign at the Ministry because "we have opened our archives."[156]

These demands for information, when coupled with the massive propaganda efforts of competitors, convinced many of the need for a permanent institutional means to inform and influence public opinion. Major innovations were necessary, argued various proposals, to expand the relatively small wartime Press Bureau into a more efficient and elaborate department.[157] In response, Schüler created the new and enlarged Press and Information Service under the joint responsibility of the Chancellor's office and the Ministry for Foreign Affairs. Placed in the hands of an official with the important rank of *Ministerialdirektor*, this division now began using publications, news releases, and press conferences in order to tell both foreign and domestic correspondents about Germany's external policies and internal affairs.[158]

Such mechanisms designed to provide contact between Wilhelmstrasse's diplomats and bureaucrats on the one hand, and legislators, journalists, and the general public on the other, increasingly indicated the expanding circle of "outsiders" with which the

154. Among many examples, see the *Kabinettsitzung* of 18 November 1918, in Germany, Volksbeauftragen, *Die Regierung der Volksbeauftragen*, 1, p. 102.

155. A. S. 2565, letter from Müller "An den Vorsitzenden des parlamentarischen Untersuchungsausschusses Herrn Abgeordneten Senator Dr. Petersen," 11 December 1919; and the note of 17 December 1919 from Mechler; both in PA/AA, Abteilung IA, Deutschland 149, Band 31.

156. Hermann Müller, 23 October 1919, in Germany, Nationalversammlung, *SB*, 330, p. 3357.

157. Among others, see "Reorganisationspläne," dated 15 April 1919 from Naumann (director of the Presseabteilung at that time), in PA/AA, Handakten des Unterstaatssekretär Töpffer, Aktenzeichen 13, Band 1.

158. See Chapter Six for more discussion.

Ministry had to deal. The once-secluded organization was transformed even more by maintaining regular communication with other Reich ministries, foreign countries, international bodies, and German commercial concerns on matters of external relations. By establishing a collective Cabinet, for example, the Weimar Constitution provided new opportunities for mutual discussions between the Foreign Minister and his cabinet-level colleagues.[159] Participation in multilateral commissions increased with the creation of such positions as the *Delegierter in den Stromkommissionen* for international rivers and the *Kommissars des Auswärtigen Amts für die Gemischten Schiedsgerichtshöfe* for mixed courts of arbitration.[160] The institution of *Sonderreferat Völkerbund* (Special Office for the League of Nations) gave the Wilhelmstrasse administrative means to manage affairs and maintain communications with this experiment in international organization.[161] Such innovations as financial attachés, foreign trade experts, commercial intelligence specialists, and the *Zweigstellen des Auswärtigen Amts für Aussenhandel* (Branch Offices of the Foreign Ministry for Foreign Trade) all indicated that officials henceforth would have many avenues of contact with German business interests.[162] Furthermore, innovators made sure that the Wilhelmstrasse's entrance examining committee now included men drawn from the outside ranks of manufacturers, exporters, bankers, and professors.[163]

*   *   *   *

When announcing the reasons for instituting reforms and innovations in the Wilhelmstrasse, Brockdorff-Rantzau spoke of the "disintegration of the old order" and of the indispensable need for

159. See PA/AA, Politisches Archiv, "Geschäftsverteilungspläne," Band 1, "Verteilung der sich aus der Durchführung des Friedensvertrags ergebenden Aufgaben."

160. Ibid., Politisches Archiv, "Geschäftsverteilungspläne," Band 1, "Zuständigkeit und Besetzung der Arbeitseinheiten des Auswärtigen Amts vom 1920," and "Stand vom August 1923."

161. Ibid., "Stand vom August 1923."

162. See Chapter Five.

163. See PA/AA, Büro des Reichsministers, Aktenzeichen 2, Band 3, I.F. 124/25, note from Rathenau to "Die Herren Mitglieder des Prüfungsausschusses" dated 22 February 1922.

"change" and "reconstruction."[164] He, Schüler, and other officials realized that many critics were correct in their claims that the rigorous demands of diplomacy in this century necessitated significant reorganization within the Ministry for Foreign Affairs. Responding to the pressures of both international and domestic politics, therefore, ministerial orders established new institutional means to administer German external relations more effectively.

Like the response of the French Quai d'Orsay, these changes reorganized the Ministry's central administration by unifying political and commercial matters, creating geographical divisions and technical experts, developing more elaborate administrative offices, applying modern managerial procedures, and introducing new equipment. Revised standards of recruitment, examination, payment, advancement, and discipline followed for personnel matters. Other actions unified the diplomatic and consular services, abolished antiquated posts abroad, and established new missions and specialized attachés in accordance with need rather than tradition. Additional innovations even created mechanisms to maintain permanent contact between the Wilhelmstrasse and the "outsiders" in parliament, in other ministries, in foreign governments, in international organizations, and in private business concerns.

Considering the difficulties of instituting bureaucratic change, these reforms and innovations represent a remarkable accomplishment. Observers almost immediately began to notice the contrast between the new and the old Ministry and to praise the achievements. Articles in the press and in official publications described them as "sound," "beneficial," and "practical" institutional responses to twentieth-century diplomacy.[165] "For the first time," said one former critic with satisfaction "the work of the Wilhelmstrasse now is carried out on the basis of a logically studied plan, and the advantages are enormous and unmistakable."[166]

---

164. Brockdorff-Rantzau, 10 April 1919, in Germany, Nationalversammlung, *SB*, 330, p. 933.

165. *Deutsche Allgemeine Zeitung*, 25 January 1921; *Frankfurter Zeitung*, 25 December 1920; and Report Nr. 862 from Finance Minister Wirth to the President of the Reichstag, "Organisationpläne der Reichsministerien," dated 8 November 1920, p. 3, in PA/AA, Büro des Reichsministers, Aktenzeichen 2, Band 1.

166. Theodor Wolff, in *Berliner Tageblatt*, 27 December 1920.

PART III

— 5 —

Diplomatic Pouches and Pocketbooks:
New and Expanded Responsibilities
for International Commerce

It is a matter of general knowledge that international relations in the twentieth century depend increasingly on commercial relations.

> –Vice Consul
> Joseph Pyke

Prior to the twentieth century, Ministries for Foreign Affairs had relatively little involvement with commercial matters. Although cooperation between government officials and business interests had a long tradition, overseas transactions always remained within restricted bounds. In part, this was due to the limited amount of foreign trade, to philosophical assumptions regarding the value of laissez-faire, and to the inability of businessmen to sufficiently pressure their governments for more protection or assistance. This condition also resulted from the attitude among professional diplomats that their time should be spent on solving the vastly more "important" political problems rather than mundane questions of "inferior" commercial matters. As a result, foreign ministries created administrative structures that reinforced these prejudices, assumed few responsibilities for commercial matters, employed staffs inexperienced with graphs or figures, and maintained little contact with the business world.[1] In the words of one diplomat: "The great flaw in the system was that economics had no place in it; the subject slightly alarmed a world still struggling against a predominance of prose."[2]

1. See Chapter One, Sections 2 and 3. Holstein, 1, p. 28, notes that "the safest place for a tactless person was in the Commercial Division."
2. Vansittart, p. 40.

The luxury of this traditional approach no longer could be maintained after 1900. Europe began to experience a period of bursting economic growth and of unparalleled expansion in foreign trade. This development, combined with the pressures arising from the First World War, led to demands by many business groups for active state support and demonstrated the increasing invasion of commercial affairs into diplomatic intercourse. The Quai d'Orsay and the Wilhelmstrasse thus were forced to break with past practices and to create elaborate institutional mechanisms designed to assume new and expanded responsibilities for international commerce.

1. The Expansion of International Commerce and Demands for Government Assistance

In the opinion of many European economic and business leaders, the best thing about the nineteenth century was its passing.[3] Particularly throughout the seventies, eighties, and early nineties, the national economies remained in a state of depression. Prices on manufactured goods declined, real wages fell, land values decreased, and investment rates remained low. Slumps continually blighted most hopes for economic advance and prosperity seemed impossible. In 1896, however, indicators suggested the gradual development of an encouraging new trend toward sustained growth.

With the new century, Europe was the center of a booming world economy. Advancing prices, increased investment, expanding production, rising wages, and full employment marked this as a time of remarkable economic progress. Karl Helfferich, Director of the *Deutsche Bank*, boasted of "intensified productivity," "increased efficiency," "the spirit of an impetuous forward impulse," and "a new beginning."[4] He and others maintained that this change resulted largely from the combined influence of a development in scientific techniques and rational organization for business and industry, the application of technological advances in physics and chemistry, a mobilization and concentration of capital, improvements in transportation and communication—and the remarkable

3. See Hale, p. 54.
4. Karl Helfferich, *Deutschlands Volkswohlstand, 1888–1913*, 7th ed. (Berlin: Stilke, 1917), pp. 4, 5, 10.

expansion of international commerce.[5]

The rise of prosperity increased foreign commercial transactions. Unprecedented production rates of manufactured goods in Europe required massive imports of raw materials like rubber, jute, cotton, mineral oils, tin, and copper from India, the Congo, Indonesia, and Latin America. Opportunities for profit abroad encouraged the growth of international cartels and shipping firms, and produced a dramatic rise in the flow of exports to expanding foreign markets. Increasing industrialization and rising population levels necessitated greater importation of foodstuffs. The use of the internal combustion engine and the conversion of modern navies from coal to oil demanded enlarged quantities of foreign petroleum from the Netherlands East Indies, the United States, and the Baku fields on the Caspian Sea. In addition, the generation of great wealth at home led to an extensive movement of investment capital overseas and the financing of railroads in the Balkans and Canada, factories in Russia, roads in Turkey, electrical companies in Argentina and Norway, mines in South Africa, port construction in Brazil, and businesses in the Far East and Africa.

Nations began to import and export to one another on a scale altogether unknown. Modern merchant marines, railroads, and transcontinental telegraph cables made nearly every location on the globe a potential market. Owing to the easy transfer and movement of the joint stock share, investors in one country became part owners in another nation's resources to an extraordinary degree. It is not surprising, therefore, that observers sensitive to these developments began to speak of global transactions, the interdependence of international trade, and the twentieth-century emergence of a *world* economy.[6]

5. Also see MAE/Chambre, Rapport No. 1230 (1908), p. 70; and PRO/FO 371/260, Despatch No. 238, "Confidential," from Lascelles (Berlin) to Grey, 24 May 1907.

6. J. H. Clapham, *The Economic Development of France and Germany, 1815–1914*, 4th ed. (Cambridge: Cambridge University Press, 1955), pp. 359, 362, 400–1; and Renouvin, pp. 136–43. The titles of new journals reflected this emergence of a world economy, as evident in Bernhard Harms, "Weltwirtschaft und Weltwirtschaftslehre," in *Weltwirtschaftliches Archiv*, 1 Band, Heft 1 (January 1913, pp. 1–36; the first publication in 1903 of *Les Annales diplomatiques et consulaires. Revue hebdomadaire d'expansion économique mondiale: propagande économique, politique extérieure, commerce international;* and the first publication in 1910 of *Weltwirtschaft: Zeitschrift für Weltwirtschaft und Weltverkehr.*

These new conditions led to closer ties between those managing foreign affairs and those responsible for particular business interests. Governments increasingly recognized that the distribution of goods and capital abroad might be utilized as an instrument of diplomacy. Investment could buy friendships or build and solidify alliances, while monies withheld or economic reprisals could coerce opponents into making certain diplomatic concessions. Financial penetration could facilitate political hegemony in developing countries. Commercial advantages offered to foreign suppliers of strategic raw materials could strengthen security. Moreover, profits from overseas markets could contribute to national wealth and perhaps increase international prestige.[7]

Many diplomats, however, watched this rising importance of economics in international relations with uncertainty. Some feared that finance might "dominate diplomacy,"[8] while others noted that it seemed as though "every financier considers himself a born Secretary of State for Foreign Affairs."[9] Kiderlen-Wächter informed Reichstag deputies that in this century commercial matters and external politics would become increasingly "interlocked."[10] Foreigners observed that due to growing involvement abroad, "the banks resembled embassies."[11] This change seemed to be symbolized by one French professor who, in passing the huge *Crédit Lyonnais*, warned his young friends in the diplomatic corps: "Look, *Messieurs*, for here is the real Ministry for Foreign Affairs."[12]

Large numbers of businessmen and investors welcomed a more intimate interaction with foreign policy decision makers. Government officials, in their opinion, might prove very useful in sustaining economic prosperity and in promoting commercial expansion. Diplomatic and consular agents, for example, could acquire overseas

7. MAE/Chambre, Rapport No. 2661 (1906), p. 2; and Herbert Feis, *Europe, the World's Banker, 1870–1914: An Account of European Foreign Investment and the Connection of World Finance with Diplomacy before the War* (New Haven: Yale University Press, 1930).

8. Paléologue, *Un grand tournant*, p. 398.

9. Note by William Tyrell filed immediately following C 13484/725/18 in PRO/FO 371/7538, referring specifically to Stinnes in Germany and Lord Beaverbrook in England.

10. Kiderlen-Wächter, 11 November 1908, in Germany, Reichstag, *SB*, 233, p. 5433.

11. Feis, p. 47.

12. Saint-Aulaire, *Confession*, p. 30.

markets, spheres of influence, or trade concessions. They could help secure orders for exports, offer protection against hazardous investments, aid branch offices and subsidiaries located abroad, and procure greater representation on the directing boards of foreign firms. Official backing could regulate tariff policy against competitors and lend assistance in guaranteeing the uninterrupted flow of goods across the oceans.

Such ideas of active governmental support and protection gained support within the business communities of France and Germany, among others. After the strain of the Great Depression of 1873–1896, proponents of laissez-faire capitalism were less dogmatic and less enthusiastic than formerly. Those deeply involved in foreign trade and investment increasingly asked the state to assume the role of their defender. They alternately pleaded softly and demanded vociferously that the Ministries for Foreign Affairs venture upon new and expanded resposibilities for international commerce.

Although businessmen did not always speak with a single voice, these pleas for state protection were heard around the world as commercial interests in many countries turned to their respective governments for assistance. Demands poured into the Foreign Office in London calling for effective steps to safeguard trade abroad[13] and complaining that British officials demonstrated "less energy and activity than those of Germany and France."[14] A Conference of the Association of Chambers of Commerce urged immediate action and encouraged the Chancellor of the Exchequer to announce before its delegates: "We are prepared . . . to give the assistance of the Government to the development of foreign trade in order to ensure that those rivals who are now our bitter enemies shall not have the control of foreign trade which they have enjoyed in the past."[15] As one journal noted, "Chambers of Commerce have passed resolutions on the subject, business men have written letters to newspapers, and individual sufferers have been loud in proclaiming their grievances."[16]

---

13. Among many examples, see PRO/FO 369/970 and PRO/FO 369/971.
14. Steiner, p. 168.
15. Mr. McKenna, as cited in *The Times*, "State Aid for Traders," 1 March 1916.
16. "A Plea for Cinderella," *United Empire*, 8, 5 (May 1917), p. 312.

In America the Department of State came under similar pressure. The President of the National Association of Manufacturers told the Convention for the Extension of Foreign Commerce that, due to the new extent of business transactions overseas, the active participation of federal authorities must be expanded and applied "to all countries and all important products which we sell."[17] His counterpart in the prestigious Chamber of Commerce of the United States later echoed this theme by declaring that "the increased importance of international relationships . . . makes it necessary for the United States Government to follow foreign affairs more closely in all sections of the world" and to promote and protect "our commercial interests."[18] Before the hearings on the proposed reform of the American foreign service, one consul general bluntly asserted:

> Mr. Chairman, this bill is a business bill. Its outstanding purpose is to protect, encourage and assist our commercial and other business relations abroad, which are so intimately intertwined with our political relations as to be practically inseparable.[19]

Indeed, it was precisely this difficulty of maintaining the strict traditional distinction between "political" and "commercial" affairs that presented one of the fundamental reasons for reforming the antiquated administrative structures of the Quai d'Orsay and Wilhelmstrasse.[20] French and German businessmen provided the first spearhead of this larger movement calling for massive protection and assistance from their Ministries for Foreign Affairs. Trade associations, chambers of commerce, industrial groups, shipping firms, consular agents, and private citizens loudly expressed dissatisfaction over governmental neglect of their international business interests. With the beginning of the twentieth century, they argued, it became imperative to obtain active and aggressive state

17. James W. Van Cleave, "What America Must Do to Make an Export Business," *The Annals of the American Academy of Political and Social Science,* 29, 3 (May 1907), p. 32.

18. Julius H. Barnes, in a letter of 23 December 1922 to Representative John Rogers, as reproduced in U.S. Congress, House of Representatives, Committee on Foreign Affairs, Document No. 24470, p. 98.

19. Robert Skinner, in ibid., p. 76.

20. See above, Chapter Two, Sections 2 and 3; Chapter Three, Section 2; and Chapter Four Section 2.

support for securing markets, safeguarding investments, and promoting trade overseas. The accomplishment of these tasks would require employing qualified specialists and terminating "honorary" consuls, creating new departments and commercial attachés, developing closer relations with businessmen and other ministries, providing economic training for diplomats, expanding consular representation, and assuring that reports on conditions of international commerce be transmitted immediately to the business community.[21] "The role of universal protector must fall on the Ministry for Foreign Affairs and its officials," stated one report, but noted that without expanded responsibilities the existing programs would remain "insufficient to respond to the needs of our times."[22]

During the First World War these pleas for state protection multiplied. Lengthy conflict resulted in economic disruptions, scarcities, and regulations. Political and military leaders began to realize how much modern warfare had become a function of industrial and financial capacity, and consequently imposed comprehensive programs regulating prices, resource allocation, production schedules, distribution, consumption, and forms of mixed public and private management. Because of these forced sacrifices, many businessmen felt justified in insisting anew on governmental assistance. In France, for instance, *Le Petit Havre* urged an intelligent response to changed conditions and a "united front " for "tomorrow's economic struggle," asserting that "the war has created new requirements and concerns, and has necessitated urgent reforms, even for the most venerable institutions."[23] *Le Figaro* called upon the Quai d'Orsay to mobilize "modern men," "scientific organization," and a "rational utilization of specialization" to promote foreign trade.[24] One group of parliamentarians claimed that economic rivalries now were rising to the forefront of international politics and declared: "At the very least the State must suppress

21. Among many pre-war examples, see MAE/Chambre, Rapport No. 333 (1907), pp. 206–11, summarizing the complaints for specific chambers of commerce; idem, Rapport No. 2749 (1910), p. 47; PA/AA, Abteilung IA, Deutschland 122 Nr. 2 *secr.*, Band 1, A.S. 1752, *Denkschrift* from Dernburg to Stemrich, 26 November 1908; Deutschland 122 nr. 2, Band 3; Gustav Stresemann, 15 March 1910, in Germany, Reichstag, *SB*, 260, pp. 2133–40; and *Deutsche Marke*, 5 January 1913.

22. France/Chambre, Rapport No. 2661 (1906), pp. 4, 194.

23. *Le Petit Havre*, "Nos Consulats," 20 July 1916.

24. *Le Figaro*, "La Réforme des Consulats," 1 July 1916.

anything that would hinder the development of our foreign commerce and must adapt existing organizations to these new circumstances."[25]

Similar wartime demands for state support bombarded the German government. The *Hamburger Denkschrift* represented only one among hundreds of explicit statements insisting that foreign trade should be the prime objective of world politics and that the Wilhelmstrasse therefore should assume major new responsibilities for promoting international commerce.[26] The *Frankfurter Zeitung* warned that without immediate reforms or innovations "a national disaster" would ensue, and asserted that since "extraordinarily large amounts of money" were at stake, "all our resources should be placed at the disposal of our overseas trade."[27] In a memorandum to the Imperial Chancellor, the Chambers of Commerce from Bremen, Hamburg, and Lübeck proclaimed:

> Because all policy is to a large extent economic policy, one of the principal means of furthering German foreign interests must lie in the activities of our diplomats and consuls in the economic sphere, whether in warding off foreign attacks or in assisting in the capture of new markets. The whole export trade is together in the conviction that the reconquest of our former position in the world market will be possible only if all our forces coalesce toward this end and if the Government and trading interests work together in close and constant cooperation.[28]

These insistent cries sounded with even greater force during the harsh postwar period when the complex economic clauses of the peace treaties, massive balance of payments deficits, disruptions in

25. France, Chambre, Rapport No. 2234, "Proposition," p. 2.

26. PA/AA, *Hamburger Denkschrift,* passim. Also see idem, Abteilung IA, Deutschland 122 Nr. 2, Band 5, A. 40292, letter of 29 November 1917 from one hundred prominent merchants, bankers, and shippers to Bethmann Hollweg.

27. *Frankfurter Zeitung,* "Die Förderung unseres Aussenhandels," 17 June 1917.

28. The joint memorandum submitted to Chancellor Hertling from the Bremen, Hamburg, and Lübeck Chambers of Commerce in June, 1918, as cited in Despatch No. D/3391 from the War Intelligence Department to the Foreign Office, 31 August 1918, in PRO/FO 371/3481. Also see Max M. Warburg, "Betr. Amtliche Vertretung Deutschlands im Auslande," "Geheim", in PA/AA, Handakten des Unterstaatssekretär Töpffer, Aktenzeichen 13, Beilage.

supplies, loss of foreign markets and investments, and mounting inflation presented innumerable problems to those involved in international commerce. The Quai d'Orsay must assume new responsibilities in these commercial matters in order to advance material prosperity, announced Senator Hubert, "for now more than ever before, France needs to demonstrate her strength and vitality to the world."[29] Representatives of the Ministry for Foreign Affairs must realize that their task "consists more and more of directing, informing, guiding, protecting, supervising, and representing the overseas enterprises of our merchants, financiers, and industrialists," stated Deputy Noblemaire.[30] "Our diplomats still do not understand," he claimed, "that today Politics and Economics are twin sisters and have complete equality."[31] Requests poured into the Wilhelmstrasse urging the immediate expansion of efforts and mobilization of means to assist German commercial interests. To compete adequately with foreign rivals, they asserted, required that diplomats and businessmen learn to work "hand in hand."[32]

The urgency for diplomatic institutions to take greater responsibility for international commerce was heightened by the activities of rival states. During and after the war commercial competition reached new levels of intensity. It became commonplace to hear bitter French and German rivals speak of each other and their mutual struggle in terms of "business enemies," "financial weapons," "commercial battles," "captured markets," and "economic war."[33] The activities of one encouraged similar responses in degree and kind from the other. Those making demands upon the

29. MAE/Sénat, Rapport No. 145 (1921), p. 2. Also see LaRoche, p. 112.

30. MAE/Chambre, Rapport No. 802 (1920), p. 9.

31. Ibid., Rapport No. 2020 (1921), p. 73. Also see idem, Rapport No. 3131 (1922), pp. 11ff.; and idem, Rapport No. 6339 (1919), pp. 79, 103; and MAE/Sénat, Rapport No. 818 (1922), p. 248.

32. *Berliner Börsenzeitung*, "Förderung des Aussenhandels," 27 January 1919; *Berliner Tageblatt*, "Eine Kundgebung des Deutschen Wirtschaftskongresses," 30 January 1919; and *Zollwarte:Zeitschrift des preussischen Landesverbandes und des Bundes deutscher technischer Zoll- und Steurbeamten*, 14. Jahrgang, Nr. 11/12 (10 June 1919); all filed in PA/AA, Handakten des Unterstaatssekretär Töpffer, Aktenzeichen 13, Band 1.

33. See *Le Figaro*, "La Réforme des Consulats," 1 July 1916; MAE/Chambre, Rapport No. 4108 (1918), p. 14; idem, Rapport No. 802 (1920), p. 9; *Frankfurter Zeitung*, "Die Förderung unseres Aussenhandels," 17 June 1917; and PA/AA, *Hamburger Denkschrift; Die Hamburger Warte*, "Das Neue Auswärtige Amt," 9 August 1919.

Ministry for Foreign Affairs in Paris constantly pointed to the support given to their German rivals by the Wilhelmstrasse,[34] while those seeking changes in Berlin bolstered their own arguments by drawing attention to the ever-closer relationship between their French competitors and the Quai d'Orsay.[35]

2. Commerce and the Quai d'Orsay

The pressure applied by commercial interests, said Philippe Berthelot, constituted one of the primary reasons for instituting reforms and innovations in the French Ministry for Foreign Affairs. Businessmen were correct in their claims that the "new necessities" of twentieth-century diplomacy required more involvement in the details of international trade. The Reform Commission agreed that "political and commercial questions have become fused," and noted that "in all countries commerce and politics now are equal and in constant interaction with each other." As a consequence, observed Berthelot, it would be not only logical, but necessary, "to respond to the unanimous wishes of the chambers of commerce, industrialists, and businessmen."[36]

In recognition of these external demands and the impossibility of maintaining a strict separation between "political" and "commercial" affairs, the first reforming decree established a unified *Direction des affaires politiques et commerciales*.[37] Under this department, as previously described,[38] these heretofore separated matters would be treated together in an effort to guarantee greater consistency in policy management. The task of providing specialized

34. AN, Ministère du Commerce et de l'Industrie, Carton F^{12} 9302, "Enquête sur l'activité industrielle et la propagande commerciale des allemands dans les pays étrangèrs, 1919–1922"; Ministère de l'Intérieur, Direction des Renseignements, Folder No. 34, "Confidentiel," dated 13 April 1921 from MAE to Minister of the Interior, in Carton F^7 13.424; *Le Petit Havre*, "Nos Consulats," 20 July 1916; and France, Chambre, Rapport No. 2234, "Proposition," p. 17.

35. PA/AA, Abteilung IA, Frankreich 87 series and Frankreich 108 series, passim; the lengthy letter of von Schwabach to Töpffer, 23 January 1919, in idem, Handakten des Unterstaatssekretär Töpffer, Aktenzeichen 13, Band 1; and Theodore Schuhart, *Die deutsche Aussenhandelsförderung* (Berlin: Simon, 1918).

36. Berthelot, "Commission des réformes administratives," pp. 3269–70.

37. Decree of 29 April 1907, in France, *JO*, 3 May 1907, p. 3268.

38. See Chapter Three, Section 2.

assistance was assigned to the new position of *Conseiller commercial et financier*, whose responsibilities included advising all geographical bureaus on the economic consequences of policy, preparing treaties of commerce, observing international financial fluctuations, and collecting reports on foreign market conditions. In creating this post, Berthelot and Stephen Pichon emphasized that the performance of such duties required a "technical expert" possessing the ability to conduct dealings with "French financial and industrial associations that operate in the diverse parts of the world with the support of the Ministry for Foreign Affairs."[39]

The Quai d'Orsay continued to assume additional responsibilities for international commerce during and after the First World War. A *Bureau des services économiques* (Bureau of Economic Services) and a *Bureau des études financières* (Bureau of Financial Studies) were instituted to assist with those immediate problems resulting from the war's massive confusion and disruption.[40] The size of the task soon proved so great that innovators merged these bureaus into two new units: the *Office des biens et intérêts privés* (Office of Personal Property) designed to deal with private interests in former enemy territories,[41] and the *Sous-direction des relations commerciales* (Subdivision of Commercial Relations). The latter's assignment included responsibility for "the flow of exports and imports; accords and conventions with foreign countries; and the resumption, reorganization, and the development of the commercial relations of France."[42]

These administrative offices enabled the Ministry for Foreign Affairs to take a more active role in promoting French commercial interests overseas. Studies were made of means to develop trade relations, of ministerial representation on financial commissions, and of predicting economic conditions for the future.[43] Businessmen were provided with "up-to-date information" through published

39. Berthelot, "Commission des réformes administratives," p. 3271; and France, *JO*, 3 May 1907, p. 3268.

40. Decree of 23 July 1918, in France, *JO*, 31 July 1918, p. 6643. Also see MAE/Chambre, Rapport No. 2020 (1921), pp. 58–60.

41. Decree of 4 March 1920, in France, *JO*, 9 March 1920, p. 3878.

42. Decree of 1 May 1919, in France, *JO*, 4 May 1919, p. 4599.

43. MAE, Comptabilité, "Décrets et décisions ministérielles," Carton 69, Decree of 18 May 1916; Decree of 22 April 1915, in France, *JO*, 29 April 1915, p. 2698; and MAE/Chambre, Rapport No. 4108 (1918), p. 12n, among others.

reports or articles on overseas markets, on foreign resources, on investment opportunities, and on tariff policies.[44] Early in this activity observers expressed pleasure at the Quai d'Orsay's support during "long and delicate negotiations" to obtain foreign contracts.[45] Pichon announced that his Ministry now acted "so that our commerce and industry are enabled to profit as much as possible," and claimed that "thanks to the intervention of the Ministry for Foreign Affairs, in accord with the Ministries of Commerce and Finance, we have been able to secure important orders from abroad."[46]

This cooperation between the Quai d'Orsay and other government agencies in matters of international commerce consciously became closer and more frequent than ever before. Reformers realized that the complexity of foreign trade required the mobilization of as much expertise as possible, and therefore urged greater attempts toward mutual consultation and the sharing of information among interested ministries.[47] Attention centered upon establishing more permanent ties between the Ministries for Foreign Affairs and Commerce, for as Senator Dupuy reminded Pichon: "The Minister of Commerce is there to aid you, inform you, and furnish you with his advice."[48]

Evidence of this increased collaboration between the Quai d'Orsay and the Ministry of Commerce became apparent with their respective roles in the creation, enlargement, and operation of the new *Office national du Commerce extérieur* (National Office of External Commerce). Together they signed legislation charging this special organization with "furnishing French industrialists and merchants, either by reports, general publicity or any other means, with commercial intelligence of every kind capable of developing

44. "Rapports commerciaux des agents diplomatiques et consulaires de France," printed as supplements to the *Moniteur officiel du Commerce;* France, Chambre, Rapport No. 2234, "Proposition," p. 4; MAE/Chambre, Rapport No. 3131 (1922), p. 194.

45. Feis, p. 128.

46. Pichon, 13 January 1911, in France, Chambre, *DP,* p. 90.

47. Archival material, for example, shows an increase in the amount of information shared between the Quai d'Orsay, the Ministère du Commerce, the Office national du commerce extérieur, the Etat-Major de l'Armée—Section économique, and the Etat-Major de la Marine. See AN, Ministère du Commerce et de l'Industrie, Carton F12 7955, "Informations économiques provenant de diverses sources."

48. Charles Dupuy, 15 January 1907, in France, Sénat, *DP,* p. 90.

overseas commerce and extending trade outlets in foreign countries."[49] To accomplish such an assignment, agents gathered and centralized data on opportunities in external markets, customs regulations, import and export statistics, transportation carriers and costs, procurement of raw materials, contract law and foreign litigation, consular services, and new industrial processes and methods employed by competitors of other countries. A large central office in Paris and various regional bureaus throughout France distributed this information by means of publications, private correspondence, consultations, meetings, and comprehensive collections of library resources on the latest details of international commerce.[50] The program so impressed one American consular official that he described it as "complete and ambitious," and asserted: "In fact, the task to which the National Office of External Commerce has set itself may be said to include the application of every conceivable means for the promotion and extension of foreign trade and commerce."[51]

In establishing the *Comité consultatif du Commerce extérieur* (Consultative Committee of External Commerce) innovators drew upon a variety of governmental agencies and specialists "to study and examine all questions concerning international commerce."[52] Besides representatives from the Ministry for Foreign Affairs, delegates on this committee came from Commerce, Finance, Colonies, Agriculture, and Public Instruction. The list included

49. *Loi* of 25 August 1919 signed by Pichon, Clémental, and Klotz, in France, *JO*, 27 August 1919, p. 9170. Also see France, Ministère du Commerce et de l'Industrie, *Loi et Décrets relatifs à l'Office national du commerce extérieur* (Paris: Imprimerie nationale, 1920); Decree of 27 April 1921, in France, *JO*, 28 April 1921, pp. 5101-2; MAE/Chambre, Rapport No. 333 (1907), pp. 211-12; and Legendre, p. 380, noting that the creation of this office in 1898 signalled the beginning of a dynamic new phase in the history of these administrative institutions involved in foreign commerce.

50. AN, Ministère du Commerce et de l'Industrie, Carton F^{12} 9288, "Office national du commerce extérieur;" various issues of *Moniteur officiel du Commerce et de l'Industrie,* "Rapports commerciaux des agents diplomatiques et consulaires de France," and "Dossiers commerciaux."

51. Report of 3 February 1921 by Consul Clement Edwards, entitled "Changes Made Since 1914 in the Organization of the French Diplomatic and Consular Services, Foreign Office and Coordinating Ministries, Especially Relating to Foreign Trade," pp. 23, 26, enclosed in Despatch of 11 February 1921 from Thackera (Paris) to Secretary of State, NA/DS, Index 851.021/2 [hereafter cited as Edwards, "Changes Made," NA/DS, Index 851.021/2].

52. France, *JO*, 30 October 1919, p. 12126.

senators, deputies, economists, and the Directors of the National Office of External Commerce, and the National Bank of External Commerce.[53] The creation of such institutional mechanisms, noted foreign observers, permitted the Quai d'Orsay and other official organizations to achieve a new cooperation and "team work" in advancing French commercial interests overseas.[54]

Reformers of the Ministry for Foreign Affairs also applied this principle of ministerial cooperation to matters regarding those representatives of France assisting businessmen abroad. In addition to the newly-elevated status, increased salaries, guaranteed security, and strengthened posts in the consular service,[55] further innovations created means for increased contact between these agents and other governmental administrations. Decrees conferred upon the Ministry of Commerce the right to advise on matters of French overseas representation and to correspond directly with consuls on "all questions having an economic character."[56] Moreover, the Ministries for Foreign Affairs and Commerce were given *joint* responsibility for nominations, entrance requirements, and examinations for the foreign service—conditions that, in the words of one proposal, would stress "a strong preparation in practical commerce" and emphasize "commercial, industrial, and technical abilities."[57]

Further collaborative efforts between these two ministries resulted as they managed still other innovations designed to support businessmen in the field: *attachés commerciaux* and *agents commerciaux*. These officials attempted to satisfy that long-standing desire to have "agents specially charged with researching commercial questions and entering into direct relations with French producers."[58] They represented, in the words of Foreign Minister Jean Cruppi, "a type of economic missionary."[59] Stationed in foreign

---

53. Decree of 28 October 1919, in ibid., 30 October 1919, pp. 12126–27.

54. Among others, see Edwards, "Changes Made," pp. 7ff., NA/DS, Index 851.021/2; and the Report enclosed in Despatch No. 445 from John Simons (Paris) to Secretary of State, 24 April 1925, p. 12, in Index 851.021/14.

55. See Chapter Three, Section 4.

56. *Le Temps*, "La Réorganisation du Ministère du Commerce," 1 November 1906; MAE/Chambre, Rapport No. 1230 (1908), 2, p. 79; idem, Rapport No. 1237 (1912), pp. 99–100; idem, Rapport No. 4108 (1918), p. 15; and idem, Rapport No. 3131 (1922), p. 12.

57. France, Chambre, Rapport No. 2234, "Proposition," pp. 13–14.

58. MAE/Chambre, Rapport No. 333 (1907), p. 214.

59. Jean Cruppi, as cited in Legendre, p. 380.

countries and under the supervision of the diplomatic chief of mission, the commercial attachés were responsible for "the investigation and treatment of all economic questions."[60] This involved conducting studies on local customs, sale and delivery conditions, transportation facilities, raw materials and the activities of competitors, seeking out new markets and opportunities for investment, and lending "all possible assistance" to chambers of commerce and other business organizations.[61] In these tasks the attachés were aided by special commercial agents who also reflected the change from limited to extensive government support as they became charged with actively "studying, protecting, and expanding French commercial interests abroad."[62]

3. Commerce and the Wilhelmstrasse

The steady influence exerted by dissatisfied business groups, Schüler's own determined interest in international commerce, and the desperate need to restore trade after the First World War all combined to force major changes within the German Ministry for Foreign Affairs as well. Brockdorff-Rantzau and others began to realize that in this century, diplomacy increasingly involved "an interaction between foreign trade, international economics and high politics."[63] They no longer could ignore the fact that the critics demanding reforms, innovations, and "a new, free, and practical spirit in the old halls of the Wilhelmstrasse" now "accurately represented the broad mass of commercial interests."[64]

In response to such pressures. Schüler initiated the "most significant feature"[65] of his entire reorganization: the abolition of the

60. Decree of 25 August 1919, in France, *JO*, 27 August 1919, p. 9170. According to Deschanel, a small number of commercial attachés were first established in 1908 and a small number of commercial agents in 1906. See MAE/Chambre, Rapport No. 333 (1907), p. 213; and idem, Rapport No. 361 (1911), p. 158.

61. Edwards, "Changes Made," pp. 16–19, NA/DS, Index 851.021/2.

62. Decree of 25 August 1919, in France, *JO*, 27 August 1919, p. 9170. Also see Decree of 26 December 1919, in idem, 7 January 1920, pp. 263–64; and Decree of 30 April 1920, in idem, 2 May, p. 6579.

63. Schifferdecker, p. 54; Brockdorff-Rantzau, 14 February 1919, in Germany, Nationalversammlung, *SB*, 326, p. 67; and 10 April 1919, in idem, 327, p. 933.

64. Letter No. 17 from von Rechenberg (Hamburg) to Brockdorff-Rantzau, 9 August 1919, in PA/AA, Abteilung IA, Deutschland 149, Band 6.

65. Schuman, "The Conduct of German Foreign Affairs," p. 190.

distinction between "political" and "commercial" affairs. He recognized with so many others that in foreign relations these matters had become inextricably intertwined. Under his new regional system, therefore, all aspects of policy—including those of a commercial nature—were administratively unified under geographical divisions along the French pattern.[66] This innovation raised the status of economic questions within the Wilhelmstrasse, thus setting the stage for further changes and expanded responsibilities in the area of international commerce. Such developments, said Hermann Müller, represented "an integral part of the entire reform of the Foreign Ministry and its services."[67]

Once given the authority to institute major changes, Schüler launched his favorite and most elaborate creation: the *Aussenhandelsstelle* (Office of Foreign Trade).[68] Occupying over one hundred and twenty rooms and employing a very large staff,[69] this office centralized the management and promotion of external commerce within the Ministry for Foreign Affairs.[70] Schüler established numerous subdivisions charged with supervising economic relations with every geographical location in the world, improving the commercial training of diplomats, furnishing assistance to businessmen, publishing reports for exporters, and organizing resource data on all financial matters. Additional bureaus became responsible for agriculture, textiles, heavy industry, optics, gold flows and banking, foreign stock exchanges, chemicals, machinery, transportation, and communications systems, to name only a few.[71] A special *Eildienst* was designed to collect the most recent commercial intelligence and distribute it as fast as possible to businessmen by means of

---

66. PA/AA, Politisches Archiv, Geschäftsverteilungspläne, Band 1; and the examples of weekly reports in PA/AA, Abteilung III, Geschäftsgang 1a, Band 1.

67. "Rede des Reichsministers des Auswärtigen," Anlage to A.H. 26779, in ibid., Abteilung III Geschaftsgang 1, Band 1.

68. The history of the *Aussenhandelsstelle,* or *Abteilung X,* is recounted briefly in the Anlage to A.H. 26779, "Tätigkeitsbericht des Auswärtiges Amtes, Abteilung Aussenhandelsstelle," in ibid.

69. Ibid., Band 2, "Uebersicht über die Unterbringung der einzelnen Abteilungen des Auswärtigen Amts."

70. See the early description in ibid., Abteilung IA, Deutschland 149, Band 29, Despatch of 14 April 1919, "Geheim," from Mathieu to missions abroad.

71. Ibid., Band 31, Nr. 368, "Geschäftseinteilung der Aussenhandelsstelle des Auswärtigen Amtes," 18 November 1919.

the latest electronic equipment.[72] The creation of this administrative machinery, noted one observer, marked a fundamental change from the old Commercial Division's traditional philosophy of simply "looking after" the general economic interests of Germany abroad to a new aggressiveness by the Wilhelmstrasse in actively giving aid, seeking markets, and promoting foreign trade.[73]

To assist the Ministry's new regional divisions and other interested parties, Schüler also designed the position of *Staatssekretär W (Wirtschaft)* (State Secretary for Economic Affairs) and a separate *Büro des wirtschaftlichen Unterstaatssekretärs* (Office of the Assistant State Secretary for Economics). One section of this bureau he charged with coordinating the activities of the *Aussenhandelsstelle* with the Wilhelmstrasse as a whole, and with advising the Minister for Foreign Affairs, German chambers of commerce, business organizations, missions and consulates abroad. Another department was responsible for "all matters concerning German and international economic policy," particularly those questions relating to finance, tariffs, taxation, and currency values overseas.[74] The monetary costs, personal rivalries, and sheer bulk of these huge departments soon proved to be impractical, however, and the large administrative units were replaced with bureaus of a more manageable size.[75]

Many responsibilities once under the auspices of the enormous *Aussenhandelsstelle* and the office of the State Secretary for Economic Affairs therefore were distributed to smaller, more

---

72. Ibid., Abteilung III, Geschäftsgang 1, Band 1, Anlage to A.H. 26779, "Tätigkeitsbericht des Auswärtigen Amtes, Abteilung Aussenhandelsstelle"; and in idem, Band 2, Anlage to 15628 from Asmis to Abteilung VI, 18 April 1921, "Vertraulich!," "Der Funkdienst des Eildienstes."

73. Report, "Secret," "The Reorganisation of the Foreign Office," from D.M. 1 (Rotterdam) to Foreign Secretary, 13 December 1920, in PRO/FO 371/4851; and PA/AA, Politisches Archiv und Historisches Referat, Aktenzeichen 13, "Geschichte der Handelspolitischen Abteilung des A.A., 1885–1920," pp. 27–36.

74. Circular Nr. 110, "Vfg. betr. das Büro des wirtschaftlichen Unterstaatssekretärs (Büro W)," in PA/AA, Abteilung IA, Deutschland 149, Band 31; and the "Geschäftsverteilung innerhalb des Auswärtigen Amtes," signed by Schüler, 19 March 1920, in idem, Politisches Archiv, Geschäftsverteilungspläne, Band 1.

75. See ibid., Presse Abteilung, Beiakten II, Band 1, I.A. 3640, Circular of 23 December 1921 from Gneist, and idem, I.A. 985/A. 9555, Circular of 14 April 1923 from Rosenberg; and *Industrie und Handels Zeitung*, 19 December 1921, "Die Auflösung der Aussenhandelsstelle."

specialized bureaus. The *Sonderabteilung für Wirtschaftspolitik* (Special Department for Economic Policy) assumed duties for reparations payments, indebtedness, imports and exports, relations with chambers of commerce, overseas trade statistics, and those "affairs of foreign politics affecting the interests of German commercial policy."[76] A position of *Kommissar für Handelsvertragsverhandlungen* dealt with negotiations for international commercial agreements.[77] *Referat Schiffahrtwesen* and a *Kommissar für internationale Verhandlungen in Schiffahrtsangelegenheiten* managed all affairs concerning maritime commerce, the German merchant marine, harbor facilities, and shipping issues, while *Referat Rohstoffwirtschaft* supplied information concerning the availability of raw materials around the world.[78] Finally, a new *Referat für wirtschaftliches Nachrichtenwesen* (Economic Intelligence Service) gathered commercial information, supervised the activities of the *Eildienst*, directed correspondence with industrial and financial circles, and distributed any economic data able to benefit German exporting firms.[79]

To help overseas trading interests even further, Schüler and other innovators sought to establish and maintain close contact between the Ministry for Foreign Affairs and German businessmen. A significant step toward this objective proved to be the creation of new *Zweigstellen des Auswärtigen Amts für Assenhandel*—official bureaus of the Wilhelmstrasse actually located in the major commercial cities throughout Germany including Bremen, Flensburg, Hamburg, Munich, Nürnberg, and Stuttgart.[80] Working in intimate

---

76. See PA/AA, Politisches Archiv, Geschäftsverteilungspläne, Band 1, "Auswärtiges Amt, Geschäftsverteilungsplan, Stand vom August 1923."

77. Ibid., Presse Abteilung, Beiakten II, Band 2, Circular Nr. 248 of 27 November 1923 from Maltzan. The name was soon changed to *Kommissar für Wirtschaftsverhandlungen*.

78. See ibid., Politisches Archiv, Geschäftsverteilungspläne, Band 1. A simple form of *Referat S* was created first in 1907–1908.

79. See ibid., Politisches Archiv, Geschäftsverteilungspläne, Band 1, "Auswärtiges Amt, Geschäftsverteilungsplan, Stand vom 15. February 1922," and other listings thereafter. The activities of the *Eildienst* eventually were transferred to a newer service called the *Aussenhandelnachrichtendienst*.

80. Ibid., Presse Abteilung, Beiakten II, Band 2, Anlage to IA 3635/290, dated 3 January 1922 from Simons, "Die Zweigstellen des Auswärtigen Amtes für Aussenhandel"; and idem, Abteilung III, Geschäftsgang 1, Band 1, Anlage to A.H. 26779, "Tätigkeitsbericht des Auswärtigen Amtes, Abteilung Aussenhandelsstelle."

cooperation with the multiple departments of the central administration, these various Branch Offices of Foreign Trade could transmit requests from local firms directly to headquarters in Berlin. They also disseminated valuable information about business opportunities, costs, and overseas regulations from ministerial officials to interested parties. This entire administrative apparatus now enabled the Mininistry to answer specific inquiries on economic matters, to analyze future financial trends, to assist in publishing consular reports, to send speakers to chambers of commerce meetings, and to rapidly collect and distribute information about international commerce as never before.[81] Included in such activities was the annual publication of a massive loose-leaf collection of quantitative data, including such things as charts and graphs analyzing commercial transactions, specific products, natural resources, and the activities of competitors.[82]

Reformers of the Wilhelmstrasse realized that the effectiveness of these enlarged responsibilities and activities was dependent upon the cooperation of other government agencies. As described in the journal *Export*:

> Stress must be laid on the fact that in international questions, the Ministry for Foreign Affairs and the Ministry of Economics must work in closest touch with one another. . . . In their daily work at home and abroad these two departments must exchange experiences and at all times be fully informed of each other's aims and measures.[83]

The rationale of this argument led Schüler and others to solicit advice from the Ministry of Economics and to design institutional means for assuring mutual consultation. Both ministries, for example, played major roles in the creation and performance of the

81. Ibid., Sonderreferat W, Politik Nr. 25, Band 1; Abteilung III, Geschäftsgang 1, Band 1; AN, Ministère du Commerce et de l'Industrie, Carton F¹² 9302, "Enquête sur l'activité industrielle et la propagande commerciale des allemands dans les pays étrangers, 1919–1922"; and NA/DS, Index 862.021/2, Despatch No. 3093, dated 23 July 1919.

82. Germany, Auswärtiges Amt, *Sammelmappe des Auswärtigen Amts. Deutschland und die weltwirtschaftliche Lage,* the first volume of which was published in 1919.

83. From a memorandum submitted to the Chancellor by German chambers of commerce as reproduced in *Export*, and as cited in Despatch No. D/3391 from War Intelligence Department to FO, 31 August 1918, in PRO/FO 371/3481.

Aussenhandelsstelle.[84] On the *Verwaltungsrat der Aussenhandelsstelle des Auswärtigen Amts* (Governing Board of the Office of Foreign Trade) representatives from the Wilhelmstrasse sat side by side with those from the Ministries of Economics, Finances, and Transportation.[85] Furthermore, the creation of a special position for *Vertreter des Reichswirtschaftsministeriums* established a direct and permanent liaison between the Ministries for Foreign Affairs and Economics.[86] Additional measures sought to make those German foreign service officers stationed abroad more responsive to business interests and more capable of promoting international trade. Besides the other reforms instituted for overseas representatives,[87] many *Wahlkonsuln* (honorary consuls) were replaced with more qualified professional *Berufskonsuln.*[88] Greater efforts were made to assure increased cooperation between the diplomatic and consular missions in the field,[89] and special technical advisers for commercial and trade affairs continued to be attached to overseas posts.[90] Even the entrance requirements reflected a change in the Wilhelmstrasse toward new and expanded responsibilities for international commerce, for they stressed the ability ''to become shrewd and accurate observers of political and economic developments'' and advised all

84. See PA/AA, Abteilung III, Geschäftsgang 1, Band 1, Anlage to A.H. 26779, ''Tätigkeitsbericht des Auswärtigen Amtes, Abteilung Aussenhandelsstelle.''

85. Ibid., Anlage to A.H. 26779, ''Niederschrift über die Grundungssitzung des Verwaltungsrats der Aussenhandelsstelle des Auswärtigen Amts.''

86. Ibid., Politisches Archiv, Geschäftsverteilungspläne, Band 1, ''Auswärtiges Amt, Geschäftsverteilungsplan, Stand vom 15. February 1922''; and idem, Abteilung III, Geschäftsgang 1, Band 2, N 2063/14286, letter of 3 April 1922 from Knipping.

87. See Chapter Four, Section 4, on the reforms in the diplomatic and consular corps.

88. Schuman, ''The Conduct of German Foreign Affairs,'' p. 199.

89. See R. von Scheller-Steinwartz, ''Reform des Auswärtigen Dienstes,'' in Gerhard Anschütz, et al. (eds.),*Handbuch der Politik,*3rd ed. (Berlin: Rothschild, 1921), pp. 355–59; Wolgast pp. 63–64; and Schifferdecker, pp. 68–69.

90. Wolgast, p. 65. In the use of special attachés the post-war reformers were assisted to a very large degree by the fact that special technical advisers had been developed and used sporadically since the beginning of the century. See PA/AA, Abteilung IA, Deutschland 122 Nr. 2, Band 5, Abschrift zu J. Nr. 2307/11, ''Technisch-diplomatische Vertretungen,'' of 1911; B. von König, ''Die konsularische Berichterstattung und der amtliche Nachrichtendienst,'' *Bank-Archiv,* X. Jahrgang, 19 (1 July 1911), pp. 291–95.

applicants to "secure practical business experience in a branch office of the A. A. [*Zweigstellen*] for foreign trade, in a chamber of commerce or of agriculture, in a business association, a factory, or a commercial or industrial enterprise."[91]

4. Businessmen and Diplomacy

Due to these many reforms and innovations in both the Quai d'Orsay and the Wilhelmstrasse, business interests increasingly became represented in the councils of foreign policy decision making. In France, representatives of the Ministry for Foreign Affairs were joined on the new *Comité consultatif du commerce extérieur* by delegates from precisely those pressure groups that had demanded more state assistance and protection: large business associations and companies, industrial syndicates, exporters, and chambers of commerce.[92] Merchants and manufacturers were guaranteed positions on the examining boards of commercial attachés and agents in order to place a premium upon "commercial competency."[93] The Quai d'Orsay sought direct advice from businessmen,[94] and those appointed as *Conseillers du commerce extérieur* came only from "French industrialists and traders highly prominent in import and export affairs who have personally contributed to the development of overseas commerce."[95] Such programs, said the Minister of Commerce, demonstrated "the indisputable utility of uniting governmental action with private efforts."[96]

In the Wilhelmstrasse as well, persons with commercial interests made their appearance as never before. Businessmen, bankers, and industrialists increasingly were called upon to serve either as inter-

91. Schuman, "The Conduct of German Foreign Affairs," p. 200. In addition, successful candidates were required to spend part of their probationary period in the *Aussenhandelsstelle*.

92. Decree of 28 October 1919, in France, *JO*, 30 October 1919, pp. 12126–27.

93. Decree of 26 December 1919, in ibid., 7 January 1920, pp. 263–64.

94. See among many examples, Decree of 22 April 1915, in ibid., 29 April 1915, p. 2698.

95. Decree of 6 March 1921, in ibid., 9 March 1921, p. 3001.

96. Report of 6 March 1921 from Dior to Millerand, in ibid.

mediaries or as active participants in diplomatic negotiations.[97] Others sat as delegates on the new *Verwaltungsrat der Aussenhandelsstelle des Auswärtigen Amts* to promote overseas commerce.[98] They dominated so many conversations and issues that one ambassador described Foreign Minister Hans von Simons as being "at a considerable disadvantage with his colleagues" because, unlike them, he did "not really understand figures."[99] Yet their influx helped to fulfill Brockdorff-Rantzau's promise to the German public "to employ men of more practical experience"[100] by drawing from commercial circles to fill positions once held only by professional diplomats.[101] Indeed, Walter Rathenau as part owner or director of eighty-six domestic and twenty-one international enterprises even assumed the duties of Minister for Foreign Affairs. By so doing he symbolized, in the words of one scholar, "the role that large-scale business now was to play in international politics."[102]

Men from business groups also entered significant diplomatic positions by being named to official posts abroad. The postwar French embassy in Berlin witnessed first the banker Charles Laurent and later the financier André François-Poncet presiding over an elaborate battery of economic experts and serving as Ambassador.[103] Germany sent the banker von Berenberg-Gossler to Rome, the businessman Dufour-Féronce to London, and several others with

97. See PRO/FO 371/7536, Despatch No. 85, "Secret," from D'Abernon (Berlin) to Foreign Secretary, 24 January 1922; the earlier Despatch No. 470, "Secret," from Goschen (Berlin) to Grey, 19 December 1913, in PRO/FO 371/1654; Alfred Vagts, "M.M. Warburg und Co.: Ein Bankhaus in der deutschen Weltpolitik, 1905–1933," *Verteiljahrschrift für Sozial- und Wirtschaftsgeschichte*, 45 Band, Heft 3 (September 1958), pp. 289–388.

98. PA/AA, Abteilung III, Geschäftsgang 1, Band 1, Anlage to A.H. 26779, "Niederschrift über die Gründungssitzung des Verwaltungsrats der Aussenhandelsstelle des Auswärtigen Amts am 17. Februar 1920."

99. PRO/FO 371/6025, letter, "Private and Confidential," from D'Abernon (Berlin) to Crowe, 19 April 1921.

100. Brockdorff-Rantzau, 14 February 1919, in Germany, Nationalversammlung, *SB*, 326. p. 67.

101. See PA/AA, Büro des Reichsministers, Aktenzeichen 2, Band 2, the undated, unsigned document describing the previous occupations of new officials in the Wilhelmstrasse. Among the businessmen one finds Behrendt, de Haas, and Wallroth. Helmuth Töpffer was himself a very wealthy merchant in private life.

102. The words are those of Craig, *From Bismarck to Adenauer*, p. 45.

103. See PRO/FO 371/4851, enclosure to Despatch No. 1337 from Kilmarnock (Berlin) to Foreign Secretary, 22 December 1920; MAE/Chambre, Rapport No. 3131 (1922), pp. 188–89; and the later *Le Petit Parisien*, 14 January 1935.

commercial interests as consuls to various locations around the globe.[104] In some cases, businessmen with no official positions began to initiate and conduct bilateral negotiations between themselves, leading then-Senator Raymond Poincaré to speculate that future transactions may be conducted "not between Governments, but between commercial, industrial, and financial organizations of the various countries."[105]

Although most contemporaries viewed these developments as necessary and intelligent responses to new conditions, a few also saw in the changes a potentially dangerous threat to the traditional norms and integrity of diplomatic behavior. Critics observed that "profound and lasting" problems resulted as politics and economics became so "inextricably bound up" with each other.[106] They feared that this greater intimacy between diplomats and commercial interest groups—between the pouch and the pocketbook—would encourage intrigue for personal gain. In France, journalists and parliamentarians watched with alarm when, in return for special favors, the names of distinguished ambassadors increasingly appeared on the directing boards of banks, industrial establishments, exporting firms, and international financial companies.[107] Parisian press articles warned that under such arrangements, "those *representing the interests of France*" might be seduced "to fill their own pockets."[108] In Germany, Deputy Walter Stoecker complained that these many new appointments now enabled "men from the world of finances and industry" to control foreign as well as domestic policy.[109] Such thoughts prompted the future French Foreign Minister Paul-Boncour to warn that it would be necessary to guard against "cases of collusion between diplomacy and finance."[110]

104. PA/AA, Büro des Reichsministers, Aktenzeichen 2, Band 2, the undated, unsigned document describing the previous occupations of those holding overseas positions.

105. Raymond Poincaré, as cited in *Morning Post*, "M. Briand's Declaration," 2 January 1922.

106. See Alfred Zimmern, *The League of Nations and the Rule of Law, 1918–1935* (London: Macmillan and Co., 1939), pp. 500–501.

107. Feis, pp. 158–59.

108. *L'Humanité*, "Diplomatie et Finances," 22 July 1921.

109. Walter Stoecker, 17 March 1921, in Germany, Reichstag, *SB*, 348, p. 3106.

110. See the discussion of Deputies Paul-Boncour and Barthe, in France,

* * * *

In assuming new and expanded responsibilities for international commerce, the French and German Ministries for Foreign Affairs demonstrated a remarkable ability to respond to change. The creation of elaborate offices and departments, the development of innovative agencies, the establishment of contact with other ministries and commercial groups, the employment of special attachés and agents, the revamping of consular representation abroad, and the appointment of businessmen to decision-making positions indicated a twentieth-century commitment to protect and promote overseas trade. Criticisms were lost in the wave of praise as observers hailed these particular reforms and innovations as "well-planned," "far reaching," "practical," and indicative of "a new spirit."[111] They represented part of that larger movement under which diplomatic institutions, in the words of one authority, began to evolve "in order to adapt themselves to changes in the nature and conduct of foreign relations. The influence that had been at work in shaping their evolution was the development of diplomacy itself—the growth, in terms of sheer bulk and of intrinsic importance, of foreign relationships, and the gradual invasion of these relationships by economic and publicity problems."[112]

Chambre, *DP*, 2ᵉ séance du 8 July 1921, pp. 905–8, prompted by the financial scandal involving Berthelot himself.

111. See MAE/Chambre, Rapport No. 2020 (1921), p. 76; Edwards, "Changes Made," NA/DS, Index 851.021/2, and Index 851.021/14, Report enclosed in Despatch No. 445 from Simons (Paris) to Secretary of State, 24 April 1925; PA/AA, Abteilung III, Geschäftsgang 1, Band 1, Anlage 1 to A.H. 26779, "Rede des Reichsministers des Auswärtigen"; and *Die Hamburger Warte*, "Das neue Auswärtige Amt," 9 August 1919; among others.

112. Strang, p. 67.

— 6 —

Civilisation and Kultur:
New and Expanded Responsibilities
for International Propaganda

Next to economic and political struggles, the
battles of culture and language now have become
one of the most significant forms of international
competition.

–L'Opinion

In the nineteenth century, Ministries for Foreign Affairs not only lacked involvement in commercial matters but had relatively little to do with propaganda. This condition resulted from a number of factors, including a restricted political franchise, low literacy among the general populace, and technological limitations upon the dissemination of information. Of equal importance was the attitude among diplomats that any effort made to influence popular opinion would stand in sharp contrast with their professional sense of responsibility. Traditional norms dictated that diplomatic negotiations and transactions be conducted with privacy, self-restraint, discretion, and even secrecy if necessary—not with press conferences, published statements, public displays, or appeals to emotion. For these reasons, therefore, diplomats and bureaucrats generally maintained a "discreet silence" and "abstained assiduously" from creating any mechanism that deliberately would draw the masses into the elite gentleman's game of international politics.[1]

1. Benjamin Akzin, *Propaganda by Diplomats* (Washington, D.C.: Digest Press, 1936), pp. 1–3.

Such attitudes and conditions began to change dramatically with the extension of voting rights, the advancement of compulsory education, and the emergence of the mass circulation newspaper. In the new century, many observers became aware of the potential of these developments. The temptation to use them as a means of manipulating large numbers of people for particular purposes grew rapidly. Especially during the First World War when nations fought for their very survival, pressures mounted for governments to mobilize all possible resources in support of their cause, including public opinion at home and abroad. Vicious, unprecedented competition for the hearts and minds of the world's citizens convinced many of the necessity for immediate action. In response, reformers and innovators of the Quai d'Orsay and Wilhelmstrasse broke with past practices and created elaborate institutional mechanisms designed to assume new and expanded responsibilities for international propaganda.

1. The Development of International Propaganda and Demands for Government Involvement

In 1829 Lord Palmerston noted: "There is in nature no moving power but mind, all else is passive and inert; in human affairs this power is opinion; in political affairs it is public opinion; and he who can grasp this power, with it will subdue the fleshly arm of physical strength, and compel it to work out his purpose."[2]

At the time of this statement little effort was expended to influence or to use this opinion. Restricted electoral franchise, the lack of educational opportunities, indifference, and inadequate means of disseminating news prevented the general populace of any country from knowing much about either national or international politics.[3] Particularly in questions of foreign affairs, the additional factors of jealously-guarded executive prerogative and traditional diplomatic custom successfully kept discussions out of "the public street" and

2. Lord Palmerston, 1 June 1829, in Britain, House of Commons, *The Parliamentary Debates*, New Series, XXI (London: Hansard, 1829), col. 1667.
3. See the excellent discussion by Oran Hale, *Germany and the Diplomatic Revolution: A Study in Diplomacy and the Press, 1904–1906* (Philadelphia: University of Pennsylvania Press, 1931), p. 7.

confined to the "inner sanctum" of a select few.[4] With little exception, such practices helped to maintain what one ambassador termed
"those happy days" when "diplomats hardly knew what was to be
understood by the word 'Propaganda.' "[5]

As time passed these earlier conditions began to change.
Technological invention played a monumental role by increasing the
scope, range, and speed of information distribution. Electrical
transmissions from telegraph and telephone lines brought news from
the far corners of the globe. Mechanical discoveries of high-speed
rotary presses, stereotypes, rapid multiplication of plates, and
typesetting machines revolutionized the production of printed
media. New chemicals and modern techniques reduced the cost of
newsprint, enabling the volume and diffusion of information to
expand. Technology provided a means by which millions of persons
could share the news of public events, and for the first time in history
placed the printed page within the reach of all working men and
women.

Educational reforms encouraged further transformations by assuring that such men and women actually could read this newly-
available material in print. The democratization of popular education began to replace the limited opportunities of earlier times.
Campaigns against illiteracy, the growth of state-supported secular
schools, and curricula changes away from classical Greek and Latin
toward modern languages and sciences contributed to the rapid
growth of a new reading public. Demands for printed materials
grew, causing presses to produce quantities of books, periodicals,
and—most important—mass circulation newspapers. The daily
press brought information, entertainment, and excitement to readers heretofore confined to their own small world and its monotonous
routine. In addition, the newspaper provided a potential means of
access into the home of every citizen.

With the expansion of electoral franchise, these new readers also
became new voters. Consequently, politicians began to realize that
the printed media could be used as an instrument for influencing
voting behavior. They needed only to look at the successful adver-

4. See Chapter One, Section 4.
5. Bernstorff, p. 47. A few exceptional early and rudimentary propaganda
efforts can be found in Robert Holtman, *Napoleonic Propaganda* (Baton Rouge:
Louisiana State University, 1950), pp. 55–57, 94–96, and 72–76; and R. Mowat,
Diplomacy and Peace (New York: McBride, 1936), pp. 232–33.

tising techniques developed by the business community to see vivid examples of consumer manipulation. A new breed of publishers seeking wide circulation repeatedly verified that the reading public frequently wanted quantity rather than quality, and sensationalism rather than education. In their choice of materials, readers demonstrated that they did not always require discriminating accuracy, subtle nuance, or a complete rendition of all facts. Shrewd political leaders, like many advertisers and publishers, saw that they could elicit desired responses by presenting complex ideas in terms sufficiently easy or interesting to hold attention. In an emerging era of mass culture and yellow journalism, according to one authority, this enabled the unscrupulous to use the press as a means of exploiting "the ignorance, repressions, and emotions of the masses."[6] As such, communication channels to the reading, voting public became forces "of the first importance," and potential media of propaganda to influence popular opinion.[7]

Seeing the advantages of using propaganda in domestic affairs, politicians began considering the application of similar techniques to diplomacy. If public support could be aroused for internal political purposes, so it also might be enlisted to strengthen bargaining positions in foreign relations. Popular sentiment could furnish a convenient excuse for refusing concessions that negotiators for other reasons had no intention of granting. The press could be employed to stir patriotism for uniting a country behind its leaders in time of international crisis or war. It could be used to justify particular claims or simply to explain the government's official position. In addition, inspired information could be directed toward foreign audiences. The media could be manipulated to launch trial balloons to test the reaction of other powers without unduly exposing one's own hand. It could be aimed at allies, neutrals, or opinion within an opponent's territory to gain support or weaken resolve.[8] In more

6. Ralph D. Casey, "Communication Channels," in Bruce Smith, Harold Lasswell, and Ralph Casey, *Propaganda, Communication, and Public Opinion* (Princeton: Princeton University Press, 1946), p. 6.

7. See Joseph Ward Swain, *Beginning the Twentieth Century* (New York: W. W. Norton and Co., 1933), p. 13; and Jacques Ellul, *Propaganda: The Formation of Men's Attitudes* (New York: Knopf, 1965), pp. 89, 108.

8. On some of these points, see Paul Gordon Lauren, "Ultimata and Coercive Diplomacy," *International Studies Quarterly*, 16 (June 1972), pp. 159–61; and E. M. Carroll, *Germany and the Great Powers, 1866–1914: A Study in Public Opinion and Foreign Policy* (New York: Prentice-Hall, 1938), p. 11.

ambitious terms, propaganda could be designed to convince others around the world of the glories and wonders of one's own civilization and culture.

Although statesmen considered these uses of the press, those of even the late nineteenth century approached the potential of propaganda in diplomacy with extreme caution. To many, such activities seemed to stand in sharp conflict with their professional sense of responsibility and tantamount to opening Pandora's box. In the past, legal constraints and traditional practice had managed to keep negotiations among nations under accepted norms of discreet behavior and within relatively manageable bounds. The prospects of destroying this secure system by aroused public opinion brought visions of chaos. As a consequence, self-imposed restrictions contributed in keeping foreign policy debates infrequent, press reports short, pressure groups small, and overseas schools limited.[9] Even Bismarck, who used the media on occasion to promote his policies, warned that one "must not provoke people unnecessarily"[10] and condemned newspapers whenever they accorded "exaggerated attention" to foreign affairs.[11] The press was used "for the purpose of making pronouncements, or putting out feelers, to foreign governments [rather] than as a means of influencing public opinion at large."[12] As described by one distinguished journalist, the game played by the diplomats and bureaucrats required secrecy. "They were all agreed that the peace and safety of the world absolutely depended on letting nobody else know what they were doing. And very often they were right. So long as the game went on, its dangers were limited by excluding an audience which must have taken sides . . . . Keep the public out of it, and it was a relatively safe game; let the public in, and it instantly became full of deadly peril."[13]

9. E. M. Carroll, *French Public Opinion and Foreign Affairs, 1870–1914* (New York: Century, 1931), pp. 7–8.

10. Busch, 1, p. 11. Also see Morsey, pp. 110–12; and W. Boelcke, "Presseabteilung und Pressearchive des Auswärtigen Amts, 1871–1945," *Archivmitteilungen*, Heft 2, IX Jahrgang (1959), p. 43.

11. Detlef Albers, *Reichstag und Aussenpolitik von 1871–1879* (Berlin: Ebering, 1927), p. 14; and Carroll, *Germany and the Great Powers*, p. 6.

12. E. H. Carr, *Propaganda in International Politics* (New York: Farrar and Rinehart, 1939), p. 9.

13. J. A. Spender, 2, pp. 40–41.

With the beginning of the twentieth century, however, the temptation to use any available instrument for diplomatic success began to outweigh previous restraints or calculations of future risk. Indeed, according to one observer, at precisely this time "there was a noticeable increase of attention to the questions [of foreign affairs] in the press."[14] This change resulted from deliberate policy. Among those responsible was Théophile Delcassé who, when first entering the Quai d'Orsay, represented a man "too conscious of the power of the press to neglect to use it when he became foreign minister."[15] Once placed in a position of authority he introduced a policy of inspiring articles, of "purchasing" newspapers, and of maintaining such strong ties with the media that he became described as "more open to journalists than to diplomats."[16]

In the same period, Bernhard von Bülow became the man most responsible for introducing the use of propaganda into German diplomacy. On his appointment as Imperial Chancellor in 1900, he made use of the means of government to foster his "artful posturing," "superficiality," "bombast and fustian," and the "gestures of statecraft" rather than its substance.[17] Before Bülow, according to his associate, no statesman paid as much attention to public opinion or worked so hard to manipulate it.[18]

The tenure of Delcassé in France and of Bülow in Germany corresponded with the period in which the press began to be used "as a great engine of publicity and propaganda."[19] Both men recognized that their official position gave them valuable information that they could "release or withhold or color at will."[20] Delcassé, to quote one authority, initiated the practice of dictating items each evening to appear in the following day's press, "taking special care to vary his style according to the newspaper concerned."[21] Style

14. Carroll, *French Public Opinion*, p. 10.

15. Christopher Andrew, *Théophile Delcassé and the Making of the Entente Cordiale: A Reappraisal of French Foreign Policy, 1898–1905* (New York: St. Martin's Press, 1968), p. 67.

16. British Ambassador Monson, as cited in ibid., p. 68.

17. These words are from the perceptive essay on Bülow in Craig, *From Bismarck to Adenauer*, pp. 33–35.

18. Otto Hammann, *Bilder aus der letzten Kaiserzeit* (Berlin: Hobbing, 1922), p. 41.

19. Hale, *Germany and the Diplomatic Revolution*, p. 213.

20. Ibid., p. 15.

21. Andrew, p. 67.

also played a role in the practices of Bülow, who manipulated the press into expressing barious forms of silence, criticism, praise, or resentment, depending upon the circumstances.[22] Such activities, when combined with publishers seeking mass circulation, contributed to an embittered atmosphere in which diplomacy was conducted with "suspicion and hostility in the public mind" and with "misunderstandings, false statements, malicious suppositions, invidious criticisms, and acrimonious polemics."[23] This marked the beginning of a twentieth-century condition described by an authority as one in which "the newspapers of two countries often took up some point of dispute, exaggerated it, and made attacks and counterattacks, until a regular newspaper war was engendered, which thoroughly poisoned public opinion, and so offered fertile soil in which the seeds of real war might easily germinate."[24]

This ability of the media to influence international relations by manipulating public opinion convinced many people of the accuracy of *Le Temps'* early assertion that "each day the press becomes . . . more of a diplomatic force of the first order."[25] Parliamentarians, publicists, and diplomats in France argued that appropriate action by the government itself must be taken to assure that circulating publicity be as favorable as possible. They demanded that the Ministry for Foreign Affairs assume new responsibilities for propaganda matters. Deputy Gervais urged the Quai d'Orsay to concentrate less on "the ancient methods of brutal conquest and territorial domination" and more on "the new methods" using "the force of intelligence, reason, and national conscience."[26] Others argued that the effective management of opinion required a comprehensive program and a permanent, rationally-designed administrative apparatus rather than the simplistic, *ad hoc* arrangements then in existence. Proposals submitted to the Ministry stressed that foreign opinion

22. See the Instructions, for example, in Germany, Auswärtiges Amt, *GP*, XX, pp. 313, 403n.

23. Hale, *Germany and the Diplomatic Revolution*, p. 211. Also see the comments of Eyre Crowe in W 18 39911/37537, note of 16 November 1908, in PRO/FO 371/463; and *Vossische Zeitung*, 28 December 1912.

24. Sidney B. Fay, *The Origins of the World War* (New York: Macmillan, 1928), 1, p. 48.

25. *Le Temps*, "La politique étrangère," 5 April 1900.

26. MAE/Chambre, Rapport No. 2661 (1906), pp. 2–3.

could be swayed best by "the extension of French culture abroad," and urged officials to establish overseas schools and hospitals and to mobilize the press, library resources, religious missionaries— "valuable instruments of influence"—and professors toward this end.[27] The need for such action appeared to be urgent. Ambassador Jules Cambon reminded his superiors: "Ideas and sentiments are effective tools" and in diplomacy easily can "become useful instruments of propaganda."[28]

Similar proposals besieged the Wilhelmstrasse. Many Germans concerned with questions of foreign affairs realized the potential power of the media and its impact upon one's international "image." The 1906 Algeciras Conference provided such evidence by hosting nearly as many journalists as diplomats and by its description as "the first international congress to be exploited by the new journalism for the instruction and entertainment of the masses."[29] After this humiliation, observers claimed that they had learned "a special lesson"—namely, that they must develop "a desire and a will to create a more efficient and efficacious organization . . . to direct public opinion abroad."[30] Some claimed that the best means of reducing hostility and suspicion would be the universal spreading of national art, music, literature, and language "because German culture is really the culture of the civilized world."[31] Others urged the Ministry to create favorable opinion by employing agents to influence the foreign press or by subsidizing a worldwide news service to combat the prejudicial "false views" presented by the

27. MAE, Allemagne, politique étrangère, dossier général, NS 18, proposal from Gustave Mendel, entitled "Note sur un projet qui semble propre à fortifier et à étendre l'action économique, intellectuelle et morale de la France dans le Levant," dated March, 1914.

28. Ibid., Despatch No. 380 from Jules Cambon (Berlin) to MAE, 30 June 1914.

29. See Hale, *The Great Illusion*, p. 247; and André Tardieu, *La Conférence d'Algésiras* (Paris: Alcan, 1909), pp. 92ff., 502–4.

30. *Allgemeine Zeitung*, "Die Presse und die deutsche Weltpolitik," 16 April 1906.

31. *Handbuch des Deutschtums im Auslande*, as cited in PRO/FO 371/258, Despatch No. 20 from Cartwright (Munich) to Grey, 22 February 1907. Also see *Das Deutschtum im Ausland*, Heft 3 (March 1910), p. 1, and the many articles in subsequent issues; and Allen Croneberg, Jr., "The Volksbund für das Deutschtum im Ausland: Volkisch Ideology and German Foreign Policy, 1881–1939 (Stanford: unpublished dissertation, 1969), pp. 32–34.

British Reuters and the French Havas agencies.[32] To project the country in a favorable light, said the *Deutsche Marke*, would require increasing the contact between officials and journalists and performing an "essential" task: "the modernization of the Wilhelmstrasse's so-called Press Division."[33]

These suggestions, requests, and demands for more government activity in the realm of foreign propaganda poured in with torrential force during the First World War. In all belligerent countries it appeared that years of armed conflict and destruction required more than the mobilization of soldiers and equipment. Endurance seemed to depend upon the ability to manage opinion and attitudes by "direct manipulation."[34] To quote one of the world's foremost propagandists:

> It was in this recognition of Public Opinion as a major force that the Great War differed most essentially from all previous conflicts. The trial of strength was not only between massed bodies of armed men, but between opposed ideals . . . [and] raised issues that had to be fought out in the hearts and minds of people as well as on the actual firing line.[35]

"It was shown only during the War," agreed Adolf Hitler, "to what enormously important results a suitably applied propaganda may lead."[36] Patriots therefore encouraged the use of inspired information to stir their own nation toward unity, to inflame hatred

---

32. Otto Hötzsch, "Auswärtige Politik und Presse," *Deutsche Monatschrift*, Heft 2 (November 1906), pp. 160–72; clipping of the *Frankfurter Zeitung* filed on 21 December 1908 in PA/AA, Abteilung IA, Deutschland 122 Nr. 2, Band 3; Adolph von Flöckher, *Was muss der Deutsche von auswärtiger Politik wissen?* (Berlin: Curtius, 1908); "Deutschlands weltwirtschaftliche Bestrebungen: Ein Syndikat für den Auslandsnachrichtendienst," *Deutsch Export-Revue*, 5 June 1914.

33. *Deutsche Marke*, "Arbeit für den Staatssekretär von Jagow!," 5 January 1913. This statement was considered important enough to be specially marked and filed, as evidenced in PA/AA, Abteilung IA, Deutschland 122 Nr. 2, Band 5. Also see Schoen, p. 117, for mention of a proposal submitted in 1910.

34. See Harold Lasswell, *Propaganda Technique in the World War* (New York: Peter Smith, 1938), p. 9.

35. George Creel, *How We Advertised America* (New York: Harper and Brothers, 1920), p. 3.

36. Adolf Hitler, *Mein Kampf* (New York: Reynal and Hitchcock, 1939 ed.), p. 227.

against opponents, to justify war aims or assign guilt, to preserve friendship among allies or procure cooperation from neutrals, and to demoralize enemies. Citizens declared that "thoughts are bullets,"[37] spoke of the "War of Ideas"[38] or "the fight for the *minds* of men,"[39] and urged their governments to devise means of pursuing war on the military front, the economic front, and now on the propaganda front.[40] The experiences of the Quai d'Orsay and Wilhelmstrasse once again formed an integral part of this international wartime milieu. Frenchmen and Germans alike bombarded their respective Ministries for Foreign Affairs with demands that they assume increasing responsibility for directing propaganda abroad. Proposals in Paris urged diplomats and bureaucrats to use every conceivable means of influence. Some advocated the massive utilization of the press, posters, handbills, telegraphs, cables, professional associations, schools, and the new invention of motion pictures—described as "the most powerful medium of modern times" because "people believe what they see"[41]—for propaganda purposes.[42] Others urged the Quai d'Orsay to use musical and dramatic presentations, claiming that "in an era of international transactions theatrical art is a force that the Government cannot disregard."[43] Another report

37. United States, War Department, General Staff, Military Intelligence Division, *Propaganda and its Military and Legal Aspects* (Washington, D.C.: 1918?), introduction, citing George Curtis.

38. Walter Raleigh, "The War of Ideas," in *United Empire*, 8, 1 (January 1917), pp. 13–23.

39. Creel, p. 3.

40. See Lasswell, p. 214; Lord Francis Bertie, *The Diary of Lord Bertie of Thame, 1914–1918* (London: Hodder and Staughton, 1924), II, p. 203; James Mock and Cedric Larson, *Words That Won the War* (Princeton: Princeton University Press, 1939), pp. 50–51; *Corriere della Sera*, "Diplomazia o diplomatici?" 27 June 1917; and Mayer, p. 276; among others.

41. MAE, Direction politique et commerciale, Papiers des Agents: Philippe Berthelot, Carton 9, undated letter from LaVoy to Beatty; and idem, Carton 8, report dated 1916 entitled "Avant-Projet de Propagande en Amerique latine," p. 24.

42. Ibid., Philippe Berthelot, Carton 1, undated report from Deschanel to Briand; idem, Carton 9, report of 5 June 1916 entitled "Considerations générales en vue de l'organisation de l'influence française aux Etats-Unis"; and several hundred other examples throughout the Berthelot papers.

43. Ibid., Philippe Berthelot, Carton 1, unsigned, untitled report dated September 1916, p. 8.

said, "It is high time to change the methods of our activities overseas," and advised the Ministry to propagandize French *civilisation*
by employing "the voice of our orators," "the pen of our writers,"
and "the elite of our knowledge: geographers, historians, jurists,
economists, and specialists in the study of languages and foreign
affairs."[44]

Officials in Berlin heard the same demands, as anxious patriots
urged the Ministry to increase its use of propaganda. The *Hamburger Denkschrift* argued that "kid-glove policies" from the past
no longer would work, and advocated deliberate manipulation of
opinion to generate sympathy abroad. Statesmen must learn to work
"hand in hand" with "the mighty power of the press." It asserted:
"Above all, the authorities must attach great importance to German
Kulturpropaganda. . . . First-class means of persuasion exist in the
schools, missions, churches of all denominations, and the cinema,
and these should be used in the service of our nationalist endeavors
abroad."[45]

Such demands increased during the postwar period. A "wave of
'propaganda consciousness' " seemed to follow the conclusion of
armed conflict.[46] One French deputy declared in a lengthy report on
foreign affairs that "today one subject must dominate and direct
everything: *la Propagande*. A system for the coordination, liaison,
and inspiration of all forms of propaganda therefore must be created
within the Quai d'Orsay. . . . French propaganda now must take an
incomparable burst, providing an intensity and effectiveness without precedent."[47] Others recommended that the Ministry be given
the necessary resources "to rationally intensify our propaganda
overseas."[48]

To many Frenchmen, the press, pamphlets, novels, photographs,
films, foreign schools, and missions appeared as valuable diplomatic

44. MAE/Chambre, Rapport No. 4108 (1918), pp. 81–83.

45. PA/AA, *Hamburger Denkschrift*, pp. 15–18 and 36–37. Among many
others, see E. H. Schmidt, "Nationale Propaganda," in *Mitteilungen des Vereins
deutscher Reklamefachleute*, Heft 9 (September 1918), pp. 129–36; *Berliner
Tageblatt*, "Propaganda," 12 May 1918; and *Leipziger Neuesten Nachrichten*,
"Das Trommelfeuer des Geistes!," 24 March 1918.

46. Bruce Smith, "The Political Communication Specialist of Our Times," in
Lasswell, et al., p. 31.

47. MAE/Chambre, Rapport No. 802 (1920), pp. 2, 67, 154.

48. MAE/Sénat, Rapport No. 339 (1920), p. 5.

tools for justifying their action in war, their achievement of "victory," the terms of the Versailles settlement, and the "superiority" of their civilization as "the teacher of humanity."[49] To many Germans the use of these same means by the Wilhelmstrasse seemed like useful instruments for claiming their innocence of "war guilt," their suffering under the "dictated" peace, and the universal benefits of their own cultural achievements for mankind.[50] In short, said one influential proposal, the Ministry for Foreign Affairs must respond to the "modern necessities" of twentieth-century diplomacy by assuming new and expanded responsibilities for international propaganda.[51]

This necessity for diplomats and bureaucrats to assume such tasks appeared particularly pressing because of the action taken by foreign rivals. Advocates of increased propaganda argued that the deliberate manipulation of opinion by other states compelled them to respond immediately in degree and kind. Here competition played the same motivating role as it did for those businessmen demanding greater government assistance for commercial interests.[52] In the minds of many, business and propaganda were but two sides of the same coin of external influence.[53] Patriots in France and Germany urged their respective governments to use all available means in their joint struggle for world opinion, and spoke with intense expressions like psychological "weapons" and "attacks," "ideological warfare," "cultural struggles," "the offensive of words," and the "conquest of convictions."[54] Frenchmen continually directed attention to the new manipulating techniques employed

49. See MAE/Chambre, Rapport No. 6339 (1919), pp. 42, 115–41; among others.

50. C. H. Becker, *Kulturpolitische Aufgaben des Reiches* (Leipzig: Quelle and Meyer, 1919); Schiffer, 9 April 1919, in Germany, Nationalversammlung, *SB*, 327, p. 908; *Vorwarts,* 19 December 1920; and *Deutsche Allgemeine Zeitung,* 25 January 1921, as filed in PA/AA, Büro des Reichsministers, Aktenzeichen 2, Band 2.

51. PA/AA, Nachlässe Ulrich von Brockdorff-Rantzau, Aktenzeichen 14, Band 1, report of 18 March 1919 entitled "Reorganisationspläne."

52. As described in Chapter Five, Section 1.

53. MAE/Chambre, Rapport No. 6339 (1919), p. 115; PA/AA, *Hamburger Denkschrift;* Schmidt, "Nationale Propaganda," and PRO/FO 371/4851, Report, "Secret," "The Reorganisation of the Foreign Offiice," from D.M. 1 (Rotterdam) to Foreign Secretary, 13 December 1920.

54. See, for example, MAE, Allemagne, politique étrangère, dossier général,

by the Wilhelmstrasse,[55] and were horrified to hear that people from other lands had learned to say *bitte* or *danke schön* rather than *s'il vous plaît* or *merci beaucoup.*[56] Germans making demands upon their Foreign Ministry, on the other hand, strengthened their own contentions by pointing to the increased propaganda activities of the Quai d'Orsay.[57]

2. *Propaganda and the Quai d'Orsay*

The growing importance of public opinion and newspapers, reported Philippe Berthelot, represented another of the "new conditions of modern diplomacy."[58] He recognized that those demands for more involvement in propaganda activities had the merit of facing this changing reality of international politics. Since opinion at home and abroad could affect policy to a significant degree, conscious attempts should be made by diplomats and bureaucrats to influence the public. Insofar as journalists, parliamentarians, and many citizens at large were asserting their right to obtain more information about foreign affairs,[59] they should be supplied with material as favorable as possible. For such reasons, Berthelot and the Reform Commission recommended that appropriate changes be instituted immediately within the Ministry for Foreign Affairs.

In response to these pressures, the first major decree reorganizing

---

NS 18, proposal from Gustave Mendel, entitled "Note sur un projet qui semble propre à fortifier et à étendre l'action économique, intellectuelle et morale de la France dans le Levant," dated March 1914; MAE/Chambre, Rapport No. 802 (1920); PA/AA, *Hamburger Denkschrift;* and *Leipziger Neuesten Nachrichten,* "Das Trommelfeuer des Geistes!," 24 March 1918.

55. MAE, Allemagne, politique étrangère, dossier général, NS 18, Despatch No. 305 from Bompard (Constantinople) to MAE, report entitled "Programme en vue du développement de l'influence allemande. Mesures à prendre pour y répondre"; idem, Direction politique et commerciale, Papiers des Agents: Philippe Berthelot, Carton 9, letter from Jusserand (Washington) to Berthelot, 1 January 1916.

56. M. Wilmotte, "La Langue française en Orient," *L'Opinion,* 13 (27 March 1909), p. 399.

57. PA/AA, Abteilung IA, Frankreich 87, Band 88, Despatch No. 73, from Radolin (Paris) to von Bülow, 26 February 1909; the material in idem, Deutschland 122, Nr. 2, Bände 4–6; and idem, *Hamburger Denkschrift,* p. 17.

58. Berthelot, "Commission des réformes administratives," p. 3269.

59. See Chapter Two, Section 2, and Chapter Three, Section 5.

the Quai d'Orsay's entire administration included a provision creating a new office specifically designed to influence public opinion: the *Bureau des Communications*. To understand what the public read and what publicists wrote, the men of this department became responsible for purchasing and analyzing all significant French and German publications. Then, to influence opinion through the media they were charged with issuing direct "communications to the press and public."[60] The bureau therefore initiated a program of subscribing to many newspapers and periodicals, and of receiving French and foreign journalists on a regular basis, including Sundays and legal holidays.[61] One contemporary diplomat observed that as a result of these innovations, "relations between the press and the Quai d'Orsay have certainly become closer than in the past" and that ministerial officials dealing with public opinion were receiving "more importance than ever before."[62]

After initiating this modest entrance into publicity activities, reformers turned toward more ambitious programs for extending French culture and propaganda abroad. Another new department soon appeared in the Ministry for Foreign Affairs: the *Bureau des Ecoles et des Oeuvres françaises à l'étranger.*[63] The responsibilities of this office included corresponding with those interested in the expansion of their language and thought overseas, recruiting the services of teachers and professors, and supervising the distribution of money to various French religious institutions, charitable organizations, schools, and hospitals located in foreign countries.[64] Enthusiasts urged that even these seemingly neutral education and health programs could be used for "scholarly propaganda" and

60. Decree of 29 April 1907, in France, *JO, 3 May 1907, p. 3268. The creation of this *Bureau* more or less replaced the earlier *Service de la Presse* which had been composed simply of a small number of individuals within the *Cabinet du Ministre*.

61. See MAE/Chambre, Rapport No. 2015 (1909), p. 22.

62. PRO/FO 371/666, report from Grahame, as enclosed in Despatch No. 44, "Confidential," from Bertie to Grey, 24 January 1909. I am indebted to David Miller for this reference.

63. Created first as a *service* by Pichon's ministerial *arrêté* of 4 April 1909, and then elevated to a *bureau* by the Decree of 13 August 1910.

64. France, MAE, *Annuaire diplomatique et consulaire,* 1911 and thereafter; and MAE/Sénat, Rapport No. 28 (1912), pp. 58–59. Money had been distributed to these overseas establishments for several years, but the amounts had always been relatively small and, before the creation of the *Bureau,* in no way had been systematically managed.

"medical propaganda."[65] Through such means officials hoped to reach the most influential citizens throughout the world, and thus to nurture a strong international sympathy for France and her *civilisation*.

The greatest impetus to this assumption of new and expanded responsibilities by the Quai d'Orsay came with the onslaught of the First World War and its flood of propaganda. Caught in the middle of this "struggle for the minds of men," the imaginative but modest prewar ministerial programs became grossly inadequate.[66] Pressure increased for bigger staffs, larger budgets, more extensive facilities, and aggressive involvement. In response, the creative and energetic Berthelot instituted and personally directed an elaborate administrative apparatus called the *Maison de la Presse*. As "one of the first to understand the role that propaganda would be able to play in diplomacy,"[67] Berthelot placed this bureau under the authority of the Ministry for Foreign Affairs where, in the words of one diplomat, "it rendered real service" to France.[68] Even allies knew the *Maison* as "the official French Propaganda Department."[69] With the men and women of this bureau, Berthelot funneled money to, and helped coordinate the activities of, the *Union des grandes associations françaises contre la propagande ennemie* and its multiple private organizations. He utilized newspapers, books, pamphlets, tracts, telegraphs, telephones, films, photographs, and even works of art.[70] Furthermore, he sent agents to legations abroad and he instituted extensive programs throughout the world to help spread the message of France.[71] "This system," said Berthelot with pride, "responded well to the existing necessities."[72]

65. MAE, Comptabilité, "Décrets et décisions ministérielles," Carton 64, item No. 257, annex to "Note pour le Ministre. Année 1913—Chapitre 23."

66. MAE/Chambre, Rapport No. 802 (1920), p. 15.

67. LaRoche, p. 31.

68. Ibid.

69. PRO/FO 371/3474, item 99085, F50910.

70. One propaganda exposition planned by the *Maison* included some of the great paintings of Cézanne, Renoir, Degas, Gauguin, Monet, and Toulouse-Lautrec, Gobelin tapestries, and various *objets d'art* borrowed from the Louvre. See MAE, Direction politique et commerciale, Papiers des Agents: Philippe Berthelot, Carton 6, dossier "Hollande: Propagande artistique."

71. See material on Berthelot's activities with the *Maison* in ibid., Cartons 1–12.

72. Ibid., Carton 7, letter from Berthelot to the French Ambassador in Rome, 28 July 1916.

The activities inspired by Berthelot and the *Maison* continued throughout the war, although the organization itself took the new name of *Services de l'information à l'étranger*.[73] One staff group, for example, organized all international communications, received journalists, and supplied them with information. In addition, they arranged for visits to the front lines because these were considered "one of the most effective means of propaganda."[74] Another section studied and published accounts from the foreign press. Still another group mobilized books, brochures, films, and photographs "to spread French thought abroad."[75] It was no exaggeration, therefore, to claim that during the war, the responsibilities of the Quai d'Orsay in propaganda affairs grew with "a considerable extension."[76]

After the war, it appeared more important than ever before that the Ministry for Foreign Affairs should "spread French views with unprecedented intensity and efficiency."[77] As described by one determined senator:

> It is necessary that France appear in the eyes of even the most remote people as a great victorious nation in full possession of her strength and her genius . . . [and] this responsibility, in large measure, is up to our diplomatic agents.[78]

The task for the Quai d'Orsay, therefore, became one of convincing the world of the incalculable price paid by Frenchmen for victory, of their innocence for the war's outbreak, and of Germany's corresponding guilt in initiating a holocaust. To demonstrate German "inhumanity," "despotic arrogance," or "cunning," might make the harsh terms of the Versailles Treaty at least seem more like impartial justice rather than deep revenge.[79]

73. MAE/Chambre, Rapport No. 802 (1920), p. 16.

74. Ibid., Rapport No. 4108 (1918), p. 78.

75. Ibid.

76. Ibid., Rapport No. 802 (1920), p. 58. Also see Georg Huber, *Die französische Propaganda im Weltkrieg gegen Deutschland, 1914 bis 1918*, (Munchen: Pfeiffer, 1928).

77. MAE/Chambre, Rapport No. 802 (1920), p. 13.

78. MAE/Sénat, Rapport No. 145 (1921), p. 2.

79. MAE/Chambre, Rapport No. 802 (1920), pp. 13–14; and idem, Rapport No. 6339 (1919), p. 115.

In order to accomplish this, innovators instituted a department that soon began "to contribute significantly to the propaganda work of the Ministry for Foreign Affairs—the *Service d'Information et de Presse*."[80] Due to the sudden public interest in diplomacy after the war, the first responsibilities of this division became answering requests for information and receiving French and foreign journalists. Reporters now obtained permission to discuss questions of foreign affairs "at any time"[81] and to attend daily press conferences. The Press and Information Service was responsible for sending news reports abroad by means of the latest telegraphic and telephonic devices. Such instruments in the hands of the Quai d'Orsay, asserted several deputies, would provide diplomats and bureaucrats with "the most powerful and the most rapid means of spreading information."[82] Additional tasks included the analysis and translation of articles appearing in foreign periodicals, and the publication of abstracts to keep officials abreast of world opinion.[83] With so many expanded responsibilities, the handful of men from the once-quiet prewar Communications Bureau became transformed into a bureaucracy staffed by eighty persons.[84] Still others were hired to serve as special press attachés or to publish and distribute documentary collections carefully selected from the "arsenal" of the archives.[85]

Extensive propaganda activities also became the primary task of one of the Ministry's most elaborate and ambitious innovations: the *Service des Oeuvres françaises à l'étranger*. Created by a special decree, this department was organized to spread superior French

80. Ibid., Rapport No. 802 (1920), p. 58.

81. Norton, p. 66.

82. MAE/Chambre, Rapport No. 802 (1920), p. 63; and idem, Rapport No. 2020 (1921), p. 150.

83. Such publications included the *Bulletin périodique de la presse, Bulletin quotidien de presse étrangère,* and the *Recueil de documents étrangers.*

84. Le Temps, "Le nombre des fonctionnaires des affaires étrangères," 22 July 1921.

85. See MAE/Chambre, Commission des Affaires étrangères, Rapport No. 5377, "Rapport . . . d'examiner la proposition de loi," par Louis Farges, p. 9. Also see the resulting publications of the *Livre jaune,* various short *Documents diplomatiques* on special problems, and the *DDF* series of 38 volumes covering the period from 1871–1914.

civilisation to all parts of the globe.[86] It sought " to centralize and coordinate all appropriate means of action to enlighten world opinion about France; about her sentiments, her resources, her work, and her achievements in the realm of art, science, commerce, and industry."[87]

Attaining such objectives hopefully would make "the genius of France known, admired, and loved."[88] Toward this end, one group called the *Section universitaire des Ecoles* was responsible for creating educational institutions, arranging exchanges, giving lectures, building libraries, and supporting associations teaching the French language. "Our universities and our schools in foreign lands," declared one report, "are veritable centers of favorable propaganda."[89] Another unit, the *Section artistique et littéraire,* was charged with keeping libraries abroad filled with appropriate books, sponsoring theatrical and musical entertainment, promoting exhibits and conferences, and maintaining contact with foreign literary critics. The *Section de tourisme et des sports* was assigned the task of encouraging foreigners to visit France and of assisting international athletic competitions. Finally, all additional activities not falling under the purview of these other sections were charged to the general *Section des Oeuvres diverses,* including financial support distributed to the propaganda committees of French religious denominations operating overseas.[90]

With this *Service des Oeuvres,* officials of the Quai d'Orsay found themselves immediately involved in a wide variety of propaganda activities throughout the world. They established professional chairs for French literature at universities in Finland, Latvia, Poland, Czechoslovakia, Hungary, Rumania, Bulgaria, Yugoslavia, Turkey, and Japan. They created scholarly institutes for French studies in Spain, Portugal, Italy, Great Britain, Belgium, Shanghai, Argentina, and Brazil. They gave financial assistance to French

86. Decree of 15 January 1920, according to MAE, Division des Archives, Papiers du Cabinet, "Décrets concernant l'organisation du Ministère des Affaires étrangères, 1870–1947." This replaced the *Bureau des Ecoles* created in 1910.
87. MAE/Chambre, Rapport No. 6339 (1919), p. 176.
88. Ibid., p. 115.
89. Ibid., Rapport No. 802 (1920), p. 49.
90. Ibid., pp. 47–57; and MAE/Sénat, Rapport No. 309 (1923), pp. 45–47.

schools in Syria, Palestine, China, India, Mexico, Cuba, and the United States including those in such cities as New York, San Francisco, Seattle, and New Orleans. They distributed thousands of books, brochures, photographs, and films to overseas libraries. They sponsored art exhibits in Copenhagen and Prague, and arranged for French athletes to compete in Sweden and Switzerland.[91]

Such wide-ranging activities conducted by the Ministry for Foreign Affairs itself gave dramatic demonstration of the new commitment to "cultural diplomacy." Henceforth, French diplomats and bureaucrats clearly would use the Quai d'Orsay and other government agencies in order to influence opinion as never before.[92] Indeed, the claim by one deputy that "the propagation of intellectual *civilisation* now is a very important part of our foreign policy"[93] is confirmed by the expanding annual expenditures for precisely this purpose:[94]

1900	353,850	current value francs
1905	883,340	
1910	2,277,971	
1915	2,309,000	
1920	14,214,351	
1925	27,817,950	
1930	37,112,205	
1935	66,881,803	

Such amounts received parliamentary approval year after year, although reductions occurred elsewhere and in other ministries. In part, the reason for this strong constant support—some called it an

91. See MAE/Sénat, Rapport No. 145 (1921), pp. 49–56; and MAE/Chambre, Rapport No. 4792 (1923), pp. 49–131.

92. See, for example, the discussion of the *Office d'expansion nationale* in France, *JO*, 8 December 1919, pp. 14187–88.

93. Charles Daniélou, *Les Affaires étrangères* (Paris: Figuière, 1927), p. 63.

94. Current value amounts taken from the figures indicated specifically for "Oeuvres" in the Quai d'Orsay's annual budget as found in France, MAE, *Compte définitif des dépenses de l'exercice 1900–1935*, except for the 1915 wartime figures which are from the less accurate MAE/Chambre, Rapport No. 802 (1920), p. 159. The 1935 figure includes a new item entitled "Fonds spéciaux pour information française à l'étranger."

"extraordinary mania"[95]—could be seen in the fear expressed by one deputy that "German propaganda . . . has resumed with the most feverish activity. . . . Although the Reich cannot find a single pfennig to spend on repairing the devastated regions of France that it destroyed, it is finding millions and millions of marks . . . to preach the supremacy of its *Kultur* over all parts of the world."[96]

3. *Propaganda and the Wilhelmstrasse*

With the first wave of popular uproar caused by the *Daily Telegraph* affair, many Germans became convinced that their own Ministry for Foreign Affairs should seek to influence public opinion. They too cried out that the few *ad hoc* contacts with newspaper correspondents as initiated by Bismarck would become more and more antiquated. They feared that unless the Wilhelmstrasse actively engaged in such activities, France and other nations would use international propaganda against them. Twentieth-century diplomacy required an urgent response in the form of new and expanded responsibilities for propagandizing those attitudes favorable to German foreign policy.[97] When these demands first reached Chancellor von Bülow, they fell on the receptive ears of not only the man most able to institute reforms and innovations, but also the man described by one contemporary as "a modern statesman who grasped with remarkable perspicacity the potential usefulness of the press."[98]

Under Bülow's administration, the *Pressebureau* of the Wilhelmstrasse "became one of the most important agencies in the government."[99] Directed by the shrewd former journalist and trusted bureaucrat, Otto Hammann, the Press Bureau soon gained considerable power and influence.[100] It was charged with the responsibility

---

95. PRO/FO 371/8257, comment by R. H. Campbell on W 9912/185/17.
96. MAE/Chambre, Rapport No. 802 (1920), p. 14.
97. See Section 1 of this chapter.
98. G. V. Williams, "The German Press Bureau," *The Contemporary Review,* 97 (March 1910), p. 322.
99. Hale, *Germany and the Diplomatic Revolution,* p. 6.
100. Holstein, 2, p. 732.

for maintaining close touch with public opinion and for guiding it whenever possible. Hammann and his enlarged staff systematically began to read, clip, and classify articles appearing in the German and foreign press.[101] They received newspaper correspondents, arranged interviews with ministerial officials, and prepared news releases for distribution. By either granting or withholding information, they could inspire friendly comments throughout the press. This deliberate practice led one openly hostile journalist to assert that German newspapers "could only be likened to a powerful and well-attuned organ on which the Press Bureau . . . knew how to play with every variety of skilfully contrived effect, sometimes *piano*, rarely *pianissimo*, and more often pulling out all the stops in succession for an impressive *largo* rising to a resounding *forte* or violent *fortissimo*."[102]

Other efforts concentrated upon involving the Wilhelmstrasse more deeply in the overseas propagation of *Kultur*. One diplomat soon noticed that "the Imperial Government is well aware of the importance of stimulating German culture all over the world and provides it practically by allowing annual grants to the various schools."[103] Ministerial expenditures increased significantly for the constuction and maintenance of schools, libraries, institutes, and missions scattered from China to the Middle East to Argentina.[104] Assistance and encouragement were provided to private educational and propaganda associations such as the *Verein für das Deutschtum in Ausland*.[105] Some observers viewed the expansion of these new responsibilities as a direct result of "a modern spirit," "methodical organization," and "vigorous and continuous action."[106] Others

---

101. The subscription list of foreign periodicals can be found in PA/AA, Abteilung IA, Deutschland 149, Band 12, A. 2843.

102. Chirol, p. 277. Also,see *Das Kleine Journal*, "Reorganisation des offiziösen Pressebureaus," 23 November 1911; and the later job description provided in the note of 30 July 1912, in PA/AA, Abteilung IA, Deutschland 122 Nr. 2, Band 5.

103. PRO/FO 368/984, Despatch No. 197, Commercial, from Goschen (Berlin) to Grey, 29 December 1913.

104. PA/AA, Politisches Archiv, Haushalt des Auswärtigen Amtes, 1901–1914. Although funds had been allocated to these schools for several years, the amounts were very small. In 1912 a new budget item also appeared: "Förderung des deutschen Nachrichtenwesens im Ausland."

105. See Croneberg, passim.

106. "Note sur un projet", pp. 21–22, in MAE/Allemagne, politique étrangère, dossier général, NS 18.

saw the subsequent activities "as all directed toward the same goal: the spreading of German culture and genius around the entire surface of the globe."[107]

In Germany, as in France, the most dramatic change toward further ministerial involvement in these affairs occurred with the cataclysmic experience of the First World War. Here, in the words of one authority, "Propaganda became an obsession."[108] Foreign opinion seemed to crystalize almost immediately against the German invasion of neutral Belgium, and in response innovative diplomats and bureaucrats began to organize new institutional means for conducting massive propaganda campaigns. Within just a few weeks they created an office within the Ministry for Foreign Affairs designed to coordinate the efforts of other government agencies also trying to influence opinion abroad: the *Zentralstelle für Auslandsdienst*. Directed by former ambassador Freiherr von Mumm, the staff of this department disbursed huge sums of money to buy "friendly" journalists overseas, to print foreign language newspapers, and to support private patriotic groups. They collected press clippings from foreign papers and published detailed summaries of these articles on a regular basis.[109] They also supervised the distribution of countless books, brochures, photos, posters, and motion pictures throughout the world to elicit sympathy from citizens in other lands for German policies.[110] Such activities made the *Zentralstelle* "a very busy bureau" and one responsible for "an imposing array of propaganda material."[111]

Additional innovations instituted during the heat of war included transformation of the small Press Bureau into the new and enlarged *Nachrichtenabteilung* (Press and Information Division). Directives made clear that its responsibilities now should "encompass not only

107. Despatch No. 380, from Jules Cambon (Berlin) to MAE, 30 June 1914, in ibid.

108. Lucy M. Salmon, *The Newspaper and Authority* (New York: Oxford University Press, 1923), p. 336.

109. Included in this list of publications are the various *Wochenbericht* of the Zentralstelle fur Auslandsdienst—Zeitungskontrolle entitled *Französische Presse, Italienische Presse,* or the *Deutsche und Österreichische Presse.*

110. PA/AA, Abteilung IA, Deutschland 149, Band 21, A.N. 11807, note from Mumm, 30 December 1915.

111. Lasswell, p. 24.

foreign, but domestic politics as well."[112] To manage the resulting increase of duties, Wilhelmstrasse officials created a wide variety of bureaucratic subdivisions. Some became responsible for supplying news to the German press and for acting as general censor. Others gave interviews to foreign correspondents and distributed information to all geographical areas overseas. Some sections specialized in topical matters such as war aims or "commercial propaganda." Still others devoted their energies to various means of influence including illustrated literature, caricatures, pamphlets, or films. One office concentrated specifically on *Kulturpropaganda*, utilizing art, music, drama, and even variety shows if necessary to gain public support for external policies.[113]

The use of such means by the Ministry for Foreign Affairs represented a mere prelude to those activities of the postwar period. Upon receiving the victor's imposed peace terms, many citizens screamed that their national propaganda should be multiplied to unparalleled proportions. "Hatred engendered by the most refined methods and fantastic lies contributed considerably to our defeat," claimed Admiral von Tirpitz. "Hatred of France is therefore of vital necessity for us," asserted this master of influencing popular opinion, and urged his countrymen to continue counter-propaganda programs "because we now need hatred to maintain ourselves and we wish to see it live in the hearts of all Germans."[114] He and many others felt that such a campaign should be directed by the Wilhelmstrasse. They believed that it should persuade people at home and abroad of the guilt among others for starting the war, of the ruthlessness of the treaty *Diktat,* and of the necessity for civilization to have Germany stand as a bulwark against the spectre of Bolshevism.[115] If they could convince people of the "sadistic hatred" and "inexorable cruelty" of France, perhaps they could

112. PA/AA, Abteilung IA, Deutschland 122 Nr. 2, *secr.,* Band 2, A.S. 4180, note concerning the "Sitzung des Königlichen Staatsministerium," 20 October 1916.

113. Ibid., Presse Abteilung, Beiakten I, Band 1, A.N. 1335, "Geschäftsverteilung der Nachrichtenabteilung," February 1916 with Hammann; and idem, Abteilung IA, Deutschland 149, Band 25, circular of 2 October 1917 from Radowitz.

114. Admiral von Tirpitz, in *Deutsche Allgemeine Zeitung,* 22 February 1923.

115. See PA/AA, Nachlässe Ulrich von Brockdorff-Rantzau, Aktenzeichen 14, Band 1, report of 18 March 1919 entitled "Reorganisationspläne," and *Vossische Zeitung,* "Auslandsdeutsche und Republik," 7 June 1921; among others.

win sympathy by posing as the injured party and thus discredit the moral condemnation and the oppressive obligations contained within the Treaty of Versailles.

Part of this propaganda campaign became the responsibility of the newly-created *Vereinigte Presseabteilung der Reichsregierung*. Supervised by a high-ranking official of the Wilhelmstrasse and placed under the direction of the Foreign Minister and the Chancellor, this division served as the authorized spokesman for all government ministries. It assumed the tasks of presenting, explaining, and supporting official policy before the news media. In order to perform these functions effectively, bureaus were organized for complete coverage of the globe. Individual sections specialized in Western Europe, Central Europe and the Balkans, the Americas, England and the Near East and Africa, Russia with Poland and Scandinavia, and Asia. Other sections coordinated matters of press conferences on both domestic and foreign politics with German journalists, telegraph and telephone communications, contact with the Wolff Bureau, and the dissemination of books, brochures, films, and other forms of propaganda.[116] A special office called the *Reichszentral für Heimatdienst* provided assistance with various publications or news releases on questions of economics, society, culture, and, of course, foreign policy.[117]

Still another institutional innovation designed for the Wilhelmstrasse's new efforts to influence world opinion found form in the *Schuldreferat* (War Guilt Section) whose purpose was the mobilization of all available means that might convince people of Germany's innocence for the outbreak of the First World War. It acted as censor over archival evidence on prewar diplomacy by giving documents to some and denying them to others, by subsidizing "objective" (i.e., friendly) writers and historians, and by publishing numerous collections of primary source material such as the massive *Die Grosse Politik* series. The *Schuldreferat* also financed and utilized front organizations for its work, including the *Zentralstelle für Erforschung der Kriegschuldfrage* (Center for the

116. PA/AA, Presse Abteilung, Beiakten I, Band 1, directive of 24 November 1919; and idem, Politisches Archiv, Geschäftsverteilungspläne, Band 1, relevant sections on "Presseabteilung."

117. See Germany, *Handbuch für das Deutsche Reich, 1922*, p. 57; and Johannes Richter, *Die Reichszentrale für Heimatdienst* (Berlin: Landeszentrale für politische Bildungsarbeit, 1963).

Study of the War Guilt Question) to insure that revisionist literature would receive wide circulation among academicians and publicists. By producing the monthly journal *Die Kriegsschuldfrage,* it provided a prominent forum for propagating favorable views against the Versailles "lie." In addition, it used the *Arbeitsausschuss Deutscher Verbände* (Working Committee of German Associations) "to guide virtually every patriotic organization in matters of German war guilt" by means of "all the modern propaganda techniques"[118]—"word, print, and picture."[119]

To complete this propaganda machinery within the Ministry for Foreign Affairs, Schüler created one final department: the *Kultur Abteilung* (Cultural Division). Its responsibility was the proliferation of *Deutschtum* (German culture) throughout the world. One section, the *Auswanderung Referat,* dealt with emigration, maintaining contact with ethnic Germans living abroad, and with the distribution of funds to various missionary establishments. The *Schulen Referat* specialized in supporting overseas schools teaching the German tongue and in granting scholarships to enable foreign students to study in Germany. Another bureau, the *Kunst Referat,* managed the use of fine art exhibits, musical and theatrical performances, and sporting events. Finally, the *Literatur Referat* supplied overseas libraries with book after book on German literature, language, and philosophy in order to win sympathy abroad.[120]

Equipped with such an administrative apparatus, diplomats and bureaucrats of the Wilhelmstrasse discovered themselves spending more time and more money on propagandizing efforts than ever before. In 1919 the first-year operations of the *Vereinigte Presseabteilung* cost three and one-half million marks. Only one year later its expenses in current values exceeded eleven million marks.[121] Even

---

118. Herman Wittgens, "The German Foreign Office Campaign against the Versailles Treaty" (Seattle: unpublished dissertation, 1970), pp. iv, 43, which provides the best treatment of the *Schuldreferat* available in English. Also see F. Stieve, "Der Kampf gegen die Kriegsschuldlüge, 1922–1928," *Berliner Monatshefte,* 15 (March 1937), pp. 194–201.

119. Hans Dreager, "Der Arbeitsausschuss Deutscher Verbände," *Berliner Monatshefte,* 15 (March 1937), p. 262.

120. PA/AA, Politisches Archiv, Geschäftsverteilungspläne, Band 1, I.A. 2482,*Verfügung* of 10 September 1920, signed by Schüler; and the relevant material on the *Kultur Abteilung.*

121. Ibid., "Haushalt des Auswärtiges Amtes," 1919, 1920.

the amounts allocated to a single budget item for "Promotion of German Information Abroad" demonstrate a striking expansion within just a few years:[122]

1918	300,000	current value marks
1919	3,000,000	
1920	17,600,000	
1921	25,000,000	
1922	610,000,000	

Expenditures of this magnitude permitted officials to initiate an extensive propaganda program considered to be one "conducted with method, perserverance, ingenuity, and prodigious means."[123] They subsidized overseas schools, educational institutions, religious missions, hospitals, nationalistic associations, and cultural organizations. They sponsored lectures, courses, seminars, expositions, shows, and athletic competitions. They inspired the content of material appearing on the screen, over the radio, and in the press, magazines, professional journals, books, and documentary collections.[124] In addition, they deliberately began to involve publicists in the affairs of diplomacy.

4. Publicists and Diplomacy

While instituting these dramatic changes officials in both the Quai d'Orsay and the Wilhelmstrasse realized that they now would need the active assistance of those persons most qualified in propaganda activities. The diplomats and bureaucrats understood that their own inclination, training, and experience certainly had not prepared them in the techniques of influencing "the masses." To succeed, they needed the talents and expertise of those persons most able to reach, to teach, and to mobilize public opinion. Such activities, said

---

122. Current value amounts taken from ibid., 1918-1922.

123. *La Tribune de Lausanne,* "L'Organisation de la propagande allemand," 16 March 1921.

124. See PA/AA, Abteilung VI (Kultur), Allgemeines, Band 1, passim; and idem, Sonderreferat W, Politik Nr. 25, Band 1, I.G. 95, "An sämtliche Arbeitseinheiten."

one report, required collaborators "recruited from the outside: professors, scholars, businessmen, and other publicists noted for their particular competence."[125] In France, the Ministry began to utilize teachers, authors, missionaries, artists, film directors, and athletic champions among others—all "representatives of the French spirit and culture."[126] In Germany as well, "journalists, deputies, permanent officials, speakers, writers, and even young ladies were harnessed to the cart."[127] As a consequence, publicists of various kinds were to become conspicuous actors in twentieth-century diplomacy.

One of the most readily available sources of these outside publicity experts could be found in the many private propaganda organizations flourishing throughout France and Germany, Here, the Ministries for Foreign Affairs discovered patriotic men and women eager to devote considerable energy to spreading the glory of their respective nations. Efforts by the Quai d'Orsay increasingly used the skills of personnel from language associations such as *Alliance française*, religious groups like *Amitiés catholiques françaises* or *Comité protestant de propagande française à l'étranger*, and friendship societies such as the *Comité France-Amèrique*. Within just a short period of time, their valuable assistance became described as "one of the essential elements of French overseas propaganda."[128]

The Wilhelmstrasse similarly drew upon the talents of these groups specializing in influencing popular opinion. By means of the *Arbeitsausschuss Deutscher Verbände* it soon established contact with over one thousand different organizations, including the *Deutscher Frauenausschuss zur Bekämpfung der Schuldlüge, Akademischer Arbeitsausschuss gegen Versailles Dikat und Kriegsschuldlüge, Arbeitsgemeinschaft für Vaterländische Auf-*

---

125. MAE/Chambre, Rapport No. 6339 (1919), p. 177.
126. Ibid., Rapport No. 802 (1920), p. 48; idem, Rapport No. 2020 (1921), p. 146; and idem, Rapport No. 3131 (1922), p. 34.
127. *Acht Uhr Abendblatt*, "Erzberger," 27 August 1921.
128. Daniélou, p. 73. Also see MAE, Direction politique et commerciale, Papiers des Agents: Philippe Berthelot, Carton 1, undated report from Deschanel concerning the Fédération Nationale des Grandes Associations Françaises, and Carton 3, untitled "France. Comités."

klärung, and the *Volksbund für das Deutschtum im Ausland*.[129] Such collaboration between public and private sectors, said one authority, gave diplomats and bureaucrats the new means "to reach a vast audience that otherwise could not be touched with so-called 'official' propaganda."[130]

In addition, the French and German Ministries for Foreign Affairs began to employ publicists directly. With his well-known affinity for those with "literary or artistic skills,"[131] Berthelot encouraged the Quai d'Orsay to hire individuals like Charles Daniélou, the politician-journalist, and Jean Giraudoux, the playwright-novelist, to manage the important *Service des Oeuvres françaises* for cultural propaganda. Paul Claudel, the celebrated man of letters, received appointments as ambassador to Washington and then to Tokyo. Under Schüler's direction, the Wilhelmstrasse similarly opened its once-sacrosanct doors to those with publicity experience. Prolific writer-propagandists such as Friederich Heilbron or Friedrich Stieve and art curators like Johannes Sievers were employed in the *Vereinigte Presseabteilung, Schuldreferat,* and *Kultur Abteilung.* Several journalists even secured assignments as mission chiefs abroad, including Adolf Müller in Berne, Ulrich Rauscher in Warsaw, and Adolf Köster in Riga and then in Belgrade.[132]

Officials also commissioned publicists to perform specific tasks. The Quai d'Orsay began hiring professors to deliver occasional lectures or instructors to teach the French language overseas. In return for cash payments, agents of the wire services distributed information, theatrical groups gave performances, and famous personalities traveled abroad to represent the achievements of France.[133] The Wilhelmstrasse itself employed "a host of writers

129. PA/AA, Sonderreferat W, Politik Nr. 25, Band 1, I.G. 95, memorandum of 15 March 1922 "An sämtliche Arbeitseinheiten"; Wittgens, pp. 41–48.

130. Daniélou, p. 74.

131. Challener, in Craig and Gilbert, 1, p. 72.

132. PA/AA, Büro des Reichsministers, Aktenzeichen 2, Band 2, the unregistered, unsigned document listing previous occupations; and Sievers, pp. 288, 456.

133. MAE, Direction politique et commerciale, Papiers des Agents: Philippe Berthelot, passim; France, Ministère des Affaires culturelles, *Les Archives de l'Agence Havas* (Paris: S.E.V.E.N., 1969), pp. xvi–xvii and xxiii; MAE/Chambre, Rapport No. 4792 (1923), pp. 13–17 and 126–30.

. . . engaged as part-time propagandists."[134] These free-lance authors received subsidies for writing three or four pieces each month exonerating Germany from war guilt. The resulting numbers of monographs, articles, and reviews are described by one scholar as "nearly incredible."[135]

Though many observers considered such changes as imperative and as shrewd responses to "the new conditions,"[136] a few also viewed them as a perilous menace to established diplomatic practice. They argued that to replace with propaganda the traditional norms of private conversations, restraint, and discretion would lead only to public displays, to misunderstandings, and to uncontrollable emotions. Several French ambassadors complained of professional diplomats being "deposed" by press correspondents and warned against the potential dangers of this "inflamation of national passions."[137] Others claimed that propaganda was an "insidious weapon," a "terrible invention," or an "engine of mental corruption."[138] One German diplomat referred to this attempt to influence opinion as another of the "horrors and abortions" produced by the First World War and sagaciously advised against excessive reliance upon it. "I am convinced," he said, "that propaganda itself is useless. It is just like advertisement in private business. If a firm supplies good products, advertisement produces excellent results. But if the products are poor, the firm and its advertisement will soon break down together. In the same way, the best political propaganda, equipped today with wireless and every modern method, cannot transform a mistaken foreign policy into a successful one."[139]

*   *   *   *

With the assumption of these new and expanded responsibilities for international propaganda, the Quai d'Orsay and Wilhelmstrasse

134. Imanuel Geiss, "The Outbreak of the First World War and German War Aims," *Journal of Contemporary History*, 1, 3 (July 1966), p. 76.

135. Wittgens, p. 190.

136. Daniélou, p. 74.

137. See Saint Aulaire, *Confession*, pp. 48, 776–77; Cambon, p. 103; and Albert Mousset, *La France vue de l'étranger; ou le déclin de la diplomatie et le mythe de la propagande* (Paris: L'Ile de France, 1926).

138. Sir Rennell Rodd, "The Old and the New Diplomacy," *Quarterly Review*, 239, 474 (January 1923), p. 82; Nicolson, *Diplomacy*, p. 93; and Salmon, p. 366.

139. Bernstorff, p. 47.

further demonstrated their ability to respond to a rapidly changing environment. Contemporaries praised these reforms and innovations as "particularly encouraging," "the greatest success," and "excellent."[140] The creation of specialized divisions and bureaus, the enlargement of staffs, the utilization of innovative techniques and instruments designed to influence popular opinion, and the placing of publicists in decision-making positions all signified a dramatic break with the past. The new activities of this elaborate apparatus were described as "indispensable" and as "an important and integral part" of the operations of both the French and German Ministries for Foreign Affairs.[141] Such developments indicated an unprecedented determination to use propaganda in diplomacy.

Indeed, conscious efforts to influence public opinion at home and abroad now became a major hallmark of diplomacy in the twentieth century. Within just a short period of time, commentators began to reflect upon the contrast existing between new and traditional diplomatic practices. "Thirty years ago," said one scholar, "the word propaganda was hardly known to students of politics. Today no word is of more frequent occurrence in newspapers, in books, in conversation, whenever international relations are discussed. The importance of propaganda is recognized, willingly or reluctantly, by all; and every government in the world pays ever-increasing attention to it."[142] For this reason propaganda became described as "a decisive factor" in diplomacy, "of prime importance" in foreign politics, and as "one of the most powerful instrumentalities in the modern world."[143] One astute observer predicted that "even in peace, propaganda seems likely for the future to be recognized as a regular instrument of foreign policy."[144]

140. See MAE/Chambre, Rapport No. 3131 (1922), pp. 16, 25, 26, 30; idem, Rapport No. 4792 (1923), p. 16; Pfeiffer, 23 October 1919, in Germany, Reichstag, *SB*, 330, p. 3366; Hoetzsch, 16 April 1923, in idem, 359, p. 10539; among others.

141. MAE, Commission de Réorganisation, "Rapports," p. 91; and Wittgen p. v.

142. Preface to Carr.

143. See Akzin, pp. 3, 12; Lasswell, p. 220; Bernstorff, p. 47; Norton, p. 64; Vansittart, p. 159; Allard, pp. 57–63, 167–92; Paul-Boncour, 2, pp. 398ff.; Nicolson, *Diplomacy*, pp. 92–94; and Strang, pp. 22, 43.

144. Carr, p. 12.

PART IV

— 7 —

Epilogue:
On the Nature of Institutional Responses
and Twentieth-Century Diplomacy

> *It must be considered that there is nothing more
> difficult to carry out, nor more doubtful of suc-
> cess, nor more dangerous to handle, than for a
> reformer to initiate a new order of things.*
> –Niccolo Machiavelli

The reforms and innovations instituted for the Quai d'Orsay and
Wilhelmstrasse demonstrated an ability to respond creatively to the
rigorous demands of twentieth-century diplomacy. Their achievements are all the more remarkable because of their striking similarity. They did not reflect national differences between France and
Germany because they both addressed themselves to the larger and
more universal problems faced by modern diplomats and bureaucrats everywhere. For this reason, their accomplishments served as
a model to stimulate major administrative changes in the Foreign
Ministries of many other countries.[1] It is hardly surprising, therefore, that the French responses became described as "logical,"

1. Among many examples, see "La Riforma del Ministero degli Esteri," *La
Vita Italiana* (April 1917), pp. 337–68; "Belgique: La réforme consulaire," *Les
Annales diplomatique et consulaires*, No. 44 (15 February 1920), p. 6; *Züricher
Post*, "Unsere Konsularvertretung," 4 July 1917; PRO/FO 371/900, Despatch No.
11, "Confidential," from Langley to Bertie (Paris), 12 January 1911; Britain, Royal
Commission of the Civil Service, Command Paper No. 7748, "Fifth Report of the
Commissioners: The Diplomatic Corps and the Foreign Office; The Consular
Service," and Command Paper No. 7749, "Appendix to the Fifth Report,"
particularly pp. 80, 84, 86, in *Sessional Papers 1914–1916*, XI (London: H.M.S.O.,
1914); Young, pp. 54–55, 60–63 and passim; PA/AA, Abteilung III, Geschäftsgang
Ia, Band 1, L512, letter from Coffin (American Commission) to von Lohneysen, 12
January 1921; U.S. Congress, House of Representatives, Committee on Foreign
Affairs, Document No. 24470, "Hearings . . . for the Reorganization and
Improvement of the Foreign Service" (Washington: G.P.O., 1922).

"most important," and "most advantageous," "well-conceived," "gradually and systematically developed."[2] Admirers referred to the German responses as "a reformation from top to bottom," "highly up-to-date," "an improvement without question," and "a great reform of modernization."[3]

These praises are well-deserved, for the initiation of a new order of things requires confrontation with innumerable difficulties. To overcome the inertia, tradition, and vested interests of bureaucratic institutions often involves serious monetary, psychological, and political costs. The relative importance of change over stability or of technical competence above ideological belief is not easy to determine, and no solution is acceptable to everyone. Struggles, compromises, and the ever-transforming environment complicate these problems even further. As the experience of the French and German Ministries for Foreign Affairs indicates, the obstacles confronting reformers and innovators are enormous.

1. The Hard Realities

Sweeping institutional responses, by their very nature, are disruptive. Since reforms restructure existing arrangements and since innovations create entirely new ones, they introduce change, disturb traditional patterns, upset entrenched interests, and compel altered performance for the future. The problems resulting from these upheavals become particularly acute in bureaucratic settings, where the essence of operational continuity depends upon established routine, predictable behavior, and general stability. Even Max Weber, who idolized this form of organization, observed that once bureaucracy is fully developed, it is one of society's most difficult creations to modify.[4] It is not surprising, therefore, that the first institutional responses to twentieth-century diplomacy in

2. See MAE/Chambre, Rapport No. 361 (1911), p. 139; idem, Rapport No. 4108 (1918), p. 11; and Report by Consul C. Edwards (Paris) entitled "Changes Made," in NA/DS, Index 841.021/2, among others.

3. Schifferdecker, p. 45; Hindenburg, p. 15; "Grosses Reinemachen im Auswärtigen Amt," *Roland: Gesellschaft, Kunst, Finanz*, Heft 3 (19 January 1921), p. 5; and PA/AA, "Ministerialdirektor a. D. Schüler," and Schuman, p. 193, among others.

4. Weber, 2, 577ff.

France and Germany should be subjected to many practical difficulties—or to what one ambassador called "the hard realities."[5]

One such problem is that presented by the resistance of existing arrangements. Reformers and innovators must contend with commitments to the established order, with fear of the unfamiliar, with inertia, with apathy, and with those who stand to lose something if change is instituted. As many writers have noted, these forces are magnified even more in bureaucracies where the prevailing philosophy tends to sanctify the *status quo* and to suppress criticism.[6] The tendency to emphasize loyalty, to stress adherence to the rules, and to glorify traditional ways of doing things deliberately discourages individuals who detect shortcomings from voicing their opinions. Those who express discontent by proposing the introduction of reforms or innovations indicate by their very suggestion that, in contrast to their colleagues, they do not share the prevailing values or accepted norms. For this reason, they are considered by others to be deviants, and therefore must overcome the fact that they may be regarded as being unworthy of receiving either respect or cooperation in their efforts.

Other difficulties are raised by the inherently disruptive character of change itself. It is a form of creative destruction in that the old order is broken down to pave the way for the new. The transformation of old offices, duties, chains of command, and various power relationships can cause great uncertainty and confusion in the regular operations of an organization. People are pushed from the familiar to the unknown, from the tried to the untried, and from the predictable to the unpredictable. They are forced away from their comforts of habit and vested interests. They are required to learn new skills and performance patterns, and made to adapt to those adjustments in their responsibilities, routines, and authority structures. In the process, tensions frequently come to the surface and generate even further confusion. It is hardly surprising, therefore, that observers saw efforts to create institutional responses to

5. Schoen, p. 112, who also notes on pp. 118–19 that these difficulties must never be underrated. In addition, see James McCamy, *The Administration of American Foreign Affairs* (New York: Knopf, 1950), pp. 82–83.

6. Among others, see Peter Blau and Marshall Meyer, *Bureaucracy in Modern Society* (New York: Random House, 1971 ed.), pp. 50–55; and Everett Rogers, *Diffusion of Innovations* (New York: Free Press, 1969), p. 193.

twentieth-century diplomacy as often meeting "with strong opposition from the permanent officials."[7] In both the Quai d'Orsay and the Wilhelmstrasse, there were complaints that reforms and innovations had "disorganized the Ministry,"[8] introduced "defects" and "serious inconveniences,"[9] exhibited "kaleidoscopic changing," and produced "complete chaos."[10]

Besides creating initial disruption, the introduction of elaborate changes can impose serious burdens upon available resources. They require extensive investigations, evaluations, and decisions—all of which divert time, energy, and money away from normally heavy responsibilities.[11] Even when approved, such expenditures are a calculated risk for there is no guarantee that modifications will produce beneficial results. When reforms or innovations actually take place, financial allocations must be increased to correspond with the expansion of services, the growth of staffs, the salary raises, and the purchase of new equipment. In the French and German Ministries for Foreign Affairs these difficulties were exacerbated by postwar financial problems, by competition with other ministries for limited funds, and by vociferous demands by taxpayers that all developments "stay within the limits of the budget."[12]

7. Report of 31 October 1919, "Secret," from the Director of Military Intelligence (War Office) to Under Secretary of State for Foreign Affairs, in PRO/FO 371/3778.

8. Private letter from Paul Cambon (London) to Jules Cambon, 31 January 1911, in MAE, Direction politique et commerciale, Papiers des Agents: Jules Cambon, Carton 6. I am indebted to David Miller for this reference. Also see Millet, p. 190; and Pognon, pp. 37 and 120–21.

9. MAE/Chambre, Rapport No. 1237 (1912), p. xix; and idem, Rapport No. 148 (1913), p. 44.

10. Private letter from Simons (Bärenfels) to Haniel, 30 December 1920; and private letter from Simons (Berlin) to Lersner (Nieder-Erlenbach), 18 September 1920; both in PA/AA, Büro des Reichsministers, Aktenzeichen 2, Band 1. Also see Schifferdecker, p. 48.

11. See James March and H. Simon, "Planning and Innovation in Organizations," in Joseph Litterer (ed.), *Organizations: Systems, Control and Adaptation* (New York: Wiley, 1969 ed.), 2, 328–44.

12. MAE/Chambre, Rapport No. 2015 (1909), p. 38; MAE/Sénat, Rapport No. 28 (1912), p. 28; MAE/Chambre, Rapport No. 802 (1920), p. 4ff.; Brockdorff-Rantzau, 10 April 1919, in Germany, Nationalversammlung, *SB*, 327, p. 931; the unnumbered report entitled "Aufzeichnung für die Besprechung mit dem Reichskommissar für die Vereinfachung und Vereinheitlichung der Reichsverwaltung," dated December 1920, in PA/AA, Büro des Reichsministers, Aktenzeichen 2, Band 1; and Seabury, p. 19.

Among the other "hard realities" are those problems presented by the daily external pressures of international affairs and domestic politics which continue unabated and sometimes demand immediate attention themselves. Those who introduce institutional change do not have the luxury of conducting their tasks in peace. In fact, many observers note that reforms and innovations are most likely to occur not during times of stability, but rather in the midst of some traumatic crisis—at a critical time when a particular event or combination of events temporarily unhinges the strength of those forces resistant to change.[13] This may provide the spark that ignites the situation, giving reformers or innovators their chance, but it also complicates their difficulties. The frustration caused by this dilemma was apparent to Brockdorff-Rantzau, who said: "It is in some ways unfortunate that peace and reform should coincide. More peaceful conditions would be necessary to bring the foreign service to the highest level of perfection by reforms, and a highly developed apparatus would be needed to attain a tolerable peace in the unprecedented difficult situation in which Germany finds itself today."[14]

Additional obstacles are produced by the inevitable criticisms that result when abstract ideas are translated into concrete reality. Constant expressions of scepticism and displeasure or even violent protest over substantive changes are common problems. Critics in both Paris and Berlin complained that in their reorganized Ministries for Foreign Affairs it was dangerous to separate different features of international relations into so many diverse geographical, functional, and administrative divisions. Some trained in traditional methods warned of the resulting hazards in "the dispersing of efforts and crumbling of responsibilities,"[15] while others claimed that certain questions of a universal nature actually defied such division.[16] Sceptics said that "only a circus driver" could manage so many different departments,[17] and argued that the new organization

13. See Albert Lanza, *Les Projets de réforme administrative en France de 1919 à nos jours* (Paris: Presses Universitaires de France, 1968), p. 161; Brecht, p. 13; Rogers, p. 125; and Caiden, p. 134.

14. Brockdorff-Rantzau, in Germany, Nationalversammlung, *SB*, 327, p. 931.

15. Millet, p. 193.

16. See MAE/Chambre, Rapport No. 1237 (1912), pp. xix, 119–20.

17. *Kölnische Volkszeitung*, "Unser Auswärtiges Amt," 30 May 1921.

was "suited for a museum of natural history—but not a Foreign Ministry."[18]

Practical difficulties also can be increased by criticisms directed against the methods of instituting change. Even though agreement may exist on objectives, emotion-charged disputes frequently ensue concerning the ways in which decisions are made and implemented. Particularly susceptible to attack are the men responsible for directing these operations. They are likely to find that opponents fail to appreciate their efforts, ridicule their ideas, distort their words, suspect their motives, or plot to subvert their plans. Critics frequently complained of Berthelot's heavy-handed methods and accused Pichon of enacting reforms with "an autocratic temperament."[19] Schüler too was charged with being "inaccessible,"[20] creating "numerous enemies"[21]—"about as many foes as an average person ever can make"[22]—and establishing a "personal regime."[23] Some officials in their private correspondence referred to him as an "autocrat" and "dictator,"[24] and eventually organized their opposition to the point where they could successfully force Schüler from office.

Such vindictive complaints—when occurring simultaneously with expressions of lavish praise—emphasize that reform and innovation invariably involve conflict. Complex and difficult problems abound in balancing between competing ideas, interests, and individuals. Moreover, as Chancellor Wirth once remarked, there is always the struggle "between those who look backwards and dream of byegone splendor, and those who strive passionately, perhaps too

---

18. Freiherr von Griesinger, "Aufbau, Umbau und Abbau des Auswärtigen Amt," *Deutsche Revue*, 47 (March 1922), p. 195.

19. Pognon, p. 37. Also see MAE/Sénat, Rapport No. 165 (1911), p. 36; MAE/Chambre, Rapport No. 4108 (1918) p. 12; and idem, Rapport No. 802 (1920), pp. 7, 81.

20. See the Military Intelligence report, "Secret," "The Reorganization of the Foreign Office," from D.M. 1 (Rotterdam) to Foreign Secretary, 13 December 1920, in PRO/FO 371/4851.

21. *Freiheit*, "Politischer Geist und politische Technik," 25 May 1921.

22. *Berliner Tageblatt*, 27 December 1920.

23. *Frankfurter Zeitung*, "Das Auswärtige Amt," 25 December 1920.

24. Private letter from Kuno Tiemann to Simons, 2 July 1920; and private letter, "Streng vertraulich und persönlich!" from Schubert (London) to von Haniel, 28 July 1920; both in PA/AA, Büro des Reichsministers, Aktenzeichen 2, Band 1.

eagerly, forward."[25] The necessity of compromise in these circumstances makes complete satisfaction an exception, as evidenced in the Quai d'Orsay and Wilhelmstrasse where actions perceived as "too much" by some were seen as "not enough" by others.[26] With good cause, therefore, one diplomat noted very early that in instituting change "it is not easy to devise a remedy."[27] At the time when a spirit of compromise, good-will and cooperation are needed most, reforms and innovations only seem to make disagreement and strife flourish. As Schüler said himself, they actually encourage extremism both "for and against."[28]

These difficulties manifest a larger and more serious problem: that reform or innovation is a highly political matter. In the words of Gerald Caiden, both represent sheer "power politics in action."[29] They entail struggles for control of services and people, fights between people and institutions, campaign strategies and obstructive tactics, compromises, and concessions. The availability of opportunities, number of constraints, strength of opposition, allocation of resources, comprehensiveness of program, timing and sequence of implementation, interdependence with other changes, and the power of the individuals involved are determined to a very large degree by politics. This means that a successful reformer or innovator must be able to manipulate the various pressures and competitors of his political environment. As Samuel Huntington describes it, such a person must become "a master politician."[30]

25. Dr. Wirth, as cited in Despatch No. 1040 from D'Abernon (Berlin) to Foreign Secretary, 12 August 1921, in PRO/FO 371/5970.

26. See, for example, MAE/Chambre, Rapport No. 1237 (1912), p. 131; France, Chambre, Commission des Affaires étrangères, Rapport No. 5377, Annexe au procès-verbal de la 2ᵉ séance du 28 décembre 1922, "Rapport fait au nom de la Commission des Affaires étrangères chargée d'examiner la proposition . . . à répartir en zones administratives nos postes et agents diplomatique ou consulaires et à organiser, sur cette specialisation, les services des affaires étrangères," par Louis Farges, p. 3; and PA/AA, Büro des Reichsministers, Aktenzeichen 2, Band 2; passim.

27. Heinrich von Tschirschky, as cited in Despatch No. 348, "Very Confidential," from Lascelles (Berlin) to Grey, 9 November 1906, in PRO/FO 371/80.

28. Schüler's letter to Gneist, 1 January 1921, in PA/AA, Büro des Reichsministers, Aktenzeichen 2, Band 2. Also see Pognon, passim.

29. Caiden, p. 9.

30. Samuel Huntington, *Political Order in Changing Society* (New Haven: Yale University Press, 1968), p. 345.

This burden is compounded by the fact that very few people possess the ability to direct the multiple forces of politics. Reforms and innovations are rare, it has been said, because the political talents necessary to make them a reality are rare.[31] Not many individuals have the requisite skill to introduce change without threatening the stability of the institution, stiffening resistance of vested interests, or causing lasting impairments in personal relations. Nor are many able to inspire believers, to reassure and entice neutrals, and to coerce or disarm opponents all at the same time.[32] As Honoré de Balzac illustrated with his discouraged characters in *Les Employés:*

> The Minister: "Bah! There will never be any scarcity of schemes of reform—"
> de la Brière: "Yes, we have ideas in plenty, but what we lack are the men that can carry them out."[33]

He knew that it is extremely hard to find those who are capable of achieving selective change instead of total convulsion, of promoting adaptability rather than rigidity, and of managing a large number of human participants—each with his own particular beliefs.

2. Political Beliefs

Reforms and innovations for inanimate organizational structures and procedures, although confronted with innumerable difficulties, still are more easily introduced than those directly involving personnel. The shuffling or dismissal of existing staff members, installation of "new blood," and application of different salary scales and promotion practices all involve the delicate sensitivities of individual careers. The dynamics of interpersonal relations, of rivalries for advancement or connections with superiors, of demands that services be sufficiently rewarded, of established interests, of competition among strong personalities for influence, and of human

31. Ibid.
32. Caiden, p. 184.
33. Honoré de Balzac, *Les Employés*, in *Oeuvres complètes* (Paris: Calmann-Lévy, 1875 ed.), XI, p. 276.

friendships or animosities can throw one obstacle after another in the path of someone trying to institute change. Yet, these personnel problems typical of any bureaucratic organization are magnified in the special case of public servants, for here there exists a particularly crucial factor: political beliefs.

"The civil service, of which the diplomatic service is a branch," writes one authority on diplomacy, "is supposed to possess no politics. Its duty is to place its experience at the disposal of the Government in power, to tender advice, and if need be to raise objections. Yet, if that advice be disregarded by the Minister, as representative of the sovereign people, it is the duty and function of the civil service to execute his instructions without further questions."[34] This principle, of course, expresses an abstract ideal rather than providing an accurate description of reality. Bureaucratic performance indicates that officials are not neutral machines, but instead discharge their responsibilities with particular attitudes, values, operational codes, and belief systems.

For this reason, those who wield political power need to be conscious of the problems involved in the oppositional or supportive behavior of a civil service.[35] "If you intend to make a decisive revolution," warned Independent Socialist Haase, "you must expel all the old officials. If the civil servants remain, the revolution will fail."[36] He realized that the degree of loyalty and sense of obligation among permanent officials is indispensable to the existence of a political regime. Consequently, stated the Duc de Broglie: "The purge of personnel, as we know from experience, is the first act of all triumphant revolutions."[37]

With the establishment of *la République radicale* and the announcement of comprehensive reforms in France, Clemenceau declared that diplomats and bureaucrats of the Quai d'Orsay must bear the imprint of the new political regime and its institutions.[38] The

34. Harold Nicolson, *Diplomacy*, p. 42.

35. On this point, see Seabury, p. x. For evidence of the continuing nature of this problem with particular reference to diplomats, see *Die Zeit*, "Sattelfest in Urdu und Marxismus: Wie Ost-Berlin Diplomaten auswählt und ausbildet," 27 April 1973.

36. Hugo Haase, as cited in Sasse, *Auswärtiges Amt*, p. 33.

37. Broglie, p. 20.

38. See Georges Clemenceau, 5 November 1906, in France, Chambre, *DP*, pp. 5–6.

press openly used the word "purge," while government leaders expressed their determination to "republicanize" these officials.[39] The use of this criterion of private convictions was deplored by many professionals,[40] noted in the press,[41] and recognized by foreign visitors.[42] "Only diplomatists of approved Republican opinions," concluded one observer, "can hope for advancement in the French diplomatic service under the present regime."[43] The purpose of such a policy, asserted Pichon, was to assure that missions abroad contained "true representatives of our philosophy."[44]

In building the democratic principles of Weimar upon the ruins of traditional monarchy, German politicians also declared that their diplomats and bureaucrats must "give expression in both form and spirit to our republican ideals."[45] "It is quite obvious," said Müller, "that whoever harbors the intent of intriguing against the Republic under no circumstances shall be appointed to any post."[46] The resulting dismissals, transfers, and promotions brought many comments from officials,[47] newspapers,[48] and foreign observers[49] that political leanings were an important factor in personnel policy. Simons confirmed these judgments when he declared:

> With regard to complaints about the occupants of particular posts, I absolutely agree with the principle that every civil servant who

39. *L'Echo de Paris*, 18 November 1906.

40. Charles-Roux, p. 95; Pognon, pp. 103, 142; among others.

41. *Journal des Débats*, "Le Mouvement diplomatique," 3 January 1907; and *L'Aurore*, "Diplomatie républicaine," 5 January 1907.

42. See PA/AA, Abteilung IA, Frankreich 105 Nr. 1, Band 24; idem, Abteilung IA, Frankreich 108, Band 16; and Despatch No. 4, "Confidential," from Bertie (Paris) to Grey, 6 January 1907, in PRO/FO 371/250.

43. Note on the cover of W 17 788/788, in PRO/FO 371/250.

44. Stephen Pichon, as cited by Marcel Hutin in *L'Echo de Paris*, 18 November 1906.

45. The words are those of Socialist Eduard Bernstein, 17 March 1921, in Germany, Reichstag, *SB*, 348, p. 3094.

46. Hermann Müller, 23 October 1919, in ibid., Nationalversammlung, *SB*, 330, p. 3355.

47. PA/AA, Büro des Reichsministers, Aktenzeichen 2, Band 1, personal letter from Haniel to Simons, 20 August 1920; Tiemann, p. 35.

48. *Deutsche Allgemeine Zeitung*, "Die Besetzung der Gesandtsachaftsposten," 17 April 1919; and *Berliner Börsen-Zeitung*, "Das Amterbedürfnis der Sozialdemokratie," 16 October 1920; among others.

49. See MAE, Allemagne, Mission Haguenin, Volume 12, Report No. 275,

cannot bring himself to serve the present Constitution must be dismissed. . . . Officials of the foreign service must do nothing by word or deed to discredit or depreciate the prestige of the German Reich in its present form.[50]

The historical development of the diplomatic profession, however, had not encouraged the growth of such liberal democratic ideals among its elite practitioners. As described, a fundamental criticism leveled against diplomats and bureaucrats of the "old school" centered upon their aristocratic nature and the monopolistic clique of wealth and birth. Many of those trained in the traditional modalities and convictions of the nineteenth century, therefore, could not hope to qualify under this new requirement of loyal republicanism. As a consequence, both the French and German Ministries for Foreign Affairs began seeking to fill their positions with politically acceptable persons from other professions.

To professionals of the Quai d'Orsay and Wilhelmstrasse, these unappreciated newcomers soon became known contemptuously as the "outsiders."[51] French deputies noted that the Ministry's personnel increasingly seemed to be "chosen from outside the diplomatic and consular career," and composed of "industrialists, businessmen, engineers, and professors" among others.[52] In Germany, press articles wrote of the growing presence of "new men" in the most significant posts.[53] Appointments began to consist of individuals previously active in democratic political parties, journalism, governmental administration, and various forms of commercial activity.[54] Such practices contained inherent risks, however, for

"La Répresentation diplomatique allemande à l'étranger," from Berlin, 26 September 1919; and Despatch No. 972, from D'Abernon (Berlin) to Foreign Secretary, 23 December 1923, in PRO/FO 371/7536.

50. Simons, 24 January 1921, as cited in *Berliner Tageblatt*, "Reichsminister Dr. Simons über das Auswärtige Amt," 25 January 1921.

51. The English word "outsider" was used in both the French and German Foreign Ministries. Among others, see Charles-Roux, p. 95; Saint-Aulaire, *Je suis diplomate*, p. 77; and the unsigned, unnumbered note "für Klubgeschwätz," dated 15 September 1920, in PA/AA, Büro des Reichsministers, Aktenzeichen 2, Band 1.

52. MAE/Chambre, Rapport No. 6339 (1919), p. 179.

53. *Frankfurter Zeitung*, "Das Auswärtige Amt," 25 December 1920; among others.

54. See the unregistered, unsigned document listing previous occupations, filed under July–August 1921, in PA/AA, Büro des Reichsministers, Aktenzeichen 2, Band 2.

Simons and others clearly understood that "this employment of outsiders has its advantages—but also its dangers."[55]

To introduce new individuals into positions requiring highly developed skills raises a major problem for reformers: Does a person with *loyalty* to a particular party or ideology also possess sufficient *ability*?[56] Career officials in Paris, for example, readily expressed their opinion that political appointments resulted in a serious lack of competence within the Quai d'Orsay.[57] One expert recognized that if selection by political affiliation were applied by the French, "it may debar from the diplomatic service a number of able men who although theoretical royalists or imperialists by tradition, may yet be eminently useful and devoted public servants."[58] In Berlin cautious deputies warned of the dangers "in today's difficult times of sending such men to fill diplomatic posts abroad whose entire qualifications for these positions consist merely of parliamentary or feuilletonistic activity or a combination of both."[59] According to an article in the press: "Nowadays suitable men will not easily be found outside the old school of diplomacy. But from fear of incurring the ill-founded reproach that a reactionary spirit prevails in the Foreign Ministry, is it right to place incompetent men in posts of the greatest importance?"[60]

This is the fundamental dilemma for those instituting reforms or innovations in personnel policy among civil servants. The necessity for professional ability to manage responsibilities successfully must be weighed against the significance to a regime of loyal political support among its officials. In the French and German Ministries for

55. Simons, as cited in *Berliner Tageblatt*, 25 January 1921.

56. On this point, see Pichon's early comments in *L'Echo de Paris*, 18 November 1906; Barth's later remarks in Germany, Volksbeauftragen, *Die Regierung der Volksbeauftragen*, I, 397; and RK 4566, "Geheim," letter from Erzberger to Scheidemann, 26 April 1919, and RK 4752, letter from Erzberger to Scheidemann, 2 May 1919; both in Bundesarchiv, Akten der Reichskanzlei 1919—1933, R 43 I, Friedensverhandlungen, Band 2. I am indebted for this last reference to Sybil Milton.

57. Pognon, pp. 132–33.

58. Note by Eyre Crowe, 20 November 1906, written on Despatch No. 455 from Bertie (Paris) to Grey, 18 November 1906, in PRO/FO 371/74.

59. Dr. Becker, 30 May 1922, in Germany, Reichstag, *SB*, 355, p. 7724. Also see the comments of Dr. Hoetzsch on 16 April 1923, in idem, Band 359, p. 10538.

60. *Kölnische Volkszeitung*, "Unser Auswärtiges Amt," 30 May 1921.

Foreign Affairs, many recognized the complicated nature of this problem. Instead of choosing between one solution or the other, however, they continually connected the two.[61] Individuals proposing greater "standardization," "efficiency," "rationalization," "competitive recruitment," and "professionalism" among personnel were often those who advocated a "democratization" of diplomats and bureaucrats and a policy of "republicans to represent the Republic." This linkage between what Berthelot termed *"le mérit professionel"* and *"le point du vue politique"*[62] confirms the judgment of one scholar who writes:

> The questions of bureaucratic "efficiency" and the responsible exercise of bureaucratic power are inseparably linked. Together they constitute one of the most crucial dilemmas of modern industrial society. For, if a bureaucracy is to serve as an effective instrument of democratic policy, it must be tolerably "efficient." But a rationally organized, efficient bureaucracy, with its own *esprit de corps* boasting of a highly competent personnel, need not necessarily be responsible to its constitutional superiors. Nor is it necessarily imbued with the same political philosophy. . . .[63]

Such dependence upon technical ability presents a formidable obstacle to reformers and innovators and thus provides bureaucracy with its greatest strength to resist change. Political zeal of new regimes is seldom sufficient to satisfy the demands of administration and statecraft, particularly in the twentieth century. The need for expertise, the difficulty of sustaining reforming fervor, and the importance of maintaining stability increase the influence of established bureaucratic skills, of routine, of norms of behavior, and of tradition. Career officials with experience and tenure are provided with great security, for if money becomes tight they will remain while newcomers will be among the first to go. Moreover, their

61. Among many examples, see the comments of Berthelot in France, *JO*, 3 May 1907, p. 3273; Pichon's statement in idem, p. 3266; MAE/Chambre, Rapport No. 2020 (1921), p. 125; Hermann Müller, in Germany, Nationalversammlung, *SB*, 330, p. 3355; and Simons in *Berliner Tageblatt*, 25 January 1921. Only gradually was this dilemma more or less resolved by considering certain positions such as the Minister for Foreign Affairs and some ambassadorships as "political" appointments, whereas most of the others were "professional."

62. Berthelot, "Commission des réformes administratives," p. 3273.

63. Seabury, p. 15.

nearly monopolistic ability to control information places them in a position to modify the sudden impact of any reforms or innovations. For this reason, as one writer observed: "If the officials want to dispose of a new Minister they know how to do it. First, by giving him too many documents so that he is unable to ascertain the simple facts, and then by giving him too few in order that he may know nothing. It is much more difficult, however, for a Minister to slay a civil servant."[64]

These questions of professional competence arise in any public administrative organization, but they are particularly difficult when dealing with diplomacy. In both the Quai d'Orsay and the Wilhelmstrasse, the argument was raised that—unlike the abilities necessary for other professions—the special talents required of a diplomat or a bureaucrat concerned with foreign affairs could not be subject to structured education, to systematic training, or to the new standardized examinations. Some claimed that such criteria became irrelevant in this sphere because, in the words of Bülow the elder, "diplomacy is neither a science nor, unfortunately, a branch of ethics—but an art."[65] Some deplored the new methods of treating complicated political problems as technical matters,[66] while others asserted that instinct, not merely knowledge, was the indispensable quality needed in foreign politics.[67] It is not surprising that these debates over the talents and abilities needed for international relations should arise, for during this period of reform and innovation the nature of diplomacy itself seemed to be in transformation.

---

64. Veit Valentin, in *Berliner Börsen-Courier*, 21 August 1923, referring specially to the power of a *Geheimrat*. Also see MAE, Allemagne, politique intérieur, dossier général, NS 4, Despatch No. 269, "Très confidentiel," from Berckheim (Berlin) to Pichon, 16 July 1909; MAE/Sénat, Rapport No. 148 (1913), p. 44; Wolfgang Elben, *Das Problem der Kontinuität in der deutschen Revolution* (Düsseldorf: Droste, 1965), particularly pp. 159–76; and Seabury's comments on the remaining strength of the old guard careerists, pp. 18, 20, 152.

65. Bülow, 4, p. 273. Also see R. von Scheller-Steinwartz, "Auswärtige Politik und Diplomatenkunst," and "Reform des Auswärtigen Dienstes," in Anschütz, pp. 351–59.

66. See, for example, the later private letter, "Personnelle," from Paul Claudel (Brussels) to Berthelot (Paris), 16 November 1933, in MAE, Direction politique et commerciale, Papiers des Agents: Philippe Berthelot, Carton 12; and Outrey, 3, 4, particularly pp. 721ff. on "La crise des institutions diplomatiques traditionnelles depuis 1914."

67. Theodore Wolff, in *Berliner Tageblatt*, 6 October 1919.

3. Twentieth-Century Diplomacy

The institutional responses creating complex organizational structures of elaborate departments, expanded staffs, enlarged budgets, new personnel policies, and sophisticated inventions not only reflected many of the changing features of diplomacy, but contributed to them as well. When compared with previous institutions and practices, it became evident to many diplomats that the nature of their craft recently had been, and was becoming, dramatically transformed. The necessity of ministerial efficiency became greater, the entrance requirements more difficult, the diplomatic community more diverse and extended, the tempo faster, the work loads heavier, and the pressure of domestic politics more demanding than ever before. For some of those trained in the tradition of relative stability, of simplicity and seclusion, such changes were traumatic. Indeed, several emphasized this transformation by contrasting the "old" diplomacy of the past with the "new" diplomacy of the twentieth century.[68]

"The old order changed, yielding place to the new . . . and slow motion was not regained," recalls one professional diplomat in stressing this difference. "The pace of progress was more killing than at any time since the invention of gunpowder. Everything went faster."[69] Others spoke of the "furious gallop of events" and of the "extraordinary acceleration in means of communication," noting that each new technical invention brought "an increase in the task imposed upon the Minister for Foreign Affairs."[70] In comparison with times past, officials in the Wilhelmstrasse now described their work as "strenuous."[71] "What makes the difference between the old Quai d'Orsay and the one after 1918," concluded a French

68. MAE/Chambre, Rapport No. 6339 (1919), "La Diplomatie nouvelle," pp. 3ff.; Saint-Aulaire, *Je suit diplomate*, pp. 74ff.; Albrecht Mendelssohn Bartholdy, *Diplomatie* (Berlin: Rothschild, 1927), pp. 11–13; Ludwig Zimmermann, *Deutsche Aussenpolitik in der Ära der Weimarer Republik* (Göttingen: Musterschmidt, 1958), p. 21; A. L. Kennedy, *Old Diplomacy and New*; and George Young, *Diplomacy Old and New* (London: Swarthmore, 1921).

69. Vansittart, pp. 236–37.

70. MAE/Chambre, Rapport No. 802 (1920), p. 59; Ambassador de Fleuriau, in Levis-Mirapoix, p. x.

71. Dirksen, p. 55. Also see Hindenburg, p. 10; and Sasse, "Zur geschichte des Auswärtigen Amts," Heft 7, p. 168.

diplomat, "is the acceleration in the rhythm of work, swelling of services, avalanche of paper, abundance of telephone calls, flood of visitors, and the entire congestion of business."[72]

Additional changes in the subject matter and techniques of diplomacy compounded such burdens and stressed the difference even further. The new global features of international relations stood in marked contrast with the previously limited focus of continental Europe, imposing enlarged responsibilities upon the Ministries.[73] Greater complexities in commercial and propagandistic matters were unfamiliar to those trained in traditional political affairs and presented problems "over the heads of the old-time diplomats."[74] Once-discreet and quiet conversations among professionals gave way to the unfamiliar noise and clamor of press conferences, public appearances, publications, films, and cultural exchanges. Private discussions between a few individuals appeared superseded by large meetings with business groups, multilateral commissions, international organizations, and the growing frequency of "diplomacy by conference."[75]

Dramatic changes in the composition of the diplomatic community also transformed the nature of diplomacy for the twentieth century. The decline of Europe as the epicenter of international politics, the growth in the numbers of nations actively participating in affairs, and the influx of "outsiders" all contributed to end the former cultural homogeneity among the diplomats themselves. Gone was the earlier degree of cohesiveness within the *corps diplomatique* gained by speaking the same language, by belonging to the same families, by attending the same schools and—most importantly—by sharing a consensus on the legitimate methods and

72. Charles-Roux, p. 96. Also see Simons, in *Berliner Tageblatt*, 25 January 1921; Hindenburg, p. 10; and Herbert Butterfield, "The New Diplomacy and Historical Diplomacy," in Butterfield and M. Wight eds., *Diplomatic Investigations* (London: Unwin, 1966), pp. 186–89.

73. See MAE/Chambre, Rapport No. 6339 (1919), p. 20; Tiemann, pp. 36ff.; and Vansittart, p. 28.

74. The words are those of Hajo Holborn, "Diplomats and Diplomacy in the Early Weimar Republic," in Craig and Gilbert, 1, p. 150.

75. See MAE/Chambre, Rapport No. 6339 (1919), pp. 17, 114ff., 146ff.; Saint-Aulaire, *Je suis diplomate*, pp. 84–86; Friedrich von Prittwitz und Gaffron, *Aussenpolitik und Diplomatie* (München: Isar, 1951), pp. 6–7; Seabury, pp. 153–54; and Sir Maurice Hankey, "Diplomacy by Conference," *Proceedings of the British Institute of International Affairs*, 1 (London: Smith and Son, 1920).

objectives of diplomacy. After all, said one professional, the practices of the old school "could flourish only so long as there was
general agreement to behave more or less like gentlemen."[76] The
destruction of this former unity and the subsequent introduction of
new ground rules opened the door to ideological rivalries, soon
permitting exponents of communism, fascism, and democracy to
contort the traditional forms of diplomacy into unrecognizable
ones.[77]

The burdens arising from such changes prompted many diplomats
and bureaucrats to complain about "the enormous increase in the
volume and complexity of international business" and about new
"problems of the greatest difficulty."[78] One observer said, "Their
solution frequently requires resources beyond those of the most
competent and qualified diplomatist," concluding that "they require
an even wider perspective than in the past to keep them abreast of
the times."[79] A professional contrasted the "calm" of former days
with the "storm clouds" of the twentieth century.[80] At the Quai
d'Orsay conditions were considered "more serious" than heretofore,[81] while officials of the Wilhelmstrasse used adjectives like
"terrible" and "extremely difficult" to describe their new tasks.[82]
Other contemporaries concurred in this judgment, stating that "the
new era presents for diplomacy tasks of greater complication and
difficulty than it has ever had to deal with,"[83] and describing the
problems as "more *numerous*, more *varied*, more *technical*, more
urgent and, we may add, more intractable, both in themselves and

76. Vansittart, p. 234.

77. Gordon A. Craig, "Totalitarian Approaches to Diplomatic Negotiation,"
in *War, Politics and Diplomacy*, pp. 220–47; and Harold Nicolson, *The Evolution
of Diplomatic Method* (London: Constable, 1956), p. 90.

78. Hankey, p. 25. Also see the comments on the increased difficulties of
twentieth-century diplomacy in John Harr, *The Professional Diplomat* (Princeton:
Princeton University Press, 1969), pp. 28ff.

79. Hankey, p. 25.

80. Vansittart, p. 187. Also see the chapter entitled "The End of the Old
Order," in Steiner, pp. 209–13.

81. MAE/Chambre, Rapport No. 802 (1920), p. 8.

82. Foreign Minister von Rosenberg, as cited in PRO/FO 371/7536, Despatch
No. 910, "Confidential," from D'Abernon (Berlin) to Foreign Secretary, 28
November 1922.

83. Rodd, p. 82.

because of the popular passions liable at any moment to gather around them.''[84]

The latter point emphasizes that the difficulties imposed upon diplomacy by technical problems seemed mild when compared with those emerging from domestic politics. Isolation and insulation crumbled under intrusions by legislative commissions, by political parties, by special interests, and by the press. The immediate objective for many groups, in the words of the *Kölnische Volkszeitung*, seemed "to secure by a resolute effort the share in foreign policy and service personnel to which it is entitled.''[85] This led one careerist to declare: "Each day the task of diplomatic agents is becoming more difficult. The press, parliamentary lobbies, activities of businessmen, ignorance of the public, and the impatience of popular opinion insisting upon knowing everything does not help.''[86]

In negotiations, these encroachments greatly compounded the problems of diplomats and bureaucrats. The innovative liaisons connecting the Quai d'Orsay and the Wilhelmstrasse with "outsiders" provided information to those concerned with foreign affairs, yet these furnished facts also provoked unrestrained discussion. Officials found the substantive matters of their confidential transactions openly debated in parliament and the press. Uncertain legislative majorities, the "irresponsibility" and unaccustomed bluntness of the public, and the political preference for quick solutions, for vague formulae, and for stereotypes only added to their difficulties.[87] Old school professionals feared that these manifestations of popular chauvinism would harm international understanding and would impede the ability to reach agreement. They worried when they listened to the "extraordinary language" now used in negotiations,[88] and cringed upon hearing domestic politicians call their foreign opponents "vampires.''[89]

---

84. Zimmern, p. 496.

85. *Kölnische Volkszeitung*, 30 May 1921.

86. Jules Cambon, *Le diplomate* (Paris: Hachette, 1926), p. 68.

87. See Nicolson's discussion of "democratic diplomacy" in *Diplomacy*, pp. 46–50.

88. LaRoche, p. 122.

89. Frau Clara Zetkin of the German Communist Party, as cited in Despatch No. 633 from Kilmarnock (Berlin) to Curzon, 29 July 1920, in Britain, FO 371/4740.

The intrusion of internal political struggles into diplomacy became evident in issues of personnel selection as well. Contemporaries observed that politicians were interfering with questions of appointments and assignments in staggering proportions.[90] Socialists petitioned that negotiating delegations include representatives of "the workers"—"whose blood has flowed more freely than that of any other class"[91]—and businessmen insisted that their interests also be represented in the new voices of diplomacy.[92] Political parties fought over positions for their own members, particularly over the biggest prize of all: the post of Minister for Foreign Affairs itself.[93]

To many diplomats and bureaucrats the legitimation of such partisan activities seemed to confirm a frightening politicization of their craft. Politicians rejected the earlier notion that diplomatic matters stood outside the arena of party conflict and the traditional premise that "the ways of diplomacy are proverbially dark . . . and beyond the understanding of those who have not been trained in its methods."[94] They argued instead that diplomacy constituted a political activity, and therefore should reflect shifts in internal power relations, in public opinion, and in prevailing philosophies. Indeed, according to Harold Nicolson, this attitude became the factor most responsible for bringing about "the transition from the old diplomacy to the new. It was the belief that it was possible to apply to the conduct of *external* affairs, the ideas and practices which, in the conduct of *internal* affairs, had been regarded for generations as the essentials of liberal democracy."[95]

90. Norton, pp. 32, 35.

91. The demands issued to Clemenceau, as cited in Despatch No. 1584 of 23 November 1918 and Despatch No. 1627 of 27 November 1918, both from Derby (Paris) to Balfour, in PRO/FO 371/3215. Also see LaRoche, p. 121, discussing the role of Herr Hué at Versailles as a "representative of the German workers."

92. PA/AA, *Hamburger Denkschrift,* passim; Germany, Reichskanzlei, *Akten der Reichskanzlei, Weimarer Republik: Das Kabinett Scheidemann* (Boppard am Rhein: Boldt, 1971), pp. 63–65; and LaRoche, p. 121.

93. MAE, Allemagne, Mission Haguenin, Volume 15, Report of 10 December 1919 from Haguenin; PRO/FO 371/2935, Despatch No. 1118 from Bertie (Paris) to Foreign Secretary, 22 October 1917; FO 371/5970, Despatch No. 720 from D'Abernon (Berlin) to Foreign Secretary, 21 May 1921; and the comments of Schultz, in Germany, Reichstag, *SB,* 330, p. 3377.

94. *The Times* (London), "The German Emperor and German Policy," 5 December 1907.

95. Nicolson, *The Evolution of Diplomatic Method,* p. 84.

The impact of this philosophy upon diplomacy became evident as elected heads of state began to conduct negotiations themselves. Being either unfamiliar with or in contempt of traditional diplomatic practices, these politicians introduced their own personal styles, slogans, and ideologies into the realm of international affairs. Professionals heard their political superiors proclaim that the nature of diplomacy itself must be transformed as a matter of policy. National leaders spoke of the "Old" and "New Diplomacy," denouncing past methods and objectives and preaching an unorthodox message of "democratic diplomacy," "open convenants of peace openly arrived at," "diplomacy in the public view," "reign of law," "equality among nations," "self-determination," "free trade," "disarmament," "enlightened reason of mankind," and "universality."[96] Even the locations and dress of diplomatic intercourse, as described by Gordon Craig, became stamped with the heretical imprint of politicians like Aristide Briand, Gustav Stresemann, Lloyd George, and Stanley Baldwin:

> Conclaves of ambassadors at the Quai d'Orsay, the Wilhelmstrasse, and the Ballplatz—names now of sinister connotation—gave way to 'frank and friendly conversations' in such charmingly unconventional places as the golf course at Cannes, the bosom of the Lago Maggiore, the mountain tavern at Thoiry, and a certain mossy log on the banks of the Potomac. The correctly dressed and distressingly uniform diplomats, who until now had held the center of the stage, ceded their places to a succession of politician-diplomats with such striking and memorable characteristics as plus-fours, Scots brogues, shaggy coiffures, white linen neckties, underslung pipes, and various kinds of umbrellas.[97]

Many career diplomats and bureaucrats reacted angrily against such attempts to discredit their hallowed profession and efforts to transform the form and substance of traditional diplomacy for the

96. See Mayer, pp. 8, 14–16, 53–58, 290, 358; MAE/Chambre, Rapport No. 6339 (1919), pp. 3–9; Herbert von Dirksen, *Diplomatie: Wesen, Rolle und Wandlung* (Nürnberg: Abraham, 1950), p. 10; von Prittwitz, pp. 6–7; and Zechlin, pp. 14–15.

97. Gordon A. Craig, "The Professional Diplomat and His Problems, 1919—1939," in *War, Politics and Diplomacy*, p. 209.

twentieth century. Internal efficiency and more modern administrative techniques within the family might be endurable, but this outside political "interference" clearly was not. They denounced these developments and warned against "the ruin of professional diplomacy."[98] Careerists at the Quai d'Orsay spoke of the "contamination of foreign policy by domestic politics."[99] "The old officials," said one in the Wilhelmstrasse, "were accustomed from earlier times to work under the direction of a professional. But . . . after 1919 the men in charge of the Foreign Ministry were changed frequently and regarded by us as amateurs."[100] Others deplored "the danger of parliamentary intrigues"[101] and "the irresponsible seeking for sensation,"[102] warned of "disaster,"[103] and in private even referred to politicians as "imbeciles" and "idiots."[104]

4. The Limits of Institutional Responses

These complaints about transformations in diplomacy and the innumerable problems incurred when introducing change draw attention to the fundamental influence of environmental forces upon institutions. Throughout this study it has been emphasized that organizations do not function within a vacuum, but are conditioned by their political, social, economic, and cultural surroundings. Just as those many pressures first necessitated elaborate responses from the French and German Ministries for Foreign Affairs, so they helped determine how these reforms and innovations would be utilized. The difficulties caused by this continuous interaction became known to men like Berthelot, Pichon, Schüler, Brockdorff-Rantzau, and others as they gradually realized that internal and external conditions can present an infinite number of

98. Vansittart, pp. 294–95.

99. Saint-Aulaire, *Je suis diplomate*, pp. 102–5.

100. Weizsäcker, p. 80, who also notes, of course, the exception of Gustav Stresemann's lengthy tenure.

101. Pognon, p. 159.

102. Dirksen, *Diplomatie*, p. 10.

103. Harold Nicolson, *Curzon: The Last Phase, 1919–1925: A Study in Post-War Diplomacy* (New York: Houghton Mifflin, 1934), p. 245.

104. Saint-Aulaire, *Confession*, p. 82.

problems entirely beyond an individual's ability to control. As such, their experience also serves to demonstrate some of the inherent limitations of institutional responses.

Elaborate reforms and innovations, however "successful," are unable to eliminate the basic problems created by the nature of bureaucracy. Although well-designed modifications can increase the advantages of bureaucratic institutions, they can only be expected to reduce in partial form the disadvantages. In order to maximize the pursuit of organizational objectives, to illustrate, bureaucracy must constrain each participant to suppress his individual needs for the common good. The elements of formalized divisions of labor, specialization, a hierarchy of authority, and highly defined rules of behavior all contribute toward this goal. Yet, by their very nature, they also produce a high degree of rigidity, of impersonalization, and of strata isolation. For this reason, people caught up within a complex bureaucracy frequently find themselves feeling like a mere cog in a gigantic wheel. They resent the inherent restrictions, the entanglement of "red tape" (or what the French call *la paperasserie*), the monotonous routine, the close supervision, the insistence on conformity, and the stifling of initiative. Such resentment, in turn, seriously can affect their motivation to perform well within the organization.[105]

This performance of bureaucrats itself presents another limitation upon the extent of any institutional response. Writers from the beginning of the nineteenth century to the present have warned potential reformers and innovators to recognize in advance that legal decrees cannot change the fundamental fact that bureaucracy is geared for *average* performance. Those mechanisms necessary for constraining individuals to work for the larger organizational goals make little room for aberrations or genius, and produce what Balzac contemptuously called "a system devised by mediocrity to please mediocrity."[106] As Henry Kissinger noted more recently, "institutions are designed for an average standard of performance—a high

---

105. Among many writers on this subject, see Crozier, pp. 257–59, 268–69, 291–92; Blau and Meyer, pp. 23, 50ff.; Jacoby, pp. 197–208; and Chris Argyris, *Personality and Organization* (New York: Harper and Brothers, 1957), passim.
106. Balzac, p. 182.

average in fortunate societies, but still a standard reducible to approximate norms."[107] With specific reference to foreign affairs, he maintains that this makes the spirit of policy and that of bureaucracy "diametrically opposed" to each other since the essence of policy is perpetual change, contingency planning, and the adjustment of risks, whereas the essence of bureaucratic organization is safety, routine, and the avoidance of deviation.[108]

In addition, reforms and innovations simply are unable to solve the problem of how to determine whether or not a governmental bureaucracy is efficient. Those who had hoped to introduce "scientific management" and "greater efficiency" into the Quai d'Orsay and the Wilhelmstrasse ultimately had to recognize that they could create no empirical means by which to calculate performance or determine the precise ratio of output to input. Diplomats and bureaucrats provided numerous services and assumed certain responsibilities, but they did not manufacture a tangible product that could be weighed, measured, or otherwise counted. Their "efficiency" or "inefficiency" could not be determined by dividing the number of memos or despatches produced in a day by the number of officials. Nor could it be calculated by the "success" or "failure" of foreign policy itself, for this could take years to determine and what would be used as criteria? A solution to this problem, in short, seems to elude even the most sophisticated of responses.

Moreover, the mere *creation* of institutional changes can give no assurance that they actually will be *used* as originally intended. Official regulations cannot prevent the emergence of unsanctioned or informal arrangements, malfunctions, conflicts, human failures, and group dynamics from either modifying or undermining formal organizational structures and standard operating procedures.[109] As many people in the French and German Ministries for Foreign Affairs discovered, contempt, ambition, or lack of confidence in the

107. Henry A. Kissinger, "The White Revolutionary: Reflections on Bismarck," *Daedalus*, 97, 3 (Summer 1968), p. 889.

108. Henry A. Kissinger, *A World Restored* (Boston: Houghton Mifflin, 1973 ed.), pp. 326–27.

109. See George, p. 766; Harold Wilensky, *Organizational Intelligence* (New York: Basic Books, 1967), pp. 173–91; Destler, pp. 41–51; and James March and Herbert Simon, *Organizations* (New York: Wiley, 1959), pp. 112–71.

bureaucratic machinery can lead individuals to take action independent of the established channels. Undisciplined behavior by subordinates who boasted of "steering their own course" or "raping"
their superiors subverted some of the most carefully planned designs
of the reformers and innovators.[110] "Intruding" politicians and their
roving emissaries deliberately ignored the considered advice of the
professionals charged with managing foreign affairs and refused to
inform them of what had been negotiated with other countries.[111]
When generals and other so-called "experts" decided to play a
greater role in international politics outside of the official bureaucracy, the problems became all the more exacerbated.[112]

This tendency to bypass formal organizations, to ignore professionals, and to discard advice indicated a marked diminution in the
use of diplomatic institutions themselves. Many diplomats and
bureaucrats felt that in the twentieth century they were becoming
technologically obsolete, politically superseded, and placed in a
position where their own trained judgments "mattered less and
less."[113] In the Quai d'Orsay, careerists deplored the passing of
ambassadors as "central figures on the international scene," observing that they were being demoted from the important *notaires* to
the mere *greffiers* of history.[114] Officials of the Wilhelmstrasse
complained that they frequently had nothing to do with the formulation of vital decisions, but became "degraded to the level of a mere
technical apparatus."[115] One contemporary observer wrote that
"ambassadors lost a good deal of their importance in the great
capitals. On the whole, they were abased to the level of ushers,

110. Dirksen, *Moskau, Tokio, London,* p. 43; and Wipert von Blucher, *Deutsch-lands Weg nach Rapallo* (Wiesbaden: Limes, 1951), p. 161n.

111. France, Chambre, Commission d'enquête parlementaire, Rapport No. 2344, Annexe au procès-verbal de la 2ᵉ séance du 8 août 1947, "Rapport fait au nom de la Commission chargée d'enquêter sur les événements survenus en France de 1933 à 1945," par Charles Serre, particularly pp. 86–87; among others.

112. See LaRoche, pp. 58, 59, 72, 98; and Friedrich von Rabenau, *Seeckt: Aus seinem Leben, 1918–1936* (Leipzig: Hase und Koehler, 1941), who points out that General von Seeckt believed that he possessed the right to help determine external policy whenever the interests of Germany and his army were at stake.

113. Vansittart, p. 269.

114. Saint-Aulaire, *Je suis diplomate,* p. 106.

115. Weizsäcker, p. 129.

messengers and mailboxes. Essential negotiations no longer were channeled into their care. The heads of government, or the Foreign Ministers . . . became the supreme negotiators."[116]

The rise and fall of these same political leaders indicated to reformers and innovators another limitation upon their creations. Although official decrees could exercise some authority over internal bureaucratic operations, they remained helplessly unable to control what one diplomat called "the storms of domestic politics."[117] The electoral success of one political party and then another caused rapid shifts in the direction of policy. The advent of more effective public accountability, much to the chagrin of the professionals, brought continuous changes among those persons occupying the position of Minister for Foreign Affairs. "The Ministers who succeed one another are not necessarily statesmen," observed one ambassador "and therefore are all the more susceptible of being influenced in their conduct of affairs by sentimentality or party prejudice."[118] As a consequence, the Quai d'Orsay and Wilhelmstrasse suffered from a lack of steady ministerial leadership, thus inhibiting stability as originally intended (and needed) for the elaborately designed machinery.[119]

Problems presented by this human inability to direct all subsequent events demonstrate further inherent limits upon the effectiveness of reforms and innovations. Institutional responses, by their very nature, are attempts to create organizational structures, procedures, and personnel policies in order to cope successfully with new environmental conditions during a particular point in time. The milieu of domestic and international pressures itself, however, does not remain in a fixed state but continually is reshaped in forms often unforeseeable. No system of regulations and assignments can

116. André Géraud, "Diplomacy, Old and New," *Foreign Affairs*, 23, 2 (January 1945), p. 267. Also see Craig, "The Professional Diplomat and His Problems," in *War, Politics and Diplomacy*, pp. 207ff.; Seabury, pp. 157ff.; and for a more recent continuation of this theme, Dean Acheson, "The Eclipse of the State Department," *Foreign Affairs*, 49, 4 (July 1971), pp. 593–606.

117. Broglie, p. 42.

118. Cambon, p. 62.

119. Joseph Paul-Boncour, *Entre deux guerres: souvenirs sur la IIIe République* (Paris: Plon, 1945), 2, p. 335; Dirksen, *Moskau, Tokio, London*, p. 44; Schmidt-Pauli, pp. 32–33; and MAE/Chambre, Rapport No. 802 (1920), p. 6.

be so finely spun that it anticipates all exigencies that may arise. Transformations in external conditions are bound to create new problems, and the very modifications introduced to solve them may have unanticipated consequences that produce further difficulties.[120] This becomes particularly acute in the special case of diplomats and those bureaucrats concerned with foreign affairs, for unlike their counterparts in other types of public administration, they operate in an area where most of the subject matter with which they deal is beyond the control of their country's authority. Accordingly, said one ambassador, "any organization of a foreign ministry will never be definitive, and it therefore must proceed with perpetual changes."[121] Particularly in our twentieth century when the rate and directions of change are greater than ever before, institutions must be reorganized constantly in response to always newer needs. This is essential, in the words of a recent author, to prevent collision with "future shock."[122] Those who were concerned with the operations of the Quai d'Orsay and Wilhelmstrasse warned that institutional responses must be more than a one-time occurrence, and argued that these reforms and innovations should be considered as only a beginning of additional changes to come.[123] As Schüler himself asserted in the last memorandum issued to his colleagues: "The work of reform is incomplete. Novel and difficult tasks still stand before you, and they will require even further efforts."[124]

120. See Blau and Meyer, p. 57; among others.

121. Comment by de Fleuriau, in Levis-Mirapoix, pp. x–xi.

122. Toffler, particularly Chapter 7, "Organizations: The Coming Adhocracy." Also see Butterfield, p. 181. Both authors, however, emphasize that continuity also serves a useful function in providing stability.

123. Proposals for further changes, to illustrate, continued throughout the century. For early examples, see MAE/Chambre, Rapport No. 189, Annexe au procès-verbal de la séance du 13 janvier 1920, "Proposition . . . à fixer par loi les cadres des services diplomatiques et consulaires," and idem, Rapport No. 190, "Proposition de loi tendant à répartir en zones administratives nos postes et agents . . . et à organiser sur cette spécialisation les services des Affaires étrangères," par Louis Marin; Jacques Seydoux, "Suggestions pour une réorganisation du Ministère des Affaires étrangères," *L'Europe Nouvelle* (26 March 1927), pp. 428–30; the various items throughout the series of "Organisation, Personalfragen," in PA/AA, Büro des Reichsministers, Aktenzeichen 2; and the speech by Hoetzsch, 16 April 1923, in Germany, Reichstag, *SB*, 359, pp. 10536–39; among others.

124. Memorandum from Schüler to Gneist and Abteilung I, 1 January 1921, in PA/AA, Büro des Reichsministers, Aktenzeichen 2, Band 2.

Finally, as one perceptive French deputy noticed, reforms and innovations are limited by the fact that "the evolution made suddenly in *things* cannot be done as quickly with the human *spirit.*"[125] The changing of attitudes is one of the most difficult and most crucial of all objectives to achieve. Diplomats and bureaucrats in the French and German Ministries for Foreign Affairs learned that the ability of even their most carefully or imaginatively designed organization to perform its responsibilities can be no better than the motivations and values of its political leaders and permanent staff. Decisions are made and policies are executed by living men and women whose attitudes must either change or be changed. Precisely for this reason, said a contemporary statesman, "We must look for a new spirit and purpose among nations, not to a change of method, to secure better things."[126] One ambassador advised that governments would have to recognize that the best means available for conducting international relations was not sophisticated mechanisms but rather "the word of an honest person."[127]

Thoughts such as this prompted Brockdorff-Rantzau to reflect upon the nature of institutional responses to twentieth-century diplomacy and to observe: "Even with the best organization and the best staff, good foreign policy cannot be made if the source from which we derive the strength for our service is poisoned or runs dry—if the nation for which we should work wastes itself in inner conflict and renders itself incapable of creating new values."[128]

125. MAE/Chambre, Rapport No. 6339 (1919), p. 18 [my emphasis].

126. Viscount Grey, *Twenty-Five Years, 1892–1916* (New York: Stokes, 1925), II, p. 278.

127. Cambon, p. 120.

128. Brockdorff-Rantzau, 10 April 1919, in Germany, Nationalversammlung, *SB*, 327, p. 933.

Diplomats and Bureaucrats
in the French Ministry for Foreign Affairs,
1900–1925*

ADMINISTRATIVE

I. *Foreign Ministers*

Delcassé	6.1898 – 6.1905
Rouvier	6.1905 – 3.1906
Bourgeois	3.1906 – 10.1906
Pichon	10.1906 – 3.1911
Cruppi	3.1911 – 6.1911
de Selves	6.1911 – 1.1912
Poincaré	1.1912 – 1.1913
Jonnart	1.1913 – 3.1913
Pichon	3.1913 – 12.1913
Doumergue	12.1913 – 6.1914
Bourgeois	6.1914 – 6.1914
Viviani	6.1914 – 8.1914
Doumergue	8.1914 – 8.1914
Delcassé	8.1914 – 10.1915
Briand	10.1915 – 3.1917
Ribot	3.1917 – 10.1917
Barthou	10.1917 – 11.1917
Pichon	11.1917 – 1.1920
Millerand	1.1920 – 9.1920
Leygues	9.1920 – 1.1921
Briand	1.1921 – 1.1922
Poincaré	1.1922 – 6.1924
Lefebvre du Prey	6.1924 – 6.1924
Herriot	6.1924 – 4.1925
Briand	4.1925 – 7.1926

*Compiled from the yearly *Annuaire diplomatique et consulaire, Almanac de Gotha,* and, in some cases, the *Journal officiel de la République française.* The dates of service for some officials, therefore, can be only of an approximate nature.

II. *Secretaries General*
(post created in 1915)
Cambon (Jules)   10.1915 – 12.1917
(position abolished in 1917 and
then reestablished in 1920)
Paléologue   1.1920 –   9.1920
Berthelot   9.1920 – 12.1921
(position abolished in 1922 and
then reestablished in 1925)
Berthelot   4.1925 –   2.1933

III. *Chefs of the Cabinet*
Beau   1898 – 1902
Delavaud   1902 – 1906
Thiébaut   1906 – 1908
Dutasta   1908 – 1911
Herbette   1911 – 1913
Aynard   1913 – 1914
Margerie   1914 – 1914
Piccioni   1914 – 1915
Berthelot   1915 – 1917
Legrand   1917 – 1920
Petit   1920 – 1920
Hermite   1920 – 1924
(internal reorganizations in
1907, 1912, 1918, and 1920)

IV. *Chefs of the Personnel Bureau*
Beau   1892 – 1902
Jullemier   1902 – 1903
Delavaud   1903 – 1906
Thiébaut   1906 – 1907
Maruéjouls   1907 – 1914
Lemonnier   1914 – 1923
(reorganized in 1920 with transfer
from the Cabinet du Ministre)
Hermite   1922 – 1924

V. *Chefs of the Fonds and Comptabilité Division*
Roger   1884 – 1902
Thiboust   1902 – 1906
Hamon   1906 – 1912

Bizot	1912 – 1913
Delamontte	1913 – 1920
Dobler	1920 – 1926

(internal reorganizations in
1902, 1907, 1912, and 1918)

VI. *Directors of Administrative and Technical Affairs*
(post created in 1907)

Gavarry	1907 – 1917
Herbette	1917 – 1922
Daeschner	1922 – 1924

(internal reorganizations in
1911, 1912, and 1913)

VII. *Sous-Directeurs of Chancellery Affairs and Contentieux Administratif*
(combined post created in 1907)

Piccioni	1907 – 1910
Chatain	1910 – 1911
Aynard	1911 – 1913
Martin	1913 – 1914
Auzovy	1914 – 1920
Hermite	1920 – 1923
Vieugue	1923 – 1926

(internal reorganizations in
1911, 1913, 1914, 1918, and 1920)

GEOGRAPHICAL

I. *Sous-Directeurs du Nord*

Dumaine	1899 – 1905
Soulange-Bodin	1905 – 1907

(post reorganized in 1907)

II. *Sous-Directeurs du Midi*

Saint-René-Taillandier	1895 – 1902
Horric de Beaucaire	1902 – 1907

(post reorganized in 1907)

III. *Chef of Colonial Affairs*

Lecomte	1899 – 1904 (05)

(post reorganized in 1904–1905)

IV. *Sous-Directeurs of Europe, Africa, and Oceania*
(post created in 1907)

Soulange-Bodin	1907 –	1909(10)
Conty	1910 –	1913

(reorganized in 1912 with transfer of
Oceania to Asia and addition of Levant)

Margerie	1913 –	1914

(reorganized in 1914 with creation of
separate posts for Europe and for Africa)

V. *Sous-Directeurs of the Levant*
(post created in 1907)

Defrance	1907 –	1910
Gout	1910 –	1912

(reorganized in 1912 with transfer to
Sous-Direction d'Europe)

VI. *Sous-Directeurs of Asia*
(post created in 1907)

Berthelot	1907 –	1913

(reorganized in 1912
with addition of Oceania)

Gout	1913 –	1920
Kammerer	1920 –	1923
Clinchant	1923 –	1926

VII. *Sous-Directeurs of America*
(post created in 1907)

Conty	1907 –	1910
Piccioni	1910 –	1911
Chevalley	1911 –	1914
Gauthier	1914 –	1920
Dejean	1920 –	1928

(internal reorganization in 1914)

VIII. *Sous-Directeurs of Europe*
(post created in 1914)

Berthelot	1914 –	1920
Laroche	1920 –	1922
Vignon	1922 –	1923
de Lacroix	1923 –	1925

IX. *Sous-Directeurs of Africa*
(post created in 1914)

la Rocca	1914 – 1920
Beaumarchais	1920 – 1925

FUNCTIONAL

I. *Directors of Political Affairs*

Raindre	1899 – 1903
Cogordan	1903 – 1904 (05)
Louis	1905 – 1907

(post reorganized in 1907)

II. *Directors of Consulats and Commercial Affairs*

Bompard	1895 – 1903
Louis	1903 – 1905
Henry	1905 – 1907

(post reorganized in 1907)

III. *Directors of Political and Commercial Affairs*
(post created in 1907)

Louis	1907 – 1910
Bapst	1910 – 1913
Paléologue	1913 – 1914
Margerie	1914 – 1919
Berthelot	1919 – 1920
la Rocca	1920 – 1925

IV. *Sous-Directeurs of Consular Affairs*

de Cazotte	1895 – 1905
Blanchard de Farges	1905 – 1907

(post reorganized in 1907)

V. *Sous-Directeurs of International Unions and Consular Affairs*
(post created in 1907)

Veillet-Dufrèche	1907 – 1911
Herbette	1911 – 1918
Péan	1918 – 1925

(internal reorganizations in
1910, 1911, 1912, 1918, and 1920)

VI.   *Sous-Directeur of Commercial Relations*
                  (post created in 1920)
            Seydoux   1920 – 1925

VII.   *Jurisconsultes of the Legal Department*
            Renault   1892 – 1920
            Fromageot   1920 – 1930

VIII.   *Chef of the French Service at the League of Nations*
                  (post created in 1920)
            Gout   1920 – 1925

IX.   *Chefs of the Press Bureau*
                  (post created in 1907 as Bureau des
                  Communications, although earlier press
                  work conducted under the Cabinet)
            Herbette   1907 – 1911
            Clinchant   1911 – 1913
            Montille   1913 – 1914
            Vignon   1914 – 1920
                  (reorganized in 1920 as the Press and
                        Information Service)
            Corbin   1920 – 1925

X.   *Chefs of French Cultural Propaganda*
                  (post created in 1910)
            Gauthier   1910 – 1913
            Pingaud   1913 – 1920
            Milhaud   1920 – 1922
            Giraudoux   1922 – 1925
                  (internal reorganizations in 1910,
            during the First World War, and in 1920)

Diplomats and Bureaucrats in the German Ministry for Foreign Affairs, 1900–1925*

ADMINISTRATIVE

I. *State Secretaries*

von Bülow	8.1897 –	10.1900
von Richthofen	10.1900 –	1.1906
von Tschirschky	1.1906 –	11.1907
von Schön	11.1907 –	6.1910
von Kiderlen-Wächter	6.1910 –	12.1912
von Jagow	12.1912 –	11.1916
Zimmermann	11.1916 –	8.1917
von Kühlmann	8.1917 –	7.1918
von Hintze	7.1918 –	10.1918
Solf	10.1918 –	12.1918
Brockdorff-Rantzau	12.1918 –	4.1919
von Haimhausen	7.1919 –	12.1922

(reorganized in 1919 with the creation
of an additional post for Wirtschaft)

Boyé (W)	11.1919 –	7.1921
Simon (W)	11.1921 –	7.1922

(reorganized in 1922 with the creation
of one position for State Secretary)

von Maltzan	12.1922 –	12.1924
von Schubert	12.1924 –	6.1930

*Compiled from the *Catalogue of Files and Microfilms of the German Foreign Ministry Archives, 1867–1920*, Volume I of *A Catalog of Files and Microfilms of the German Foreign Ministry Archives, 1920–1945*, and the respective Geschäftsverteilungspläne located in the Politisches **Archiv** in Bonn.

II. *Foreign Ministers*
(post created in 1919)

Brockdorff-Rantzau	4.1919 –	6.1919
Müller (Hermann)	6.1919 –	4.1920
Köster	4.1920 –	6.1920
Simons	6.1920 –	5.1921
Rosen	5.1921 –	10.1921
Wirth	10.1921 –	1.1922
Rathenau	1.1922 –	6.1922
Wirth	6.1922 –	11.1922
von Rosenberg	11.1922 –	8.1923
Stresemann	8.1923 –	10.1929

III. *Under State Secretaries*

von Richthofen	12.1897 –	10.1900
von Mühlberg	10.1900 –	11.1907
Stemrich	11.1907 –	5.1911
Zimmermann	5.1911 –	11.1916

(reorganized 24 November 1916
with the creation of two posts)

von dem Bussche-Haddenhausen	1916 –	12.1918
von Stumm	11.1916 –	12.1918
David	10.1918 –	2.1919
Langwerth von Simmern	1.1919 –	6.1919
Töpffer	2.1919 –	7.1919

(reorganized in 1919 with
elevation to State Secretary)

IV. *Directors of the Personnel Department*
(post created in 1879 as Abteilung IB)

von Eichhorn	2.1895 –	10.1902
von Schwarzkoppen	4.1903 –	12.1912
Matthieu	1.1913 –	8.1918
Schüler	8.1918 –	12.1920

(reorganized in 1920 as Abteilung I)

Gneist	12.1920 –	7.1924
von Stoher	8.1924 –	11.1926

(internal reorganizations in
1920, 1921, 1922, 1923, and 1924)

GEOGRAPHICAL

I. *Directors of Colonial Affairs*
(post created in 1890 as Abteilung IV)

Stuebel	6.1900 –	11.1905
Hohenlohe-Langenburg	11.1905 –	9.1906
von Dernburg	9.1906 –	5.1907

(reorganized in 1907 as post
transferred from the Ministry)

II. *Directors of Western Europe*
(post created 15 March 1920.
as Abteilung II)

von Simson	3.1920 –	7.1921
von Mutius	7.1921 –	4.1923

(reorganized 1 January 1922
as Abteilung IIa)

Köpke	5.1923 –	2.1936

(internal reorganizations in
1920, 1921, 1922, 1923, and 1924)

III. *Directors of Central Europe and the Balkans*
(post created 15 March 1920
as Abteilung III)

von Stockhammern	3.1920 –	12.1921

(reorganized 7 November 1921 with the
transfer of Turkey to the new
Abteilung III which also included
England and America)
(reorganized 1 January 1922
as Abteilung IIb)

Rümelin	1.1922 –	2.1922
Köpke	3.1923 –	2.1936

(internal reorganizations in
1922, 1923, and 1924)

IV. *Directors of Russia, Poland, and Scandinavia*
(post created 15 March 1920
as Abteilung IV)

Behrend	3.1920 –	11.1921

von Maltzan   11.1921 – 12.1922
(reorganized 1 January 1922
as Abteilung IVa)
Wallroth   1.1923 –   3.1925
(internal reorganizations in
1920, 1921, 1922, 1923, and 1924)

V. *Directors of Great Britain and Its Empire*
(post created 15 March 1920
as Abteilung V)
Rhomberg   3.1920 –   8.1920
von Schubert   8.1920 – 12.1921
(reorganized 7 November 1921 as new
Abteilung III with addition of the
Americas and Turkey)

VI. *Directors of Americas, Spain, and Portugal*
(post created 15 March 1920
as Abteilung VI)
Graf von Wedel   3.1920 –   6.1920
Pauli   6.1920 –   9.1920
von Erckert   9.1920 –   3.1921
Grunenwald   3.1921 – 10.1921
von Schubert   10.1921 – 12.1921
(reorganized 7 November 1921 when
Americas transferred to the new
Abteilung III with Portugal and
Spain transferred to Abteilung II)

VII. *Director of Asia*
(post created 15 March 1920
as Abteilung VII)
Knipping   3.1920 –   3.1925
(reorganized 1 January 1922
as Abteilung IVb, with internal
reorganizations in 1922, 1923, and 1924)

VIII. *Directors of England, the Americas, the Near East, and Africa*
(post created 1 January 1922
as Abteilung III)
von Schubert   1.1922 – 12.1924

de Hass 12.1924 – 9.1930
(internal reorganizations in
1922, 1923, and 1924)

FUNCTIONAL

I. *Directors of the Political Department (IA)*
(position created in 1910)

Zimmermann	4.1910 –	5.1911
von Stumm	5.1911 –	11.1916
Langwerth von Simmern	11.1916 –	1.1919
von Bergen	1.1919 –	6.1919
Boyé	9.1919 –	11.1919

(Haniel von Haimhausen, von Rosenberg,
and Göppert also acted as Dirigent at
various times during 1919)
(position reorganized in 1919–1920)

II. *Vortragende Räte of the Political Department (IA)*

von Holstein	1878 –	1906
von Lindenau	1894 –	1907
Hammann	1894 –	1915
Klehmet	1896 –	1908
von Mühlberg	1898 –	1900
Prince Lichnowsky	1899 –	1904
Rosen	1900 –	1904
von Rücker-Jenisch	1901 –	1902
von Kries	1902 –	1907
von Below-Schlstau	1904 –	1907
Zimmermann	1905 –	1910
von Jagow	1906 –	1907
von dem Bussche-Haddenhausen	1907 –	1910
von Eckert	1907 –	1910
von Flotow	1907 –	1910
von Griesinger	1908 –	1911
von Stumm	1909 –	1911
Graf Wedel	1910 –	1917
von Romberg	1910 –	1912
Langwerth von Simmern	1910 –	1916
von Montgelas	1911 –	1919

von Mirbach-Harff	1911 – 1913
von Rosenberg	1912 – 1919
von Bergen	1915 – 1919
Rhomberg	1916 – 1920
Nadolny	1917 – 1919
Göppert	1919 – 1919
Trautmann	1919 – 1920

(post reorganized in 1920)

III. *Directors of the Commercial Department (II)*

| von Körner | 1899 – 1914 |

(internal reorganization in 1907)

| Johannes | 1914 – 1918 |
| von Stockhammern | 1918 – 1920 |

(post reorganized in 1920)

IV. *Director of the "Aussenhandelsstelle" (Commerce)*

(post created in 1919)

| Wiedenfeld | 1919 – 1922 |

(reorganized in 1920 as Abteilung X)
(reorganized again in 1922 with functions
being dispersed to the Reichswirtschafts-
ministerium and the new Referat N)

V. *Director of "Referat N" (Economic Intelligence)*

(post created in 1922)

| Rössler | 1922 – 1925 |

VI. *Directors of "Referat S" (Maritime Affairs)*

| Seelinger | 1908 – 1920 |

(reorganized in 1920 from Referat II-S
to the new Referat S)

Bleyert	1920 – 1921
Breiter	1921 – 1922
Bleyert	1922 –

VII. *Directors of "Sonderreferat W" (Economic Policy)*

(post created in 1920)

| Bücher | 1920 – 1922 |
| de Haas | 1922 – 1923 |

(reorganized in 1923 as Abteilung W for
Wirtschafts- und Reparationspolitik)

Ritter   1923 –
(reorganized in 1925 as Sonderreferat **W**)

VIII. *Directors of the Legal Department*
    (post created in 1885 as Abteilung III)

Hellwig	4.1885 – 10.1902
von Franzius	10.1902 – 9.1911
Kriege	10.1911 – 9.1918
Simons	9.1918 – 7.1919
von Simson	7.1919 – 3.1920

    (reorganized in 1920 as Abteilung VIII)

Eckardt	3.1920 – 8.1920
Göppert	8.1920 – 5.1921
Köpke	5.1921 – 5.1923

    (reorganized in 1922 as Abteilung V)

Gaus	5.1923 – 5.1936

    (internal reorganizations in
    1920, 1921, 1922, 1923, and 1924)

IX. *Directors of "Abteilung F" (Peace)*
    (post created in 1919 as Friedensabteilung)

Mertens	1920 – 1921
Göppert	1921 – 1923
Moraht	1923 –

X. *Director of "Sonderreferat Volkerbund"*
    (post created in 1923)

von Bülow	1923 – 1928

XI. *Directors of "Referat D" (Deutschland)*
    (post created in 1919)

von Prittwitz und Gaffron	10.1919 – 10.1920
Rümelin	10.1920 – 2.1923
von Brentano	2.1923 – 5.1925

XII. *Directors of the "Schuldreferat" (War Guilt)*
    (post created in 1920)

Freytag	1920 – 1921
Delbrück	1921 – 1923
Stieve	1923 –

XIII. *Directors of the Press Department*
    (post created in 1915, although Hammann
    conducted similar work earlier under
    Abteilung IA)

Hammann	4.1915 –	12.1916
Deutelmoser	1.1917 –	11.1918
Naumann	11.1918 –	12.1919
Rauscher	1.1920 –	7.1920

(reorganized in 1920 as Abteilung P)

Heilbron	8.1920 –	6.1921
Müller (Oskar)	1921 –	1922
Heilbron	1.1923 –	8.1923
Spiecker	8.1923 –	1925

(internal reorganizations in
1920, 1921, 1922, 1923, and 1924)

XIV. *Directors of German Cultural Propaganda*
    (post created in 1920 as Abteilung IX)

von Schnitzler	3.1920 –	9.1920
Moraht	9.1920 –	10.1921
Heilbron	10.1921 –	1.1923

(reorganized 1 January 1922 as Abteilung VI)

Söhring	1.1923 –	8.1923
Heilbron	8.1923 –	7.1926

(internal reorganizations in
1920, 1921, 1922, 1923, and 1924)

Bibliography

A study of this nature requires utilization of a wide range of diverse source material. Since the subject centers around foreign ministries, considerable use first must be made of their own records. This entails evidence found within several archival collections in different countries. Of this material, particular emphasis is placed upon those items not intended for external consumption, including despatches sent from abroad providing first-hand observations of administrative practices, internal memoranda and reports issued in confidence, private papers, and personnel files. Among the most useful of these documents are special annual budget reports containing eyewitness accounts of organizational operations, structures, personnel, and expenditure priorities. Further information concerning procedures is found in official handbooks, manuals, and regulation lists.

This study also examines the new impact of domestic pressures upon these ministries, so attention is given to those expressions of public opinion. These include the speeches of parliamentary debates, contemporary books and pamphlets, novels, essays in journals of special interest groups, and the articles published in newspapers of the time advocating a particular course of action. Consideration is afforded those materials produced to influence this opinion as well, such as official documentary publications, "inspired" news items, and personal memoirs of the diplomats and bureaucrats themselves.

In addition, it is necessary to take account of the large amounts of secondary literature bearing upon institutional responses and twentieth-century diplomacy. Within these sources one finds interdisciplinary monographs and articles on bureaucratic institutions, reform and innovation, the dynamics of change, administrative science, various types of history, political science, diplomacy and international politics, commercial development, technological advancement, decision making, and organizational theory, among others.

In an effort to assist those readers who search for the needles of specific bibliographical references within the haystack of entries, the items below are divided into several categories. These include archival sources, government publications, memoirs, contemporary monographs, secondary monographs, contemporary articles, secondary articles, and contemporary newspapers. Individual items under each classification are listed alphabetically according to standard practice. The only exception to this arrangement is the extensive archival section where the material is separated first by national source, then either alphabetically according to series title (as in the case of the Auswärtiges Amt or Ministère des Affaires étrangères) or numerically according to the series classification (as in the case of the British Foreign Office), and finally in chronological order according to internal filing systems.

Archival Sources

1. *France. Archives diplomatiques du Ministère des Affaires étrangères, Paris.*
   Archives diplomatiques, Nouvelle série:
   Correspondance politique et commerciale.
   Europe, 1896-1918.
   Allemagne. Politique intérieur, dossier général.
   Volume NS 3 (1901–1906)
   Volume NS 4 (1907–1918)

   Allemagne. Politique étrangère, dossier général.
   Volume NS 17 (1907–1909)
   Volume NS 18 (1910–1914)
   Europe, 1918–1929.

   Allemagne. Mission Haguenin.
   Volume 10 (1919)
   Volume 11 (1920)
   Volume 12 (1920)
   Volume 15 (1920)
   Volume 16 (1920)

   Allemagne. Politique étrangère, dossier général.
   Volume 375 (1920)
   Volume 376 (1921)
   Volume 377 (1921)

Direction du Personnel.

*"Affaires étrangères. Textes et projets de réforme antérieur à 1912."
Carton 85

*"Commission de Réorganisation de la comptabilité et de l'architecture, 1911."
Carton 86

*"Organisation du Ministère. II. Décrets, Arrêtés, Rapports, Ordonnances, Circulaires, Notes, Etc., 1860–1896."
Carton 27

*"Projet de Réorganisation de l'Administration centrale, 1899–1900."
Carton 28

Direction politique et commerciale.

Papiers des Agents.

*Berthelot, Philippe.
"Propagande. Dossier général et France."
Carton 1
"Propagande. Groupements divers."
Carton 2
"Propagande. France. Comités."
Carton 3
"Propagande. Pays Scandinaves et Angleterre."
Carton 4
"Propagande. Belgique et Hollande."
Carton 6
"Propagande. Italie."
Carton 7
"Propagande. Russie et Amerique latine."
Carton 8
"Propagande. Etats-Unis."
Carton 9
"Propagande. Afrique du Nord, . . . Chine."
Carton 10
"Propagande de guerre à l'étranger, 1915–1916."
Carton 11
"Papiers Berthelot."
Carton 12

*Indicates special authorization required for use.

*Cambon, Jules.
  Carton 6

*Pichon, Stephen.
  "Negociation d'Armistice. Reparation des negociations de
  la Paix. 1918–1919."
  Volume 6

Division des Archives.

  *Papiers du Cabinet (card file).
  "Décrets concernant l'organisation du Ministère des Affaires
  étrangères, 1870–1947."

Série: Comptabilité.
  "Décrets et décisions ministerielles."
  Cartons: 44 (1900), 50 (1906), 51(1906), 52 (1907), 53 (1907),
    58 (1910), 59 (1910), 61 (1911), 62 (1912), 63 (1912), 64 (1913),
    69 (1916), 70 (1916)

Série: Personnel.
  "Lois, Ordonnances, Décrets et Arrêtés."
  Cartons: 29 (1907), 38 (1916), 40 (1918), 42 (1919), 43 (1920),
    44 (1920)

*Bibliothèque du Ministère (special collections and reports of lim-
ited circulation):

Assemblée nationale. Chambre des Députés.

  Rapport No 2234. Annexe au procès-verbal de la séance du 22
  juin 1916. "Proposition de loi ayant pour objet la réform de
  l'organisation des consulats."
  par Henry Lémery, et al.

  Rapport No 189. Annexe au procès-verbal de la séance du 13
  janvier 1920. "Proposition . . . à fixer par la loi les cadres des
  services diplomatiques et consulaires: les emplois, traite-
  ments, zones de cherté de vie."
  par Louis Marin

  Rapport No 190. Annexe au procès-verbal de la séance du 13
  janvier 1920. "Proposition de loi tendant à répartir en zones
  administratives nos postes et agents diplomatiques ou
  consulaires et à organiser sur cette spécialisation les services
  des Affaires étrangères."
  par Louis Marin

Assemblée nationale. Chambre des Députés, Commission des Affaires étrangères.

Rapport No 5377. Annexe au procès-verbal de la 2ᵉ séance du 28 décembre 1922. "Rapport fait au nom de la Commission des Affaires étrangères chargée d'examiner la proposition de loi de M. Louis Marin tendant à répartir en zones administratives nos postes et agents diplomatiques ou consulaires."
par Louis Farges

Assemblée nationale. Chambre des Députés, Commission du Budget (reports given each year to, and about, the Ministère des Affaires étrangères).

Rapport No 1871. Annexe au procès-verbal de la séance du 10 juillet 1900. "Rapport fait au nom de la Commission du Budget chargée d'examiner le projet de loi portant fixation du Budget général de l'exercice 1901 (Ministère des Affaires étrangères)."
par Henry Boucher

Rapport No 2640. Annexe au procès-verbal de la séance du 6 juillet 1901. "Rapport fait . . . de l'exercice 1902 (Ministère des Affaires étrangères)."
par Fernand Dubief

Rapport No 2661. Annexe au procès-verbal de la 2ᵉ séance du 13 juillet 1905. "Rapport fait . . . de l'exercice 1906 (Ministère des Affaires étrangères)."
par A. Gervais

Rapport No 333. Annexe au procès-verbal de la 2ᵉ séance du 13 juillet 1906. "Rapport fait . . . de l'exercice 1907 (Ministère des Affaires étrangères)."
par Paul Deschanel

Rapport No 1230. Annexe au procès-verbal de la 2ᵉ séance du 11 juillet 1907. "Rapport fait . . . de l'exercice 1908 (Ministère des Affaires étrangères)."
par Paul Deschanel

Rapport No 2015. Annexe au procès-verbal de la séance du 13 juillet 1908. "Rapport fait . . . de l'exercice 1909 (Ministère des Affaires étrangères)."
par Paul Deschanel

Rapport No 2749. Annexe au procès-verbal de la séance du 27 juillet 1909. ''Rapport fait . . . de l'exercice 1910 (Ministère des Affaires étrangères).''
par Paul Deschanel

Rapport No 361. Annexe au procès-verbal de la 2e séance du 12 juillet 1910. ''Rapport fait . . . de l'exercice 1911 (Ministère des Affaires étrangères).''
par Paul Deschanel

Rapport No 1237. Annexe au procès-verbal de la 2e séance du 12 juillet 1911. ''Rapport fait au nom de la Commission du Budget chargée d'examiner le projet de loi portant fixation du Budget général de l'exercice 1912 (Ministère des Affaires étrangères).''
par Paul Deschanel

Rapport No 1873. Annexe au procès-verbal de la 2e séance du 30 mars 1912. ''Rapport fait . . . de l'exercice 1913 (Ministère des Affaires étrangères).''
par Paul Deschanel

Rapport No 3318. Annexe au procès-verbal de la séance du 22 décembre 1913. ''Rapport fait . . . de l'exercice 1914 (Ministère des Affaires étrangères).''
par Louis Marin

Rapport No 3617. Annexe au procès-verbal de la 2e séance du 4 mars 1914. ''Rapport supplémentaire fait . . . de l'exercice 1914 (Ministère des Affaires étrangères).''
par Louis Marin

Rapport No 1542. Annexe au procès-verbal de la séance du 9 décembre 1915. ''Rapport fait au nom de la Commission du Budget chargée d'examiner le projet de loi portant conversion en crédits définitifs des crédits provisoires ouverts au titre du Budget général et au titre des budgets annexes de l'exercice 1915.''
par Raoul Péret

Rapport No 2703. Annexe au procès-verbal de la séance du 21 novembre 1916. ''Rapport fait . . . des budgets annexes de l'exercice 1916.''
par Raoul Péret

Rapport No 4294. Annexe au procès-verbal de la 2e séance du 7 février 1918. ''Rapport fait . . . des budgets annexes de

l'exercice 1917.''
par Louis Marin

Rapport No 4108. Annexe au procès-verbal de la séance du 20 décembre 1917. ''Rapport fait au nom de la Commission du budget chargée d'examiner le projet de loi portant fixation du Budget ordinaire des services civils de l'exercice 1918 (Ministère des Affaires étrangères).''
par M. Raiberti

Rapport No 6339. Annexe au procès-verbal de la 1re séance du 19 juin 1919. ''Rapport fait au nom de la Commission du Budget chargée d'examiner le projet de loi portant fixation du Budget général de l'exercice 1919 (Ministère des Affaires étrangères).''
par M. Raiberti

Rapport No 802. Annexe au procès-verbal de la 1re séance du 28 avril 1920. ''Rapport fait . . . de l'exercice 1920 (Ministère des Affaires étrangères).''
par M. Noblemaire

Rapport No 2020. Annexe au procès-verbal de la séance du 20 janvier 1921. ''Rapport fait . . . de l'exercice 1921 (Ministère des Affaires étrangères).''
par M. Noblemaire

Rapport No 1538. Annexe au procès-verbal de la séance du 25 septembre 1920. ''Rapport fait . . . de l'exercice 1921 (Ministère des Affaires étrangères, chapitres 43 et 44 concernant les dépenses de la Société des Nations).''
par M. Noblemaire

Rapport No 3131. Annexe au procès-verbal de la 2e séance du 12 juillet 1921. ''Rapport fait . . . de l'exercice 1922 (Ministère des Affaires étrangères).''
par M. Noblemaire

Rapport No 4792. Annexe au procès-verbal de la 2e séance du 8 juillet 1922. ''Rapport fait . . . de l'exercice 1923 (Ministère des Affaires étrangères).''
par M. Noblemaire

Assemblée nationale. Sénat, Commission des Finances.

Rapport No 65. Annexe au procès-verbal de la séance du 21 mars 1905. ''Rapport fait au nom de la Commission des Finances, chargée d'examiner le projet de loi, adopté par la Chambre des

Députés, portant fixation du Budget général de l'exercice 1905 (Ministère des Affaires étrangères)."
par Charles Dupuy

Rapport No 140. Annexe au procès-verbal de la séance du 27 mars 1906. "Rapport fait . . . de l'exercice 1906 (Ministère des Affaires étrangères)."
par Albert Decrais

Rapport No 439. Annexe au procès-verbal de la séance du 18 décembre 1906. "Rapport fait au nom de la Commission des Finances, chargée d'examiner le projet de loi, adopté par la Chambre des Députés, portant fixation du Budget général de l'exercice 1907 (Ministère des Affaires étrangères)."
par Charles Dupuy

Rapport No 337. Annexe au procès-verbal de la séance du 19 décembre 1907. "Rapport fait . . . de l'exercice 1908 (Ministère des Affaires étrangères)."
par Charles Dupuy

Rapport No 323. Annexe au procès-verbal de la séance du 8 décembre 1908. "Rapport fait . . . de l'exercice 1909 (Ministère des Affaires étrangères)."
par Charles Dupuy

Rapport No 114. Annexe au procès-verbal de la 1re séance du 17 mars 1910. "Rapport fait . . . de l'exercice 1910 (Ministère des Affaires étrangères)."
par Charles Dupuy

Rapport No 165. Annexe au procès-verbal de la séance du 18 mai 1911. "Rapport fait . . . de l'exercice 1911 (Ministère des Affaires étrangères)."
par Raymond Poincaré

Rapport No 28. Annexe au procès-verbal de la séance du 26 janvier 1912. "Rapport fait . . . de l'exercice 1912 (Ministère des Affaires étrangères)."
par Stephen Pichon

Rapport No 148. Annexe au procès-verbal de la séance du 29 mars 1913. "Rapport fait . . . de l'exercice 1913 (Ministère des Affaires étrangères)."
par Paul Doumer

Rapport No 272. Annexe au procès-verbal de la séance du (date unknown). "Rapport fait . . . de l'exercice 1914 (Ministère

des Affaires étrangères)."
par Paul Doumer

Rapport No 226. Annexe au procès-verbal de la séance du (date unknown). "Rapport fait . . . de l'exercice 1919 (Ministère des Affaires étrangères)."
par Lucien Hubert

Rapport No 375. Annexe au procès-verbal de la séance du (date unknown). "Rapport fait au nom de la Commission des Finances, chargée d'examiner le projet de loi, adopté par la Chambre des Députés, portant fixation du Budget général de l'exercice 1919 (Ministère des Affaires étrangères)."
par Lucien Hubert

Rapport No 339. Annexe au procès-verbal de la séance du 10 juillet 1920. "Rapport fait . . . de l'exercice 1920 (Ministère des Affaires étrangères)."
par Lucien Hubert

Rapport No 145. Annexe au procès-verbal de la séance du 15 mars 1921. "Rapport fait . . . de l'exercice 1921 (Ministère des Affaires étrangères)."
par Lucien Hubert

Rapport No 818. Annexe au procès-verbal de la séance du 22 décembre 1921. "Rapport fait . . . de l'exercice 1922 (Ministère des Affaires étrangères)."
par Lucien Hubert

Rapport No 309. Annexe au procès-verbal de la séance du 29 mars 1923. "Rapport fait . . . de l'exercice 1923 (Ministère des Affaires étrangères)."
par Lucien Hubert

Rapport No 144. Annexe au procès-verbal de la séance du 17 mars 1925. "Rapport fait . . . de l'exercice 1925 (Ministère des Affaires étrangères)."
par M. Reynald

Ministère des Affaires étrangères, Comité chargé de rechercher et de proposer toutes mesures tendant à la suppression ou à la réduction des dépenses publiques.

"Rapport général au Président du Conseil."
Août 1935.

Ministère des Affaires étrangères, Commission de Réorganisation.

"Rapports présentes à la Commission de réorganisation de l'Administration centrale."
Année 1933.

2. *France. Archives nationales, Paris.*

Archives Privées.

Fonds Albert Thomas (94 AP).
Cartons: 181, 182, 185, 190, 357, 358, 406

Ministère du Commerce et de l'Industrie.

"Enquête sur l'activité industrielle et la propagande commerciale des allemands dans les pays étrangers, 1919–1922."
Carton F ^{12} 9302
"Informations économiques provenant de diverses sources."
Carton F ^{12} 7955
"Office national du commerce extérieur."
Carton F ^{12} 9288
"Rapports consulaires postérieurs à la circulaire du 26 décembre 1906 . . . —Allemagne."
Carton F ^{12} 7216

Ministère de l'Intérieur, Direction des Renseignements.

Pays étrangers. Allemagne.
"Notes générales, 1922."
Carton F ^{7} 13.425
"Rapports d'agents secrets, de commissaires spéciaux, correspondance entre les commissaires spéciaux et les Préfets et la Direction de la Sûrete . . . , 1915–1921."
Carton F ^{7} 13.424

3. *Germany. Bundesarchiv, Koblenz.*

Akten der Reichskanzlei, 1919–1933.

R 43 I
Friedensverhandlungen.
Volume 2 (April–May 1919)

4. *Germany. Politisches Archiv des Auswärtiges Amt, Bonn.*

Aktengruppe: Abteilung IA

Deutschland 122 Nr. 2
Das Auswärtige Amt.
Volume 1 (1885–1904)
Volume 2 (1904–1906)

Volume 3 (1907–1909)
Volume 4 (1909–1910)
Volume 5 (1910–1918)
Volume 6 (1918–1919)
Deutschland 122 Nr. 2 *secr.*
Das Auswärtige Amt.
Volume 1 (1906–1914)
Volume 2 (1915–1919)
Deutschland 149
Der Geschäftsgang bei der politischen Abteilung.
Volume 9 (1904–1906)
Volume 10 (1906–1906)
Volume 11 (1907–1907)
Volume 12 (1908–1909)
Volume 13 (1909–1910)
Volume 14 (1910–1911)
Volume 15 (1911–1912)
Volume 16 (1912–1914)
Volume 17 (1914–1914)
Volume 18 (1914–1915)
Volume 19 (1915–1915)
Volume 20 (1915–1915)
Volume 21 (1915–1916)
Volume 22 (1916–1916)
Volume 22a (1916–1916)
Volume 23 (1916–1917)
Volume 24 (1917–1917)
Volume 25 (1917–1917)
Volume 26 (1918–1918)
Volume 27 (1918–1918)
Volume 28 (1918–1919)
Volume 29 (1919–1919)
Volume 30 (1919–1919)
Volume 31 (1919–1920)
Deutschland 149 *secr.*
Der Geschäftsgang bei der politischen Abteilung.
Volume 1 (1889–1914)
Volume 2 (1915–1919)
Frankreich 87
Allgemeine Angelegenheiten Frankreichs.
Volume 87 (1908–1909)

Volume 88 (1909–1909)
Volume 89 (1909–1910)
Volume 90 (1910–1910)
Volume 91 (1911–1913)
Volume 93 (1918–1920)

Frankreich 105 Nr. 1
Französische Staatsmänner.
Volume 24 (1906–1906)
Volume 25 (1907–1907)
Volume 26 (1907–1908)
Volume 27 (1908–1909)
Volume 28 (1909–1911)
Volume 29 (1911–1912)
Volume 30 (1912–1914)
Volume 31 (1915–1916)
Volume 32 (1917–1917)
Volume 34 (1918–1920)

Frankreich 108
Die diplomatische Vertretung Frankreichs im Auslande.
Volume 16 (1906–1907)
Volume 17 (1907–1908)
Volume 18 (1908–1910)
Volume 19 (1910–1912)
Volume 21 (1914–1920)

Weltkrieg 11 adh. 1
Die Sozialdemokratie bezw die Arbeiterschaft.
Volume 1 (1914–1915)

Aktengruppe: Handakten des Unterstaatssekretär Töpffer.

Aktenzeichen 13
Reform des Ausw. Amtes.
Volume 1 (1919)
Beilage (1919)

Aktengruppe: Abteilung III

Geschäftsgang 1
Allgemeines. Dienstbetrieb im Auswärtigen Amt im allgemeinen.
Volume 1 (1912–1920)
Volume 2 (1921–1922)

Geschäftsgang 1a
Neuorganisation des Ausw. Amtes.
Volume 1 (1921–1935)

Aktengruppe: Abteilung VI—Kultur

Allgemeines.
Förderung des Deutschtums im Auslande.
Volume 1 (1920–1921)

Aktengruppe: Büro des Reichsministers

Aktenzeichen 2
Auswärtiges Amt.—Organisation, Personalfragen.
Volume 1 (1920–1920)
Volume 2 (1921–1921)
Volume 3 (1922–1923)

Aktengruppe: Nachlässe Ulrich von Brockdorff-Rantzau

Aktenzeichen 14
Ministerialsachen (enthält auch Material zur Reorganisation des AA).
Volume 1 (1918–1919)

Aktengruppe: Politisches Archiv und Historisches Referat

*Aktenzeichen 10
Geschichte der Personalienabteilung 1879–1920.
Volume 1

*Aktenzeichen 11
Geschichte der Politischen Abteilung 1870–1920, sowie der Kolonialabteilung 1890–1907.
Volume 1

*Aktenzeichen 12
Geschichte der alten 2. (staatsrechtlich-handelspolitischen) Abteilung, 1871–1885.
Volume 1

*Aktenzeichen 13–14
Geschichte der Handelspolitischen Abteilung des A.A., 1885–1920.
Volume 1

Aktengruppe: Presse Abteilung

Beiakten I
Geschäftsordung, Referats und Diensteinteilung.
Volume 1 (1915–1924)

Beiakten II
Geschäftsordung des Ausw. Amt; Geschäftsverteilungsplan.
Volume 1 (1916–1921)
Volume 2 (1922–1932)

Aktengruppe: Referat Deutschland

Aktenzeichen Gg. la Neuorganisation des Auswärtigen Amts.
Volume 1 (1920–1922)

Aktengruppe: Sonderreferat Wirtschaft

Politik Nr. 25
Deutschtum im Auslande.
Volume 1 (1920–1934)

Auswärtiges Amt. Politisches Archiv

*Geschäftsverteilungspläne.
Volume 1 (1919–1924)
Volume 2 (1925–1940)

Auswärtiges Amt. Politisches Archiv

*Haushalt des Auswärtigen Amtes.
(1901–1924)

Auswärtiges Amt. Politisches Archiv (special file).

*Personal.
Edmund Schüler.

5. *Great Britain. Public Record Office, London.*

Foreign Office Correspondence

F.O. 368 (Commercial Correspondence).

Volumes
(1906): 21
(1907): 98, 102, 107
(1911): 628
(1912): 679
(1914): 984, 987
(1917): 1744
(1919): 2126

F.O. 369 (Consular Correspondence).

Volumes
(1908): 186
(1912): 466, 540
(1913): 646, 648
(1914): 707
(1916): 873, 874
(1917): 933, 970, 971
(1918): 996

F.O. 371 (Political Correspondence).

Volumes
(1906): 74, 76, 77, 78, 79, 80
(1907): 250, 252, 254, 256, 257, 258, 259, 260, 262, 263
(1908): 455, 456, 459, 461, 462, 463, 530
(1909): 669, 671
(1910): 899, 900, 903
(1911): 1116, 1117, 1125, 1168
(1912): 1366, 1374, 1378, 1555
(1913): 1647, 1654
(1914): 1974, 1978, 1981, 1986, 1990, 2198
(1915): 2365, 2366
(1916): 2677
(1917): 2934, 2935, 2936, 2938, 2939, 2941, 3085
(1918): 3214, 3215, 3223, 3436, 3474, 3478, 3481
(1919): 3752, 3757, 3759, 3763, 3765, 3768, 3778, 3782, 3786,
3787, 3790, 3799, 3800, 3801
(1920): 4725, 4740, 4742, 4827, 4839, 4851, 5468
(1921): 5970, 5974, 5985, 5989, 6008, 6025, 6976, 6977, 6979,
6989, 6991, 6993
(1922): 7535, 7536, 7538, 7539, 7577, 8247, 8255, 8256, 8257,
8265, 8301
(1923): 8513, 8669, 8699, 8798, 8817, 9391, 9394, 9397

F.O. 372 (Treaty).

Volumes
(1918): 1125
(1919): 1248

F.O. 382 (Contraband).

Volume
(1918): 1835

F. O. 395 (News).

Volume
(1917): 98

F.O. 800 (Private Papers).

The Private Papers of Sir Francis Bertie
Volumes: 165, 168, 169

F.O. 881 (Confidential).

Volume
(1905): 1296

6. *United States. National Archives, Washington D.C.*
   Department of State
   Political, Legal and Diplomatic Correspondence.
      "Records of the Department of State Relating to Internal
      Affairs of France, 1910–1929."
      Decimal File 851.02
      —Executive Departments
   "Records of the Department of State Relating to Internal
   Affairs of Germany, 1910–1929."
   Decimal File 862.02
   —Executive Departments

Published Documents

American Historical Association, Committee for the Study of War
Documents. *A Catalogue of Files and Microfilms of the German
Foreign Ministry Archives, 1867–1920.* Oxford: Oxford University
Press, 1959.

Ausschuss für Neugestaltung des Auslandsdienstes, Hamburg. *Hamburger Vorschläge zur Neugestaltung des deutschen Auslandesdienstes.* Hamburg: April 1918.

France. *Almanach Impérial.* Paris: Guyot & Scribe, 1805, 1860.

——. Assemblée nationale, Chambre des Députés. *Annales de la Chambre des Députés, Débats parlementaires.* Paris: Imprimerie des Journaux officiels, 1890–1936.

——. Assemblée nationale, Chambre des Députés, Comité secret du 1er juin 1917. *Comptes-rendus in-extenso des comités secrets de la Chambre des Députés, 1916–1917* extracts du *Journal officiel de la République française*, 17 mai 1925. Paris: Imprimerie des Journaux officiels, 1925.

——. Assemblée nationale, Chambre des Députés, Commission de l'Administration générale. Rapport No. 1213, Annexe au procès-verbal de la 2e séance du 11 juillet 1907. "Rapport fait au nom de la Commission de l'administration générale, départementale et communale, des cultes et de la décentralisation chargée d'examiner le projet de loi sur les associations de fonctionnaires." Paris: Imprimerie de la Chambre des Députés, 1907.

——. Assemblée nationale, Chambre des Députés, Commission de l'Administration générale. Rapport No. 4285, Annexe au procès-verbal de la séance du 6 février 1918. "Rapport fait au nom de la

Commission de l'administration générale, départementale et communale chargée d'examiner les propositions de loi et de résolution concernant la réorganisation administrative de la France.'' Paris: Imprimerie de la Chambre des Députés, 1918.

———. Assemblée nationale, Chambre des Députés, Commission d'enquête parlementaire. Rapport No. 2344, Annexe au procès-verbal de la 2ᵉ séance de 8 août 1947. ''Rapport fait au nom de la Commission chargée d'enquêter sur les événements survenus en France de 1933 à 1945.'' Paris: Presses Universitaires de France, 1947.

———. Assemblée nationale, Sénat. *Annales du Sénat, Débats parlementaires*. Paris: Imprimerie des Journaux officiels, 1890–1936.

———. L'Ecole nationale d'administration. *Concours d'entrée et scholarité*. Paris: Imprimerie nationale, 1951.

———. *Journal officiel de la République française. Lois et Décrets*. Paris: Imprimerie nationale, 1890–1936.

———. Ministère des Affaires culturelles. *Les Archives de l'Agence Havas*. Paris: S.E.V.E.N., 1969.

———. Ministère des Affaires étrangères. *Annuaire diplomatique et consulaire de la République française*. Paris: Berger-Levrault and Imprimerie nationale, 1871–1936, 1971.

———. Ministère des Affaires étrangères. *Bulletin périodique de la Presse*. Paris: Ministère des Affaires étrangères, 1916–1930.

———. Ministère des Affaires étrangères. *Bulletin quotidien de Presse étrangère*. Paris: Ministère des Affaires étrangères, 1916–1930.

———. Ministère des Affaires étrangères. *Chefs d'état, ministres, grands traités de la France*. Paris: Palais des Affaires étrangères, 1960.

———. Ministère des Affaires étrangères. Commission de publication des documents relatifs aux origines de la Guerre de 1914. *Documents diplomatiques français (1871–1914)*. 38 volumes. Paris: Imprimerie Nationale, 1929–.

———. Ministère des Affaires étrangères. *Compte définitif des dépenses de l'exercice 1881–1938*. Paris: Imprimerie nationale, 1883–1896 and Melun: Imprimerie administrative, 1897–1942.

———. Ministère des Affaires étrangères. *Le Ministère des Affaires étrangères, residence des chefs d'état, hôtes de la France*. Paris: Ministère des Affaires étrangères, n.d.

———. Ministère des Affaires étrangères. Office des biens et intérêts privés. *Guide pratique*. Paris: Imprimerie nationale, 1920.

———. Ministère du Commerce et de l'Industrie. *Loi et Décrets relatifs à l'Office national du Commerce extérieur*. Paris: Imprimerie nationale, 1920.

————. Ministère du Commerce et de l'Industrie. Office national du Commerce extérieur. *Bibliothèque d'information économique et technique internationale: Catalogue de périodiques*. Paris: Société Fermière, 1925 ed.

Germany. Auswärtiges Amt. *Die Grosse Politik der Europäischen Kabinette, 1871–1914: Sammlung der diplomatischen Akten des Auswärtigen Amtes*. 40 volumes. Berlin: Deutsche Verlagsgesellschaft für Politik, 1922–1927.

————. Auswärtiges Amt. *Sammelmappe des Auswärtigen Amts: Deutschland und die weltwirtschaftliche Lage*. Berlin: Auswärtiges Amt, 1919, 1925.

————. Nationalliberalen Zentralvorstandes. *Von Bassermann zu Stresemann: Die Sitzungen des nationalliberalen Zentralvorstandes, 1912–1917*. Edited by Klaus-Peter Reiss. Band 5 of *Quellen zur Geschichte des Parlamentarismus und der politischen Parteien*. Düsseldorf: Droste, 1967.

————. Nationalversammlung. *Stenographische Berichte über die Verhandlungen der Verfassunggebenden deutschen Nationalversammlung*. Berlin: Norddeutschen Buchdruckerei, 1919–1921.

————. Prussia, Landtag. *Stenographische Berichte über die Verhandlungen des Preussischen Hauses der Abgeordneten*. Berlin: Preussische Verlagsanstalt, 1917.

————. Reichsamt des Innern. *Handbuch für das Deutsche Reich*. Berlin: Carl Heymanns Verlag, 1874–1918.

————. *Reichsgesetzblatt*. Berlin: Reichsdruckerei, 1871–1936.

————. Reichskanzlei. *Akten der Reichskanzlei, Weimarer Republik: Das Kabinett Scheidemann*. Boppard am Rhein: Boldt, 1971.

————. Reichsministerium des Innern. *Handbuch für das Deutsche Reich*. Berlin: Carl Heymanns Verlag, 1922–1936.

————. Reichstag. *Reichstags-Handbuch*. Berlin: Norddeutschen Buchdruckerei, 1912.

————. Reichstag. *Stenographische Berichte über die Verhandlungen des Reichstags*. Berlin: Norddeutschen Buchdruckerei, 1890–1933.

————. Volksbeauftragten. *Die Regierung der Volksbeauftragten 1918–1919*. Edited by Erich Matthias and Susanne Miller. Band 6 of *Quellen zur Geschichte des Parlamentarismus und der politischen Parteien*. Düsseldorf: Droste, 1969.

Germany (Federal Republic). Auswärtiges Amt. Kommission für die Reform des Auswärtigen Dienstes. *Bericht der Kommission*. Bonn: Auswärtiges Amt, 1971.

Great Britain. Foreign Office. *Index to the Correspondence of the Foreign Office, 1920–1938*. London: Her Majesty's Stationery Office, 1969.

———. Parliament, House of Commons. *The Parliamentary Debates*. Volume XXI. London: Hansard, 1829.

———. Parliament, House of Commons. *The Parliamentary Debates*. Volume CIV. London: His Majesty's Stationery Office, 1918.

———. Parliament, House of Lords. *The Parliamentary Debates*. Volume CII. London: His Majesty's Stationery Office, 1902.

———. Royal Commission of the Civil Service. Command Paper No. 7748, "Fifth Report of the Commissioners: The Diplomatic Corps and the Foreign Office; The Consular Service." Command Paper No. 7749, "Appendix to the Fifth Report." *Sessional Papers, 1914–16*. Volume XI. London: His Majesty's Stationery Office, 1914.

Schmoeller, G., *et al.*, *Acta Borussica. Die Behördenorganisation und die allgemeine Staatsverwaltung Preussens im 18. Jahrhundert*. Berlin: Parey, 1894–1908.

United States. Congress, House of Representatives, Committee on Foreign Affairs. Document No. 24470, "Hearings . . . for the Reorganization and Improvement of the Foreign Service of the United States." Washington: Government Printing Office, 1922.

———. Congress and Office of the President. Commission on the Organization of the Government for the Conduct of Foreign Policy. "Mandate." COG/FP Staff 1. 15 April 1974.

———. Congress and Office of the President. Commission on the Organization of the Government for the Conduct of Foreign Policy. "Tentative Program." COG/FP COM D 1. 1 August 1973.

———. Department of State, Historical Office. *A Catalog of Files and Microfilms of the German Foreign Ministry Archives, 1920–1945*. 4 volumes. Edited by George O. Kent. Stanford: Hoover Institution Press, 1962–1972.

———. War Department. General Staff, Military Intelligence Division. *Propaganda in its Military and Legal Aspects*. Washington: 1918?

Memoirs

Adams, Henry. *The Education of Henry Adams: An Autobiography*. Boston: Houghton Mifflin, 1918.

Bernstorff, Graf Johann Heinrich. *Erinnerungen und Briefe*. Zürich: Polygraphischer Verlag, 1936.

Bertie, Lord Francis. *The Diary of Lord Bertie of Thame, 1914–1918*. 2 volumes. Edited by Lady Algernon Lennox. London: Hodder & Stoughton, 1924.

Blücher, Wipert von. *Deutschlands Weg nach Rapallo*. Wiesbaden: Limes, 1951.

Bonnet, Georges. *Le Quai d'Orsay sous trois républiques, 1870–1961*. Paris: Fayard, 1961.

Bülow, Bernhard Fürst von. *Denkwurdigkeiten*. 4 volumes. Berlin: Ullstein, 1931.

Busch, Moritz. *Bismarck: Some Secret Page of His History*. 2 volumes. New York: Macmillan, 1898.

Callières, François de. *On the Manner of Negotiating with Princes*. Translated by A. F. Whyte. Notre Dame: University of Notre Dame Press, 1963 ed.

Charles-Roux, F. *Souvenirs diplomatiques d'un âge révolu*. Paris: Librairie Rayard, 1956.

Chirol, Sir Valentine. *Fifty Years in a Changing World*. London: Cape, 1927.

Creel, George. *How We Advertised America*. New York: Harper & Brothers, 1920.

Curtius, Julius. *Sechs Jahre Minister der deutschen Republik*. Heidelberg: Winter, 1948.

Dirksen, Herbert von. *Moskau, Tokio, London: Erinnerungen und Betrachtungen zu 20 Jahren deutscher Aussenpolitik, 1919–1939*. Stuttgart: Kohlhammer, 1949.

Frédéric II. *Oeuvres historiques de Frédéric II, Roi de Prusse*. Berlin: Decker, 1846.

Grey, Viscount. *Twenty-Five Years, 1892–1916*. 2 volumes. New York: Stokes, 1925.

Guizot, François. *Mémoires pour servir à l'histoire de mon temps*. 5 volumes. Paris: Michel Lévy Frères, 1858–1862.

Hammann, Otto. *Bilder aus der letzten Kaiserzeit*. Berlin: Hobbing, 1922.

———. *Deutsche Weltpolitik, 1890–1912*. Berlin: Hobbing, 1925.

Hitler, Adolf. *Mein Kampf*. New York: Reynal & Hitchcock, 1939 ed.

Holstein, Friedrich von. *The Holstein Papers*. Edited by Norman Rich and M. H. Fisher. 4 volumes. Cambridge: Cambridge University Press, 1955.

Kordt, Erich. *Nicht aus den Akten*. Stuttgart: Union Deutsche Verlagsgesellschaft, 1950.

LaRoche, Jules. *Au Quai d'Orsay avec Briand et Poincaré, 1913–1926.* Paris: Hachette, 1957.

Machiavelli, Niccolò. *Il principe.* Milano: Mursia, 1969 ed.

Monts, A. Graf von. *Erinnerungen und Gedanken.* Edited by K. Nowak and F. Thimme. Berlin: Verlag für Kulturpolitik, 1932.

Morand, Paul. *Giraudoux, Souvenirs.* Geneva: La Palatine, 1948.

———. *Journal d'un attaché d'ambassade.* Paris: Gallimard, 1963.

———. *1900.* Paris: Les Editions de France, 1931.

Nicolai, W. *Nachrichtendienst, Presse und Volksstimmung im Weltkrieg.* Berlin: Mittler & Sohn, 1920.

Paléologue, Maurice. *Un grand tournant de la politique mondiale, 1904–1906.* Paris: Plon, 1934.

———. *Journal de l'affaire Dreyfus, 1894–1899: L'affaire Dreyfus et le Quai d'Orsay.* Paris: Plon, 1955.

Paul-Boncour, Joseph. *Entre deux guerres: Souvenirs sur la IIIe République.* 3 volumes. Paris: Plon, 1945–46.

Pognon, H. *Lettre à M. Doumergue, Président du Conseil, Ministre des Affaires étrangères, au sujet d'une réforme du Ministère des Affaires étrangères.* Paris: Figuière, 1914.

Radowitz, Joseph Maria von. *Aufzeichnungen und Erinnerungen.* 2 volumes. Edited by Hajo Holborn. Berlin: Deutsche Verlags-Anstalt Stuttgart, 1925.

Richelieu, Duc de. *Testament politique.* Edited by Louis André. Paris: Robert Laffont, 1947.

Saint-Aulaire, Comte de. *Confession d'un vieux diplomate.* Paris: Flammarion, 1953.

———. *Je suis diplomate.* Paris: Editions de Conquistador, 1954.

Schmidt-Pauli, Edgar von. *Diplomaten in Berlin.* Berlin: Mauritius, 1930.

Schoen, Wilhelm von. *Erlebtes: Beiträge zur politischen Geschichte der neuesten Zeit.* Berlin: Deutsche Verlags-Anstalt, 1921.

Sievers, Johannes. "Aus meinem Leben." Berlin: unpublished manuscript, 1966.

Spender, J. A. *The Public Life.* 2 volumes. London: Cassell, 1925.

Spitzemberg, Baronin. *Am Hof der Hohenzollern: Aus dem Tagebuch der Baronin Spitzemberg, 1865–1914.* Edited by Rudolf Vierhaus. München: Deutscher Taschenbuch Verlag, 1965.

Thayer, Charles W. *Diplomat.* New York: Harper & Brothers, 1959.

Vansittart, Lord. *The Mist Procession.* London: Hutchinson, 1958.

Warburg, Max M. *Aus meinen Aufzeichnungen*. London: privately printed, 1952.

Weizsäcker, Ernst von. *Erinnerungen*. München: Paul List, 1950.

Contemporary Monographs

Albers, Detlef. *Reichstag und Aussenpolitik von 1871–1879*. Berlin: Ebering, 1927.

Akzin, Benjamin. *Propaganda by Diplomats*. Washington, D.C.: Digest Press, 1936.

Allard, Paul. *Les dessous de la guerre révélés par les comités secrets*. Paris: Editions de France, 1932.

————. *Le Quai d'Orsay: Son personnel, ses rouages, ses dessous*. Paris: Editions de France, 1938.

Anschütz, Gerhard, et al. *Handbuch der Politik*. III. 3rd edition. Berlin: Rothschild, 1921.

Balabanoff, Angelica. *Die Zimmerwalder Bewegung, 1914–1919*. Leipzig: Hirschfeld, 1928.

Balzac, Honoré de. *Les Employés. Oeuvres complètes*. Vol. XI. Paris: Calmann-Lévy, 1875 ed.

Barthélemy, Joseph. *Démocratie et politique étrangère*. Paris: Félix Alcan, 1917.

————. *Essai sur le travail parlementaire et le système des commissions*. Paris: Delagrave, 1934.

Becker, C. H. *Kulturpolitische Aufgaben des Reiches*. Leipzig: Quelle & Meyer, 1919.

Benoist, Charles. *La crise de l'état moderne. L'organisation du travail: le travail, le nombre et l'état*. Paris: Plon, 1905.

Bernstein, Eduard. *Die parlamentarische Kontrolle der auswärtigen Politik*. The Hague: Nijhoff, 1916.

Berthelot, Philippe. "Rapport de la Commission des réformes administratives du Ministère des Affaires étrangères." [As reproduced in France, *Journal officiel de la République française. Lois et décrets*, 3 May 1907.]

Boell, Paul. *Les scandales du Quai d'Orsay*. Paris: Nouvelle Librairie Parisienne, 1893.

Bréal, Auguste. *Philippe Berthelot*. Paris: Gallimard, 1937.

Bülow, Bernhard Wilhelm von. *Der Versailler Völkerbund: eine vorläufige Bilanz*. Stuttgart: Kohlhammer, 1923.

Cambon, Jules. *Le Diplomate*. Paris: Hachette, 1926.

Carr, E. H. *Propaganda in International Politics*. New York: Farrar & Rinehart, 1939.

Chardon, Henri. *L'Administration de la France: les fonctionnaires*. Paris: Perrin, 1908.

————. *Le pouvoir administrative*. Paris: Perrin, 1912 ed.

Chow, S. R. *Le contrôle parlementaire de la politique étrangère en Angleterre, en France et aux Etats-Unis*. Paris: Sagot, 1920.

Comité de propagande socialiste pour la Défense nationale. *Les Socialistes dans la Nation et pour la Nation*. Paris: Librairie de l'Humanité, 1916.

Comité pour la Reprise des Relations Internationales. *Seconde conférence socialiste internationale de Zimmerwald: Les résolutions*. Paris: Féderation des Métaux, 1916.

Daniélou, Charles. *Les Affaires étrangères*. Paris: Figuière, 1927.

Demartial, Georges. *La réforme administrative: ce qu'elle devrait être*. Paris: Cornély, 1911.

Duguit, Léon. *Les constitutions et le principales lois politiques de la France depuis 1789*. 4th edition. Paris: Librairie générale de Droit et de Jurisprudence, 1925.

Eltzbacher, P. *Die Presse als Werkzeug der auswärtigen Politik*. Jena: Eugen Diederichs, 1918.

Falkenberg, Albert. *Die deutsche Beamtenbewegung nach der Revolution*. Berlin: Verlag für Sozialwissenschaft, 1920.

Fay, Sidney B. *The Origins of the World War*. 2 volumes. New York: Macmillan, 1928.

Fayol, Henri. *Administration industrielle et générale: Prévoyance, organisation, commandement, coordination, contrôle*. Paris: Dunod, 1920.

Fitzgerald, F. Scott. *Tender is the Night*. New York: Scribner, 1951 ed.

Fleiner, Fritz. *Institutionen des deutschen Verwaltungsrechts*. Tübingen: Mohr, 1928 ed.

Flöckher, Adolf von. *Was muss der Deutsche von auswärtiger Politik wissen?* Berlin: Curtius, 1908.

Garden, Guillaume de. *Traité complet de diplomatie, ou théorie générale des relations extérieures des puissances de l'Europe*. 3 volumes. Paris: Librairie de Treuttel et Würtz, 1833.

Grabowsky, Adolf. *Die Reform des deutschen Beamtentums*. Gotha: Perthes, 1917.

Griolet, H. *Le Ministère des Affaires étrangères*. Paris: Charles-Lavauzelle, 1900.

Haas, Albert. *Die Propaganda im Ausland*. Weimar: Kiepenheuer, 1916.

Helfferich, Karl. *Deutschlands Volkswohlstand, 1888–1913*. 7th edition. Berlin: Stilke, 1917.

Hindenburg, Herbert von. *Das Auswärtige Amt im Wandel der Zeiten*. Frankfurt am Main: Societäts-Verlag, 1932.

Hoeniger, R. *Das Deutschtum im Ausland*. Berlin: Teubner, 1918 ed.

Huber, Georg. *Die französische Propaganda im Weltkrieg gegen Deutschland 1914 bis 1918*. München: Pfeiffer, 1928.

Jusserand, J. J. *The School for Ambassadors and Other Essays*. New York: Putnam's Sons, 1925.

Kehr, Eckart. *Der Primat der Innenpolitik*. Edited by Hans-Ulrich Wehler. Berlin: Walter de Gruyter & Co., 1970 ed.

Kennedy, A. L. *Old Diplomacy and New*. London: John Murray, 1922.

Kraus, Herbert. *Der Auswärtige Dienst des deutschen Reiches (Diplomatie und Konsularwesen)*. Berlin: Georg Stilke, 1932.

Labadie, Jean (editor). *L'Allemagne, A-t-elle le secret de l'organisation?* Paris: Bibliothèque de l'opinion, 1916.

Lefas, Alexandre. *L'Etat et les fonctionnaires*. Paris: Giard & Briere, 1913.

Levis-Mirapoix. *Le Ministère des Affaires étrangères: Organisation de l'administration centrale et des services extérieurs, 1793–1933*. Angers: Société anonyme des Editions de l'Ouest, 1934.

Lewinsohn, Richard [pseud. Morus]. *Wie Sie gross und reich wurden*. Berlin: Ullstein, 1927.

Lutz, Hermann. *E. D. Morel: Der Mann und sein Werk*. Berlin: Verlagsgesellschaft für Politik und Geschichte, 1925.

Masson, Frederick. *Le Département des Affaires étrangères pendant la Révolution, 1787–1804*. Paris: Plon, 1877.

Mendelssohn Bartholdy, Albrecht. *Diplomatie*. Berlin: Rothschild, 1927.

Mousset, Albert. *La France vue de l'étranger; ou le déclin de la diplomatie et le mythe de la propagande*. Paris: L'Ile de France, 1926.

Mowat, R. B. *Diplomacy and Peace*. New York: McBride, 1936.

Nicolson, Sir Harold. *Curzon: The Last Phase, 1919–1925; A Study in Post-War Diplomacy*. New York: Houghton Mifflin Co., 1934.

Parti Socialiste et Confédération Générale du Travail. *Le Memorandum des socialistes des pays alliés*. Paris: Simart, 1918.

Piccioni, Camille. *Les premiers commis des Affaires étrangères au XVIIe et au XVIIIe siècles.* Paris: Boccard, 1928.

Pohl, Heinrich. *Völkerrecht und Aussenpolitik in der Reichsverfassung.* Berlin: Dümmlers, 1929.

Rabenau, Friedrich von. *Seeckt: Aus seinem Leben, 1918–1936.* Leipzig: Hase & Koehler, 1941.

Rathenau, Walther. *Deutschlands Rohstoffversorgung.* Berlin: Fischer, 1918.

Remarque, Erich Maria. *All Quiet on the Western Front.* New York: Fawcett World Library, 1968 ed.

Salmon, Lucy. *The Newspaper and Authority.* New York: Oxford University Press, 1923.

Sass, Johann. *Die deutschen Weissbücher zur auswärtigen Politik, 1870–1914.* Berlin: Walter de Gruyter & Co., 1928.

Schifferdecker, O. R. *Die Organisation des Auswärtigen Dienstes im alten und neuen Reich.* Heidelberg: privately printed, 1932.

Schmitt, Bernadotte. *Triple Alliance and Triple Entente.* New York: Holt, 1934.

Schrameier, Wilhelm Ludwig. *Auswärtiges Amt und Auslandsvertretung; Vorschläge zur Reform.* Berlin: K. Curtius, 1918.

Schuchart, Theodore. *Die deutsche Aussenhandelsförderung unter besonderer Berücksichtigung des Wirtschaftsnachrichtenwesens.* Berlin: Simion, 1918.

Schuman, Frederick L. *War and Diplomacy in the French Republic.* New York: McGraw-Hill, 1931.

Sharp, Walter Rice. *The French Civil Service: Bureaucracy in Transition.* New York: Macmillan, 1931.

Sorel, Georges. *La révolution Dreyfusienne.* Paris: Rivière, 1909.

Swanwick, H. M. *Builders of Peace, Being Ten Years' History of the Union of Democratic Control.* London: Swarthmore Press, 1924.

Tiemann, Kuno. *Das Auswärtige Amt, die Notwendigkeit seiner Reorganisation.* Berlin: Verlag Neues Vaterland, 1920.

Tardieu, Andrè. *La conférence d'Algésiras.* Paris: Alcan, 1909.

Valéry, Paul. *The Outlook for Intelligence.* New York: Harper & Row, 1963 ed.

Weber, Max. *Gesammelte Aufsätze zur Wissenschaftslehre.* 2nd edition. Tübingen: Mohr, 1951.

———. *Wirtschaft und Gesellschaft.* 4th edition. Tübingen: Mohr, 1956.

Weill, Georges. *Le Journal: origines, évolution et rôle de al presse périodique*. Paris: La Renaissance du Livre, 1934.

Young, George. *Diplomacy Old and New*. London: Swarthmore Press, 1921.

Zechlin, Walter. *Diplomatie und Diplomaten*. Stuttgart: Deutsche Verlags-Anstalt, 1935.

Zimmern, Alfred. *The League of Nations and the Rule of Law, 1918–1935*. London: Macmillan & Co., 1939.

Secondary Monographs

Allison, Graham. *Essence of Decision*. Boston: Little, Brown & Company, 1971.

Andrew, Christopher. *Théophile Delcassé and the Making of the Entente Cordiale: A Reappraisal of French Foreign Policy, 1898–1905*. New York: St. Martin's Press, 1968.

Argyris, Chris. *Personality and Organization: The Conflict Between Systems and the Individual*. New York: Harper & Brothers, 1957.

Baillou, Jean and Pelletier, Pierre. *Les Affaires étrangères*. Paris: Presses Universitaires de France, 1962.

Basdevant, J. et al. *Les Affaires étrangères*. Paris: Presses Universitaires de France, 1959.

Baumont, Maurice, et al. *L'Europe de 1900 à 1914*. Paris: Sirey, 1966.

Bendix, Reinhard and Roth, Günther. *Scholarship and Partisanship: Essays on Max Weber*. Berkeley: University of California Press, 1971.

Bennis, Warren. *Changing Organizations*. New York: McGraw-Hill, 1966.

Blau, Peter and Meyer, Marshall. *Bureaucracy in Modern Society* (2nd ed.). New York: Random House, 1971.

Brecht, Arnold and Glaser, C. *The Art and Technique of Administration in German Ministries*. Cambridge: Harvard University Press, 1940.

Butterfield, H. and Wight, M. *Diplomatic Investigations*. London: Unwin, 1966.

Caiden, Gerald. *Administrative Reform*. Chicago: Aldine, 1969.

Carroll, E. M. *French Public Opinion and Foreign Affairs, 1870–1914*. New York: Century, 1931.

———. *Germany and the Great Powers, 1866–1914: A Study in Public Opinion and Foreign Policy*. New York: Prentice-Hall, 1938.

Challaye, Félicien. *Georges Demartial:sa vie, son oeuvre*. Paris: Lahure, 1950.

Chevallier, J.-J. *Histoire des institutions politiques de la France moderne, 1789-1945*. Paris: Dalloz, 1958.

Clapham, J. H. *The Economic Development of France and Germany, 1815-1914*. Fourth Edition. Cambridge: Cambridge University Press, 1955.

Craig, Gordon A. *From Bismarck to Adenauer: Aspects of German Statecraft*. Revised edition. New York: Harper & Row, 1965.

————. *War, Politics and Diplomacy: Selected Essays*. New York: Praeger, 1966.

Craig, Gordon A. and Gilbert, Felix (editors). *The Diplomats, 1919-1939*. 2 volumes. New York: Atheneum, 1968 ed.

Croneberg, Allen, Jr. "The Volksbund für das Deutschtum im Ausland: Volkisch Ideology and German Foreign Policy, 1881-1939." Ph.D. dissertation, Stanford University, 1970.

Crozier, Michel. *Le phénomène bureaucratique*. Paris: Editions du Seuil, 1963.

Demartial, Georges. *La réforme administrative: ce qu'elle devrait être*. Paris: Cornély, 1911.

Destler, I. M. *Presidents, Bureaucrats and Foreign Policy: The Politics of Organizational Reform*. Princeton: Princeton University Press, 1972.

Deuerlein, Ernst. *Der Bundesratsausschuss für die auswärtigen Angelegenheiten, 1870-1918*. Regensburg: Josef Habel, 1955.

Dirksen, Herbert von. *Diplomatie: Wesen, Rolle und Wandlung*. Nurnberg: Abraham, 1950.

Dischler, Ludwig. "Der auswärtige Dienst Frankreichs." Ph.D. dissertation, Hamburg, 1952.

Dockhorn, Robert. "The Wilhelmstrasse and the Search for a New Diplomatic Order, 1926-1930." Ph.D. dissertation, Madison, 1972.

Dorn, Walter. *Competition for Empire*. New York: Harper & Brothers, 1940.

Dorwart, Reinhold August. *The Administrative Reforms of Frederick William I of Prussia*. Cambridge: Harvard University Press, 1953.

Drachkovitch, Milord. *Les socialismes français et allemand et le problème de la Guerre*. Genève: Droz, 1953.

Duguit, Léon. *Les constitutions et le principales lois politiques de la France depuis 1789*. 4th edition. Paris: Librairie générale de Droit et de Jurisprudence, 1925.

Elben, Wolfgang. *Das Problem der Kontinuität in der deutschen Revolution*. Dusseldorf: Droste, 1965.

Ellul, Jacques. *Propaganda: The Formation of Men's Attitudes*. New York: Knopf, 1965.

Feis, Herbert. *Europe, The World's Banker, 1870–1914: An Account of European Foreign Investment and the Connection of World Finance with Diplomacy Before the War*. New Haven: Yale University Press, 1930.

Fischer, Fritz. *Germany's Aims in the First World War*. London: Chatto & Windus, 1967 ed.

Frank, Elke. "The Wilhelmstrasse During the Third Reich: Changes in its Organizational Structure and Personnel Policies." Ph.D. dissertation, Cambridge, Mass., 1963.

Gawthrop, Louis C. *Bureaucratic Behavior in the Executive Branch: An Analysis of Organizational Change*. New York: The Free Press, 1969.

Gay, Peter. *Weimar Culture: The Outsider as Insider*. New York: Harper & Row, 1968.

Gilbert, Felix. *Towards the Farewell Address*. Princeton: Princeton University Press, 1961.

Gladden, E. N. *A History of Public Administration*. 2 volumes. London: Cass, 1972.

Gottlieb, W. W. *Studies in Secret Diplomacy During the First World War*. London: Allen & Unwin, 1957.

Hale, Oran J. *Germany and the Diplomatic Revolution: A Study in Diplomacy and the Press, 1904–1906*. Philadelphia: University of Pennsylvania Press, 1931.

————. *The Great Illusion, 1900–1914*. New York: Harper & Row, 1971.

Harr, John. *The Professional Diplomat*. Princeton: Princeton University Press, 1969.

Hintze, Otto. *Soziologie und Geschichte*. Second edition. Göttingen: Vandenhoeck & Ruprecht, 1964.

Holtman, Robert. *Napoleonic Propaganda*. Baton Rouge: Louisiana State University, 1950.

Huber, Ernst Rudolf. *Deutsche Verfassungsgeschichte seit 1789*. 4 volumes. Stuttgart: Kohlhammer, 1963.

Huntington, Samuel. *Political Order in Changing Society*. New Haven: Yale University Press, 1968.

Huyghe, René and Rudel, Jean. *L'Art et le monde moderne*. 2 volumes. Paris: Larousse, 1969.

Jacoby, Henry. *The Bureaucratization of the World*. Berkeley: University of California Press, 1973.

Kehrig, Manfred. *Die Wiedereinrichtung des deutschen militärischen Attachédienstes nach dem Ersten Weltkrieg (1919–1933)*. Boppard am Rhein: Boldt, 1966.

Kindleberger, Charles P. *Power and Money: The Economics of International Politics and the Politics of International Economics*. New York: Basic Books, 1970.

King, James E. *Science and Rationalism in the Government of Louis XIV, 1661–1683*. Baltimore: Johns Hopkins, 1949.

Kissinger, Henry A. *A World Restored*. Boston: Houghton Mifflin, 1973 ed.

Lanza, Albert. *Les projets de réforme administrative en France de 1919 à nos jours*. Paris: Presses Universitaires de France, 1968.

Lasswell, Harold. *Propaganda Technique in the World War*. New York: Peter Smith, 1938.

Legendre, Pierre. *Histoire de l'administration de 1750 à nos jours*. Paris: Presses Universitaires de France, 1968.

Litterer, Joseph (editor). *Organizations: Systems, Control and Adaptation*. II. New York: Wiley, 1969 ed.

Luckau, Alma. *The German Delegation at the Paris Peace Conference*. New York: Columbia University Press, 1941.

Lyons, F. S. L. *Internationalism in Europe, 1815–1914*. Leyden: Sythoff, 1963.

March, James and Simon, Herbert. *Organizations*. New York: Wiley, 1959.

Mayer, Arno J. *Wilson vs. Lenin: Political Origins of the New Diplomacy, 1917–1918*. New York: World, 1964.

Mock, James and Larson, Cedric. *Words That Won the War*. Princeton: Princeton University Press, 1939.

Morsey, Rudolf. *Die oberste Reichverwaltung unter Bismarck, 1867–1890*. Münster: Aschendorffsche Verlagsbuchhandlung, 1957.

Morstein Marx, Fritz. *The Administrative State: An Introduction to Bureaucracy*. Chicago: University of Chicago Press, 1957.

Mosher, Frederick C. *Governmental Reorganizations*. Syracuse: Inter-University Case Program, Inc., 1967.

Muncy, Lysbeth W. *The Junker in the Prussian Administration under William II, 1888–1914*. Providence: Brown University Press, 1944.

Nicolson, Sir Harold. *Diplomacy*. Third edition. London: Oxford University Press, 1968.

———. *The Evolution of Diplomatic Method*. London: Constable, 1956.

Peyrefitte, Roger. *La fin des ambassades, roman*. Paris: Flammarion, 1953.

Prittwitz und Gaffron, Friedrich von. *Aussenpolitik und Diplomatie*. München: Isar, 1951.

Renouvin, Pierre. *Histoire des relations internationales*. VI. *Le XIXe siècle, II: de 1871 à 1914, l'apogée de l'Europe*. Paris: Hachette, 1955.

Rich, Norman. *Fredrich von Holstein: Politics and Diplomacy in the Era of Bismarck and Wilhelm II*. 2 volumes. Cambridge: Cambridge University Press, 1965.

Richter, Johannes. *Die Reichszentrale für Heimatdienst: Geschichte der ersten politischen Bildungsstelle in Deutschland*. Berlin: Landeszentrale für politische Bildungsarbeit, 1963.

Ritter, Gerhard. *Frederick the Great: A Historical Profile*. Translated with an introduction by Peter Paret. Berkeley: University of California Press, 1968.

Rogers, Everett. *Diffusion of Innovations*. New York: The Free Press, 1969.

Rosenberg, Hans. *Bureaucracy, Aristocracy and Autocracy: The Prussian Experience, 1660–1815*. Cambridge: Harvard University Press, 1958.

Sallet, Richard. *Der diplomatische Dienst*. Stuttgart: Deutsche Verlags-Anstalt, 1953.

Sasse, Heinz. *100 Jahre Auswärtiges Amt, 1870–1970*. Bonn: Auswärtiges Amt, 1970.

Seabury, Paul. *The Wilhelmstrasse: A Study of German Diplomats Under the Nazi Regime*. Berkeley: University of California Press, 1954.

Smith, Bruce; Lassewell, Harold; and Casey, Ralph. *Propaganda, Communication, and Public Opinion*. Princeton: Princeton University Press, 1946.

Steiner, Zara. *The Foreign Office and Foreign Policy, 1898–1914*. Cambridge: Cambridge University Press, 1969.

Strang, Lord. *The Foreign Office*. New York: Oxford University Press, 1955.

Swain, Joseph Ward. *Beginning the Twentieth Century*. New York: W. W. Norton & Co., 1933.

Swartz, M. *The Union of Democratic Control in British Politics During the First World War*. Oxford: Clarendon Press, 1971.

Toffler, Alvin. *Future Shock*. New York: Bantam Books, 1970.

Tuchman, Barbara. *The Proud Tower: A Portrait of the World Before the War, 1890–1914*. New York: Macmillan, 1966.

Wilensky, Harold. *Organizational Intelligence*. New York: Basic Books, 1967.

Wittgens, Herman J. "The German Foreign Office Campaign Against the Versailles Treaty." Ph.D. dissertation, Seattle, 1970.

Wörner, Karl. *Die Musik in der Geistesgeschichte*. Bonn: Bouvier, 1970.

Wright, Gordon. *France in Modern Times*. Chicago: Rand McNally & Co. 1966.

Wright, Quincy. *A Study of War*. Second edition. Chicago: University of Chicago Press, 1965.

Zimmermann, Ludwig. *Deutsche Aussenpolitik in der Ära der Weimarer Republik*. Göttingen: Musterschmidt, 1958.

Contemporary Articles

"Belgique. La réforme consulaire." *Les Annales diplomatiques et consulaires*, 44 (15 February 1920), 6.

Bergson, Henri. "Correspondance au Directeur." *Revue philosophique*, 60 (July–December 1905), 229–230.

Bloch, Marc. "Pour une histoire comparée des sociétés européenes." *Revue de synthèse historique*, 46 (December 1928), 15–50.

"Deutschlands weltwirtschaftliche Bestrebungen: Ein Syndikat für den Auslandsnachrichtendienst." *Deutsche Export-Revue*. 5 June 1914.

Dochow, Franz. "Aufgaben der deutschen Diplomatie." *Weltwirtschaft*. V. Jahrgang, Nr. 9 (December 1915), 177–78.

Drascher, Wahrhold. "Zur Organisation unseres Auslandsdienstes." *Das neue Deutschland*, 5. Jahrgang, Heft 23 (1 September 1917), 639–42.

Dreager, Hans. "Der Arbeitsausschuss Deutscher Verbände." *Berliner Monatshefte*. XV (March 1937), 258–71.

Frauendienst, Werner. "Das Kriegsschuldreferat des Auswärtigen Amtes." *Berliner Monatshefte*. XV (March 1937), 201–14.

Griesinger, Freiherr von. "Aufbau, Umbau und Abbau des Auswärtigen Amtes." *Deutsche Revue*. XLVII (March 1922), 193–207.

"Grosses Reinemachen im Auswärtigen Amt." *Roland: Gesellschaft, Kunst, Finanz*. Heft 3 (19 January 1921), 5–8.

Hankey, Sir Maurice. "Diplomacy by Conference." *Proceedings of the British Institute of International Affairs*. No. 1. London: Smith & Co., 1920.

Hanotaux, Gabriel. "L'Europe qui naît." *La revue hebdomadaire*. 48 (30 November 1907), 561–70.

Harms, Bernhard. "Weltwirtschaft und Weltwirtschaftslehre." *Weltwirtschaftliches Archiv*. 1. Band, Heft 1 (January 1913), 1–36.

Hintze, Otto. "Die Entstehung der modernen Staatsministerien." *Historische Zeitschrift*. 100 (1907), 53–111.

Hötzsch, Otto. "Auswärtige Politik und Presse." *Deutsche Monatschrift*. Heft 2 (November 1906), 160–72.

Jannasch, R. "Die Förderung des deutschen Aussenhandels." *Export: Organ des Centralvereins für Handelsgeographie und Förderung deutscher Interessen im Auslande*. XXXX. Jahrgang, Nr. 35–38 (27 August 1918), 105–7.

König, B. von. "Die konsularische Berichterstattung und der amtliche Nachrichtendienst." *Bank-Archiv*. X. Jahrgang, Nr. 19 (1 July 1911), 291–95.

Koser, R. "Die Gründung des Auswärtigen Amtes durch König Friedrich Wilhelm I. im Jahre 1728." *Forschungen Zur Brandenburgischen und Preussischen Geschichte*. II (1889), 160–97.

"La Langue Française en Orient." *L'Opinion*. No. 10 (6 March 1909), 299–301.

"The Loss of Mr. Moore," *Literary Digest*. XLVII, No. 11 (14 March 1914), 539–40.

Löwe, Dr. "Die Reform des Auswärtigen Dienstes." *Der Volksstaat*. Nr. 4 (25 January 1919).

Millet, René. "Les Ministères: Ministère des Affaires étrangères." *La revue hebdomadaire*, 10 (11 March 1911), 177–203.

Norton, Henry Kittredge. "Foreign Office Organization." *The Annals of the American Academy of Political and Social Science*, Supplement to CXLIII (1929).

"A Plea for Cinderella." *United Empire*. Vol. VIII, No. 5 (May 1917), 309–15.

Quessel, Ludwig. "Die Kontrolle der auswärtigen Politik." *Sozialistische Monatshefte*, 22. Jahrgang, 3 (1916), 1087–91.

Raffalovich, A. "L'Organisation du service consulaire allemand et les renseignements commerciaux." *L'Economiste français*. (30 September 1911), 489–91.

Raleigh, Walter. "The War of Ideas." *United Empire*. Vol. VIII, No. 1 (January 1917), 13–23.

"La Riforma del Ministero degli Esteri." *La Vita Italiana*. (April 1917), 337–68.

Rodd, Sir Rennell. "The Old and the New Diplomacy." *Quarterly Review*. Vol. 239, No. 474 (January 1923), 71–82.

Rolland, Romain. "Aux peuples assassinés." *Demain: pages et documents*. 11/12 (November–December 1916), 257–66.

Roloff, Gustav. "Die Neuorganisation des Ministeriums des Auswärtigen von 1798–1802." *Forschungen zur Brandenburgischen und Preussischen Geschichte*. 7 (1894), 97–111.

Schmidt, E. H. "Nationale Propaganda." *Mitteilungen des Vereins deutscher Reklamefachleute*. Heft 9 (September 1918), 129–36.

Schuman, Frederick. "The Conduct of German Foreign Affairs." *The Annals of the American Academy of Political and Social Science*. Vol. 176 (November 1934), 187–221.

Seydoux, Jacques. "Suggestions pour une réorganisation du Ministère des Affaires étrangères." *L'Europe nouvelle*. (26 March 1927), 428–30.

Stieve, F. "Der Kampf gegen die Kriegsschuldlüge, 1922–1928." *Berliner Monatshefte*. XV (March 1937), 194–201.

Strupp, Karl. "Zur Frage der Reform der Ausbildungsvorschriften für deutsche Diplomaten." *Niemayers Zeitschrift für Internationales Recht*. XXV. Band, 1–3 Heft (1915). 23–129.

Thudichum, Friedrich. "Die Leitung der auswärtigen Politik des Reichs." *Jahrbuch für Gesetzgebung, Verwaltung und Rechtspflege des Deutschen Reiches*. (1876), 323–47.

Van Cleave, James W. "What America Must Do to Make an Export Business." *The Annals of the American Academy of Political and Social Science*. Vol. XXIX, No. 3 (May 1907), 30–37.

"Verein für das Deutschtum im Ausland." *Das Deutschtum im Ausland*. Heft 3 (March 1910), 1.

Vogelstein, Theodor. "Der Stil des amerikanischen Geschäftslebens." *Süddeutsche Monatschefte*. II (July–December 1906), 80–100.

Wahl, Kurt. "Die deutschen Länder in der Aussenpolitik." *Tübinger Abhandlungen zum öffentlichten Recht*. 22 Heft (1930).

Whelpley, James D. "Our Disorganized Diplomatic Service." *Century*. LXXXVII (November 1913), 123–27.

Williams, G. V. "The German Press Bureau." *The Contemporary Review*. Vol. 97 (March 1910), 315–25.

Wilmotte, M. "La Langue française en Orient." *L'Opinion*. No. 13 (27 March 1909), 397–99.

Wolgast, H. "Die auswärtige Gewalt des Deutschen Reichs unter besonderer Berücksichtigung des Auswärtigen Amtes: ein Ueberblick." *Archiv des öffentlichen Rechts*. N.F. 5, Heft 1 (1923), 1–112.

"Zollbeamte als Konsuln." *Zollwarte: Zeitschrift des preussischen Landesverbandes und des Bundes deutscher technischer Zoll- und Steurbeamten*. 14 Jahrgang. Nr. 11/12 (10 June 1919).

Secondary Articles

Acheson, Dean. "The Eclipse of the State Department." *Foreign Affairs*. Vol. 49, No. 4 (July 1971), 593–606.

Allison, Graham and Halperin, Morton. "Bureaucratic Politics: A Paradigm and Some Policy Implications." *World Politics*. XXIV Supplement (Spring 1972), 40–79.

Baumgart, Peter. "Zur Gründungsgeschichte des Auswärtigen Amtes in Preussen, 1713–1728." *Jahrbuch für die Geschichte Mittel- und Ostdeutschlands*. VII (1958), 229–48.

Boelcke, Willi. "Presseabteilung und Pressarchive des Auswärtigen Amts, 1871–1945." *Archivmitteilungen*. IX. Jahrgang, Heft 2 (1959), 43–49.

Cairns, John C. "Politics and Foreign Policy: The French Parliament, 1911-1914" *The Canadian Historical Review*. XXXIV (September 1953), 245–76.

Düwell, Kurt. "Staat und Wissenschaft in der Weimarer Epoche: Zur Kulturpolitik des Ministers C. H. Becker." *Historische Zeitschrift*. Beiheft 1 (1971), 31–74.

Frankel, Charles. " 'Culture,' 'Information,' 'Foreign Policy.' " *Public Administration Review*. Vol. 29, No. 6 (November–December 1969), 593–600.

Geiss, Imanuel. "The Outbreak of the First World War and German War Aims." *Journal of Contemporary History*. Vol. 1, No. 3 (July 1966), 75–91.

George, Alexander L. "The Case for Multiple Advocacy in Making Foreign Policy." *American Political Science Review*, LXVI, 3 (September 1972), 751–85.

Géraud, André. "Diplomacy, Old and New." *Foreign Affairs*, XXIII, 2 (January 1945), 256–70.

Kissinger, Henry A. "The White Revolutionary: Reflections on Bismarck." *Daedalus*, Vol. 97, No. 3 (Summer 1968), 888–924.

Lauren, Paul Gordon. "Ultimata and Coercive Diplomacy." *International Studies Quarterly*, Vol. 16, No. 2 (June 1972), 131–65.

Leaman, Bertha R. "The Influence of Domestic Policy on Foreign Affairs in France, 1898–1905." *Journal of Modern History*, XIV (December 1942), 449–79.

Marshall, Charles Burton. "The Golden Age in Perspective." *Journal of International Affairs*, XVII, 1 (1963), 9–17.

Mosher, Frederick. "Some Observations about Foreign Service Reform: 'Famous First Words.'" *Public Administration Review*. Vol. 29, No. 6 (November–December 1969), 600–610.

Outrey, Amédée. "Histoire et principes de l'administration française des affaires étrangères." *Revue française de science politique*, III, 2 (April–June 1953), 298–318; III, 3 (July–September 1953), 491–510; III, 4 (October–December 1953), 714–38.

Sasse, Heinz. "Die Entstehung der Bezeichnung 'Auswärtiges Amt.'" *Nachrichtenblatt der Vereinigung deutscher Auslandsbeamten*, 19. Jahrgang, 10 (October 1956), 85–89.

―――. "Die Entwicklung des gehobenen Auswärtigen Dienstes." *Nachrichtenblatt der Vereinigung deutscher Auslandsbeamten*, 22. Jahrgang, 10 (October 1959), 198–204.

―――. "Von Equipage und Automobilen des Auswärtigen Amts." *Nachrichtenblatt der Vereinigung deutscher Auslandsbeamten*, 20. Jahrgang, 10 (October 1957), 145–48.

―――. "Zur Geschichte des Auswärtigen Amts." *Mitteilungsblatt der Vereinigung der Angestellten des Auswärtigen Dienstes*, 4. Jahrgang, 5 (May 1960), 105–18; 6 (June 1960), 133–41; 7 (July 1960), 161–68; 8 (August 1960), 189–217.

"Sattelfest in Urdu und Marxismus: Wie Ost-Berlin Diplomaten auswählt und ausbildet." *Die Zeit* (27 April 1973).

Schmid, Irmtraut von. "Der Bestand des Auswärtigen Amts im deutschen Zentralarchiv Potsdam. I. Teil: 1870–1920." *Archivmitteilung*, 2/3 (1962), 71–79.

―――. "Der Bestand des Auswärtigen Amts im deutschen Zentralarchiv Potsdam. II. Teil: 1920–1945." *Archivmitteilung*, 4 (1962), 123–32.

Sewell, William H., Jr. "Marc Bloch and the Logic of Comparative History." *History and Theory*, VI, 2 (1967), 208–18.

Vagts, Alfred. "M. M. Warburg & Co.: Ein Bankhaus in der deutschen Weltpolitik, 1905–1933." *Vierteljahrschrift für Sozial- und Wirtschafts-geschichte*. 45. Band, Heft 3 (September 1958), 289–388.

Contemporary Newspapers

Acht Uhr Abendblatt.

Allgemeine Zeitung.

L'Aube: revue politique et littéraire.

L'Aurore.

Bayerischer Kurier.

Berliner Börsen-Courier.

Berliner Börsen-Zeitung.

Berliner Tageblatt.

Berliner Volkszeitung.

Corriere della Sera.

Daily Telegraph.

Dépeche coloniale.

Deutsche Allgemeine Zeitung.

Deutsche Marke.

L'Echo de Paris.

Le Figaro.

Frankfurter Zeitung.

Le Gaulois.

Hannoverscher Courier.

Industrie und Handels Zeitung.

Journal des Débats.

Kladderadatsch.

Das Kleine Journal.

Kölnische Volkszeitung.

Kölnische Zeitung.

Leipziger Neuesten Nachrichten.

Leipziger Volkszeitung.
La Liberté.
Manchester Guardian.
Morning Post.
National Zeitung.
Neue Berliner Zeitung.
Neue Preussische Zeitung.
Norddeutsche Allgemeine Zeitung.
La Petit Havre.
La Petit Parisien.
Rappel.
Le Temps.
The Times.
La Tribune de Lausanne.
Vörwarts.
Vossische Zeitung.
Die Zukunft.
Züricher Post.

Index